# passport's guide to the BUSINESS CAPITALS of THE WORLD

# passport's guide to the BUSINESS CAPITALS of THE WORLD

Edited by Graham Boynton
Introduction by David Frost

Published by Passport Books
in cooperation with the editors of
Business Traveller, London, England

Trade Imprint of National Textbook Company
Lincolnwood, Illinois U.S.A.

This edition first published in 1986 by Passport Books, Trade
Imprint of National Textbook Company, 4255 West Touhy Avenue,
Lincolnwood (Chicago), Illinois 60646-1975 U.S.A.
Originally published by Perry Books © 1986. Perry Books
is a joint imprint of Perry Publications and First Edition.


ISBN 0-8442-9491-8 (hardcover)

ISBN 0-8442-9492-6 (soft cover)

# Contents

Carlsberg Beer
Probably the best beer in the world.

# Foreword

**Graham Boynton**
Editor, Business Traveller

When *Business Traveller* was founded in the mid-1970s its avowed aims were to eschew the soft-focus, land-of-contrast school of travel writing that prevailed at the time in favour of practical, hard-hitting and factual assessments of the most unglamorous business of travelling for a living. To romanticise international jet travel, faraway capitals and foreign cultures is as naive as it is inappropriate when one's audience comprises hard-bitten and often cynical businessmen whose success is more often dependent on their ability to sidestep the cultural idiosyncrasies that so many travel writers tend to celebrate so uncritically.

To illustrate the degree of mutual back-slapping that has become traditional in the travel industry I need only refer to one of my own first assignments for *Business Traveller.* It was entitled The Etiquette of Apartheid and attempted to explain to foréign visitors the day-to-day workings of a political system that prevailed in Africa's most powerful business capital. It elicited a horrified response from the South African Tourist Corporation who claimed to be *"extremely disappointed that a travel writer of your calibre should concern himself with matters outside the theme of business travel."* And yet to the travelling executive an understanding of the social environment is just as important as a description of the architectural landscape. The so-called theme of business travel encompasses everything from the socio-political nature of its inhabitants to the price of a taxi ride from the airport. To remind readers of Seoul's emotional instability ('five minutes by bomber from the north') is as integral to our reports as noting the high cost of doing business in New York or recording London's antiquated drinking hours.

Equally, we make no apologies for refraining from providing endless lists of hotels, restaurants or nightclubs. We have chosen instead to highlight what our writers consider to be the best examples of particular types of establishment, be they deluxe or budget priced hotels, restaurants providing safe local cuisine or acceptable standards of international food, and nightlife most appropriate to a particular region.

If our brief has been too wide-ranging for the travel specialist we would argue that our audience is impossible to conveniently categorise apart from the common factor of frequent international travel. He, or indeed she, may be the owner-chairman of a small manufacturing company in the south of England, a sales director for a huge multi-national conglomerate, a partner in an international law firm, or even the manager of a touring repertory company. Theirs is anything but the glamorous and heady world of the glossy advertisements, more a catalogue of missed connections, bad hotels and alien customs and tongues.

They seldom have the time to indulge themselves in tourist attractions and are more in need of advice of a practical nature – the most efficient method of transportation within a city, whether the hotels provide efficient communication facilities, convenient restaurants, watering holes with real atmosphere. Once these basics have been mastered the business traveller is in a position to appreciate the finer aspects of the cities in question. For all the drawbacks, international travel remains a great privilege, and we trust this book conveys adequately some of the pleasures of such privilege.

# Introduction by David Frost

Rose Macaulay, the celebrated English novelist and travel writer once wrote: *"The great and recurring question about abroad is, is it worth getting there?"* This invaluable guide to the world's top business capitals sets out to persuade you that wherever your abroad is, it's definitely worth the trip.

According to the editor, I was invited to write this introduction because I have an infinite capacity for taking planes. It's certainly true that I was once introduced on a talk show as *"the man who has been on more jumbos than Sabu the Elephant Boy"*.

With more than five million miles under my seat belt, I suppose I must by now be thoroughly air-conditioned. To have flown more than five million miles, as someone pointed out the other day, I must have spent more than a year of my life in flight – which might be worth mentioning to the tax man ... almost as impressive as the record of the latest recruit to the ranks of busy travellers, Pope John Paul. He's made so many overseas visits since he became Pope that Pan Am has announced that as a Frequent Flyer, he has now qualified for a free Round-the-World trip with the companion of his choice ...

Anyway, my year aloft has certainly taught me some air traveller's ground rules. Firstly, I would advise you to steer clear of the sort of airline whose motto might be: *"Patronise us – and we'll be sure to patronise you"*. You know the ones I mean. My second piece of advice is more practical: when you're travelling long distances, change your watch the moment you leave so you have the whole of your flight to adjust to where you're going. And have a gullible body, so that when you say: *"Body – it's 7.30 here,"* it believes you.

As to the cities so informatively covered in this book, I have had the pleasure of visiting about two thirds of them with stop overs at about another sixth. So far, Jakarta, Manila, Rio and Seoul have eluded me, while Amsterdam

# The Taste.

*More difficult to describe than to afford.*

How can you describe the mild, smooth taste of a very fine whisky that has been aging in oak casks since 1968? How can you explain in words the smoothness and character distilled into a precious whisky? You can't. You must simply taste it yourself.

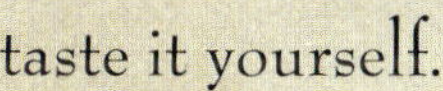

Ballantine's
17 YEARS OLD

was perhaps the most surprisingly pretty city I have ever visited, with echoes of Venice which, alas, does not qualify for this book.

Bangkok must be counted among the most romantic cities in the world as well as one of the best business cities and I suppose that the Oriental Hotel in Bangkok qualifies as one of the outstanding hotels in the world. The Oriental has a modern section, but its traditional section is particularly delightful and both the Somerset Maugham suite and the Joseph Conrad suite are memorable.

Chicago is undoubtedly an outstanding experience for any visitor. Chicago airport, however, (apparently the busiest in the world – except in the early hours of the evening when Atlanta takes over that particular title) is a devilishly designed airport where it is impossible to make a connection without having to walk the maximum number of miles and pass through the maximum number of security checks with the minimum number of luggage trolleys.

Helsinki, as far as I'm concerned, is one of the most underrated cities in the world. Before you visit Finland you have the impression that Finns live under the shadow of the Russian bear. Once you get there you find that this is not at all the case; that the Russian influence, the Russian cloud, is not as overbearing as you might expect. And there seems to be a genuine mixed economy with some of its industry among the most efficient in the world.

The car radios in Finland, for instance – and Finland has almost as many car radios, I gather, as the whole of the rest of the world put together – put even the new cellular radio telephones in the UK in the shade. Calls can be redirected to your car telephone whether you're in Helsinki or the Arctic Circle and you can telephone London and nobody would know that you were on a car telephone at all, much less in the Arctic Circle.

I found Johannesburg extremely oppressive – not so much because of specific oppression, but because the atmosphere there immediately communicates what the regime is all about. And as one tours Johannesburg one is amazed to find such a lack of tact; a lack of diplomacy; a lack of sensitivity, in which shanty town shacks are not in a different part of the city from the luxurious dwellings, but right next door. There can be no way in which the deprived of Johannesburg can be unaware of just how deprived they are; it's right at their back doors, right at their front doors.

I do have a favourite hotel in Paris but it is a rather small hotel and, lest it become overcrowded, I don't think I'll mention its name here.

But apart from London, my favourite two cities in this book have to be Sydney and New York.

The visitor to Sydney who has been educated in the Ocker language and Earls Court/Fosters Lager school of thought will be surprised by its sophistication. The wines of Australia are superb and quite unlike an Emu fortified special.

The Wentworth hotel is the grand hotel of Sydney, the Regent is the newest – almost as grand – hotel, and then there are two hotels in Sydney that are notable for their friendliness: the Boulevard and the Sebel Town House.

The restaurants of Sydney are often outstanding, too, with some wonderful local delicacies. Sydney rock oysters are undoubtedly the sweetest in the world and the carpetbag steak in Pruniers – fillet steak with Sydney rock oysters 'injected' into it – is a local delicacy that I have never found anywhere else. The Doyle's fish restaurants – they remain in the open air most of the year – are among the best in the world and the proximity of restaurants on the beach to the centre of city and business activity is a unique plus.

And then the view from Kirrabilli of the Sydney Harbour Bridge and the Sydney Opera House has to be one of the greatest man-made vistas in the world.

New York, of course, is special in so many ways. I have always tried to make my first meal in New York a steak. A New York steak is totally unobtainable anywhere in Europe. The size back home is all wrong – it's too thin and too small – and so is the taste. Baked potato skins were a New York invention, still too rarely copied in the old country.

New York is intensely theatrical. Not just on Broadway. Even the restaurants in New York are theatrical, intent on putting on a show as well as a meal. The atmosphere of Sardi's is an obvious example but it is equally true away from the theatre district. There is a razzmatazz about the Russian Tea Room, Maxwell's Plum, and the Tavern on the Green that is pure New York. All over the town the Captains enter into the spirit of the thing and 'dress the room' with a care and a flourish that a Broadway director or set designer would be proud of.

The 'non-club' clubs are special too, The camaraderie of '21' could scarcely be equalled if there were a ten-year waiting list for membership. And you will certainly find it easier to get a late-night meal in New York without the nagging fear that the chairs are about to be placed on the tables about you. One New York friend of mine recently said that he always has the feeling that he should have a taxi waiting with the meter running outside a London theatre so that he can make a headlong dash for nourishment as the curtain falls. You will have no such problems in New York, where the late-night restaurants often seem to lead on inexorably to the even later late-night clubs. Which in the case of establishments like Studio 54 and its successors takes you straight back to the world of theatre and theatricality once again.

The panoramic views available all over New York are special too, bathed as the city so often is in the crisp sunlight of a New York day – the clear blue even more memorable in winter than summer. And then at dusk there is the most well-designed and most exhilarating lighting up time of any major city. (Obviously one of those Broadway whizz kids must have been at work here too.)

The visitor will soon discover that New York has soul. Contrary to legend, this is not necessarily expressed in schmaltz. There will probably be very little bull. You know where you are with a New Yorker. They need to be tough but once you have got through the protective layer of native cunning, and you are admitted into the brotherhood of native loyalty, then a New Yorker is usually a friend for life.

Then there is the New York media. To a visitor from the UK, the radio stations of New York are special. Suddenly there is the broadcast equivalent of a magazine rack. You want to listen to 48 hours of non-stop country music? – there's a station just for you. You want to be saved from that? – there's 48 hours of gospel music just along the dial. There is all-night talk and all-day news, reggae and religion of almost every denomination.

Then there is the *New York Times.* The Sunday edition is worth every hernia that legend reports. That hefty size has an important corollary – length. *"I love those lengthy articles,"* a friend told me, *"they let you decide how long you want them to go on. Then you just stop reading."* I'm not sure that the editors have ever consciously adopted this philosophy, but certainly the *New York Times* is not a newspaper for devotees of the *Reader's Digest* approach, and the chance to dig deep can be a blessed one.

As a visitor you will be struck by the speed with which everything happens in New York. All the various sense impressions of the city's life cascade upon the visitor at an irresistible pace. There may not be the variety of tempo there is in London, but that high voltage pace is quite simply exhilarating. Exhausting too, no doubt, but at the price – a bargain.

But whichever city you choose to travel to – *Bon Voyage* and *Bon Appetit* – though the latter may well have to wait until you get off the plane!

**Note:**

The prices quoted in this guide are correct as at the beginning of 1986. They are, however, intended more as a comparative guide than definitive prices. Because of international currency fluctuations we have used local currencies.

# Amsterdam

No stranger to good fortune, Amsterdam is managing to overcome its once justified reputation as the drugs capital of Europe and to concentrate on what it really represents: a phenomenal success story of low interest and inflation rates in the face of world recession.

By Maggi O'Sullivan

The streets of Amsterdam may not be paved with gold but they are studded with diamonds. Diamond cutters. Diamond polishers. Diamond showrooms. And if the good people of this fair city singularly fail to sparkle on tram or bicycle, it is because street crime, fired by a notorious drugs problem, makes conspicuous gem-flashing a foolhardy exercise: 75 per cent of all theft in Amsterdam is now drug-related.

It wasn't always so, of course, before the drug circus, with its tawdry retinue of social misfits, came to town. Time was when the only people in Dam Square after dark were the peace-weary hippies who slept there. But times change. The hippies have all taken jobs in the city and it is heroin, rather than diamonds, that the world has come to associate primarily with the Dutch capital.

Diamonds first found the then small trading town on the Amstel in the mid-16th century. By 1750 there were more than 600 diamond workers in Amsterdam, many refugees escaping religious persecution in their own countries, and the rest, in diamond circles at least, is history. The Cullinan and the Koh-i-noor were both polished here as well as an inordinate number of lesser-known gems. Today the diamond industry in Amsterdam employs some 1,000 people and earns more than Dfl 400 million in exports annually.

But while the diamond industry suffered something of a decline during the economic recession of the 70s, the drug trade did no such thing. Substantial quantities of narcotics began to seep into Amsterdam around 1975, encouraged, it must be said, by a sublime tolerance peculiar only to the Dutch capital. Comments businessman Peter van Os: *"No other Western European society was as tolerant as Amsterdam in the 70s. We allowed everything and anything. Drugs poured into our city and we did very little about it. We simply carried on respecting the individual's right to independence and put up with the miserable consequences."* Adds Planning Consultant Benn Lateano: *"I'm not sure how much of the drug problem was caused by tolerance and how much by sheer disinterest in what anyone else was doing."*

At the end of 1984 and under the direction of the Mayor of Amsterdam, courts at least began to impose strict punishment on offenders. The police instigated a severe crackdown on anyone caught bringing drugs into the city. And, on a more positive note, advice and counselling services were made more widely available to addicts: buses and trams were plastered with the telephone numbers of Drug Advisory Centres, and pamphlets outlining the dangers of drug abuse were handed out to young visitors arriving at Amsterdam's central station, where they were most likely to first come into contact with the pushers. More recently, legislation has been passed to allow the authorities to confiscate money earned through drug dealing and seminars have been held with representatives from London to discuss more effective ways of dealing with the problem.

And it seems to be working. Figures for the first three months of 1985 showed a drop in fatalities of more than 65 per cent, and, the Tourist Office insists, Amsterdam is now no more popular with the South American dealers than London or Madrid.

But if Amsterdam has become less tolerant where drugs are concerned, it still manages to upset the Church of Rome with its liberal – some would say realistic – approach to religion. Few of Amsterdam's Catholic community would subscribe to the anti-Vatican ideas of the local youths who offered £3,500 to anyone willing to assassinate the Pope during his visit to The Netherlands, but most disagree with the Church's view on birth control, divorce, homosexuality and the barring of women from the priesthood. Most, too, object to the Vatican's recent choice of bishops for The Netherlands since all are hardline men from the old school.

Indeed, such is the feeling of dissent that when 'Popie Jopie' toured the country, Amsterdam was not even included on his itinerary.

The Vatican view is that there have been problems among the Catholic community in Amsterdam since the Reformation. The Amsterdam view is that the doctrines and values of the Catholic church are not relevant to today's needs and require urgent review.

Also slipping down the popularity polls alongside traditional Catholicism and self-destruction are: the Socialist government – the FFD – which appears to be moving further to the right; Queen Beatrix, who represents unequal distribution of wealth at its worst; a new town hall-cum-opera-house, or Stopera, which Amsterdammers feel is too expensive and unnecessarily large; and the Amsterdam Council, which is well and truly in the dog house for building hotels in the face of an acute housing shortage and for generally pandering too much to tourism and not enough to the Amsterdammers themselves.

*Amsterdam's distinctive architecture and its network of canals – a legacy from the city's golden days when The Netherlands was the world's greatest trading nation – still earn their keep as a major tourist attraction*

The latter dissatisfaction is something the council has tried to dispel with its Amsterdam *Heeft't* (Amsterdam has it) campaign. The campaign, which is aimed at people throughout The Netherlands, is intended to convince doubters that Amsterdam is not only an attractive tourist destination but *the* place in which to work and play.

Not that many people really need convincing. Most of Amsterdam's 750,000 inhabitants would never consider living anywhere else. For one thing the air is exceptionally clean – a stiff sea breeze whisks most of Amsterdam's pollution smartly into Germany. For another, the standard of living is relatively high: inflation is the lowest of all Common Market countries and interest rates hover around the eight per cent mark.

Indeed, Amsterdam really is extraordinarily prosperous given the current economic climate, with exports steadily rising each year. Most of the country's large commercial firms, agencies, buying houses and advertising agencies are located here although the extent of trade is difficult to gauge because of its very diversity. Then again, the Dutch capital is not only the financial centre of The Netherlands, but is also an important international financial centre in its own right. The number of foreign shares (455) listed on the Amsterdam stock exchange is greater than on any other European exchange. It is the largest exchange in Europe for American stocks.

All of which makes the city an exceedingly easy place in which to do business. Indeed,when it comes to attracting foreign interests, Amsterdam has it made. Explains Marriott Hotel's Director of Marketing: *"Amsterdam has something to offer that other Western European capitals simply don't have. Quite apart from the obvious historical attractions, its chief advantage is its accessibility. In many ways it is easier for a company in, say, Scotland to get to the centre of Amsterdam than the centre of London. And as far as congresses and conferences are concerned, as soon as participants start coming from more than one country, Amsterdam becomes a natural central point on the map. All we can do is try to extend and enhance that quality. And there really is a lot happening in Amsterdam. . ."*

The main event in business terms is Amsterdam's new World Trade Centre (WTC) in the heart of the business and financial district, not far from Schiphol airport. That some 80 companies had booked space at the WTC before the centre opened early in 1985 is a measure of its success.

The WTC, developed at the initiative of Amsterdam's Chamber of Commerce, is a private venture and cost between Dfl 300 and Dfl 330 million to finance. *"The pay-off period is likely to be between 15 and 20 years,"* comments the General Director of the Centre.

*"One of the goals of the World Trade Centre Asso-*

*ciation is to promote trade with the Third World and we shall develop Dutch trade with the developing countries wherever possible."*

Another advantage Amsterdam possesses, of course, is that the internationally-minded locals really do seem to have a better facility for foreign languages than any other country in Europe. Explains Robert Mul, Chairman of the Amsterdam Hotel Association, *"With only 20,000,000 Dutch-speaking people in the world, Amsterdam can't afford not to be bilingual. And most people are conversant in at least one more tongue."*

All of which will prove extremely useful should Amsterdam's bid to host the 1992 Olympics be successful. . . not that everyone is entirely in favour of that idea. *"While it certainly won't be a question of building an Olympic city from scratch, it will be a costly business,"* says one leading businessman. *"The idea at the moment is to spread the games throughout The Netherlands, building facilities that had been planned anyway. A swimming pool here, a competitors' hall there, using Amsterdam as a base."* But many Amsterdammers feel that the games will only serve to divert attention away from existing problems in the city and any boost to the unemployment figures would be short-lived. *"How can we host an Olympic games when many students can't afford to study anymore?"* demands one of a thousand students protesting against recent grant cuts.

But whether Amsterdam holds the Olympics or not, it still intends to expand its hotel capacity by another 2,000 beds by 1987. A pool-topped Holiday Inn, just off Dam Square, is the first of the new hotels on the way. The Dutch capital is already the fourth most visited city in Europe after Paris, London and Rome, and as such finds itself ill-equipped to accommodate the millions of visitors who pass through the city every year, particularly since space in central Amsterdam is limited. Yet few Amsterdammers will ever agree to cede their canal-fronted houses to tourism, preferring to live the way they have always lived – in thin, gable-topped, plant-filled buildings, close to the heart of a city that still reeks of Amsterdam's past.

*Many Amsterdammers live on houseboats due to an acute housing shortage*

# WHERE TO STAY

The last time anyone counted there were 23,000 hotel beds in Amsterdam. It wasn't enough then. It isn't enough now, and, whatever the outcome of the city's bid to host the 1992 Olympics, it certainly won't be enough in ten years' time. Three new hotels are already in the planning stages, but the present shortage does not augur too well for anyone arriving in Amsterdam without a reservation.

All of which gives Amsterdam's hoteliers ample cause for celebration. Occupancy rates rarely slide below the 80 per cent mark, rising to nearer 100 per cent during the high season. Yet there are still discounts to be had – the Amsterdam Tourist Office, for example, offers something called the Amsterdam Way package, available from November to March, which provides one to three nights' accommodation (weekends only) at five de-luxe hotels or five first class hotels from Dfl 98. The package also includes complimentary admittance to several museums, reductions on city tours, plus a welcome drink when you check in and a glass of wine with lunch or dinner.

And for visitors who arrive without a hotel reservation, the VVV office, in front of the central station, does its best to find suitable accommodation for a modest fee.

Choosing a hotel is, as usual, largely a matter of personal taste. The **Marriott** (Stadhouderskade 19-21; tel: 835 151; telex: 1508), the **Hilton** (Apollolaan 138-140; tel: 780 780; telex: 11025) and the **Okura** (Ferdinand Bolstraat 175; tel: 787 111; telex: 16182) are certainly the best of the new moderns, serving up luxury and five-star comfort.

Overlooking bustling Leidseplein, the Marriott is a shining example of a hotel chain at its best; all the usual amenities plus faultless service and careful attention to detail. Renovation has transformed the lobby area into a homely, as opposed to formal, lounge area and set the Marriott corporation back some Dfl 15 million. Standard single/double Dfl 395/Dfl 455; suite Dfl 975.

Further out of the city centre, the Hilton and the Okura are ideally suited to visitors arriving in Amsterdam under their own steam or to anyone hiring a car, since both possess that most sought after of amenities: a car park.

The Okura, a member of the Japanese-owned chain of the same name and the only Okura property in Europe, was originally built as part of a scheme to combine a hotel with an Opera House. The hotel was built in 1971. The Opera House was not – leaving a pocket of cleared land that is only recently being developed. Still, the breathtaking city view from the hotel's 23rd-floor Ciel Bleu bar more than makes up for the unattractive building site next door.

The Hilton, on the other hand, is fronted by the boulevard-like Apollolaan and edged by the Northern Amstel Canal. The first American chain hotel to open in Amsterdam during the 60s, the ultra-modern, squeeky clean hotel could hardly be anything *but* a Hilton. Hilton prices: single/double from Dfl 201.47/Dfl 251.83; suite prices on application. Okura: single/double Dfl 270/Dfl 310; suite Dfl 675-Dfl 1,300.

One of the oldest purpose-built hotels in Amsterdam, and probably the most elegant, is Inter-Continental's **Amstel** Hotel (Professor Tulpplein 1; tel: 226 060; telex: 11004). This, according to the Tourist Board, is where royalty and international celebrities stay although the Amstel itself is much too discreet to say so. Each one of the Amstel's 118 rooms is different and all are exquisitely turned out in pale gold, peach or cream. Single/double from Dfl 275/Dfl 375; suites from Dfl 600-Dfl 1,250.

An honourable alternative to the Amstel, although no cheaper, is the **Hotel de l'Europe** (Nieuwe Doelenstraat 2-4; tel: 234 836; telex: 12081), just off Rembrandtsplein. Built originally as a fortress to defend the city, the Hotel de l'Europe was completely rebuilt in 1895, renovated in 1985 and very nearly matches the Amstel for elegance and style. Its chief claim to fame, however, is its wine cellar which contains over 40,000 bottles, some of which have languished there for over 50 years. Single/double Dfl 250-Dfl 350; suites from Dfl 850.

The **American Hotel's** (Leidsekade 97; tel: 245 322; telex: 12545) main attraction, on the other hand, is its *art nouveau* café-restaurant; a registered national monument, resplendent in original Jugendstil decoration. The Café Américain is Amsterdam's very own Champs Elysée – everyone goes there sooner or later – and if there's one disappointing thing about the American, it's that the rest of the hotel is not decorated in the same style. Single/double from Dfl 165/Dfl 238.

Because building space is at such a premium in the centre of Amsterdam, ingenious conversions are the order of the day as far as many hotels are concerned. Golden Tulip's **Hotel Pulitzer** (Prinsengracht 315-331; tel: 228 333; telex: 16508) began life as 19 canal houses and is now a 200-room melange of modern-day comfort and 19th century atmosphere. Floor layout is unconventional to say the least and room service is limited by the number of steps that has to be negotiated on each of the original, interconnected winding corridors (unsuitable, of course, for food trolleys. Similarly, the **Sonesta** (Kattengat 1; tel: 212 223; telex: 17149) and the **Grand Hotel Krasnapolsky** (Dam 9; tel: 549 111; telex: 12262) – another Golden Tulip property – were respectively a Lutheran church and a Polish coffee shop. Pulitzer: single/double Dfl 225/Dfl 275. Sonesta: single/double Dfl 365/ Dfl 425; suites from Dfl 395. Grand Hotel Krasnapolsky: single/double from Dfl 215/Dfl 275; suites Dfl 500.

Slightly cheaper, although still rich in atmospere, are the Dutch-owned Crest hotels of which there are five in Amsterdam. Three, the **Doelen** (Nieuwe Doelenstraat; tel: 220 722; telex: 14399), the **Carlton** (Vijzelstraat; tel: 222 266; telex: 11670) and the **Schiller** (Rembrandtsplein 26-36; tel: 231 660; telex: 14058) are particularly comfortable and equipped with a very reasonable supply of five-star amenities. And the Schiller boasts one of the finest fish restaurants in town. Singles/ doubles from Dfl 165/Dfl 2121.

Finally, it must be said that, comfortable though Amsterdam's top hotels may be, it is the small, humble establishments that offer the best insight into the way the city really is. There are any number of well-appointed, family-owned hotels in the Dutch capital and the following are all worthy of the businessman off-duty: **Canal House** (Keizersgracht 148; tel: 225 182; telex: 10412); **Ambassade** Herengracht 341; tel: 262 333; telex: 10158); **Hotel Agora** (Singel 462; tel: 272 200); and **de Gouden Kettingh** (Keizersgracht 268; tel: 248 287). Few provide restaurants but all offer the sort of ambience possible only in a small hotel. Single rooms cost around Dfl 110; doubles are around Dfl 150.

Reservations for the Okura Hotel and Hotel de l'Europe can be made direct or through Leading Hotels of the World (tel: London 583 3050); Golden Tulip Hotels can be contacted on: London 568 0071 or worldwide through any KLM office.

# WHERE TO EAT

It's not unusual for the uninitiated to view the gastronomic delights of Amsterdam with something less than enthusiasm. Isn't this where the locals buy raw herrings from roadside carts and gulp them down whole, tail and all?

Actually, it is and they do, although to my disappointment I've never witnessed any such heroic event – most Amsterdammers these days appear to prefer the convenience of the plastic fork. Then again, this is also where French and traditional Dutch restaurants rub shoulders with the more exotic Indonesian, Japanese and Pakistani establishments; where pancake rolls, meat balls and beef croquettes spill endlessly from food dispensers; where hot waffles, sticky with syrup, are sold in bundles from street stalls and where even a simple carton of chips comes with a dressing.

Certainly there is no shortage of choice: there are more than ten pages of restaurant, bar and café listings in the Amsterdam Yellow Pages, covering virtually every national cuisine in the world. Continental cuisine, on the other hand, is probably best left to the major hotels who manage that sort of thing rather well in Amsterdam. The **Excelsior** in the Hotel de l'Europe (tel: 234 836), for instance, with its baronial atmosphere, fresh flowers and picture windows overlooking the Amstel River, is a particular favourite with Prince Bernhard while **La Rive** at the Amstel Hotel (tel: 226 060) serves French-inspired cuisine in small intimate surroundings overlooking the same river. Faultless service and exquisite fare have their price, however – in this case around Dfl 60 per person, exclusive of wine.

Otherwise, more than worthy of note are Marriott's **Port O'Amsterdam** (tel: 835 151), where the guinea fowl is quite perfect; Grand Hotel Krasnapolsky's **Reflet d'Or** (tel: 554 951) which still oozes all the pomp and splendour of *La Belle Epoque;* the **Dikker & Thijs** restaurant at the Alexander Hotel (tel: 267 721) and the Garden Hotel's **De Kersentuin** (tel: 642 121).

But while most hotel restaurants have at least some pretension to serving French cuisine, French cuisine per se is not that widely indulged in Amsterdam. **Le Tout Court** (17 Runstraat; tel: 258 637) and **'T Swarte Schaep** (Korte Leidsedwarsstraat 24; tel: 223 021) are probably the best known and as such tend to get rather crowded. Le Tout Court prides itself on 'good food without a fuss' and certainly its *mousse aux prunes* is one of the best I have tasted. Its four menus, with a choice of three, four, six or eight courses ranging from Dfl 41.50 to Dfl 72.50, are also excellent value.

Not far away, on Reestraat, is **Sancerre** (Reestraat 28-31; tel: 278 794) which, not surprisingly, specialises in wines from the Sancerre region and **Valentijn** in Kloveniersburgwal (Kloveniersburgwal 6-8; tel: 242 028), the only restaurant in Amsterdam to have been restored by the Department of Monument Care.

One cheering thing about Amsterdam restaurants, however, is that although the health bandwagon rolled into town many years ago, the traditionally heavy Dutch cuisine is still very much in evidence, witness the preponderance of *Neerlands Dis* stickers which indicate a wide choice of original Dutch and/or regional specialities.

The *grande dame* of Dutch cuisine is *erwtensoep* – a thick pea soup served traditionally between October and March. **Dorrius** (NZ Voorburgwal 336; tel: 235 875), probably the best known of all Amsterdam's Dutch restaurants, not only provides this soup as a starter but, for Dfl 21, will bring it back again as an entrée. And then there is something called *hutspot* – a mixture of potatoes, carrots and onions which, it is said, was given to the starving people of Leiden when the siege of that city was raised in 1574.

The widest selection of typically Dutch restaurants in Amsterdam is in the Student Quarter, on or near Spui. Dorrius, **Haesje Cleas** (NZ Voorburgwal 320; tel: 249 998) and the **Sherry Can Bodega** (Spui 30; tel: 231 892) are the most authentic, although visitors can be sure of getting a good feed at any of the restaurants displaying the *Neerlands Dis* emblem.

Also popular here, and throughout The Netherlands, is Indonesian cuisine – a vivid reminder of a colonial past. The best Indonesian restaurants do tend to be in The Hague but Amsterdam serves up its fair share of excellent Indonesian delicacies too. Straight Indonesian, rather than Indonesian-Chinese, restaurants are what to look for although all serve some version of that traditional *rijsttafel* – a multi-course extravaganza that normally takes some sleeping off.

Not far from the Rijksmuseum is the **Samo Sebo** (PC Hoofstraat 27; tel: 728 146) which, for my money (around Dfl 40), is the finest Indonesian restaurant in Amsterdam. Service is extremely attentive in what can only be described as slightly over the top surroundings. Reservations here are essential, though, and should be made at least one day in advance.

Other Indonesians well worth a visit are **Bali,** just off Leidseplein (Leidsestraat 95; tel: 227 878), **Djawa** (K Leidsewarsstraat 18; tel: 246 061) and **Indonesia** (Singel 550; tel: 232 035), on the second floor of the Carlton House office building and hotel. Otherwise, most of the small Indonesian places in the red light district are excellent and somewhat cheaper.

Given its water history, it's hardly surprising that fish and seafood is another thing that Amsterdammers prepare particularly well – the **Schiller Crest Hotel** (tel: 231 660), **De Oesterbar** (Leidseplein 10; tel: 263 463), **Le Pêcheur** (Reguliersdwarsstraat 32; tel: 243 121) and **Lucius** (Spuistraat 247; tel: 241 831) all serve mouthwateringly fresh sea fare for between Dfl 30 and Dfl 40. Alternatively, the afore-mentioned herring stalls not only sell herring but *paling* (young smoked eel), *gerookte aal* (mature smoked eel), *gestoomde* or smoked mackerel and shrimps. And nearly all of the *broodje* (sandwich) bars provide suitably fishy fillings.

One of the nicest things about Amsterdam cuisine, however, is that it is not exclusive to those with the time – or money. All of Amsterdam's *eet* cafés provide snacks and extensive menus for less than Dfl 15. **De Doffer** (Runstraat 12; tel: 226 686), not far from Spui, for example, turns out excellent spare ribs, steak, fish, omelettes, soups and pâtés and really is extraordinarily good value. Coffee shops, too, are perfect for snacks of the afternoon tea variety. **Prix d'Ami,** on the other hand (Reguliersdwarsstraat 29; tel: 270 333) serves cake of a slightly more stimulating nature – hash cake in chocolate or fruit flavour.

**Rum Runners** (Prinsengracht 277; tel: 274 079), Amsterdam's only Caribbean restaurant, allows customers to pick individual items from its lunch or dinner menus – such as its *chicharrones,* small pieces of fried chicken with lime and hot sauce for Dfl 5.50 – with no minimum charge.

Still on an economical note, many of Amsterdam's restaurants offer a tourist menu for Dfl 16.75, details of which can be obtained from any Tourist or VVV office. And, if a steak is what is really required then **Die Port van Cleve** (NZ Voorburgwal 178; tel: 24 00 47) offers a free bottle of wine to anyone ordering a steak with a winning number (all steaks are numbered and have been since Die Port van Cleve opened in 1870 – at the last count they were already well over 5,500,500). I'm not sure what the winning number is. . .

«"*Live shows, come in and see,*" coos the man beneath the neon. Boys in bars. Girls in windows. Men in slow cars. Gommorrah with clogs on. There can't be many first time visitors who leave Amsterdam without taking at least a cursory glance round its famous rosse buurt, or red light district, behind Dam Square.

In any case, it's worth knowing where it is simply to help the hordes of English, German and Japanese tourists who will inevitably ask for directions there. Not knowing the way to the rosse buurt is like not knowing who lives in Buckingham Palace.

Once there, it's probably best to leave the so-called live shows, that vie for custom along the canal edges, well alone. Most are very expensive and few offer particularly good value for money, and it's no good expecting the scantily-clad window sitters to provide free entertainment either – some knit, some yawn, most charge around Dfl 30 for five minutes of their time and none will have the girlish modesty to look away first should your eyes meet theirs. Staring out the voyeurs is part of their stock in trade.

Having exhausted the possibilities of the rosse burrt, one's thoughts turn, quite naturally, to drink and although some of the bars and cafés in this part of town should be entered with caution (notably those displaying a red light in the window), most are perfectly innocuous. The **Wijnand Fockink** (Pijlsteed 31; tel: 243 989) a short walk away, on the edge of the rosse buurt, is guaranteed to revive flagging spirits, not least because customers are required to take the first sip of their drink, glass on bar, hands behind back, with a maximum of slurping. The Wijnand Fockink is what is known in The Netherlands as a *proeflokaal* or tasting house and as such is stuffed with old liqueur bottles of varying sizes and shapes, small barrels and an endless supply of spirits. And nobody leaves here without first exchanging a few words with the jovial bartender (usually as the butt of one of his jokes).

Other tasting houses in a similar vein are **Bols House of Liqueurs** (36 Damstraat) and **De Drie Fleshjes** (Gravenstraat 18) behind the Nieuwe Kerk – both within easy strolling distance of the Wijnand Fockink.

But, as most visitors to Amsterdam soon discover, the place for serious drinking is a Brown Café. Here it is that the ancient art of slicing the head off beer with a wet knife was begun. Here it is, too, that centuries of smoke and animated conversation cling doggedly to sombre-coloured walls and unvarnished floors. Some of the oldest, brownest cafés remain exactly as they were in Rembrandt's time but even the relative newcomers (which for a Brown Café means built at the end of the last century) bristle with atmosphere.

**Café Nol,** in the Jordaan district, to the west of the city centre, is a typical example of a Brown café – small, crowded, friendly and, in this case, kitsch to the extreme. **De Wenteltrap** (Gravenstraat 2; tel: 248 935), **'T Smalle** (Egelantiersgracht 12; tel: 239 617) and **'T Smackzeyl** (Brouwersgracht 101; tel: 226 520) should all be included on any café crawl undertaken in this area, finishing, stamina permitting, by walking east to the **Hoppe** (Spui 18), a noisy, jolly affair, popular with tourists and locals alike.

Less atmospheric, perhaps, but growing in popularity – particularly among the young – are Amsterdam's new crop of white bars which look like they sound – light, bright and airy, a total antithesis of Brown Café. **Oblomov** (Reguliersdwarsstraat 40) is something like a wine bar with a small restaurant and cocktail bar open in the evenings. Although not a 'gay bar', Oblomov is also popular with Amsterdam's extended gay community since Reguliersdwarsstraat has become very much a gay street, with several gay coffee shops – **Down Town,** for example – and discos.

*The infamous rosse buurt*

Elsewhere, the gay scene tends to polarise around the Muntplein and those who would rather not unwittingly stumble upon gay life in full swing should simply keep an eye on who is going where.

On the whole, nightclubs and discotheques are not quite as essential to Amsterdam nightlife as they are, say, in London or Paris, particularly since many of the bars and cafés stay open until 3a.m. anyway. The Leidseplein is the best place for this sort of thing although several of the hotel clubs – **Juliana's** at the Hilton (tel: 737 313) or the **Boston Club** at the Sonesta (tel: 244 461), for example, – are worth looking into. Most of the guidebooks still list Marriott's **Windjammer** as one of the best discos in town – it isn't. Because guests were finding themselves elbowed aside by local revellers, the Windjammer has been smoothed into a somewhat slicker and altogether more dignified cabaret club, offering dinner and a show for Dfl 90.

Elsewhere, the music scene is a little more up tempo, specialising particularly in jazz. Many of the Brown Cafés have weekly jazz bands and **De Melkweg** (234a Lijnbaansgracht), just off Leidseplein, occasionally features European and American jazz artists. The place for avant-garde composed and improvised jazz, however, is **Bimhuis** (Oude Schans 73; tel: 233 373) near the east docks.

But perhaps the most relaxing way for jaded souls to spend a couple of hours after dark is drifting (or chugging) effortlessly through the canals and waterways that score the city. **Rederij P Kooij** (tel: 233 810), just opposite Spui, offers cheese and wine candelight cruises, lasting two hours, for Dfl 27.50. Alternatively, those with the legs for it can rent canal bicycles for around Dfl 15.

Further details of theatre and cinema programmes, plus information of what's on where, can be obtained from a free booklet called *Amsterdam This Week*, available at all VVV offices.

## GETTING AROUND

With 16 tram lines, 30 bus lines, a plethora of taxis and a shortage of parking, there really is little point hiring a car in Amsterdam unless business takes you beyond the city centre. If it does, however, Hertz (tel: 852 441), Europcar (tel: 184 595) and Budget Rent A Car (tel: 126 066) all have offices close to Leidseplein while Avis (tel: 262 201) can be found in Keizersgracht.

While taxis are relatively inexpensive – around Dfl 10 to most points in the city centre – something to bear in mind is that they can't be hailed in the street. Nevertheless, they are always plentiful at the central station, outside most major hotels and at certain designated taxi ranks throughout the city. Alternatively, taxis can be ordered by dialling 777 777.

Cheaper still is the network of trams and buses that reaches out to the suburbs of Amsterdam. A day ticket, which covers all zones on tram, bus or Metro, costs Dfl 7.85 and can be bought at the information and ticket office opposite central station. A 6- or 10-strip ticket can also be bought from tram and bus drivers although these are not quite as good value as the day tickets.

Buses and trams work on the honour system – it's up to you whether you buy a ticket or not but getting caught without one means a Dfl 26 fine.

Renting a bicycle is the obvious answer to rush hour traffic, and although perhaps not entirely appropriate for the image-conscious there is no real stigma attached to bicycle clips. Rental rates are around Dfl 6 per day or Dfl 30 per week, with deposit required, and bikes can be picked up at the Koenders Rent-A-Bike, outside central station.

Travel to and from Schiphol airport is easily done by bus. KLM runs a regular service between the airport and central station for Dfl 8.00, and the local bus services are even cheaper.

# Bahrain

By David Owen

**Outwardly the very model of tranquillity and prosperity, minority-ruled Bahrain is something of a potential powder keg whatever the outcome of the ongoing Gulf War. Meanwhile, the island State is pushing ahead with a masterplan to become the service centre for the entire Arab world.**

To Westerners, one of the most immediately striking aspects of Bahrain is its women. To the unaccustomed eye, these nebulous figures with beaked masks and billowing black clothes seem unaccountably sinister. This mode of dress developed from a section of the Koran which instructs *"believing women to avert their glances and guard their private parts, and not to display their charms . . . They should fold their shawls over their bosoms . . ."* (The Light 24:30-31). In Islam, a woman's beauty is for her husband's eyes alone. Islamic women who do not wear the traditional garb will always dress inconspicuously, for to do otherwise is seen as a severe breach of faith.

It is not surprising, then, that Arab men tend to see Western women as wanton and lascivious creatures; and European women in Bahrain are often subject to advances which can best be described as indelicate. The situation is not helped by the number of Western women who do exchange their favours for something more tangible than marriage – it is not unknown for a Ferrari to mark the start of an affair.

It may seem a contradiction in terms, but while Islam remains the unyielding backbone of Bahraini society, in business matters the Bahrainis have exercised a remarkable capacity for change.

Change, fuelled by oil money, has indeed been rapid: in 1960 there were 7,000 cars in Bahrain, today there are close to 100,000; before 1975 there wasn't a single offshore banking unit, by 1983 there were more than 70 with assets of $60 billion. As the first Gulf State to exploit its oil reserves in 1932, Bahrain will almost certainly be the first to run out by early in the 21st century – already national output has fallen from a peak of 75,000 barrels a day in the early 70s to the 1983 level of some 42,000 barrels a day.

Even before full independence from Britain in 1971, Bahrain had begun to use the rich pickings from its oil fields to lay the foundations of an alternative economy capable of sustaining the nation in the post oil age. Today, while oil still accounts for around 67 per cent of GNP, the island (the State is billed as an archipelago of 33 islands of which Bahrain is the largest) has successfully diversified into steel, aluminium, plastics and others and has secured 50 per cent of output from a Saudi oilfield, safeguarding crude supplies for the Bapco refinery until well into the next century. Gas is another major source of power and income. In short, the government has shown a refreshing readiness to saddle itself with short-term loss leaders for the sake of long-term prosperity.

Above all, the ruling al-Khalifa family has set about furnishing Bahrain with the infrastructure to become the service centre of the Arab world. The island was already possessed of one priceless asset when it came to selling itself to insurers and bankers: its geographical position. Opening in time to catch afternoon business in Tokyo, offices could comfortably work through the bulk of the London day and even catch early New York trading with relatively slight inconvenience. Any Middle East nation could claim as much. But by the time Bahraini strategists had finished preparing the ground for their assault, the State had three crucial advantages over potential rivals: sizable tax incentives, a communications system second-to-none (and still a vast improvement on British Telecom's archaic system) and a liberal attitude to Western life-styles and their concomitants, notably alcohol.

Indeed, tolerance towards alcohol has proved an important fringe benefit in its own right. Planeloads of Western expatriates and Arabs from neighbouring Gulf nations fly in every weekend (Thursday/Friday) to spend their hard-earned dinars and riyals on a night on the town – and frequently under the table. The flight from Dhahran (the nearest Saudi town of any consequence) on Thursday nights is always packed – despite the fact that it is allegedly the most expensive flight per km anywhere in the world.

Whatever the relative merits of Bahrain's attractions to financiers, the masterplan ultimately worked because Westerners and Arabs alike found they enjoyed doing business there and were, moreover, assured an affluent and tolerably comfortable life-style.

The last phase of the hard sell was to instil in potential 'settlers' a great deal of confidence. Not just that they would make money but that they were putting down roots in a stable oasis (in a notoriously unstable part of the world). The marketing men did – and continue to do – a good job. But then, they have much to eulogise.

Office blocks such as the Bahrain Monetary Agency and the beautiful but controversial Sheraton Tower have now completely usurped the coastal strip in the capital Manama. And most of the mosques, with their fluorescent lighting and often amplified *muezzin,* look brand new. Although more traditional and ramshackle Bahraini dwellings nestle within 100 yards of the business sector on the other side of the Government Road, and the *suq* behind Bab al-Bahrain Square thrives unabated, the quantity of construction work still proceeding is quite staggering – and there are plenty of gaps to be filled along King Faisal Highway. The most ambitious housing project yet is taking shape in the desert, not far from the police base of Isa Town: a garden city with room for 60,000 named Hamad Town.

Meanwhile, the welfare system has come on in leaps and bounds. Medical care is free and by all accounts excellent, while housing is cheap – with rents guaranteed under 25 per cent of income for the less well-off. Schools are generally regarded as the best in the Gulf (the Arab Gulf University is in Bahrain) and specialist training institutions, such as the bankers' training centre, have paved the way for the process of 'Bahraini-isation', which has seen the number of expensive Western expatriates dwindle to around 20,000 in recent years.

But the sheer speed of transformation from desert island to international financial centre has inevitably fostered new tensions to add to a number which were already present. Despite the sterling efforts of the marketing men, it does not take much probing to discover that all is perhaps not so well in the State as initial appearances tend to suggest.

One is always suspicious of a country where the press is muzzled – however benignly. The local newspapers (the daily (expect Friday) *Gulf Daily News* and the weekly *Gulf Mirror)* do what they can but are effectively emasculated – with the *Mirror* further hampered by understaffing, the legacy of its failure to make a profit for several years. Both make copious use of the international news wires, while publication of matter which might be construed as taboo necessitates a preliminary 'courtesy call' to the Information Ministry. To be fair, journalists say such a call seldom warrants an outright veto. For example, the story of the Bahraini found to be trading oil with South Africa merely rated the imprecation 'keep it off the front page in future'. On a lighter note, with both organs distributed to other Gulf States, in the words of one prominent newspaperman: *"For us, alcohol simply doesn't exist"*. The publication of ladies' 'naughty bits' eg arms and ankles is also out of the question – a restriction which has resulted in photographs of aerobics classes going out with participants clad in hastily-penned *abas* –the shapeless black smocks still *de rigueur* with Muslim women.

This manic obsession with painting a rosy picture is eminently understandable when the viewer is the outside world. As former British ambassador Roger Tomkys opined in an interview: *"However well-run Bahrain is internally, prosperity and security ultimately depend on factors outside the State's direct control."* More worrying is the apparent need to paint such a picture to its own inhabitants.

Not only is Bahrain potentially the poorest of the six Gulf Co-operation Council (GCC) States – more about that later – it is also under minority rule. Guidebooks are non-committal on the subject, maintaining the population is *"almost equally divided between Sunni and Shia Muslims"*. Most islanders put the split at around 35 per cent Sunni (the lowest proportion of any GCC State) to 65 per cent Shia. Nobody knows the precise figure since the question was omitted from forms in the 1981 census. Rapid strides in material well-being (annual per capita income is around $9,000) and a token five seats in Bahrain's 17-man cabinet have until now kept the Shias quiet and to a degree happy. But how long this would last should the economy falter (and 1983's budget deficit totalled D47m) is anyone's guess.

Bahrain's Prime Minister, Shaikh Khalifa Bin-Sulman al-Khalifa, likes to dub the security pact signed with Saudi Arabia in 1981 *"a frame on a nice picture"*. In fact security spending is another touchy subject, because a certain amount obviously finances internal security, which some might interpret to mean presiding over the current Sunni/Shia status quo. In terms of defence of the GCC region, most of the cash comes from Saudi Arabia – but the arrangement cuts both ways. Bahrain – in common with Kuwait, Qatar, UAE and Oman – is content to use Saudi money to equip its defence force, while Saudi Arabia considers it money well spent if it ensures it is surrounded by benevolent states.

The area where military activity is most pronounced on the island – the south – is now completely out of bounds. It contains nothing but desert, yet time was, the locals reminisce, when would-be voices in the wilderness could explore the region to their hearts' content (having first acquired a permit to enable them to be traced should they get lost). The American Support Unit conducts the bulk of its operations there – that much is common knowledge. But no one can say what prompted the authorities to restrict access – although there is no shortage of rumours.

One further question mark overhangs this outwardly tranquil community: the effect of the recent linking of Bahrain and Saudi Arabia by a causeway. At $564m (or $30,000 per metre) it is reckoned to be the most expensive bridging link yet built. It should certainly bring down the cost of living: food is cheaper in Saudi Arabia. And it should enable many more luxurious accoutrements of the Bahraini life-style to be trucked in, with considerable savings on freight. By the same token, local shopkeepers are worried lest the influx erode profit margins, while planners are hoping the causeway will benefit Bahrain's efficient port by providing direct access to the lucrative Saudi market and all points beyond. Some even feel it may prompt a boom in the Bahrain property market by enabling expatriates based in Saudi Arabia to set up home on the island and commute across it to work.

But the major concern is that easier access may prompt the Saudis to push for stricter regulations – particularly those pertaining to alcohol. While it seems unlikely they will risk unsettling their neighbour in the short-term, the dwindling numbers of Western expatriates on the island mean there will be fewer to upset by a turn of the screw when the process of 'Bahraini-isation' has proceeded a few more percentage points.

Meanwhile, the working day can seem long to those unused to the Gulf way of life – especially if you are having trouble adapting to the hot, humid climate. Most offices open at 8 a.m. (banks 7.30) and they may close very late – particularly if in touch with financial markets in London and New York.

Much has been made in the past of the necessity of respecting local customs and etiquette when doing business in the Gulf. Nowadays, while one should make every effort not to ride roughshod over one's host's sensibilities, the considerable increase in Bahraini attendance at US and European

*The business section stretches right down to the beach*

universities and business schools has done much to obviate their importance. Of course, one should endeavour to remember to hold one's coffee cup in one's right (as opposed to left) hand and never to show the soles of one's footwear. But such niceties are unlikely to be the difference between clinching and failing to clinch an important deal. Far more vital is to be patient and courteous initially and – if and when a bargain is struck – to back up one's product with unquestioning service and unfailing reliability.

Many feel this is why the Japanese have acquired such a stranglehold on the Bahraini consumer durable market – despite the fact that most Bahrainis claim to be pro-British. It seems the refrain *"I was a teaboy for the British army . . ."* is only half flannel. *"An Arab customer will expect you to fly halfway around the world at the drop of a hat if he has a problem,"* I was told, *"but he's quite prepared to pay for it afterwards."* This, it would appear, is something the average UK businessman has singularly failed to grasp.

Businesswomen are really up against it in Bahrain. Or so I was led to believe until I asked some. Those I spoke to were adamant that, after an admittedly long assimilation process, they found

their sex a positive advantage. *"They never keep you waiting when they might consider delaying a man,"* said one, while another found herself so well accepted by the Bahraini business community that, when invited to family functions necessitating the segregation of the sexes, she found it hard to remember she should stay with the womenfolk. Ladies are, however, expected to conform with relatively sober dress guidelines (i.e., highish neckline, lowish hemline) when a guest, while men should note that shorts in public are definitely out.

November to February is the pleasantest time to do business. During this period humidity seldom rises above 80 per cent while temperature ranges from 15-25°C. Take care to avoid Ramadan with the celebratory Eid Al Fitr national holiday to follow. Offices are open during Ramadan but restaurants stay closed during daylight hours.

One rule of thumb which is probably best to stick to is never covet an Arab's possessions: he is very likely to give you the object of your desire there and then. Only trouble is, he will expect to receive a gift of equal value as a token of your gratitude. Businessmen should also be prepared to conduct discussions in front of several unconnected onlookers. It is commonplace and polite for visitors to be received as they arrive and confidentiality will invariably be upheld.

# WHERE TO STAY

Bahrain can boast about 2,000 hotel rooms – 500 or so more than it needs. This makes it very much a buyers' market. As a result, discounts are the norm, despite attempts by the government and hoteliers themselves to prevent them. Long-stay guests and those eligible for the 'corporate' rate will usually get reductions merely by asking (the correct rate at the Diplomat is D28 – normal D38, while the Holiday Inn offers the more modest cut of D3 to D27). Others will need to be more forceful, but few hotels can afford to turn clients away, despite the usual protestations to the contrary. Indeed, the nearest many get to being full is on Thursday nights when planeloads of expatriates and Arabs from elsewhere in the Gulf fly in to take advantage of Bahrain's liberal licensing laws.

As most cannot make enough on rooms alone, hotels have taken to securing a healthy margin on services offered. Restaurants tend to be sumptuous but expensive while telephone/telex charges and exchange rates can be exorbitant.

A 1984 survey of business visits costs showed that the average charge made by a luxury hotel for a three-minute telephone call to London is 6 D084, while three minutes on the telex would cost 7 D060. Quite a mark-up from the corresponding standard charges of 3 D600 (telephone) and 4 D200 (telex). Furthermore, the telephone cost is halved if the call is made between 7p.m. and 7a.m. local time.

Simlarly, when the *Gulf Daily News* hawked a mythical £500 around the major hotels one morning in June, it received some pretty startling offers. On a day when banks were offering 514-426 fils per £, the best hotel rate was at the Diplomat, where guests would have collected 510 fils per £. Next came the Regency Inter-Continental on 505 fils, while the Delmon and the Aradous offered around 500 fils per £. Bottom of the list was the Sheraton with an astounding 459 fils per £. Some hotels demanded a room number, stating that exchange facilities were a service for guests only, while the Hilton and the Gulf pointed the inquirer to branch banks in their lobbies.

Of the eight top class hotels in Manama, the **Regency Inter-Continental** off King Faisal Highway (tel: 231 777; telex: 9400) is handy for the main business/banking district. The 384-room Regency has a compact and businesslike foyer, incorporating a pleasant tea lounge. The Clipper Bar on the Mezzanine is ideal for a relaxed business lunch and there is a swimming pool, as with all Manama's first class hotels. The rooms are not the biggest on the island but are well fitted and decorated.

Half a dozen competitors could boast likewise. What makes the Regency stand out is the service – cheerful and attentive when required but with that essential extra ingredient of discretion. Other hotels have yet to realise that service with a smile can be overdone. Rooms: single D38; double D46. Suites D100 standard; D300 de-luxe.

**Hilton International** (tel: 250 000; telex: 8288) is suffering from over-familiarity, having been the first of the chains to set up in Bahrain. It is also visibly dwarfed by the showy Sheraton across the way. Rooms are generally small and I could have done without the pink uniforms. The elegant claret and grey foyer is marred by an impassive Arab selling the local brew by the door – doubtless at inflated prices – but does possess a map (something of a rarity) together with a complete range of business services. Avoid the Cavalry Club bar with its impossibly immaculate boarded wooden walls and leather upholstery. Rooms: single D30-40; double D36-48; suites D100-245. The **Sheraton** (tel: 233 233; telex: 9440) itself is rather ritzy with an entertaining Oriental-style cocktail lounge called An Nada. Rooms D34-54; suites D100-550.

The **Diplomat** (tel: 231 666; telex: 9555) the **Holiday Inn** (tel: 241 122; telex: 9000/1) and the **Gulf Hotel** (tel: 233 000; telex: 8241) are all a five-minute taxi ride from the main business district. Nevertheless, all have their compensations. The THF-owned Diplomat enjoys a particularly good reputation amongst the locals, as much for its spacious rooms and well-appointed pool as its comparatively generous corporate reduction. Full rates – single D38; double D46; suites D100-400.

Holiday Inn is rated more for its social life than its accommodation. I found the foyer rather garish and its geometrical layout disorientating although undeniably imaginative. Rooms are a class below the best available and are unpleasantly decorated but the beds are arguably the best on the island. Prices: single D30; double D35; suites D70-105.

Time was when the Gulf Hotel (Bahrain's original five-star establishment) stood all but on the beach. An ambitious land reclamation project has changed all that but the hotel remains the most grandiose in Bahrain. An escalator takes you to the huge foyer complex and the celebrated Sherlock Holmes bar. This brazenly British-style pub incorporates draught beer (not uncommon now in Manama), British barmaids and a British telephone box but it now has a reputation as something of a pick-up joint and, like the hotel itself, has undoubtedly seen better days. Rooms: single D38; double D46; suites D50-250.

The other two hotels which aspire to luxury status are the smaller **Delmon** (tel: 234 000; telex 8224) and **Ramada** (tel: 714 921; telex: 8855). Neither has anything noteworthy to offer not available elsewhere (except perhaps a more personal touch) and neither is noticeably cheaper than their more illustrious competitors. Prices: Delmon: single D27; double D36; suites £70-90. Ramada: single D30; double D40; suites D90-120.

Better bets by far for the businessman with an eye for a bargain are the **Bristol Hotel** (tel: 258 989; telex 8504) of which you hear nothing but good (single D20; double D25; suites D75-100), the **Aradous Hotel** (tel: 241 011; telex: 8900) noted for its local flavour and American GIs (Rooms D20-33; suites D50-90) and especially the **Al Jazira** (tel: 258 810; telex: 8999) on Al-Khalifa Road near the Suq. This homely establishment boasts a genuinely relaxed atmosphere (Rooms: D20-30; suites: D45-50). As with most hotels, the 12 per cent service charge is not included in the prices.

# WHERE TO EAT

Culinary excellence in Bahrain is the exclusive preserve of the hotels. Or so the hotel staff will tell you. And with one or two exceptions they are right. What they generally don't tell you is that it is possible to eat very well elsewhere, often at about one fifth of the cost. And curry aficionados will be gratified to learn you can eat with reasonable peace of mind at most of the plethora of Indian establishments (at prices which make the average hotel menu look positively silly). One drawback: few are licensed.

Originality is at a premium wherever you eat. And anyone hoping to combine good local cuisine with an acceptable atmosphere is likely to go home disappointed. Bahraini food is generally deemed unsuitable for restaurant consumption, largely due to its blandness. (The only two examples I noted on local menus were *machbous* – spiced meat and rice – and *hamour* – a strongly flavoured local fish.) The outcome is that many restaurants offer a selection of 'Greatest Hits' from each of a dozen countries. The pick of these is probably **Al Maharah** (tel: 241 122) at the Holiday Inn. Expect to pay D35 for two including wine. More of the same can be had at **Upstairs Downstairs** (tel: 713 093) and at **Talk of the Town** (tel: 250 728) where baby leg of lamb is a speciality.

*The harbour at Manama*

The best restaurants on the island limit their geographical options. For quality and atmosphere two stand out from the pack. The Hilton's **Kei Japanese Restaurant** (tel: 250 000) is well-patronised by Oriental businessmen (never a bad sign) and offers all the stock dishes for around D20 a head – although I have heard the sushi master is usually to be found at the Thai restaurant **The Treasure House** (tel: 713 500) on days off. Everybody welcomes an invitation to the Regency's **Versailles Restaurant,** where a three-course meal with wine starts at about D25. The quality of service has to be experienced to be believed but the dishes occasionally lack a certain authenticity for those used to good French food. I can however heartily endorse *les noisettes d'agneau à la crème d'estragon* and I have been offered many a worse cheese board in the heart of Lyons.

Seafood is usually a staple of island diets and Bahrain is no exception. Patrons of the Ramada Hotel's **Atlantis Restaurant** (tel: 714 921) will tell you the staff are the finest practitioners of the art of *fruits de la mer* preparation in the Gulf. The lobster tank is of course virtually obligatory for such establishments and should you tire of watching your entrée frolicking in its natural environment, you can avert your gaze to the hotel guests doing likewise in the adjoining glass-walled swimming pool.

Outside the hotels, **The Copper Chimney** (tel: 728 699) wins plaudits for its Indian/Nepalese dishes despite its unprepossessing exterior. Expect to pay around D20 for two and a similar outlay will buy a first rate Italian dinner at **La Taverna** (tel: 259 979), although the service never quite matches that inimitable Italian combination of servility and braggadocio.

A further step down the culinary ladder (but infinitely preferable to the Wimpy/Dairy Queen/ Kentucky Fried Chicken outlets springing up in Manama and Muharraq) are establishments like **Pizza New York** (tel: 742 121) and **Sizzler's** at **Mansouri Mansions** (tel: 713 971). Sizzler's is a particularly popular haunt of the younger business community at lunchtime and specialises in joints of meat served up on hot metal plates. You will pay around 3D500 for a sizeable fillet steak. Of the downmarket Indian restaurants, I can certainly recommend the **Nataraj** on Al-Khalifa Road (tel: 259327). If you do opt to brave the dingy lighting and pyrex tableware, the lack of alcohol should help you escape for D2-3.

# NIGHT LIFE

So whatever did happen to The Hollies? Not to mention The Stylistics, Charles Aznavour and Lulu? And where does Ronnie Scott get that suntan? Not Soho in October.

All this and more will become clear if one casts an eye upon the programme for a typical Bahrain cabaret season. Chances are you will conclude it is not terribly different from any other cabaret season: a meal ticket for second-rate artistes and has-beens. Except Bahrain has the money to afford the really big names when necessary. *"We had the New York Metropolitan Opera at the Hilton last week, you know." "Really?"* I exclaimed in my ignorance, *"You mean the Hilton has an auditorium to cope with that?" "Oh no. I expect they just did a few songs as cabaret."* I later found this particular event was billed as 'A Night out with the Stars' – tickets D9 (D14.50 with dinner).

The Hilton also plays host to another Bahraini institution: The Dinner Theatre, as pioneered by Derek Nimmo – he of *Britain's Breakfast Time* and *All Gas and Gaiters.* Under the formula, Nimmo brings over a London West End success, say *Why not Stay for Breakfast?* or *No Sex Please, we're British,* which the predominantly expatriate audience shells out about D16 to watch over dinner. But beware! In the words of one guide book, *"don't expect to be served anything special: the food is often criticised as being too boring."* Not like the drama then.

Sports/leisure clubs are popular as evidenced by the success of two recent additions to their number. The **Marina Club** (tel: 271 611), opened in 1981, specialises in watersports as its name suggests. The brainchild of Shaikh Isa Bin-Abdullah al-Khalifa, undersecretary at the Ministry of Development and Industry, it has become a victim of its own success to the extent that it gets very crowded at weekends. The **Dilmun Club** (tel: 690 926), located off the Budaiya Highway, has many of the sports facilities (tennis and squash courts, riding facilities) that used to be the exclusive preserve of the hotels and the rather going-to-seed **British Club** (tel: 728 245). Last but not least,

Bahrain also boasts a rowdy, beer-swilling **Rugby Club** (tel: 690 270) at the end of Al-Bustan Gardens – a fitting accompaniment to a XV which has been the best in the Gulf for many years.

There are nine cinemas in Bahrain (six regularly showing US/European films) and most hotels have in-house shows which major heavily on adventure yarns like *Escape to Victory* and *Battle for the Planet of the Apes.* Local television has English and Arabic channels: the Arabic is amateurish in the extreme; the English, merely bland – while, if all else fails, the 24-hour coffee shops in many major hotels can be a lifesaver.

Nightclubs, once plentiful have fallen victim to the mild Islamic backlash which many feel has swept the island in recent years. Discos (like so much else) are now confined to certain hotels, with the Holiday Inn's **Thursday Night Thrash** and **Cloud Nine** at the Aradous the best-known functions. The most recent target for the authorities has been the island's burgeoning video trade. A number of shops have been closed down and one manager deported for handling banned films. Alcohol also periodically attracts their wrath, with the commonest manifestation being an insistence that patrons of Bahrain's 'lounges' eat with their refreshments. It is at times like these that queues form at the entrance to licensed premises to collect bread rolls (returnable at the end of the evening) being doled out by managers anxious to pay lip service to the ruling.

# GETTING AROUND

The answer to the usual taxi/hire car dilemma in Bahrain is relatively straightforward. If your stay is a long one or you intend leaving Manama at all, you will require a hire car. For a stay of under two weeks, exclusively in the capital, cabs will probably suffice. In many ways, a taxi is the wiser choice: Manama's traffic congestion problem is growing worse daily and accidents in the State as a whole occur at a rate of 60 per day (including minor scrapes). If you are involved in an accident, you may find yourself forking out a 'deterrent' fee at the local police station regardless of culpability – D10 for a small dent is typical.

Budget and Europcar are both in Bahrain in their own right, while Avis and Hertz masquerade under the respective titles of Bahrain Catering and Commercial Services and MTS Rent-a-Car. Outlets are mainly confined to the airport and various hotels, although Hertz/MTS operates from Twilight Building near the Central Market. Hertz are arguably the best value for money, although Europcar tariffs are also low for Groups A-D. Daily rates for a Group B vehicle such as a Honda Civic range from D10-14 unlimited mileage, while a Group E Datsun 280C/Chevrolet Impala costs D20-22. Further up the scale, the rate for a Chevrolet Caprice is D24-25. Prospective drivers require an international driving licence which, strictly speaking, must be endorsed by the Traffic Directorate at Isa Town. However, chances are the hire firm will deal with such formalities on the spot. Estimated cost of hiring is generally payable in advance.

The Bahraini taxi driver is a common and assertive breed and any foreigner who attempts to walk to his destination will proceed to a chorus of horns and shouts. There are no meters (drivers threatened to strike if they were introduced) and the prudent visitor will glance at the fare board at Muharraq airport if he wants to avoid being fleeced. As a rule of thumb, don't pay more than D3 from the airport to central Manama or D1 within the town itself. Considerable savings may be made by the simple expedient of hailing a cab from the street rather than direct from the hotel and similarly by giving a street rather than hotel name as one's eventual destination.

With petrol at 100 fils a litre, being a cabby in Manama is a tolerably lucrative business. Even so, some are not above supplementing their income via the occasional artful ruse. One such involves the visitor who arrives at the airport with no hotel booking. *"Take me to a reasonable hotel,"* he will say – an instruction with which the driver will gladly comply, prior to pocketing a not inconsiderable proportion of the room charge courtesy of whichever hotel whose pay he is in.

During the course of the journey should the conversation turn to girls (and most drivers make it their business to ensure that it does), our resourceful 'conducteur' will offer to telephone with a rendez-vous. When he does, it will be for the following night at a different hotel – *"but don't worry,"* he says, *"I'll be round to pick you up,"* hence ensuring D7 and perhaps a percentage on the girl too.

# Bangkok

**Charging in headlong, Western-style, does little to break the ice in Bangkok business circles. Extreme politeness, punctuality and an inordinate amount of patience, however, could reap immeasurable rewards.**

**By Philip Jacobson**

It is increasingly common among those who know and love Bangkok to hear complaints about how westernised it is becoming, how the rude intrusion of development is ruining the unique character and appeal of what many South East Asia hands consider the nicest capital in the region. I count myself among Bangkok's most fervent admirers, but cannot help being wary of views of this nature, expressed, as they almost always are, by foreigners residing there in some style and comfort. True, development has hit the city like a Sunday punch, swallowing up a good many of the old neighbourhoods with their cool, tree-lined compounds and comfortable houses. True, shopping malls and high-rise office blocks seem to spring up as soon as you turn your back. True, of course, that

Some of those magnificent men in their flyir

MNC&H/THA/7856

## achines were Thais.

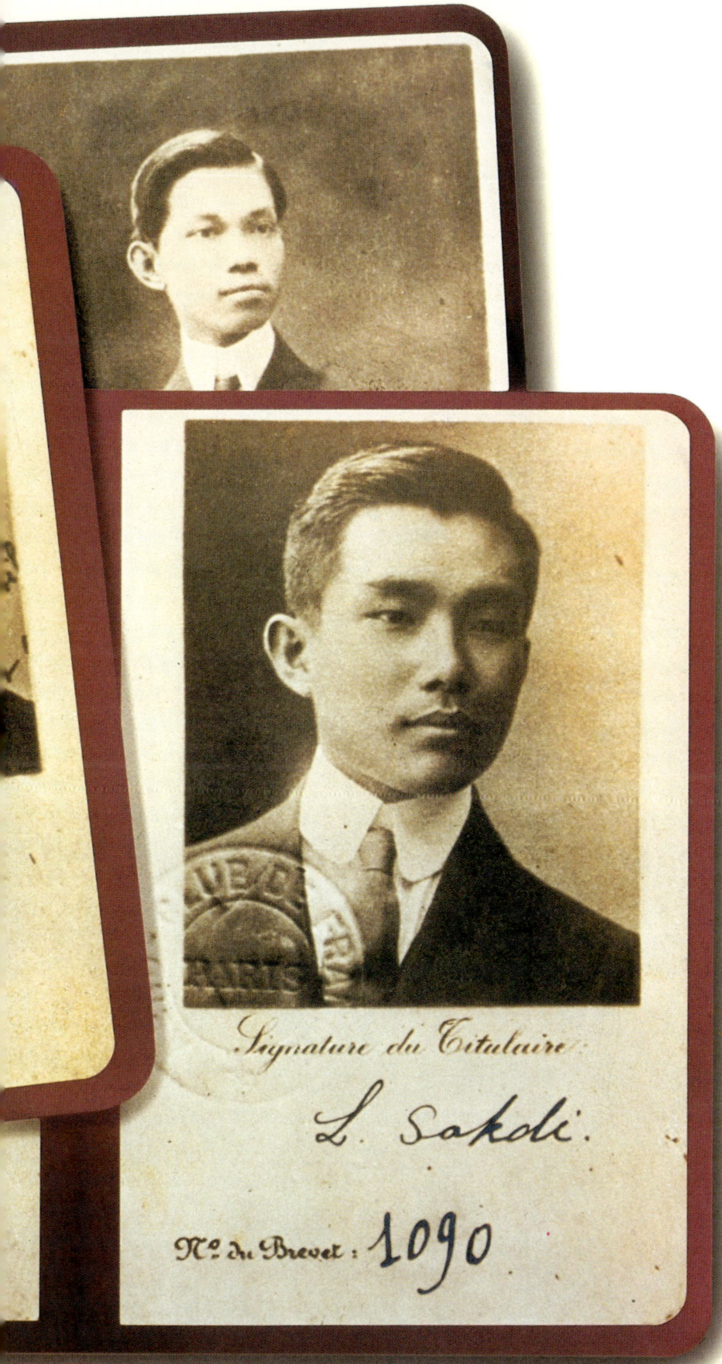

In 1912, a mere eight years after American aviation pioneers carried out the first powered flight in their 'heavier than air' machines, three Thai army officers travelled abroad to a French flying school. They learned not only how to fly aircraft but also how to build them. In quick succession the Kingdom bought airplanes, established an airport and trained new pilots.

Starting as a mail carrier, the airline quickly grew and soon a passenger service was available. Then in a major reorganisation just 25 years ago, Thai International came into being.

Thai's pioneering spirit, its attitude towards service and the importance it places on the training and skill of its pilots, has led to the airline's development as one of the world's major carriers.

Today, Thai's route network has grown to include over 41 cities in 30 countries across five continents.

And servicing these destinations is an ever-expanding fleet of magnificent 747Bs and wide-bodied A300s.

So, fly smooth as silk on Thai. The airline that's still enchanted with the wonders of flight.

getting around Bangkok tries the patience of a saint, let alone a foreign visitor running later and later on business appointments (as for the rainy season, how many cities do you know where flooding gets so bad that policemen are called upon to rule on whether lorries or boats have right of way?).

But in Bangkok perhaps more than any other Asian capital, the acid test is this: how has economic and social change affected the local people? You are unlikely to discover much about that among the expats – or if you do, it tends to come out along the lines of *"impossible to find a good houseboy these days."* I certainly wouldn't pretend to know what the Thais *really* think about the impact of progress, Western-style, on the country that they cherish with such simple and unabashed fervour. For a *farang* to achieve that would require a testing apprenticeship in Bangkok's little noodle shops after dark where Thai men gather to gossip long into the night.

What may be said, with feeling and certainty, is that the extraordinary consideration and respect for the feelings, beliefs, even foibles, of other people remain intact among Thais of every class and background. That this instinctive tolerance survives in the face of pressures pulling in quite opposite directions – political crises and threat of military coups, hard fighting and a huge influx of refugees along the border with Cambodia, the inevitable strains of mass tourism upon an immensely traditional society – makes it all the more impressive.

Good manners as much as self-respect demand that foreigners understand that behind the smiles and very real concern for their welfare they will encounter among the Thais, there is a deep and abiding respect for what translates, very approximately as 'proper form'. Some of the dos and don'ts are no more than common sense and civility. The *wai,* for instance, that graceful folding of the hands towards the face as if in prayer: it is not only the traditional Thai style of greeting, used on all occasions, formal and otherwise. In the perpetually steamy heat of Bangkok, it is also a lot better than a clammy Western handshake. Rest assured, returning a *wai,* however clumsily, will not make you seem foolish in the eyes of Thai colleagues and friends. By the same token, if you are meeting people for the first time, take the small trouble of memorising what to call them. Thai family names are long and tongue-twisting for Westerners, but it is perfectly correct to use the simpl'er first name preceded by the invaluable all-purpose *Khun* – (Mr, Mrs, Miss, even Ms): a Thai friend once referred to me as *nong,* old mate, which pleased me immoderately.

To some, probably most, visitors from the West, accustomed to the cut-and-thrust school of doing business, the unrelenting calm and politeness of Thais across the negotiating table may, frankly, become rather tiresome. But tape this piece of advice to the mirror (shaving or make-up): *"Never Lose Your Temper."* Trying to talk turkey with someone who never stops smiling and nodding understandingly, only to baulk at the dotted line stage, does become tedious but directness is not prized by the Thais and can backfire badly. Remember, too, that Thais are inclined to turn very obstinate if they feel, rightly or wrongly, that a foreigner is trying to take advantage of them, pulling a fast one. Put it down to their deep-rooted sense of independence, a quality found naturally among people of a country that has fought off countless enemies intent on subjugation (nobody has ever suceeded in colonising the Thais).

*Thai dancer*

*The Temple of the Dawn overlooks the Chao Phraya river*

Personal etiquette aside, the prudent businessman/businesswoman visiting Bangkok should stick to a fairly basic set of working rules. In view of the notorious traffic, ranging from normal jams to monstrous snarl-ups, it makes sense to ask local contacts what time to allow for the journey between A and B (then add 50 per cent, some old campaigners would say). One assumes that Thais have become accustomed to wild-eyed foreigners stumbling into their office an hour late for appointments, but punctuality is appreciated as a reflection of consideration for others. So is a measure of formality in dress, allowing for the climate: safari suits are perfectly okay, provided they don't run to shorts.

There is, incidentally, absolutely nothing to be said for saving a few baht by taking anything else than the most comfortable, roomy and icily air-conditioned cars, unless you enjoy inhaling carbon monoxide in oven-like temperatures with humidity to match. Bangkok is becoming the land of the executive limo: a man's worth may be judged by the shine on his 'Benzi' or BMW (for which there is currently a 12-month waiting list). Good to see some foreign products in Bangkok that do not come from Japan. There aren't many these days, believe me.

Entertaining clients/contacts/friends in Bangkok sometimes requires constructive cunning. In my experience, Thais are genuinely delighted if foreigners ask to be taken to a good Thai restaurant: the problem comes when they insist that being on their own ground, so to speak, they must collar the bill. If you go to one of the city's numerous Western restaurants,the argument is neatly reversed: they must pay because they have dragged you off to the sort of place you eat in every day. Wherever you end up, please do not cover your guests in shame by being masterful and assertive with waiters (clapping hands, clicking fingers, psssting etc). Thais who wish to attract attention in such circumstances favour an unobtrusive waving gesture, palm downwards, that can stop a maître d'hôtel at 30 feet.

It has been my pleasure to enjoy some long, hard nights on the town in Bangkok with Thai friends: perhaps I was lucky, but they struck me as a pretty hard-headed bunch, with firm ideas about what constitutes the correct drink for such occasions. They were distressed to hear that I have a weakness for Amarit, one of three locally-brewed beers. Upwardly mobile Thais, it appears, consider the stuff rather too working class in image (it is the most potent of local beers and has been known to produce wretched mornings after). For them, Kloster alone will do, in public at least. For real polish, though, it is Johnnie Walker Black in Bangkok's fast lane. As far as I can see, there are four political points of view for every three Thais, but remember that politics is not a noticeably genteel business there. Let the locals make the pace in conversation.

Foreigners who get to know Thais socially – not always easy but always immensely rewarding – cannot fail to be impressed by the strength of their attachment to their land and its extraordinarily rich and diverse culture. The two enduring pillars of the state throughout centuries of Thai history, Buddhism and Monarchy, have provided the country with a breathtaking heritage of palaces, temples, shrines, statues and murals, many of which continue to play a part in the everyday life of a stylised and exceptionally devout society. They also say something about the enduring pride of the Thais today. Consider, for instance, the revered King Rama IV, who decided that a nation as great as his could not reasonably be expected to conform to Greenwich Mean Time. He decided to establish Asian Mean Time instead, and to this end erected a magnificent Clock Tower in the grounds of the Grand Palace. The original long ago crumbled away, but a faithful replica has been placed in a little park nearby (Thai conservationists are hard at work protecting Bangkok's heritage in the face of pell-mell development, with the enthusiastic support of the cherished Royal Family).

So, has Bangkok today been irrevocably spoilt – whatever that may imply – by what the Australian writer Alan Moorhead described, in a different context, as the *"fatal impact"* of the West? As you will gather, I don't really think so: I remember the city in the Vietnam war days of the late 1960s, when it was an unappealing R & R centre for US troops and even the miraculous tolerance of the Thais was strained to the limit. Granted, increasing affluence is creating new problems. Many Thais feel their society is becoming depressingly materialistic, one reflection of which is a growing number of crimes against property and another a new breed of rootless, sometimes violent, young people drawn into the capital. None of this, however, is likely to affect the average business traveller too adversely. For them, I submit, Bangkok remains a destination to be savoured.

Many of Bangkok's hotels were built in the 1960s and are showing distinct signs of decay after two decades of hard use, first by US troops from Vietnam on R&R in Thailand, then in the 1970s by swarms of latent hippies in search of things Eastern. The business traveller, however, need not suffer the indignities of such accommodation since there are enough luxury hotels to cope with several international conventions at once. Facilities are universally good – almost all the hotels have swimming pools, health clubs and other sports facilities – and service is generally immaculate. The business man or woman will feel particularly pampered by the range of business services in most hotels.

British travellers will find the **Hilton International Bangkok** (Wireless Road; tel: 251 7111; telex: TH72206) convenient as it sits, resplendent in landscaped gardens, behind the British Embassy. The gardens are a necessary oasis of calm and oxygen after a day in the city. Travelling executives can recline in the comfort of a private lounge while a butler sees to all imaginable needs. Single 2,000-2,550 baht; double 2,500-3,300 baht; suite 4,300-29,000 baht.

Visitors who feel like escaping from downtown Bangkok to a self-contained haven of peace and quiet will be pleased with the **Hyatt Central Plaza** (Phaholyothin Road; tel: 270 1820; telex: TH20173). About halfway between city and airport, in an area becoming increasingly popular with major companies, banks and so on, it forms part of a spanking new complex.

The handsome 26-storey hotel offers one of Asia's biggest and most modern convention and exhibition centres. Pretty well anything the active guest desires on hand – golf course over the road, good pool, health club, tennis and jogging. Excellent shopping can be found under the same roof. The Regency Club provides everything one has come to expect from Hyatt and the Business Centre functions smoothly around the clock. There is a first-rate Dynasty Chinese restaurant, and a shuttle bus to and from city centre. Single 1,700-2,500 baht; double 1,900-2,800 baht; suite 4,500-75,000 baht.

The **Bangkok Peninsula** (Rajadarmri Road; tel: 251 6127; telex TH20004) is only a few months older than the Hilton, but is built along the neo-colonial lines of its sister property in Hong Kong. While any attempt to emulate the Hong Kong Peninsula is doomed to failure, the Bangkok hotel does succeed in seeming opulence personified. The rooms are large and lavish with murals and frescos in classical Thai motifs. In keeping with the colonial atmosphere, a traditional afternoon tea is served daily in the lobby. The hotel's Spice Market restaurant is particularly recommended for Thai food, while La Brasserie is said to have the most authentic French provincial food in Bangkok. In the absence of a true city centre, the Peninsula is amongst the best situated of hotels, being roughly halfway between the two commercial centres of Silom and Sukhumvit. Single 2,000 baht; double 2,200 baht; suite 3,600-5,400 baht.

Of the long-established hotels, **The Oriental** (Oriental Ave; tel: 234 8621; telex TH82168 or 82997) is the most famous. A new and rather dominating tower wing somewhat detracts from the atmosphere of colonial charm which so captivated Somerset Maugham in the 1920s, but the older main building is still delightful. Best of all, the staff have discovered that elusive balance between attentive and unobtrusive service, which makes staying at the Oriental a joy. In addition, the hotel is splendidly situated on the river. There are two excellent restaurants – the Normandie Grill on the top floor overlooking the river, and Lord Jim's seafood restaurant. On the opposite bank of the river sits the health club, tennis and squash courts and a running track. Single 2,900 baht; double from 3,200 baht; suite 5,400-36,000 baht.

Just a few hundred metres upstream from the Oriental is its sister hotel, the **Royal Orchid** (Captain Bush Lane: Siphya Road, tel: 234 5599; telex: TH84491). Guests are guaranteed a splendid view, since all the rooms overlook the Chao Phya river. The grill room is known for its fine roast beef, and the Benkay is reputedly one of Bangkok's best Japanese restaurants. Single 1,900-2,200 baht; double 2,100-2,400 baht; suite 3,000-15,000 baht.

The principal chain hotel is the **Siam Inter-Continental** (Rama I Road; tel: 252 9040; telex: TH81155) which has a strong following among many frequent travellers. The outside is characterised by an impressive Thai-style roof, which be-

*Royal Orchid hotel*

lies an interior that is comfortable but unexceptional. The main attraction is its 10.5 hectares of landscaped gardens – a big advantage in crowded Bangkok – where there are two tennis courts and jogging trails. Single 1,800-2,200 baht; double 2,100-2,400 baht; suite 5,100-20,000 baht.

Conveniently located in the Silom/ Suriwongse shopping and business centre and next door to the Patpong nightlife district, are the 580-room **Dusit Thani** (Rama IV Rd; tel: 233 1130; telex: TH81170 or 81027) and the 600-room **Montien** (Suriwongse Rd; tel: 233 7060; telex: TH81038, 81160 or 82938).

The Dusit Thani, with its spired tower wing, is a city landmark and boasts the largest rooms in town, plus the only hotel supper club, the Tiara, with international floor shows and superb panoramic views of the city. Again a full range of sports facilities are available. Single 2,250-2,475 baht; double 2,700-3,040 baht; suite 4,950-5,850 baht.

**The Montien,** just across the road from Patpong is another well-established property favoured for its location, with a Chinese restaurant noted for its Cantonese specialities, and good live music in the Montientong cocktail lounge. Apart from a pool, the hotel lacks sports facilities, although a health club is planned. Single 2,000-2,400 baht; double 2,200-2,620 baht; suite 3,640-17,550 baht.

Of the two properties close to Don Muang airport, the 300-room **Airport Hotel** (Chert Wundthakas Rd, Don Muang; tel: 523 9177; telex: TH87424 or 87425) is directly across the main highway from the terminal building. Facilities include a health club with 15 private massage rooms and the best *nouvelle cuisine* in town. Single 1,450-1,700 baht; double 1,550-1,700 baht; suite 3,500-4,500 baht.

The 372-room **Rama Gardens** (Vibhavadi Rangsit Rd, Bangkaen; tel: 579 5400; telex TH84250) is five miles down the main highway from the airport, amid extensive lawns and landscaped gardens, with tennis courts, squash courts and a health club. These facilities, along with a negligible noise factor, give it an edge over the Airport Hotel for anything but a brief stopover. A free shuttle bus service runs hourly to the Rama Tower hotel in town. Single 1,500-1,700 baht; double 1,650-1,850 baht; suite 3,500-6,000 baht.

Travellers should note that all hotel rates are subject to 10 per cent surcharge and a government tax of 11 per cent.

# WHERE TO EAT

Thai food should be handled with care. It is usually delicious, certainly exotic, but anyone with a delicate palate will have trouble appreciating these finer points. Thai cooks enjoy using chilli, or rather six different types of chillis, preferably in the same dish. The unabashed foreigner can overcome this difficulty by eating at one of the many restaurants catering to tourists where the food is suitably tempered for the Western tongue. Such an excursion should not be mentioned to Thai contacts, however, as Thais tend to look upon these restaurants with amused disdain.

The range of Thai food can be truly bewildering – each region has a multitude of dishes, quite different from those of the other regions. There are certain staples: rice, which appears at every meal, and fish sauce *(nam pla)* without which no meal would be complete. Apart from the ubiquitous chilli, the most common Thai spices are basil, cardamom, garlic and fresh coriander. While much of the Thai cuisine should appeal to the most unadventurous of eaters, there are those who may baulk at such northeastern specialities as pig's head and frog curry. Most restaurants print menus in English as well as Thai, so there is little danger of ordering an unwanted dish.

Every Thai has his or her favourite restaurant serving local cuisine, but visitors lacking local guidance who want to eat Thai outside the hotel won't go wrong at the **Tapkaew Garden** (236/2 Asoke-Dindaeng Road; tel: 245 2073). The **Samae Sand** (65 Sikhumvit Soi 31; tel: 258 4582) also comes well recommended, especially for seafood; try the prawns steamed in coconut.

Travellers seeking more familiar food should not feel bound by the confines of their hotel, since Bangkok also houses a vast number of excellent foreign restaurants. An established favourite is **Nick's Hungarian Restaurant** (Sathorn Tai Road; tel: 286 2258) which has been serving business men and women for over 30 years. Try lobster jubilee baked with mushrooms and peppers in a sherry and pernod sauce *au gratin,* or charcoal-broiled kobe steak served *flambé.* Nick's chocolate cake has been lavished with praise for many years, but its rising price has so outpaced inflation that it is now something of a luxury item.

Should the traveller wish to warm his or her blood before a night on the town, **Trattoria Da Roberto** (Plaza Arcade, Patpong II; tel: 234 5987) provides an Italiano setting, complete with chains of Chianti bottles hanging from the rafters. The pasta is home-made, the Parma ham imported, and the location is perfect for the start of a night of revelry.

For echos of more Northern shores, try the **Two Vikings** (Soi 35, Sukhumvit Road; tel: 391 8364), where herring aficionados will be pleased to note eight varieties of the said fish. Indeed as one of the top ten restaurants in Asia, the Two Vikings should please most palates.

Should the traveller fall victim to a sudden craving for meat and potatoes, the surest remedy is a trip to **Neil's Tavern** (Soi Ruam Rudee; tel: 251 5644) where large, Texas-style steaks are accompanied by baked potatoes and mountains of other vegetables.

For food with more Eastern tones there are several dozen Indian restaurants in Bangkok. The **Royal India** (Chakraphet Road; tel: 221 6565) set in an alley off Wang Burapaha, makes up in authenticity and good food what it lacks in piped music and elaborate decor. The dal, fish tikka and many curries are all exquisite, and prices are very reasonable.

It can be difficult to find the appropriate drink to accompany a meal since French and Italian wines are prohibitively expensive, thanks to heavy import taxes. There is Thai wine, both red and white, but it is, by all accounts, a sweet and sickly affair. Thai beer, however, more than makes up for the wine's shortcomings, and is a perfect companion for most meals.

*Market vendors*

# NIGHT LIFE

If Thai men go out for a night on the town, they almost invariably end up in a noodle shop, after imbibing vast amounts of the local Mehkong whisky. What the local whisky may lack in strength is more than made up in the quantity drunk – the Suramaharas distillers sold more than six million bottles a month at the end of 1983. But visitors to Bangkok will doubtless have other ideas about how to pass their nights in the city, and these ideas will probably run the length of Patpong, Bangkok's more than infamous Strip.

Patpong's heyday came in the late 1960s, when the streets were paved with American GIs craving recreation more than rest from the Vietnam war. The war ended and the GIs went home, but Patpong remains – a neon legacy of the Vietnam war. Every year hundreds of jumbos disgorge thousands of tourists into Bangkok, seeking their own rest and recreation away from the demands of home. The Thais may not be proud of their country's reputation for licentiousness (and indeed, prostitution is illegal, although customers are never arrested), but it is an undeniable source of foreign revenue, and has shown little sign of decline over the years.

The original Patpong has been extended to Patpongs I, II and III – three parallel streets, each catering to a different clientele. Patpong I houses the usual array of topless go-go clubs, bars and special shows, while Patpong II is said to have the best massage parlours. Travellers should note that massage parlours are exactly that: places where, for around 120 baht, you can have an hour-long massage. Anything extra is strictly between you and the masseuse, and 'tips' should be paid accordingly. Patpong III offers much the same as the other two streets, only to gay customers. There are transvestite *kra-toey* prostitutes working all three streets who, I am told, are particularly beautiful.

There is little provision for women in the official night-time circuit. The closest women come to being included as spectators is at the 'day club' along Ramadamnern Ave. These clubs differ from nightclubs only in their opening hours, yet they are considered suitable places for women to meet at lunch.

Should your desires be more in the way of sustenance, a number of outdoor seafood restaurants have sprung up along New Petchburi Road, where the nightlife can be observed from a safe distance. Travellers seeking entertainment without the sordid edge would do well not to leave their hotels. In recent years the international hotels have become popular with the more modern and affluent Thais, who can be seen dancing cheek to cheek until the early hours of the morning.

# GETTING AROUND

"*Always carry something to read,*" was the best advice I was ever given about getting around in Bangkok. Traffic congestion is rumoured to be the worst in Asia, perhaps in the world. And in the rainy season a helicopter seems the only sensible way to travel. But Bangkok is a city worth seeing, despite the frustration, so arm yourself with a large dose of patience before braving the streets.

The only way to arrive at a business appointment unruffled is to take an air-conditioned car. The choice is then between taking one of the ubiquitous Bluebird taxis or a chauffeur-driven limousine. Limousines are available at all the major hotels, they cost around twice as much as a taxi, but are well worth it. If taking a taxi, remember that there are no fare meters and the price must be settled in advance. While bargaining is expected, tipping is not. Also, unless you speak reasonable Thai, it is advisable to have the destination written out as it is unlikely the driver will speak English. A journey in town will cost around 100 baht.

If time is no object, the intrepid business man or woman should venture into a Samlor. Samlors (or *tuk tuks)* look like multi-coloured motorized tricycles; they hold two people and usually travel at no less than 50 mph. They seem extraordinarily precarious, and are only recommended for the shortest of journeys. Like taxis, the price must be arranged at the start, and should be around half the taxi fare.

There are many car hire firms in Bangkok, including Hertz (1620 New Petchburi Road; tel: 252 4903/6) and Avis (981 Silom Road; tel: 235 7745). Visitors must have an international licence, nerves of steel and adequate insurance is highly recommended. Drivers must negotiate heavy traffic and rules of the road seem to be infinitely flexible. For instance, driving on the left may be the rule, but there are many exceptions. And should there be an accident, it is usually the foreigner who is found responsible. Legal proceedings are long and costly.

Getting into Bangkok from the international airport should pose few problems for the business traveller. An eight person minibus leaves the airport every half hour between 6a.m. and 9p.m. for the Asia Hotel and costs 60 baht. For another 40 baht a similar minibus will take you to any hotel in the city. Taxis cost around 300 baht, but since the price must be negotiated in advance, it is best to check with the hotel for an approximate price.

*Save Samlors for short journeys*

# Brussels

**The EEC and the multinationals have, between them, spared Brussels the fate of becoming just another solid, provincial city slowly rotting away. The Belgian capital is, in fact, on its way to becoming the telecommunications centre of Europe.**

**By Nick Hanna**

The heart of Europe appears to be bleeding to death, with over 80,000 people leaving each year and multinationals de-camping from the capital in droves to set up elsewhere now that the government's ten-year tax holiday (which began in the early 70s) is over. Thousands of square feet of surplus office space and plummeting house prices are further indications of decline. A committee for the economic expansion of Brussels exists, but it hasn't met for years.

Brussels, they say, is slipping into a decline as slowly as the rusting Atomium, decaying as inevitably as the atomic molecules which the Atomium represents.

Or is it? More than 700 multinationals still have principal offices here; of the top 100 US corporations, over a third have a headquarters in Brussels. A new vitality in EEC-sponsored scientific research (mostly in telecommunications and computing) has encouraged businesses to keep their antennae aimed at Brussels – and to visit occasionally.

The continual comings and goings of diplomats and industrialists have led to an enormous increase in the number of aircraft movements through Brussels-National Airport (107,311 in 1984, which represents 5.5 million passengers) although nothing, unfortunately, has been done about the somewhat wretched state of the airport itself. These comings and goings have, incidentally, also led to the development of a highly competitive travel industry (at the last count there were over 5,000 travel agents for a population of just 14 million) which reacts quickly to new ideas and incentives.

Neutrality and internationalism continue to be successfully played upon to create an active business environment. Conferences for instance, are often held in Brussels merely because by so doing no one gets upset. "*It prevents arguments,*" comments Bob Buyse, manager of Brussels Conventions, who likes to see people thinking along the lines of 'Let's hold it in Brussels, and then everyone will be happy'.

The presence of the EEC and NATO, and its geographical location, equidistant between major European capitals, have also contributed to the continued growth of Brussels as a convention centre. It is hoping to soon outpace Geneva to rank third in the European league of convention centres after Paris and London, and currently holds more international (as opposed to solely national) conventions than the front-runner, London.

The slump in property prices has been partially halted as people have drifted back into the city centre from the suburbs over the last couple of years, and 'For Sale' and 'For Rent' signs on downtown office blocks aren't nearly as prolific as they used to be.

The army, nevertheless, still has separate Flemish and French-speaking tank crews to avoid misunderstandings. Presumably the same policy will be followed once NATO has finished installing its new top secret satellite-linked fully-computerised SHAPE headquarters underneath Brussels within the next couple of years – not that the Brusselois know anything about it yet.

Nothing unusual is ever likely to happen to you in Brussels (which is why some people can't stand the place): it's an extraordinarily *safe* city, where, as one resident puts it, "*you'd have to really work hard at being violently assaulted.*" This doesn't prevent the majority of Brusselois believing crime to be the third most important problem facing the city, after unemployment and immigration.

The problems of living side by side with a quarter of a million white foreigners have been overshadowed to some extent in the minds of Brusselois by the problems of co-existence with the influx of immigrants from Morocco. Of the city's 52,000 unemployed nearly 13,000 are black, and, in a recent survey, almost half the population said they thought that immigration should be stopped. But although many Brusselois reject or fear immigrants, this xenophobia is more or less confined to the suburbs and those who are less well educated or have the least amount of contact with themselves.

But residents still resent the EEC. From their point of view it has pushed up rents and increased the cost of living, and they don't take too kindly either to a foreign community which pays no taxes and swans around in cars with CD plates. But without the EEC Brussels would be just another solid, provincial city, slowly rotting away.

For their part, the foreign community feels isolated and resentful at being given the cold-shoulder by a local population whom they see as putting on stiff, affected bourgeois airs. And as for diplomatic privileges, Eurocrats are fond of pointing out that their only real perk is a somewhat meagre duty free allowance of FB1800 worth of spirits per annum.

The only negative points from the visitor's

*The 15th century cathedral, Notre-Dame-du-Sablon, was built by the city's crossbowmen*

point of view seem to be the drizzly climate and the difficulty of making friends with the locals. But there is a reason for the polite but formal attitude of Brusselois, and they weren't always like that. They just became fed up with welcoming visitors with open arms only to discover that for other people friendship wasn't permanent, and once their stint was up that was it.

Despite these minor irritations, the grafting together of the EEC and Brussels continues apace; the ghetto-isation of foreigners into suburban enclaves is not as marked as it used to be, and should become even less so with the arrival of the Spanish and the Portuguese.

Brussels continues to attract diplomats, lobbyists, journalists and those who need to keep their ear to the ground – if only because by so doing they might pick up an EEC grant or two. It's at the centre of European initiatives to beat the Americans and Japanese in high technology industries, most of which are being channelled through TFTIT (an acronym thought up by the French, who didn't realise what it would sound like when spoken in English – or perhaps they did. It stands for Task Force in Telecommunications and Information Technology).

If Europe is going to play the game at world level, though, it has to get its act together, say the Euro-optimists in Brussels, who also point out that although the Community's R&D spending is as high as that of the USA and twice that of Japan, it's much less efficient. One of their solutions is the ESPRIT programme, which focuses on information technology and telecommunications; a sister programme, BRITE, has been set up to develop ways of applying new technology in more traditional industries such as textiles and car manufacturing. Another programme, known as RACE,is intended to make sure member states are not left behind when telecommunications becomes the biggest business in the EEC, which it is forecast to do within the next decade.

Good communications and an international attitude are further reasons for continued growth, but the ease of doing business in Brussels is just as vital, as travel industry consultant Jameson Denny explains: "*The Belgians are astute, well-attuned to doing business with the outside world, very adept at the daily conduct of business, and it is easy to make contacts and maintain good business relationships with them.*" And he adds that if you're thinking of setting up in Brussels the authorities will start off by swamping you in red tape: "*You get licensed and registered up to the teeth, but once they've done that they leave you alone to get on with it. It separates those who aren't serious from those who are.*" The Brusselois, says Denny, always keep their side of a deal, and if there's a problem, well, they're calm and straightforward about dealing with it – preferably over a big lunch.

The Brusselois are likely to be fluent in at least three languages, if not four or five. They have a justifiable reputation for shrewdness: for instance, a Brusselois on holiday elsewhere in Europe will speak French in preference to English, since the French are supposedly so difficult to deal with that they always get their own way in the end.

Language is certainly less of a problem – for the visitor – than in any other country in Europe. This polyglot part-Germanic part-Latin culture is reinforced by the fact that Brussels is wired into no less than 15 TV stations; three German, three French, two Dutch, two Belgian/French, two Belgian/Flemish, one Luxembourg, and four British.

As is well known, Brussels does have considerable language problems centering on the conflict between French and Flemish speakers. But it is now accepted that bilingualism is the only practicable solution, and bilingualism has become a way of life for the majority of inhabitants. Only a small percentge of both Francophones and Flemish speakers reject this idea, and over 70 per cent on both sides would like to see the police, postmen, hospital workers and others in the public service totally bilingual. A sensible decision when the alternative, which would be to have one French and one Flemish speaker for each job, is considered.

The presence of the EEC has one particular advantage for the visitor, and that's the low cost of translators. Because of the necessity to produce every document in 12 different languages, roughly a third of the Commission's 9,000-strong staff are engaged in translation and interpretation work. Translation costs the EEC almost as much as the Common Agricultural Policy, but for the visitor, freelance translators (hired through private agencies) are cheap, since their *per diem* costs are negligible.

The people of Brussels aren't exactly the most health-conscious people in the world. Currently the authorities are trying to decide how to handle the problem of obesity in schoolchildren; joggers are such an unusual sight in the city centre that they tend to be greeted with cries of "*hup, hup, un deux, un deux*" from passers-by. Preferring endives to aerobics and gluttony to gymnasia, Brusselois haven't yet caught on to the fitness boom; the Horizon health club on the roof of the Sheraton is the exception rather than the rule. Gastronomic gifts to take home aren't hard to find in the foodie capital of Europe.

Naturally, people who live here rate the Grand'Place the most beautiful part of the city, closely followed by Notre-Dame-du-Sablon, a flamboyant Gothic edifice (built by the city's crossbowmen in the 15th century) which dominates the Place de Grand-Sablon in the middle of Brussels' antiques district.

Apart from the Baroque excesses of the guilds' houses in the Grand'Place (and possibly the Rubens and the Van Dycks of the Musée d'Art Ancien) there's not a lot else that simply *must* be seen, which has the definite advantage of relieving you of the burden of having to find time to squeeze in the sights. Certainly, the interior of the poor, aged Atomium, with its kitsch, out-of-date displays and creaking escalators, is worth a look. Other curiosities include a fabulous Chinese pavilion tucked away in the woods near the Atomium, with a five-storey Japanese pagoda placed just as improbably opposite. Both were built for the 1900 World's Fair.

When the inhabitants go out in the evenings it isn't to the touristy and mussel-and-chips-dominated Ilot Sacré area near the Grand'Place, but rather to the quieter, prettier Place Ste Catherine just a few blocks away, which houses some of the best seafood restaurants in the city. And after that? It's surprising what the supposedly dull Brusselois get up to: much to her astonishment a roving reporter from the conservative daily *Le Soir* stumbled across not only *'une nuit branchée'* (plugged in, turned on) and *'cocktails exotiques'* in the Zazoo Bar, but also *'une nuit tutti-fruit'* in the Black Bottom gay cabaret in a recent survey of the capital's nightlife, putting the lie to the popular saying that taking a trip to Liège will give you more kicks than Brussels by night. Its red light district is as raunchy, if not as extensive, as those of other European capitals. What's more, a particular bar on the Rond Pont Schuman is rumoured to be the cocaine centre of Europe, although this is hard to believe.

Hedonism and catholicity are words you often hear associated with Brussels; people who live there love ostentation – dressing up smartly, eating in smart places. Youth dissidence (except over Cruise missiles) is almost unheard of. The young are too busy tucking in with the same gusto as their parents – albeit in different restaurants.

*The flamboyant architecture of the Grand'Place is a Brussels landmark*

# WHERE TO STAY

The late 1970s and early 1980s were bad years for Brussels hoteliers. The boom days of previous decades had led to a rash of speculative construction resulting in massive overcapacity which in turn led to ferocious price-cutting and consequent bankruptcies. Grand hotels such as the Plaza and the Lendi (the latter had only been open for six months) closed their doors while others such as the Palace came under the auctioneer's hammer.

The government stepped in eventually to cut the VAT rate on hotel accommodation from 16 to 9 per cent which helped. But competition is still fierce and there are those who prophesy further closures if more visitors are not attracted.

Brussels hoteliers say that the demise of the old-style hotels can primarily be attributed to a change in what is required of hotels and their failure to recognise or adapt to this. Whereas grand hotels were formerly accustomed to trunks, servants and service-consciousness of their guests, nowadays even the average five-star traveller is quite likely to carry his own (small) bag, take the metro and grab a sandwich for lunch. Expense accounts are more tightly budgeted too, and many a business traveller looks for reasonably priced hotels.

The hotel's dilemma is a positive benefit to the traveller who now has a wide choice at international standards.

For example, the old **Palace** (3 rue Gineste; tel: 217 6200; telex: 65604) has reopened its doors after a massive restoration operation costing $4 million. (Cleaning the carpets alone cost $40,000.) The impressive halled entrance with its soft green and cream marble period furniture, side salons with their card tables and original box ashtrays recall a different age. The new owners, the Levy family, bought up the major part of the original furniture and spend their weekends scouring the flea markets for additional pieces. The idea is to offer the elegance of Palace living to travellers of moderate means. At this level they hope to ensure full capacity. The 320 rooms have been painstakingly restored to their former styles (ranging from the 20s to the 50s) and cost FB2,500 for a single, FB3,000 double, including breakfast.

On a simpler scale a similar philosophy motivated the management of the French Arcade chain to open the **Hotel Sainte Catherine** (tel: 513 7630; telex: 22476) in the Place St. Catherine. They have isolated the essential requirements of today's hotel guest and come up with specifications enabling the maximum use of space to create an ultra-modern environment at extremely low prices. Single FB1,530; double FB1,780. Breakfast is an additional FB150. A useful address for a budget trip.

The Dutch owners of the **Ascot** (1 Place Loix; tel: 538 8835; telex 25010) offer the personal touch of a family-run hotel. Service has been cut back to keep prices very reasonable: single FB1,600; double: FB2,000, including breakfast. Rooms are comfortable and the hotel is in a good position for Avenue Louise.

The Belgian Quatacker family run the medium-priced and well-known **Bedford Hotel** (135 Rue du Midi; tel: 512 7840; telex: 24059) which again wants the custom of the travelling businessman (and it can offer conference facilities). Previously it catered more for tour groups. Single FB 2,250-2,650; double FB2,870-3,310.

The **Astoria Hotel** on the rue Royale (tel: 217 6290; telex: 25040) maintains an old-world elegance. Louis XV reception rooms, splendid old bedrooms, a piano bar with concerts on Sunday mornings in what used to be the music room. The Astoria is active in catering and organises functions for the King, parliamentarians, and the EEC Commision in addition to an annual debutante ball. Single FB2,890; double FB3,735, breakfast an extra FB300.

The luxury **Amigo** (1-3 rue de l'Amigo; tel: 511 5910; telex: 21618) by the Grand'Place is arguably the best hotel in Brussels. Characterised by its Spanish brick exterior, paving stones in the lobby, and fine paintings and hangings, the Amigo is frequently thought to be older than it is (in fact it opened in 1958). Official delegations, remaining nobles, entertainers and Heads of State frequent the Amigo. Single FB3,400-4,400; double FB4,000-4,900.

The **Royal Windsor Hotel** (5 rue Duquesnoy; tel: 511 4215; telex: 62905) also close to the Grand'Place, offers more contemporary comfort. The hotel has invested heavily in re-decoration and the rooms have been lavishly refurbished. Palest of pale wood is set off with contemporary pastel shade fabrics and hessian wallpaper. Single FB5,510; double FB6,460.

Of the new hotels, the **Brussels Hilton** (38 Boulevard de Waterloo; tel: 513 8877; telex: 22744) is probably the most luxurious. It has a health club, an entire floor of conference rooms and a Japanese garden restaurant. The Enplein Gel restaurant on the 27th floor is superb and has a splendid view. A number of rooms were designed by Givenchy. Single FB4,011-4,545; double FB4,851-5,406.

The **Brussels Sheraton** (3 Place Rogier; tel: 219 3000; telex: 26887) caters to the health conscious, with a swimming pool, sauna and health club on its 30th floor with magnificent views. Single FB3,900-4,400; double FB4,400-4,900. While the **Hyatt-Regency** (250 rue Royale; tel: 219 4640; telex: 61871) has plush guest rooms, and suites. Single FB4,780; double FB5,750.

# WHERE TO EAT

Brussels may not be the same sort of jewel as London, Paris or New York but it is certainly not as dull as it might appear to the first time visitor. Even the French might admit that Belgium is justified in boasting the best French cuisine outside France (many Belgians would go further in their evaluations) and the Brussels nightlife is as varied as the city's inhabitants are cosmopolitan.

If many streets, come evening, seem ominously empty it is probably because the average Belgian and seasoned foreigners are getting down to some serious eating either at home or in one of the capital's 1,400-odd restaurants. Even a deceptively simple café is likely to have an impressive menu. Eating out is a major leisure occupation for many of the capital's one million inhabitants, and it is not only expense account holders or well-heeled Eurocrats who are prepared to lash out on an expensive meal.

Apart from its French cooking, Belgium offers plenty of home-grown specialities. *Waterzooi* and *anguille au vert, carbonnade flamande* and *lapin à la gueuze* are typical of Belgian dishes. Then there is seasonal game, mussels (mostly, admittedly, now brought in from Holland) the national vegetable endive (which easily supercedes that sprout) and of course the ubiquitous crisp *frites*. Even the sandwiches are more likely to be filled with curried prawns, goat's cheese or filet américain (a steak tartare-type preparation) than with tomatoes and lettuce or egg mayonnaise.

Charles De Gaulle complained of having problems ruling France because of its cheeses; neighbouring Belgium has its own problems. It manufactures almost 400 different beers – and the shape of the glass changes to suit the brew.

The Ilot Sacré area in the heart of Brussels has rows of brightly-lit restaurants, bars and cafés which vie for trade. Spectators of live jazz spill onto the pavements among the hawkers, walkers and potential eaters. Although it can be difficult to find a typically Belgian restaurant in terms of clientele, established places do remain to cater for the taste for national dishes. Some of them have decors reminiscent of past decades; of these one of the best-known in the medium-price range is the **Taverne du Passage** close to the Grand'Place (tel: 512 3731) where a meal for two, including wine comes to around FB2,000. The restaurant is closed on Wednesdays and also Thursdays in June and July.

Another popular family-run restaurant is **Chez Vincent** (tel: 511 2303) in the nearby rue des Dominicains. Dating from 1912, it is characterised by impressive 1900-era tiles, photos of famous (and obviously satisfied) diners and an extremely animated not to say noisy atmosphere. The *moules* and *frites* are to be particularly recommended. But you can't book so be prepared to wait your turn for a table in the café opposite. Chez Vincent is open seven days a week, and costs FB2,400 for two.

The more sophisticated Sablons area (antique shops etc) caters for a rather different mood. In addition to the well-known **Ecailler du Palais** (tel: 512 9751. Reservations required) which offers fish dishes and traditional luxury, and notably popular amongst the wealthier parliamentarians, lawyers and businessmen, a smaller more trendy venue, **Trente** (rue de la Paille tel: 512 0715), caters for sophisticated younger diners. Here, in the *nouvelle cuisine* style, small decorative portions are tastefully arranged on large plates; these are dishes designed to excite the palate (although three courses at around FB2,750-3,500 for two should satisfy all appetites).

Not far away from the Sablons lies rue Haute, another street of restaurants. **La Marée Haute** (tel: 512 6976) specialises in fish dishes, **La Cullotte de Boeuf** (tel: 511 6656) majors in grills and red meat while **Le Cheval Blanc** (tel: 512 3771) offers French cuisine at fair prices (FB3,000-3,500 for two) in an attractive upmarket brasserie-style setting.

Nearby is **Chez Christopher** (tel: 512 6957) featuring excellent French food and a very fine wine list. There you can linger over *menus de dégustation* which provide a way of tasting several different dishes – but be warned, you need a good appetite. Closed Saturday and Sunday. A meal for two is expensive at FB5,500-6,500.

In the centre of Brussels is the Place St. Catherine, site of the long-established fish market. It has been picturesquely renovated and is enchantingly illuminated at night. A square bordered on two sides by fish restaurants of every size and type, and on a third by an imposing church, this is the place to come for an impromptu fish meal (particularly lobster) if you haven't got around to booking.

On one corner of the square opposite the church, the **Cheval Marin** (tel: 513 0287) is an elegant old restaurant, popular with businessmen. Among the smaller less formal restaurants, the **Rugbyman 1** (tel: 512 5640) is worth a mention as is **Francois** (tel: 511 6089) which is almost next door.

Beer connoisseurs should visit one of the traditional cafés to sample some of the best ales made elsewhere. Not far from the Opera, **La Mort Subite** (tel: 513 1318) is a typical family-run café frequented for nearly six decades by a cross-section of Belgians and now by a fair number of expatriates. Apart from the beers (notably Brussels-brewed *gueuze, kriek, lambic* and *faro)* the café serves wine and other drinks but not spirits – the law forbids such sales in public places. The café is open seven days a week.

Different surroundings can be found in **De Ultieme Hallucinatie** (tel: 217 0614) at the wrong end of the rue Royale (not far from the Hyatt-Regency Hotel). It is named for its extraordinary *art nouveau* decoration. The drinking is fine there but the food (at FB3,000 for two) is a disappointment. Rather, eat in the smart **Den Botaniek** (tel: 281 4195) nearly next door where fish is a speciality. Den Botaniek has a garden for fine weather dining. Closed Saturday lunchtime and all day Sunday. Expect to pay around FB2,000 each.

## NIGHT LIFE

For many businessmen a trip to Brussels is no more than a day-time venture, but should you find yourself in Brussels overnight, don't despair – Brussels does offer entertainment. In addition to the national Ballet Béjart, opera, concerts or theatrical productions there are numerous clubs: sedate cocktail bars; disco dancing; live jazz; and more esoteric if not illicit entertainment like gambling which has more or less been banished to the seaside towns and spas. Entertainment guides are published in Thursday's edition of the daily *Le Soir* and the English-language weekly magazine *The Bulletin*.

That ill-famed Belgian law dating back to 1919 and forbidding the sale of spirits in public places led to the concept of the *cercle privé* with a (generally nominal) membership requirement. But the properly-dressed business visitor is seldom refused entry.

Prominent among such nightspots is the Royal Windsor Hotel's **Crocodile Club** *Cercle Privé* (tel: 511 4215) guarded by two live crocodiles; their days are numbered because they've grown too big. Drinks are reasonably priced. Green bamboo and palms lend a cool tropical air and there's a small dance floor with disco music. This is Brussels' only hotel disco and it's closed on Sunday.

Less pampered (no chairs, just bar stools at black and white marble counters) but very lively is **Rick's Club** *Cercle Privé* (tel: 647 7530) underneath the popular Rick's American Café. Friendly, noisy atmosphere and good music make it popular but it gets too hot for an extended stay. Closed on Sunday. Prices in the same range as at the Crocodile.

But the premier *Club Privé* is the **Saint-Louis** (tel: 358 3507). The visitor may need an introduction, but it's worth a try. The sufficiently well-dressed and/or important business traveller is unlikely to be turned away. Once inside he will find himself in an ultra-luxurious setting quite possibly in the company of such personalities as Jimmy Connors . . . the Saint-Louis is particularly popular with the sporting set.

Jazz enthusiasts should head for the smart **Brussels Jazz Club** (tel: 512 4093) in the Grand'-Place. The club is comfortable; the FB1,000 annual membership fee gives entitlement to free entry with a guest. Otherwise one evening's membership on a weekday costs FB100 while at the weekends (excluding Sundays when the club is closed), it is FB200.

For slightly risqué cabaret with go-go dancers your best bet is **Le Show Point** (tel: 511 5364) in the Avenue Louis area. The hostesses like you to buy champagne, at FB3,600 a bottle, but they're not pushy. Drinks are FB500 each and two each at the tables, one at the bar, is the mandatory minimum.

## GETTING AROUND

Getting into Brussels from the airport takes 20 minutes by taxi and costs around FB700. Equally easy and much less expensive is the train from the airport which leaves every 20 minutes for the city's north and central stations. The airport Tourist Office sells train tickets, and will also provide maps of the city with train and bus routes.

Once in Brussels the best way to travel is by public transport, which is extensive and easy to use. A special one day ticket allows unlimited travel on the metro, pre-metro, trams and buses, and can be bought at the information centre on rue du Marche-aux-Herbes (tel: 513 9090). There is no shortage of taxis in the city, but fares do tend to be high (although they include the tip), there is a pick up charge of FB55, and an additional FB27 per km. Out of town the fare rises by FB29 per km. Numerous care hire firms are represented in the city, most are open from 6a.m. to 11p.m.

*Trams are reliable and inexpensive*

# Chicago

**Once renowned for its gangsters and bootleggers, Chicago has grown up into an orderly, efficient and architecturally edifying modern American business centre. Even crime isn't what it used to be in the Second City.**

**By Philip Andrews**

If the south had won the War between the States, it is postulated that Chicago would have emerged as the number one city of a new inland nation rather than being relegated to the role of second fiddle to New York – which was ticketed to continue as top dog in Yankee Land. But the second-city sobriquet persists.

In 1833 the US government acquired the site (for considerations comparable to the $24 worth of rum and trinkets reportedly paid by Peter Minuit for Manhattan) from some rather unfriendly Indians who had massacred settlers at Fort Dearborn during the war of 1812. To its original inhabitants, the place was known as Checagua, a term meaning strong and powerful which apparently pertained to odours emanating from the wild onions and/or pole cats in the area. The name, in a slightly altered form, was adopted, but there were some irreverent types who maintained that the aroma remained.

Poet Carl Sandburg proclaimed Chicago as *"Hog Butcher for the World, Tool Maker, Stacker of Wheat, Player with Railroads and the Nation's Freight Handler; stormy, husky, brawling, City of the Big Shoulders . . ."*

The major meat packers have since departed, taking with them to Omaha and Kansas City the porcine appellation. But most of Sandburg's superlatives still apply. Ships plying the St. Lawrence Seaway en route to and from Europe account for 82 million tons of freight annually. Chicago still lays claim to being the nation's largest railroad centre, and O'Hare International Airport, with 50 million passengers a year, is among the world's busiest. The annual gross metropolitan product amounts to $88 billion. In addition, the Association of Commerce and Industry points with some pride to its paramount position in convention, tradeshow, and exhibition business (2.5 million attendance contributing to a total of nearly nine million visitors to the city annually), steel production, export trade, furniture marketing, commercial printing, mail order operations, industrial machinery, metal products manufacturing and tool and die making.

With a city population of 3.4 million and a metropolitan total of more than 11 million, Chicago is not only less populous than New York, but there are at least a half dozen cities in the world that are bigger. As for its area of 227 square miles, Jacksonville, Florida is now four times its size.

Baedeker's *United States 1893* recounts that in 1871 (Oct. 8-10) "*this flourishing city was the scene of a terrible conflagration which destroyed 17,500 buildings and property to the value of nearly $200,000,000 and left 100,000 homeless. About 200 people perished in the flames.*" The blaze was allegedly started when a Mrs O'Leary's cow kicked over a lantern, but she later swore under oath that she always milked her cow during daylight hours, and never took a lantern into the barn. Her story lost some credence when the wooden leg of a neighbour, who claimed to have rescued a calf, was found embedded in the scorched floorboards.

It has been said of the arts that 'form follows function', and Chicago began rebuilding the only way it knew how, purposefully, pragmatically and without regard for what Frank Lloyd Wright was later to disparage as 'the external facade'. It was in this manner that the foundation was laid for the now renowned Chicago School of Architecture by the likes of Daniel 'make no small plans' Burnham and Louis H. Sullivan, recognised as 'father of the skyscraper' for a 10-storey, steel-skeleton building constructed in 1885. As the birthplace of the skyscraper, it is perhaps appropriate that Chicago boasts the world's tallest, the Sears Tower, 110 storeys, 1,454 feet.

One might expect Chicagoans to be impressed by this flourishing forest of metal, glass and concrete structures. But you wouldn't know it to hear them talk. The John Hancock Center is known casually as Big John; the cylindrical Marina City Towers are the corn silos, and the award-winning steel-mesh parking garage on Wacker Drive is called the bird cage. One architectural item on which the natives have yet to bestow an appropriately demeaning nickname is the five-storey Picasso sculpture in front of the Civic Center, a building that continuously repaints itself, thanks to a mysterious ingredient in its naked steel.

The building of Chicago is perhaps less remarkable in what has been accomplished than that it was done without damage to its inherited resources both natural and man-made. While other cities have had to retrieve their waterfronts from deteriorating docks, unsightly wharves and warehouses, Chicago has created a series of beaches and yacht harbours along its 29-mile shoreline. In all, there are 568 parks covering more than 6,000 acres.

*Sears Tower*

The streets are straight and wide, laid out in a grid pattern, starting at the lake and radiating to the north, south and west sides. There are 'near' norths and souths, but no 'near' wests, and of course, no east at all because that's where the lake is. Street addresses progress in units of 100 per block so if you are at, say, 3400 anything, you'll know that you're just 34 blocks from the city centre – known as the Loop because this is where elevated trains (the El) make a circle in their routes to and from outlying districts.

The Loop is where you will find Frank Sinatra's *"State Street that great street"*. In recent years the pedestrian pavements have been widened and traffic restricted creating a nine-block shopping mall. Montgomery Ward and other great mercantile chains are headquartered here, but Marshall Field's still reigns as dowager queen of the district. Built in 1892, before electric lighting was consi-

*Marina Towers*

dered commercially feasible, it was designed in vertical sections, like a layer cake, with shopping areas overlooking a skylit courtyard. The store can boast generations of satisfied customers, but some of the employees haven't done badly either. One of them, a man named Selfridge, went on to establish an emporium of his own on the other side of the Atlantic.

Among the Loop's varied points of interest are the Archi-Center, which provides a graphic introduction to, and conducts tours of, Chicago sights; the Art Institute, dating from 1892 and distinguished by an outstanding collection of Impressionist and post-Impressionist paintings; the Chicago Board of Trade, largest grain exchange in the world; and the Chicago Mercantile Exchange where, if you wish, you can find out more about such fascinating subjects as pork belly futures.

Just beyond the Loop's perimeter are the Adler Planetarium – admission to the sky shows is free; the Field Museum, whose most spectacular exhibit is a pair of fighting African elephants; Shedd Aquarium, one of the largest in the world with 5,000 specimens in its 198 tanks; Lincoln Park Conservatory, where you can view a 50-foot African fiddle-leaf rubber tree or ramble through more familiar flora in Grandmother's Garden.

Newest and most dramatic addition to the Near North Side is Water Tower Place, a vertical shopping mall with a waterfall and indoor plants in an eight-floor atrium where glass-enclosed elevators take you to and from a movie theatre, restaurants, boutiques and branches of leading stores. On top of all this, with its lobby on the 12th floor, is a 22-storey hotel. Is this any way for a second city to carry on?

Second place in almost anything, however, is something for which Chicago sports fans would settle – in addition to the distinction of being the only city to support two major baseball teams in both the National and American Leagues since their beginnings (1876 and 1900 respectively). The Cubs (National) haven't won a World Series since 1917 but continue to attract a relatively polite and well-heeled clientele to Wrigley Field on the North Side.

The White Sox are not only in a different league but sometimes, it seems, in a different world – Comiskey Park on the less affluent, less inhibited South Side. In 1919 they lost the World Series to Cincinnati of the National League. Later it was found that the games had been 'fixed' and eight players were suspended in what came to be known as the Black Sox scandal. Fans waited 40 years for the next series (1959) which they lost to the Dodgers ostensibly because their 'pitchers were too polite' to indulge in their opponents' practice of 'dusting off' the batters by throwing the ball precariously close to their heads.

In professional football (American style) the Chicago Bears were long known as the Monsters of the Midway and once massacred the Washington Redskins by relentlessly running up a record score of 79 to 0. Allegations that this was in retaliation for that affair at Fort Dearborn in 1812 were vigorously denied. Owned and, until recently, coached by the venerable George 'Papa Bear' Halas, the team has lost much of its proverbial power but little of its guile – as evidenced by one instance in which a disconcerting brass band was strategically stationed directly behind the opponents' bench.

For participating sports there are 10 golf courses (six of which are open to the public) and 620 municipal tennis courts. And then, of course, there is the lake, with 15 miles of sand beaches.

*See the Cubs play baseball at Wrigley Field*

There are piers for fishing, marinas for boating and sailing which, as local mariners will caution, can be as tricky as some oceans. The waves may not be as high, but winds can reach a velocity of 40 miles per hour. For residents in general, those who reside on Lake Shore Drive (The Gold Coast) in particular, it's as though Londoners had a Brighton at their doorstep.

For a place referred to by Tin Pan Alley as *"that toddling town"* Chicago offers a plethora of cultural and after-dark diversions. *Grease* started here and made its way to Broadway but most important productions are imported in the form of 'national' companies. Still, there are more than 50 professional theatre groups in the city and the Goodman Theater, housed in the Art Institute complex, has achieved a national reputation as a fountainhead for playwrights and performers. Dinner theatres are particularly popular.

The Chicago Civic Opera House presents performances of visiting ballet troupes, musical groups and folk dancers as well as its own Lyric Opera programme during autumn and winter. Orchestra Hall is home for the world-class Chicago Symphony which can be heard during the summer at Ravinia Park, north of the city, which also presents operas in concert version, ballet and theatrical performances. The Petrillo Bandshell (named for long-time head of the musician's union) offers free concerts on the lake front next to the Art Institute.

'Chicago' as the term for a jazz-style that flourished in the 20s and 30s is as well-known to music buffs as the city itself. Today it attracts a new generation of addicts, along with mainstream dixieland, experimental blues, folk, country, rock and disco.

As for dining out, Chicago used to be pretty much a 'meat and potatoes' town. (Waiters dressed as Russian cossacks would serve a sort of kebab on a flaming sword at an establishment whose owner explained: *"Well, the customers like it and it doesn't hurt the food much"*. Unadorned steaks, chops and roasts are still favourite fare, but succeeding waves of immigrants have resulted in an eclectic cuisine. As for numbers, a Visitor's Bureau statistician calculates that one could eat out every day of his or her life without ever going back to the same restaurant.

Although Chicago has imported chefs and recipes from around the world, *"it wears no man's collar"*, as comic strip character Andy Gump used to say, when it comes to politics. But were it not for this bold and brash attitude, Abraham Lincoln might never have become president and The Great Emancipator. At the Republican convention in 1860 supporters of Illinois' favourite son erected a huge wood structure known as the Wigwam and filled it to overflowing with their delegates who had been provided with free transportation. Lincoln's opponents never had a chance.

Ever since then Chicago has been the scene of a unique kind of politics that is difficult for strangers to comprehend. (That it is widely known as The Windy City may be due not so much to occasional Lake Michigan gales as to the lung power of its politicians.) In the 1920s, for example, mayor and machine-boss William Hale Thompson (self-styled 'Big Bill the Builder' but often referred to as 'Big Bill the Boodler') threatened, for reasons known only to himself, that he would *"punch King George in the snoot"* if he ever came to Chicago. It was in the days of First Ward Aldermen 'Bath House' John Coughlin and 'Hinky Dink' Kenna, who averred *"Chicago ain't no sissy town"*, that names from tombstones in local cemeteries began to appear on voter registration lists and the admonishment *"vote early and often"* was fraught with meaning. Big Bill's reign was followed by two decades of rule by the Kelly-Nash machine, a brief respite of eight years under what might be termed a 'reform' government and, beginning in 1955, by Richard J. Daley who was returned to office regularly by overwhelming majorities. Since the death of Daley, 'last of the big-city bosses', two unthinkable things have happened.

In 1979, a woman, Jane Byrne (albeit a Daley protegé) was elected mayor and four years later it was Harold Washington, a black. Chicago politics will never be the same.

The phrase 'politics makes strange bedfellows' is perhaps nowhere more applicable than to Chicago of the Roaring 20s. The city has produced some great and famous people in many fields but among the names that are immediately recognised as being synonymous with Chicago are those of Scarface Al Capone, Baby Face Nelson, Bugs Moran, Dutch Schultz, 'Machine Gun' Jack McGurn (who actually did carry his machine gun in a violin case), Frank 'The Waiter' Ricca and Jake 'The Barber' Factor. And, yes, Eliot Ness of the FBI, whom you may have seen on TV's *Untouchables*, was a real person, and the incidents presented were essentially true.

But there is no Tower of London or Scotland's Dunvegan Castle to commemorate this gory past. The garage where seven of Moran's henchmen were gunned down (reputedly at the behest of Al Capone) by opposing gangsters dressed in police uniforms during the infamous St. Valentine's Day Massacre has been torn down. To see its wall, you'll have to go to a certain restaurant in Vancouver, B.C.

Al Capone, who netted more than $100 million in a single year, died a natural death in prison where he was sent on the only charge they could prove against him – income tax evasion. Al was buried quietly in a local cemetery, but you will have trouble finding the gravesite. About 10 years ago somebody stole the tombstone.

But crime, like politics, isn't what it used to be in Chicago. One thing that has been said of the gangsters who were primarily in bootlegging operations was that they slaked the thirst of a grateful public and confined their mayhem and murders to their business competitors. Here, as in other large cities, the new breed of criminal seems less inclined to consider his nefarious profession as an intra-mural sport.

Chicago may be the second city in many ways but there is one category in which it is probably pleased to be out of the running. It still hasn't made the list of the FBI's 30 most crime-ridden cities.

# WHERE TO STAY

In keeping with its second city status, Chicago's hotels are not quite up to New York's en masse. Individually, there are some peerless properties, but as an institution the Chicago Hotel does not have the illustrious past, and hence atmospheric present, of its New York equivalent.

The choice is simple: bright new luxury hotels operating with the efficiency and personality of a computer, or Gothic old-style Chicago, all menace and charm, where you expect to see G Men lurking around the foyer. Hotels with history like The Drake and The Knickerbocker are no more expensive than the newer hotels and one often finds the service a little more personal.

Most of Chicago's better hotels are small (200-250 rooms) by American standards, although The Drake (575 rooms) defies any suggestion that quality is the exclusive terrain of the small establishment. The other large hotel with special significance is the Palmer House (1,770 rooms) which is one of America's grand old hotels and on which Hilton have spent $35 million refurbishing. The hotel's Empire Room was Mayor Daley's favourite and in its time one of the élite's major gathering places.

Unanimously praised by Chicagoans as the best value for money in the city is **The Richmont** (162 E. Ontario; tel: 312 787 3580; telex: 910221 0501), which is similar in many ways to London's lovely 11 Cadogan Gardens. The rooms are quite small and there is no restaurant (breakfast is taken in the lounge), but it has been beautifully decorated by former general manager (now president) Mike Harney's French wife and the staff are quite charming. The prices are low – single $63-$83; double $75-$95; suites $90-$105, and the location is central (just off Michigan Avenue just north of the river).

The Richmont apart, here is a totally subjective top 10 of Chicago hotels:

**The Mayfair Regent** (181 East Lake Shore Drive; tel: 312 787 8500; telex: 256266): Quite as elegant as its New York namesake, which remains my favourite hotel in the US. This is where Sir Georg Solti lives during the Chicago Symphony's season, and where elegance Chicago-style is demonstrated at its best. The Ciel Bleu Restaurant, which overlooks the lake, is chic to be seen in and quite expensive ($85 for two). 24 hour room service. Prices: single $145-$165; double $165-$185; suites $185-$450.

**The Drake** (140 East Walton Place; tel: 312 787 2200; telex: 270278): It has been one of America's better known hotels since the 1920s and remains so. Its Cape Cod Room is the city's best seafood restaurant. Vista Executive Suites ($185) include complimentary breakfast, free cocktails and a private lounge. Prices: single $85-$185; double $95-$185; suites $200-$400.

**The Tremont** (100 East Chestnut Street; tel: 312 751 1900; no telex): Another 1920s hotel with a lobby right out of a George Raft film and no more than 137 rooms. The New Orleans brunch on Sunday is worth travelling some distance for. Prices: single $120-$150; double $140-$170; suites $325-$700.

**The Knickerbocker** (9 Walton Place at North Michigan; tel: 312 751 8100; telex: 206719). This famous establishmment opened in 1927 and the Grand Ballroom has been one of Chicago society's centrepieces since then. Prices: single $98-$128; double $118-$198; suites $160-$800.

**The Whitehall** (105 East Delaware; tel: 312 944 6300; telex: 255157): The third (with the Tremond and Knickerbocker) of Golden Mile's smaller deluxe hotels that visiting celebrities tend to favour. Notable for the Whitehall Club, which is a walnut-panelled private dining club open to hotel guests. Prices: single $130-$180; double $150-$200; suites $325-$950.

**The Park Hyatt** (800 North Michigan; tel: 312 280 2222; telex: 256216): Hyatt's small (255-room) luxury property is another élite hotel for the travelling executive on a generous expense account. The $2,000 a night penthouse suite boasts a turn of the century rosewood Steinway. Prices: single $145-$190; double $165-$190; suites $195-$495.

**Westin Hotel** (909 North Michigan Avenue; tel: 312 943 7200; telex: 206593): Modern, largish (747 rooms) business hotel which appears to function efficiently, has television sets in the bathrooms, a health club that is free to guests, and a very busy foyer. Messages always get through and room service is excellent. The Westin also boasts The Consort Room, where you can dance and dine in 20s opulence to Franz Benteler's Royal Strings. Prices: single $115-$181; double $137-$203; suites $346-$588.

**Palmer House** (17 East Monroe Street; tel: 312 726 7500; telex: 4330329): Mentioned above, this magnificent old hotel is situated in the dark canyons of The Loop and has retained the feel of old-time Chicago. Prices: single $80-$135; double $105–$155; suites $175–400.

**Ambassador East** (1300 North State Parkway; tel: 312 787 7200; no telex): Now listed on America's National Register of Historic Places, the Ambassador East has been one of the city's top hotels since it opened in 1926. Bogart and Bacall honeymooned there and JFK was a regular visitor. The celebrated Pump Room restaurant boasts dramatic Art Deco setting and pleasant if not spectacular food. Prices: single $140-$175; double $160-$205; suites $195-$400.

NOTE: Weekend rates (up to 50 per cent discount) are commonplace in American cities. Special deals should be investigated no matter how exclusive the address.

# WHERE TO EAT

Don Roth claims that dining out in Chicago is much cheaper than New York and much better. But then you would expect him to say something like that, being the owner of more than one of the city's top restaurants and recently chairman of the Chicago Convention and Tourism Bureau. There is, however, an element of truth in what he says.

According to Roth, the city was a centre for fine cuisine right through to the Second World War. It would seem that all the corrupt politicians and gangsters had discernment as well as muscle – and if Capone wanted his tagliatelli just like momma cooked it you can be sure he got just that. America's fast food revolution in the 50s and 60s apparently killed Chicago's gastronomic pretensions stone dead and it is only now recovering its reputation. And deservedly so, for there are certainly quality restaurants here to match any in New York.

Roth's own choice of top restaurant understandably takes in two of the most traditional rooms in the city – **The Pump Room** (tel: 226 0360) in the Ambassador East Hotel and The Drake's **Cape Cod Room** (tel: 787 2200). The former is scattered with photographs of celebrities enjoying the classic European and American fare while you're likely to find the real thing eating at the next booth. The New England tavern setting of the Cape Cod Room plus the reliability of the seafood for just on 50 years far outweighs the idiosyncracies of the staff.

Roth's third choice is **Mortons** (1050 North State St; tel: 266 4820) where the best and most expensive steaks in town can be found. Arnie Morton, like Roth himself, is one of Chicago's stalwart restaurateurs. The menu is limited but exceptional and the wine list is as good as you'll find in town. A dinner for two would cost in the region of $75.

For sheer extravagance though **Le Perroquet** (70 East Walton; tel: 944 7990) must be identified as Chicago's gastronomic shrine. Formerly under the auspices of Michael Beck, one of America's top chefs, and now in the equally skilled hands of Philip Weddel, the restaurant is the place for élite

*Chicago is the home of the deep dish pizza*

out-of-towners to be seen. The five course *prix fixe* dinner costs about $50 a head and is excellent. The service is impeccable and the surroundings are the essence of sombre elegance. Considered by many American food critics to be one of the best restaurants in the country.

At the other end of the gastronomic spectrum is the pizza parlour – and if Chicagoans are reluctant to discuss Al Capone they're perfectly eager to inform you that their city is the home of the deep dish pizza. Very nice they are too, and I am no great fan of this particular food. **Pizzeria Uno** (29 East Ohio; tel: 321 1000) and **Pizzeria Due** (Wabash & Ontario; tel: 943 2400) are allegedly the birthplaces of the deep dish pizza, and are conveniently a block apart. Both are usually crowded and Due is a little smarter. **Gino's East** (160 East Superior; tel: 943 1124) is another outstanding pizza restaurant. Upstairs it is quite plush, the basement is more basic and the food is as tasty as the atmosphere.

The city's other major culinary claim to fame is its rib restaurants. **Twin Anchors** (1655 North Sedgwick; tel: 266 1616) is where Frank Sinatra sends for his ribs and is a no frills establishment which serves slow-cooked ribs and generous drinks. And I am reliably informed that **The Essex Inn** (800 South Michigan; tel: 939 2800) boasts the best ribs in the US. **Carson's – The Place For Ribs** (612 North Wells St; tel: 280 9200) should also be mentioned as it was voted by *Chicago Magazine* as the top rib room.

# NIGHT LIFE

One doesn't visit Chicago to hear the revered Symphony Orchestra, to visit the blues clubs on the south side or to spend an evening in the most influential comedy club in the US. But if you happen to be in town it would be criminal to avoid them.

Electric big city blues was born in the Chicago clubs, an historic development in American popular music that completely eluded white Chicagoans until English pop began pouring into their spiritual home in the early 60s. Hardly anybody around here had heard of Muddy Waters until the Rolling Stones brought his music back into his own city.

Two of the original clubs on the south-side still exist, indeed thrive – **Theresa's Tavern** (tel: 285 2744) and **Chequerboard Lounge** (tel: 373 5948) which is owned by Buddy Guy. They're situated on East 43rd in a pretty dangerous part of town but once inside either of the clubs one is quite safe. The answer is to have a cab drop you at the door and order one to take you home in the early hours. It's well worth such extravagant tactics.

Up on the safe side of town (the Near North), there are two other blues clubs worth investigating – **B.L.U.E.S.** (tel: 582 1012) and **Kingston Mines** (tel: 477 4646), across the road from one another on North Halstead. Both are cramped smoky dives, the atmosphere is friendly, the drinks are cheap, and the cover charge on average a modest $3. Look out for Lefty Dizz, Sunnyland Slim and Jimmy Walker, blues masters all – you won't hear them outside Chicago.

Traditional jazz no longer has the pull of former days when the likes of Louis Armstrong and Bennie Goodman ruled the city. Nowadays it's confined to short engagements by travelling stars, although **Rick's American Café** (tel: 943 9200) in the Lake Shore Drive Holiday Inn, is worth a visit whoever is on. The cover charge varies between $5 and $10 depending who's playing but it's the drinking that is really expensive.

One essential diversion if you're not too daunted by the run-of-the-mill comedy the Americans serve up on celluloid, is **Second City** (1616 N. Wells; tel: 337 3992), the city's, and indeed the country's premier comedy stage. Mike Nichols and Elaine May, Alan Arkin, John Belushi, Chevy Chase and many others learned their craft at Second City. The material is far sharper than one would expect and the improvisational sessions after each scripted performance are often a riot. Second City is open Tuesdays to Sundays, tickets cost around $8.50, there is a limited menu and unlimited booze, and reservations are essential.

For those looking towards a more refined evening out on the town there are various options. Chicago takes most of the successful Broadway shows with the original casts intact at least for a short time.

During the season of course there is the Chicago Symphony Orchestra under Sir Georg Solti. I would, however, particularly recommend the Ravinia Festival which takes place in the idyllic surrounds of Highland Park, an hour's drive north of the city. The festival acts as an open air retreat for the Symphony Orchestra and showcases short seasons by such luminaries as Pavarotti, Isaac Stern, James Levine and Pinchas Zukerman. There is a restaurant at Ravinia and on a hot summer's night there is nowhere better to be.

NOTE: Nightclubs and bars usually close at 3a.m. and 4a.m. on the weekends.

Half price theatre tickets can be purchased at the Hot Tix Booth (24 South State St.) on the day of the performance. Hours: Tues-Fri 11a.m.-5.15; Sat 10-5; Sun 12-4.

# GETTING AROUND

There are 4,000 cabs in the city and they run through the night. The standard fare between O'Hare Airport and the city is $20. Some cabbies offer special rates of as little as $7 to the airport, but approach with caution.

Allow at least an hour to the airport, tailbacks on the highway can stretch for miles. Continental Air Transport buses run every 30 minutes and cost $6 each way. The underground line to O'Hare is scheduled for completion by next Spring and that may well be the quickest and cheapest method of travel.

# China

By Graham Boynton

**As Deng Xiaoping's open door policy begins to take effect, all the signs are that the door has opened too far ever to be shut. Westerners can therefore expect to find increasing signs of modernity, with Coca Cola and home computer ads ousting the traditional values and more than a hundred new international hotels going up during the next couple of years.**

Sitting in the seven-storey glass and steel atrium of Beijing's Great Wall Hotel, Chen Min sips carefully at a glass of fresh orange juice and attempts to explain the meaning of life in modern China. He is, for want of a better classification, a junior executive – the deputy public relations manager at the Western-run hotel – and, having come through the Cultural Revolution relatively unscarred, is now developing career ambitions in line with the new administration's thinking.

Like so many survivors, Chen seems to have instinctively developed a low profile personality, an easy pragmatism and an innate caution. Today, he is dressed comfortably in a snappy two-piece charcoal suit, but tomorrow he would swap it for a drab Mao uniform if circumstances dictated.

His own experiences explain his manner. At 16, midway through secondary school, the keen and talented Chen was wrenched from his studies and sent to work in a factory. This, he says, was a stroke of luck – it could have been a farm. For five years during the height of the Cultural Revolution he kept out of trouble and then, as suddenly as his education was halted, so it was recommenced – he was awarded a place at Beijing University. Through unwavering diligence Chen overcame the disadvantages of the five lost years and finally graduated in 1979 with a degree in international trade.

This was around the time that Deng Xiaoping's *kaifang* (open door) policies were beginning to take effect, and with perfect Chinese logic it was decided that with Chen's command of spoken English he was the perfect candidate for an industry that was booming and desperately short-staffed – he became a tour guide. When the Great Wall Hotel opened in 1982 he was moved into public relations and has remained there ever since.

Last year Chen applied to an American university to take an 18-month MBA course. He was accepted almost immediately and ever since has been waiting for the Chinese bureaucrats to make up their minds. And yet he shows no irritation at the cadres' extreme procrastination, but rather accepts it all as the Chinese way . . . and waits patiently.

Chen's own faltering progress is so-called modern China in microcosm. Dressed up in the picturesque language that has often been a euphemism for terrible outrage (witness Mao's Hundred Flowers Campaign which decreed *"let a hundred flowers bloom and let a hundred schools of thought contend"* and which led to a most ruthless response to the storm of criticism), the modernisation of China is understandably a hesitant and painful business. After 40 years of isolation and repression, their re-entry into the modern world must be as traumatic for the Chinese as it is curious to us.

Deng Xiaoping has set the tone by admitting that in the past party cadres, regardless of their education or aptitude, have been running the country's commerce and industry, and by calling for technocrats to take the places of bureaucrats. He has also performed with great élan the sensitive task of replacing a political leadership steeped in the old ways, whose average age is 75, with men and women in their 40s and 50s who are far less shackled by ideological convictions. Deng's Young Tigers have, according to China watchers, 20 hard years of social, intellectual and commercial reform ahead of them before China can truly be called modern.

The Chinese as a people accept the current tidal wave of change with the same thoughtful restraint that individuals like Chen Min accept bureaucratic inertia. Lu Jian He, a top official of the Guangdong Economic Commission, believes there will be a price paid for such rapid progress but that progress is not only inevitable but highly desirable. *"If you open the window to let in the fresh air, you also let in unpleasant things like flies and mosquitoes. But it is better than no fresh air at all."*

Mr Lu, who admits to being *"very lucky to have survived those terrible years and to be talking to you now"*, stresses the magnitude of the task ahead: *"At present we are perfecting our economic legislation on one hand and on the other hand we are attempting to simplify procedures to cope with the requirements of a modern economy. It is very complicated and it cannot be done in one day."*

Thus far the changes have not brought about the holocaust that the radicals led by the Gang of Four had predicted. What with a minor football riot (by European standards), small skirmishes at the successful Wham concerts and a disco-dancing craze sweeping through Beijing, life in China has changed quite dramatically in the past five years. The wall slogans have been replaced by hoardings advertising such decadent artefacts as quartz watches and video recorders, and television dramas like *The Girl Silkworm Raisers* are interspersed with alluring ads for washing machines and home computers – scarcely what Mao had in mind when

*Giant faces stare out from hoardings*

he unveiled the Great Leap Forward campaign in the late 50s.

Of course evidence of growth and development is as obvious in the statistics as it is visible in the cities. Since 1979 China has attracted well over US$17 billion in foreign investment, and since 1981 more than 2,000 joint venture projects have started up. The country's leading trade partner, the old enemy Japan, recorded total trade figures of US$13 billion in 1984. With companies like Coca Cola, Volkswagen, Sanyo and Toshiba having already established factories there and thousands more waiting in the wings, the influx of foreigners will continue to grow phenomenally, and there are more than 100 new international standard hotels scheduled for completion by the end of 1987.

The consensus, even among the wizened sceptics, is that the door has been opened too wide for it to be slammed shut again. It is the helter-skelter nature of progress that will be the major problem facing the country in the coming decade, and not the much-feared political backlash from those nostalgic for the Mao days. As the author Pang Lin observes: *"There is an innocence, natural good manners and a good humour which will be sorely tested with the invasion of modernity."*

The sceptics are those who contend that the Chinese people have endured enough misery and repression over the centuries to have tested these endearing qualities to the full. They point to the razing of Tibetan culture, the excesses of the Red Guards and the blind obedience of a nation to Mao's crazed economic experiments, and suggest that the Chinese are a people who attract oppression and who will become corrupt and ungovernable in a climate of social and economic liberty. What these observers fail to mention is that exiled Chinese communities the world over are models of discipline and diligence, which suggests that they have learned to cope with adversity by self-discipline rather than masochism.

This quality of self-discipline remains as necessary today inside China as it does in exile, for even under the current enlightened administration social deviations are not tolerated and are punished very harshly by Western standards. According to a group of international jurors, more than 10,000 people have been executed since Deng launched his anti-crime campaign in 1983. Even top bureaucrats are not immune– at a recent gang rape trial five young men, all the sons of high cadres in Bei'an, were sentenced to death and their fathers banished for trying to cover up their sons' offences.

It is against this enormously complex backdrop that the new wave of European businessmen find themselves. No doubt they have flown in on promises of unlimited opportunities ('awakening giant', 'the biggest marketplace in the world', and 'one billion potential customers' are three common catch phrases), and to be sure it is an exciting place to be. But they are certain to find their optimism sorely tested and their enthusiasm drained as this very strange society goes about its daily business. They would probably be forgiven if at times they wondered whether this particular Great Leap Forward was nothing more than a great hoax.

The Peninsula Group's Niklaus Leuenberger, who now runs the Garden Hotel in Guangzhou, was involved in the opening of China's first Western-run hotel early in 1982 and remembers rigorous daily meetings with the Chinese authorities as the two sides in the joint venture sized each other up. *"Each meeting went on for at least three hours, day after day. The biggest problem was to convince the Chinese of the benefits of our way of operating a hotel – they were used to Russian methods. It took two months of those daily meetings to convince them that our methods were not too bad. Three years later, opening in Guangzhou was much easier. I think they have come to trust us, but it has been hard work."*

Leuenberger is decidedly optimistic about China's future. *"I have faith in China . . . I feel it's nice to be here at the moment, to bring a lot of the benefits of the Western world to a country that has been closed up for 40 years. Any foreigner coming here has to realise that this was an ancient culture when we in Europe were running around naked . . . and that deserves respect. I think China is on its way back."*

His optimism is not, however, shared by others who would agree with his sentiments. Eugene Theroux, a Washington lawyer who first travelled to China with ex-President Gerald Ford and has lived there since, said recently: *"At no time since I started coming here in 1973 has there been more reason to be hopeful, yet I have never felt so little hope that China can solve its problems."*

For the moment at least there seems to be a brief lull – a number of companies which got into China early and took substantial losses are now pausing to reflect; and even more significant, the oil companies are reported to be very disappointed with their lack of success in the offshore fields, while the Chinese are claiming *"It is too early to draw conclusions."*

No doubt this is a calm before the next storm of development – this one taking the country into the 90s. I have no doubt that it is the most important five-year period China has faced since Mao's death – if it is successful and the liberalisation continues apace then the door will be well and truly open, and there can surely be no turning back.

*Uniforms have given way to Western clothing*

## DOING BUSINESS

Earlier this year a European businessman, who had spent several weeks attempting to drum up business in Guangzhou, was invited out for the evening by his potential trading partners. After a few drinks they moved on to the restaurant where the European proceeded to get rather drunk. As he did so he began telling dirty jokes and as the night wore on so the jokes got rougher. His Chinese hosts laughed heartily all the way through.

When he returned to his hotel he regaled his fellow business travellers with stories of his successful night, concluding that he had finally cracked it – he had seen behind the Chinese mask and now had their measure. The following day they all assembled for the formal meeting he assumed would seal the contract, and he was astonished when his cohorts from the previous night filed into the meeting room with stone cold expressions and an icy formality.

A week later he returned to Europe empty handed.

Whether this story illustrates the insensitivity of the European abroad or the inscrutability of the Chinese is rather difficult to tell. The conclusion drawn by European residents there is that the unfortunate businessman had not realised they were not laughing *with* him on that drunken night, but *at* him. The more cynical travellers to China claim that this is a perfect example of the deviousness of the Chinese, and that no matter how you behave it will never be right.

In China today it seems that not only are the indigenous people enigmatic, contradictory and confusing, but so are the thousands of Westerners who have been pouring through since *kaifang* was initiated. At Shanghai Airport a German businessman who had been travelling here since the early days of the Cultural Revolution, told me he considered the Chinese the best businessmen he had ever dealt with: – *"and my biggest problem in doing business here is whether my head office will let me down by not honouring our contracts to the letter."*

It came as no surprise to hear a diametrically opposed view only hours later in the bar at the Jinjiang Hotel. This time a British sales executive who had been operating in the Shanghai region since the late 70s, suggested that the Chinese were as devious and corruptible as anyone: *"They mess you around, you attend meeting after meeting never knowing who is the decision maker, 18 of them facing one or two of you, and all the time they're only after one thing – the cheapest price."*

All of which has given rise to a veritable avalanche of solemn articles in guide books and travel publications on the etiquette of doing business in China. Prefaced by the usual clichés (*"the minefield of pitfalls awaiting the unsuspecting Western businessman"* is one I saw recently), such advice seldom goes further than basic common sense that would apply to the European businessman's dealings in any foreign country, be it First or Third World. One is told that unruly behaviour and obscene gestures are not well received, that black market currency dealings are illegal, that facetiousness is not appreciated and so on, as if it were all perfectly acceptable anywhere but China.

What everyone should know about doing business in China is that patience and extreme flexibility are the two most essential virtues, that some knowledge of Chinese history over the 19th and 20th century is a useful aid to understanding the idiosyncracies of one's opposite numbers, and that the language barrier, which manifests itself in everything from giving the taxi driver instructions through to interpretation of contractual nuances, is probably the most overwhelming problem the current generation of businessman faces.

Patience and flexibility are necessary because, as the author Pang Lin says, *"Modern China dawdles in an earlier century."* The current hierarchy, including Deng Xiaoping's Young Tigers, is steeped in leaden bureaucracy; and only when the current crop of graduates shifts into positions of power in 15 to 20 years time, will this change dramatically.

For the moment business negotiations are uniformly tortuous, involving meeting after meeting, amendment after amendment, and the Chinese run them as if they have all the time in the world. This invariably leads to rearranged flights and hotel bookings which can be hellish given the shortage of hotel rooms and the unpredictability of the national airline, CAAC, which operates the only internal flight network. While the 'joint venture' hoteliers assure their clients they will do their best to extend reservations, hotels all run at occupancy rates in the high 90s, so are often genuinely full. Admittedly, a few nights at a cheap Chinese hotel in an emergency would hardly kill you, but it can be a pretty dispiriting experience and the complete lack of modern communications facilities can become a serious handicap.

CAAC is another matter altogether. At the time of going to press, the airline does not have a computerised reservations system, although it has just signed a US$9 million contract with the Sperry corporation for the installation of one, and therefore bookings are a lottery and bumping commonplace. Travellers are advised to reconfirm any internal flight three days prior to departure, but that doesn't guarantee anything – you only know you are on the flight when they hand you a boarding card.

However, my own experience suggests that however inefficient they are, inflexible they're not. I was stranded in Shanghai with a wait-listed ticket for Beijing and was grimly informed at various

CAAC offices in the city that it was unlikely I would be able to get on a flight for the following four days. Armed with the belief that even in China they would respond to a good yarn, I took myself to Shanghai Airport and put myself at the mercy of a CAAC official, and unravelled (largely in sign language) a most implausible tale of urgent meetings that very afternoon with high government officials. I was on the flight to Beijing within the hour, and I doubt that they understood me, never mind believed the tale.

Incidents like this have me believing that the Chinese are cheerful people who respond well to a friendly open attitude. It also convinces me that they are as weighed down by this combination of inefficiency and bureaucracy as their Western visitors, and the right word to the right man works as well as it does here. Of course in China the main problem is finding the right man.

The Chinese find the right man by employing what they call *guanxi* – using contacts. *Guanxi* gets you a seat on a full aircraft, and at the highest levels it gets vital documentation approved immediately or bureaucratic restrictions waived suddenly. It involves exchanges of favours and I am told gifts of considerable value. It has been the Chinese way ever since the time leaden bureaucracy was visited upon them, and it is probably the only way things moved during the dark days of the Cultural Revolution.

Understanding the Chinese way is a subject far too broad and complex to cover adequately here, and the visiting businessman is bound to find most maxims he has read contradicted within 24 hours of setting foot in the place. To add final confusion I offer one further anecdote that probably illustrates as well as anything the measure of the people one is likely to encounter.

A meeting was arranged between top officials from a Western airline and their opposite numbers, and the venue selected for a banquet lunch was Shanghai's Jinjiang Hotel. The organisers were surprised when told that the best banquet room was not available, given the importance of the occasion, and rather irritably accepted a distinctly inferior room.

On the day of the banquet the hotel management realised that the Mayor of Shanghai was one of the guests – and suddenly the main banquet room became available. When asked by the frustrated organisers how this had happened, the manager patiently explained: *"You must understand we do not measure our work against commercial considerations, but by mission, by idealism."*

*Bilingual signs welcome customers from abroad*

# Beijing

*The Imperial Palace*

There is no better place to measure the greatness of Beijing (Peking) than in Tian'anmen Square on a Sunday afternoon. To the north is the Gate Of Heavenly Peace (above which hangs the only public portrait of Chairman Mao in the city), from where China's leaders would watch over those massive military parades and rallies in the 60s and early 70s. Beyond the Gate is the Imperial Palace, an awesome creation of the Yongle Emperor in the 15th century, an extravaganza that covers 250 acres.

Equally awesome is the sheer scale of the modern palaces that flank the square – on the east side are the Museum of Chinese History and the Museum of The Chinese Revolution, opposite is the massive Great Hall of the People, and on the south flank Chairman Mao's Memorial Hall containing Mao's embalmed body. More austere certainly, but no less impressive than the palaces of former times. As one Antipodean businessman said to me, they make Europe's public buildings look like Lego-Land.

On a Sunday the Chinese come out in tens of thousands to Tian'anmen Square to pay homage to Mao and their ancestors and to spend a day out with their families. There is a sense of order and dignity about the gathering as well as a charming naiveté that you would be unlikely to see in Central Park or even Hyde Park. The adults show enormous affection for the children and the children do their bit by looking like exquisitely-made dolls. Even their speech is quieter and less percussive than the animated dialects of the south, and on a warm Sunday afternoon in Tian'anmen Square you could almost be lulled into believing that this was the perfect harmony Mao and his fellow travellers had set out to achieve.

A sideways glance at the stone-hard face of a People's Liberation Army officer in the midst of the dancing dolls, soon shakes you out of your romanticism. But there are moments when Beijing is a most seductive illusion.

The city is, from the foreigner's point of view, the easiest of the three major cities to do business in. The China hands complain about the blandness of the place compared with the excitement, both architectural and spiritual, of Shanghai or the zest of Guangzhou, but it does seem to work with something approximating smooth efficiency compared with the chaos of the other two. The telephones work more frequently, there are more Western hotels, the climate outside mid-winter is infinitely more pleasant for the European, and all the major decisions are made here.

Beijing probably boasts the two best hotels in the country and any business traveller operating in China today will tell you that these small oases of Western comfort are nothing less than lifelines. The standard of Chinese-run hotels varies from very average to quite terrible, (with the notable exception of the White Swan in Guangzhou), and travellers gladly pay the considerably higher rates of Sheraton's Great Wall and the Peninsula-run Jianguo.

The **Jianguo** (Jianguomenwei Dajie; tel: 502 233; telex: 22439) is definitely the favourite and businessmen I met spoke of it with almost patriotic fervour. That is probably because it was the first major joint venture hotel in the country and has been the Westerners' ally since 1982.

It is managed by the Peninsula Group and all the key positions are held by top class Hong Kong hotel people, both Chinese and European. The general manager, Fritz Sommerau, rates the hotel as a good quality three-star establishment, although it should be said that this is using Hong Kong as a measure. The Jianguo is American in style, small by Chinese standards (480 rooms) and rates range from Y180 to Y205 for single rooms through to Y460 for suites. It is also set on the 14-mile long Jianguomenwai, through the centre of the business district.

Most important in Beijing, as in most of China, the Jianguo has a number of very good restaurants, including probably the best Cantonese in the city, **The Four Seasons,** and a European restaurant, **Justines,** which is run by Swiss chefs. Even grizzled China hands admit that after a few weeks out there a European meal comes as welcome relief. The latter is rather expensive because of the import tax on vegetables and other European luxuries, and one can expect to pay around Y50-Y60 a head including wine. So too the Four Seasons (around Y45 per head), which is about twice the price of local restaurants and about ten times better.

The other major Western oasis is the **Great Wall Hotel** (Donghuanbei Lu; tel: 483 831/505 566; telex: 20045), about five minutes by taxi from Jianguomenwei and in the heart of the Embassy district. A dramatic steel and glass building, the Great Wall has been run by Sheraton since 1985 and is a rather classy hotel that still has some way to go to realise its potential, and is rather plagued by large groups of large American tourists, all clacking away like hens in the foyer. Room rates are that much higher than the Jianguo and it is more than twice the size with 1,007 rooms. Singles Y220; double Y250 (Y280 for a room on a higher floor); deluxe Y310; junior suite Y400; VIP suite Y1,600.

I must say I found the staff at the Great Wall a little more helpful than at the Jianguo and as one

*Jianguo hotel*

*Fitness freaks Chinese-style*

would expect for the higher prices, everything seemed a lot slicker. I did, however, meet a number of businessmen who felt the prices were too high and Sheraton admit that they still have time to go before they believe the Great Wall will be a deluxe hotel by international standards.

For the rest, **The Lido** (Jichang and Jiang Rai roads in the Dong Jiao district; telex: 22618) is now run by Holiday Inn who promise improvements. At the moment it isn't in the same class as the two mentioned above and the rates are appropriately lower. Single Y110; double Y120; suite Y200. Of the Chinese-run hotels the **Beijing Hotel** (Dong Chang Jie; tel: 506 688; telex: 22439) is the oldest and most famous but it suffers from poor service and food (like the rest). The curious thing is that when the Beijing is the venue for the many banquets that punctuate the year, it manages to serve up excellent food; on a daily basis it sometimes comes close to inedible. The coffee shop is known to foreign residents as The Bridge of Broken Dreams, as it is a sanctuary for businessmen whose dreams of sealing a contract are fading.

There are two others that are worth considering only if the others are full – **The Jinglun** (Jianguomenwai Dajie; tel: 502 266; telex: 210011) because it is situated conveniently beside the Jianguo, and the **Fragrant Hills** (Xiangshan; tel: 819 242; no telex) because it was designed by I. M. Pei and is situated in very pleasant surroundings some 40 minutes from the centre of town.

But if locally run hotels are a disappointment then local restaurants are doubly so. I'm afraid you can get better Peking Duck in London than you can in Peking, and it is generally accepted that outside the joint venture hotels there are no consistent standards maintained. The two best indigenous restaurants are the **Four Seasons** (Jianguo Hotel) for Cantonese and the **Yuen Tai** (Great Wall Hotel) for top quality Szechuan cuisine.

There is a host of well-publicised duck restaurants, aimed, presumably, at people from Milwaukee who would barely know duck from dog, with names like Small Duck, Super Duck and Sick Duck, but I am informed that only the newest, the **Beijing Roast Duck** restaurant in Guan Hua Lu near the British Embassy, is worth considering. One can expect to pay around Y25 per head there.

Another more reputable, but again inconsistent, restaurant is **Donglaishun** at the north entrance of Dongfeng Shichang, a 15 minute walk from the Beijing Hotel. It is famous for serving Mongolian hot pot and on some nights can be quite good and is rather cheap (around Y25 per head) compared with the hotel restaurants.

For all the shortcomings of a city that is hauling itself into the late 20th century at such a pace, I must re-emphasise my view that Beijing is a relatively easy city to do business in. The taxi drivers are as helpful as they can be with such limited English and are essential allies for anyone with busy schedules; the people of Beijing are extremely friendly, and if service is sloppy it is as a result of ingrained attitudes rather than malicious intent; and the city itself is full of historic and architectural treasures that will long occupy a visitor who wishes to learn more about this great city and its people.

Finally, it should be said that Beijing, like so many other aspects of China, is not all that it first appears to be. After the claustrophobia of Shanghai, Beijing at first appears to be clean and uncluttered. In fact it is one of the world's most polluted capitals. An American scientist recently measured 120 particles in a unit mass of Beijing air, which compares rather unfavourably with the internationally accepted safety level of 30 particles.

They say that to jog here in the morning is like smoking a packet of cigarettes a day.

# Guangzhou

*The odd acre of tranquillity can still be found in the urban sprawl of Guangzhou*

They say that Guangzhou (also known as Canton) is Hong Kong without the money. . . then they usually go on to say that it is probably a foretaste of Hong Kong after 1997. You may not agree, but you cannot fail to get the point.

For all the talk of this sprawling mass of a city being at the forefront of the modernisation programme because of its international links, it doesn't work very well at all. I was to discover that the chaos on the roads is common to all Chinese cities, but Guangzhou must take the biscuit for the worst telephone system, the dirtiest streets and despite its smaller population, easily matches Shanghai for overpowering congestion.

That said, there is no doubt that Guangzhou is developing faster than any of the other cities and is therefore more likely to rectify these failings sooner. The Guangdong Economic Commission highlights three major development priorities for the city – energy and energy conservation; transport and telecommunications (25,000 new telephone lines should be installed by early 1986); and power supply, which is seen as the most difficult project involving the heaviest investment.

Already, in the five years up to 1985 the province of Guangdong (which contains three of China's four special economic zones) has signed around 50,000 contracts with almost 30 countries – the potential investment value is US$6 billion. However, much depends on the success of the offshore oil drilling, and so far there has been little encouragement for the international oil companies in the first round of drilling licences. Nevertheless, there remains high optimism over oil and locals have already dubbed Zhanjiang the Houston of South China.

Guangzhou's contemporary role as China's gateway to the West began back in 1957 with the first Canton Trade Fair, which until the late 1970s was the only major forum for Western businessmen in the whole country. The China hands recall the old pioneering days before and during the Cultural Revolution as American historians conjure up the Wild West. Those were the days when their Chinese counterparts were buried in anti-West propaganda, deeply suspicious of foreign businessmen and watched constantly by political cadres who were there to ensure they exercised correct political thinking.

Like old hands everywhere they say that by comparison Guangzhou today is a doddle. They point to new international hotels, a substantial fleet of taxi cabs, professional secretarial services, telex and so on, as measures of civilisation that were unheard of up to 1979. More important, the attitudes of the people have changed and the Cantonese, probably more than any others in China, have embraced the West fervently. The fact that four-fifths of the Chinese in Hong Kong have relatives in Guangdong has something to do with it, but they are by nature a warm and hospitable people who have welcomed the political reforms and taken advantage of the freedom it has afforded them.

And the old hands are right, the facilities for the Western visitor are much improved and some of the more lavish aspects of Guangzhou's newest hotel, the 1100-room Garden Hotel, suggest that the Chinese are suckers for ostentation just like the rest of us. In the enormous foyer hangs a 24-metre-long gold and marble mural, in the top VIP suite you will find gold-plated bathroom fittings fighting with reproduction Louis XIV furniture for your attention, and at the very top you will find the traditional revolving restaurant (I thought they had gone out of fashion in the mid-70s).

The **Garden** (338 Huanshi Dong Lu; tel: 73 388; telex: 44788) is run by the excellent Peninsula Group and for all the overkill it is on the way to becoming a very good hotel. It boasts four excellent restaurants, the rooms are to Hong Kong standards with all the accoutrements like mini-bar and colour television, the service is improving, there is a well-equipped business centre and full secretarial services. Basically, it all works.

The business centre is worth stressing and although it has been suffering from teething problems it provides photocopying, telex, word processing and message taking services. The business centre is run by a doughty Australian woman called Margaret Sullivan whose company, Sullivan Secretarial Agencies, has operated out of Hong Kong for years and who was the first European typist in Beijing in 1978. They provide everything but interpreters (who can be brought in at Y100 an hour) and are open 12 hours a day.

A standard room at the Garden costs Y100 and a deluxe Y140; standard suites are Y180 and deluxe suites Y250. Reservations can be made through Cathay Pacific and Steigenberger Reservation Service and they are essential because the Garden, like all Western hotels, is often full.

Although not as well run as the Garden, the **White Swan** (1 South Street, Shamian Island; tel: 86 968; telex: 44688) is certainly more attractive, set as it is on the old British and French concession, Shamian Island. Redolent of old Shanghai, the old mansions that were once banks, embassies and even a Roman Catholic church have survived but are some way from their former glories. In a city that is not, like Beijing, blessed with historic architecture, Shamian Island is a rare treat.

Opened in 1982, the 1,000-room White Swan is regarded as the best Chinese-run hotel in the country. The rooms are pleasant, and although the service is not quite as good as the Garden the facilities are on a par. And it must be said that the lobby with its waterfalls, pools and trees is an exercise in tasteful restraint compared with the Garden. Prices: singles between Y75 and Y100; suites (2-room) between Y120 and Y140 and 3-room suites between Y160 and Y180.

The other joint venture hotel is the **China Hotel** (Liu Hua Road; tel: 66 888; telex: 44888) and its main asset is its location – opposite the Trade Fair Exhibition Hall. This one is enormous (1,200 rooms), quite comfortable and possessing the requisite modern facilities, but it is not in the class of the other two. I had some trouble making myself understood at the front desk and subsequently heard similar complaints about the hotel in general. As chauvinistic as it may appear, a hotel in

*City centre, Guangzhou*

China is only as good as its English speaking staff. Without that, the one haven available to the businessman becomes as confusing, irritating and wearying as the world beyond those air-conditioned doors. Prices at the China Hotel: Y100 to Y180 for singles; up to Y200 for doubles; and between Y285 and Y350 for suites.

If the above-mentioned hotels are full – and this is invariably the case during the two trade fairs – then there is always the **Dongfang Hotel** (120 Liu Hua Road; tel: 69 900; telex: 44139) which was once the place to stay in Guangzhou. Now it isn't but if you have to stay there you will survive. Prices: single rooms for around Y65; doubles around Y75 and suites around Y285.

Finally, a word or two about eating out in Guangzhou. Inevitably, the businessman will be showered with invitations to banquets but no doubt he will have to fend for himself occasionally. The same basic rules apply here that do elsewhere in the country: local restaurants are often inconsistent and sometimes quite dire, so the more expensive but much classier hotel restaurants are the safest bet.

I can personally recommened the **Peach Blossom** and the **Connoisseur** in the Garden hotel. The former specialises in Cantonese cuisine, naturally, and the fresh seafood and sautéed sliced pigeon are outstanding; the Connoisseur is all fluted columns, reproduction furniture and excellent continental cuisine prepared by Swiss chefs. It is very expensive (medallions of veal Y32, roast rack of lamb for two, Y56) because everything is imported, but it is the best in town.

The White Swan's **Cantonese Restaurant** is reputed to be consistently good (it also has a European style grill room called The Silk Road) and the China Hotel's **Chaozhou Restaurant,** which specialises in cuisine from northeast Guandong, serves excellent goose and Chinjie vegetables.

If you wish to eat in town there are two restaurants that do come highly recommended. **The Guangzhou** (2 Wenchang Nan Road; tel: 87 840) is open from 11 a.m. to 2.30 p.m. and from 5 to 9 p.m. and specialises in foreign groups which could be seen as a disadvantage. That it is very reasonably priced and serves consistently good Cantonese food are distinct advantages. The other restaurant is for the more adventurous but it is clean and reasonable. The **Snake Restaurant** (4 Jianglan Road; tel: 82 517) is the better of two wild animal restaurants and serves a variety of game meat as well as the infamous dragon-tiger-phoenix soup which is made from snake, cat and chicken.

Which seems a perfect way to finish – you've probably been eating snake and cat all along but it is only when they tell you what it is that it appears rather repulsive. At the Snake Restaurant you can tell – the snake is cut into cubes and the cat into strips. *Bon appetit.*

*Peach Blossom restaurant in the Garden hotel*

# Shanghai

There is something quite eerie about Shanghai, as if some omnipotent hand switched the power off sometime in the 1930s and left this great city immune and unaffected by the changes which have taken place on the rest of the planet since. Even now there seem to be no new buildings, only those great Gothic edifices built in its heyday and unchanged but for a few generations of grime. There are no architectural landmarks to say that this is a city of the late 20th century.

Only the population has grown, and with anything between 11 and 13 million inhabitants Shanghai is probably the biggest city in the world. It is also the most chaotic, most overcrowded and most run down. There is little order in the streets as pedestrians, millions of cyclists and a growing number of motor vehicles attempt to thread their way through one another in a seamless flow of movement. At intersections you will witness traffic policemen in twos and threes, but their presence appears quite superfluous to the chaos around them. I did not see them making even token arm-waving gestures all the time I was there.

Like an old film set the buildings along the Bund glower over this frenetic activity. Once the banks, clubs, offices and embassies for the foreign traders who ran Shanghai, today they are largely offices of a government that seems distinctly reluctant to develop Shanghai at the same pace as Beijing or Guangzhou.

Many theories have been raised over why Shanghai has been left out of the rush to modernise – the most popular claims that the Shanghainese have long been envied and despised by the rest of China (one local said to me that they were like the Jews of China), and that this was some sort of bureaucratic revenge. A more contentious opinion has it that the Shanghainese are traditionally a politically volatile and dissident people (it was, after all, the birthplace of Chinese communism in 1921 and the base for the Gang of Four almost 50 years later), therefore more likely to overreact to the pressures of modernisation.

Whatever the reason there is no doubt that Shanghai has been left behind. There is some building going on but not with the manic enthusiasm one encounters elsewhere in the country. And there is little evidence of the 20, 30 or 40 (depending on your source) hotels that are due to be completed between now and the end of the decade. At present there is no hotel of international standing in the city, and it was only in 1984 that the old shack at Hongqiao Airport was knocked down and a proper bricks-and-mortar terminus was built.

All of this despite Shanghai's position at the centre of the country's trade and industry – more than half of China's internal and external commerce passes through here. Shanghai trades with companies in some 150 countries, it is an important supplier of both industrial and consumer goods to central and western China and provides a huge marketplace for their goods in return, and it remains a major international port.

The very mention of the name Shanghai brings tears to the eyes of the old China hands and brings forth a flood of grand and dashing stories, some real but many imagined. To the modern business traveller the name is more likely to elicit tears of frustration. I spent several nights huddled around ill-lit bars listening to the complaints of weary businessmen – round after round of meetings, stiff banquets, terrible weather, appalling food, no nightlife, and every time they come out here they stay longer and go home with less. The Tsigtao beer's not as good as it used to be, the telephones never work and the service in the hotel stinks.

At first you feel little sympathy for these characters, you'll find them in bars all over the world, always bitching about the local customs and wishing they were somewhere else. Then after a couple of days you being to think that perhaps they aren't bigots and have a point, Shanghai, and China in general, can be hard work.

They are quite right about the hotels, at best they are average and at worst pretty diabolical, and there is always a shortage of rooms. The best known, and probably the best for foreigners, is the **Jinjiang** (59 Maoming Road; tel: 534 242; telex: 33011) which is located in the old French Concession Area. It was here that Richard Nixon stayed when he signed the 1972 Shanghai Accord and where most businessmen stay if they can get a room.

The Jinjiang now comprises four separate buildings, and the North Wing which was built in 1931 is by far the most preferable. Wood panelled rooms, art deco fixtures and the brooding menace of a bygone era conspire to make the hotel rather interesting. Sadly, the spartan facilities, indifferent service and poor food wear you down after a couple of days and you begin gathering at the bar looking for newly-arrived foreigners to unload your misery upon. One would expect such hardship if this were an adventure up the Amazon, but here you are undertaking the same tasks you would in London, Nairobi or Kuala Lumpur – and it sometimes seems like the Amazon.

The Jinjiang is, however, conveniently situated, offers telex facilities and has a most useful supermarket in the complex. Double rooms cost Y120; suites between Y200 and Y240 for the basic and up to Y1,000 for the top suites.

The alternative to the Jinjiang is the **Peace Hotel** (20 Nanjing Road; tel: 211 244; no telex), on the corner of Nanjing Road and the Bund, which, as the Cathay Hotel, was one of the landmarks of old Shanghai. Today, it is a rather spartan badly run hotel with reasonable food (at times) and a rather threadbare feel to it. The ghosts of pre-People's Revolution high society must surely haunt some of the dark corners of this once great hotel, for it was surely The Mandarin of its age. Now for around Y180 you get a large room and not much else. Some businessmen I met complained that the noise of the Bund and the river traffic were so bad that there was no peace at the Peace.

*The old have learned to accept change as a way of life*

*Shanghai carpet factory*

If neither of the above hotels have rooms there is always the **Park Hotel** (170 Nanjing Road West; tel: 225 225; no telex), which overlooks Nanjing Road on one side and Renmin Park on the other. It is slightly less expensive than the others but there is barely any difference in standards. The Park does have a lively discotheque where modern young China assembles to perform John Travolta impersonations. It might take your mind off the following day's inevitable meeting.

There is one further alternative to the main hotels – the guest house, which usually means a collection of former private homes that once belonged to the foreign residents of Shanghai: the bankers, businessmen and diplomats. The **Xing Guo Guest House** (72 Xing Guo Road; tel: 374 503; telex: 33016), comes recommended by a Washington lawyer who travels to Shanghai almost every month. The food is reasonable, the hotel air-conditioned and a double room/suite comes at around Y180 a night.

The best known of the guest houses is the **Xijiao** (191 Hongqiao Road; tel: 379 643; telex: 33004) which is set in a park in the city's western suburbs and has a number of lovely villas. The only problem here is that transport is a little difficult, otherwise guest houses are a most suitable alternative if the major hotels are full.

Despite this being the area where one would find *yangzhou* cuisine, one of four main regional types of food, eating for the foreign visitor in Shanghai is as much a lottery as it is elsewhere in the country. The hotels again provide the most sensible (and probably most consistent) restaurants – the Jinjiang serves both Chinese and Western food at its 11th floor restaurants, although I would avoid the latter; the Peace Hotel has a reasonable restaurant on the eighth floor and is worth a visit if only for the marvellous view of the Bund and the river; and the Xijiao offers a relatively pricey fixed price meal (Y30) which is pleasant by local standards.

The only way for the foreigner to get around Shanghai is in an air-conditioned taxi and they are quite cheap – the 20-minute ride from the airport to the centre of town costs about Y14.

For all the hassles, delays and frustrations the businessman will encounter in Shanghai, there remains a great charm about the place and you can see why China hands are sentimental about it. At six o'clock in the morning, before the tidal wave of traffic engulfs the place, the streets are full of sweet old Shanghainese practising *taijiquan*, scores of them all in unison. It is a silent, slow-motion mime performed in the shadows of grand old buildings, timeless testaments to a bygone age. It is a very strange place indeed.

# Delhi

**With the back of the bloody Punjab problem seemingly broken, optimists are forecasting peace and computer-based prosperity for the Indian capital. Meanwhile, Delhi remains hard work and not much play for even the most persevering of business travellers.**

**By Carol Weingott**

When the Victorian imperialists were busy making broad inroads into what they ultimately left behind, namely Delhi's impressively-proportioned boulevards, they managed to convince themselves that a failure to appreciate India was a mark of virtue. These days, while the Hindu culture has remained as writhingly evasive and paradoxical, not to say erotic, as ever, most Westerners are ashamed of having unsympathetic responses to it. They grudgingly concede that the 'difficulty' it represents is the one imposed by their own limitations.

That said, it is not at all unusual to hear stumped first-time visitors grumbling about 'bureaucracy', 'poverty' and 'disparity' with Delhi provoking less of the same comment than Bombay, Delhi being *"a dull and artificial political capital while Bombay is a fast and celluloid New York"*. Whatever the outcome of the two town debate, India is a country that comes to Westerners with prophetic utterances like Indira Gandhi's *"If I die today every drop of my blood shall invigorate the nation"* (the night before her assassination), barely dry on their lips, or hers. And it is a country that Westerners go to across a raj-channelled divide ricocheting with assassins' bullets which have left *"the faceless airline pilot who married the beautiful Italian au-pair, Sonya,"* in charge of the world's most challenging and cherished democracy.

Little wonder the place is perceived as a cavity into which it is 'all right' to pour such inanities as *"how could you stand the poverty?"* and from which it is fine to draw such insults as *"it didn't increase my spirituality"*. Little wonder the Indian Government felt it necessary to foot an enormous bill to put the Festival of India on the road for its current 18-month US tour – an event of which *Newsweek* wrote: *"It is one of the very few things outside a Bhopal and a 14-part television series to prod American curiosity beyond the clichés of crippled beggars and silent Himalayan mystics."*

The English, of course, need no such prodding. There the debate runs as far as the problem pages of women's magazines (and beyond) and centres on why it is only now that they are swooning over a past of *"so many elephants, so many servants, so much nastiness in the upper class"*. Why indeed at a time when Lord Curzon's India, which represented *"the strength and greatness of England"*, is undergoing not dissimilar 'communalism' and racial tension from that erupting sporadically in England?

But it is Indish, as Indianised English is sometimes called, that ultimately concusses the visitor. Instead of breaking down barriers as a common language is supposed to do, it effectively reinforces the fact that Westerners live a cultural world apart. The 'enigmas' that unfold daily in the half-dozen English-language newspapers put the very notion of 'making contact' or running with the herd beyond question. What, exactly, can the Westerner presume to make of the common occurrence of such incidents as bank managers on charges of bride burning, ambushes by sword-brandishing medieval dacoits and the sinister activities of communal mobs like the one that recently doused an Australian tourist in kerosene and immolated him in a lake on a suspicion of 'child-lifting'? And what are female visitors to make of the advertising slogans of nationalised banks that read *"save for your son's education and your daughter's wedding"*, and of a Post Office that has failed to devise a congratulatory telegram on the birth of a daughter?

However well-quarantined the business visitor may be from observing this sort of thing or glimpsing scenes of 'unexaggeratable poverty', he is not likely to find himself altogether spared spectacles of gross ineptitude – like those at bureaucracy-beseiged Delhi airport where officials ritually reduce otherwise 'respectable' travellers to screaming *"Why can't you speak proper bloody English?"* Nor is it beyond the realms of possibility that visitors will find themselves smashing the telephone back in its cradle when, for the tenth time, they've intercepted the Hindi/English recorded message about the line being 'overloaded'. (Visitors should not, however, smash the phones – they can take years to replace.) Various attempts are being made to sort out the communications problem. One is a mobile telephone system currently operating on an experimental basis over a 40-mile radius and requiring a security deposit of Rs30,000. The waiting list is said to be long. Another, more permanent, move comes from C-Dot, the Centre for Development of Telematics, which has introduced an indigenous exchange (a 128-line digital electronic PABX) deemed suitable for hotels, hospitals and business houses. Meanwhile, the computer-confirmed prime minister has avowed that he will use technology in a war against poverty, to do what science has done for farming – which is a lot. Though India still has lots of hungry people – with a third of its 700 million living below the official poverty line – it is in the position of being able to *export* wheat.

One of the comments that is not uncommonly being made about Rajiv Gandhi is that he is doing for his country what John F. Kennedy did for the US in the 60s – giving it a political romance. Certainly, as the grandson of India's first prime minister, Jawaharlal Nehru, he belongs to a dynasty, and a bloody one at that. He also belongs to the first generation of independence-born Indians who gave him a resounding election victory just two months after his mother's death, at 401 seats out of 528 in that citadel of democracy, the Lok Sabha, where, incidentally, the 'Ayes' still have it.

By most accounts he and the 82 (give or take the assassin's bullet) hand-picked freshers forming the vanguard of his new-look Congress (I) – including a screen siren from the 60s and a former hockey Olympian – are doing energetically and well in containing the quarrels of a continually uniting and dividing nation that grows by a million mouths a month. Rajiv Gandhi's triumph has lasted, some say spectacularly, through the ongoing bloodletting that seems to characterise Indian politics to re-emerge in the relatively calm Punjab elections.

Given that traditionally Delhi's 'constituency people' have always swarmed to their MP's homes – and remembering the string of political murders in the wake of the assassination of moderate Sikh leader Sant Longowal in 1985, Delhi visitors should not have been surprised, at that time, to see the blackened faces of commando units patrolling the otherwise quiet, tree-lined residential streets. Evidently such stringent security is not only called for, but according to the opposition Janata Party, it is not enough. After the Sant's cremation the Party issued a statement condemning Delhi as the *"crime capital of the country and a playground for political extremists"*.

It was, of course, the anti-Sikh massacre following Mrs Gandhi's assassination that lit up Delhi in Western consciousness at the end of 1984. For a short time the capital appeared to be behaving more like a Beirut or a Belfast than home to around six and a half million people in the heart of 'Mother India' – and the after-shock can still be felt. (Even fairly unobservant visitors should be able to vouch that of the 90 per cent of the drivers

*View of the old city from the Red Fort: the skyscrapers of New Delhi are on the horizon*

behind Delhi's battered black and yellow Ambassador cabs who are Sikhs, only a minority have felt it prudent to resume wearing full beards and turbans.) According to the Sikhs, after a couple of days of *"smoke rings round the city"* – while their cabs were set alight – and of *"hiding out in the forest"*, 10,000 of their number were left dead in Delhi alone.

Taking a long-term view of security in the capital, Delhi's seriously undermanned police force expresses concern that the riots have unleashed an element of criminal lawlessness now hitting West Delhi in what they describe as a 'crime wave'. Any of the dailies or the excellent weekly news magazine *India Today* can be counted on to put visitors in the *lathi*–charging, stone-throwing picture. Aside from the legendary police corruption, about which the newspaper the *Statesman* wrote *"the main purpose of giving a beat to a constable seems to be to fix the boundaries of his personal fiefdom"*, there is the hopeless task of attempting to transport police to trouble spots on an allocation of just one bicycle and jeep per station.

Much of the 'communal mayhem' and violent robbery breaks out in Delhi's resettlement colonies and shanty towns, not places that are likely to feature on the business visitor's itinerary. The closest one is likely to come is on the train to Agra to inspect the Taj Mahal, a journey disclosing scenes of back-to-back shacks assembled around water pumps, which are in turn attended by bright green overflow ponds where hopeful pigs wait for the completion of the morning's ablutions.

Any qualms visitors may have about their own security are really only justified on the roads – but that's on any road, even the clean albeit betel-stained thoroughfares of South Delhi where all the hotels and many of the business houses are found. It is the fixed stare and fatalistic spirit of those using the roads that is cause for concern. And the clunking as mechanical parts fall off your taxi ploughing its way against a reverse tide of auto-rickshaws, ice cream and parrot sellers' carts, sacred wandering cows, occasional elephants/camels and thundering buses and lorries. Even *in* the taxi your only real protection is a postcard of God taped to the dashboard – the auto-rickshaws provide none at all, their wreckage indicating that they are just as crushable as betel nuts. (Just be thankful there is no self-drive in Delhi.)

For the rest of it, physically Delhi is a sprawling city which is in fact made up of some eight – including possibly Asia's oldest settlement. The 'modern' hotels, flyovers, roundabouts and the massive sports stadium (with the appearance of a giant air-conditioning unit) all bespeak of the scramble that went on to make the city a presentable host for the '83 Asian Games. Old Delhi with its Old Fort (circa 1000 A.D.) and its Red Fort, the magnificent 17th century work of Moghul Emperor Shah Jahan, is essential if chaotic viewing. From a distance it is like a fairytale – most hotels can arrange tours. The 'essential viewing' applies equally to 'New' Delhi – the bare 15 buildings occupying a spread of land and parks the size of the City of London and constituting the political capital. These, off the drawing board of Sir Edwin Landseer Lutyens and dubbed the 'Garden City' (along with Australia's Canberra), have the appearance of being grafted on to the rest of the city, or stranded from it by mile-long vistas of hexagonal parks and grandiose monuments. 'New' Delhi doesn't in fact exist as part of the Deliwalla's frame of reference.

Rather than incidentally finding himself there, the business traveller is bound to end up in Connaught Place, the once-grand commercial circle with offices and shops running along the radial roads off it. There, having been beset by fortune tellers and purveyors of dodgy airline tickets amid dilapidated, paint-peeling pillars, he is bound to want to head back to the comparative calm of the leafy colonies (as Delhi calls her suburbs) with comforting names like Friend's, Queen's Gardens and West End, to drown the grim details of daily life in a wash of ice-cold Kingfisher or Black Label.

It is quite appropriate that Delhi's finest hotel, the **Oberoi Inter-Continental** (Dr. Zakir Hussain Marg; tel: 699 571; telex: 23723829), bears the name of the man who has done so much for India's hotel industry and tourism in general, namely M.S. Oberoi. From a 40-rupee-a-month job as a desk clerk at the Cecil Hotel in the British summer capital of Simla, 'Old Man' Oberoi (as he is known to distinguish him from his son, P.R.S. 'Biki' Oberoi) went on to acquire Clarkes Hotel in the same town, and, by mortgaging his assets and his wife's jewels, to establish an empire with 30 first class hotels in four continents. These days he and Biki live on adjoining farms outside Delhi, with the son largely running the business.

What sets the Oberoi Inter-Continental apart from the half dozen other five-star Delhi properties is, first of all, the physical green belt of the Delhi Golf Club whose 18-holes abut the property and where guests can play for a nominal fee. It is also the only five-star property that doesn't open its swimming pool to non-residents, and this, given Delhi's significant population of diplomats' children (who are just as noisy as anybody else's children) is a blessing indeed. Also, the pool is larger and cooler than anyone else's.

Another interesting point is that whereas most hotels talk about 'refurbishing' their rooms, the Oberoi Inter-Continental recently completed a multi-million dollar 're-designing' project which has upgraded guests rooms and restaurants and seen the inclusion of a business centre and executive club. Guest rooms are large and bright with decent-sized working desks and three (direct-dial) telephones, with all floors serviced by butlers and valets. The other thing, of course, is that the hotel's Taipan restaurant is widely reckoned to be the best in town. Single Rs 975; double Rs 1,075; suite Rs 2,500. Best of all though, the Oberoi guest can expect to find no fewer than six daily newspapers tucked discreetly beneath his door.

Delhi's other Oberoi, the **Maidens** (Sham Nath Marg; tel: 221 591; telex: 312702), is quite a different property, set in old Delhi with Mughal monuments all around and a façade that retains turn-of-the-century architectural elegance. I was told that *"tour groups and the Soviets"* are regulars among the guests. The atmosphere, however, was not that usually suggested by tour groups: some 70 spacious rooms, with large dressing rooms attached, and grounds adorned with bougainvillea hedges and trimmed with tennis and badminton courts. Single Rs 450; double Rs 550; suite Rs 1,000.

Oberoi's other and possibly most important Delhi connection is its hotel management and training school, opened in 1966 a year after the Oberoi Inter-Continental, whose graduates must by now occupy a high percentage of the capital's top hotel jobs. (The Oberoi School is the only one in India recognised by the International Hotels' Association.)

*The gardens of the Red Fort*

The two largest names in the industry, however, are those of the Welcomgroup, a division of ITC Ltd, one of the country's largest corporations and well-known in the cigarette business, and the Taj Group. At the Taj helm is the Parsi Tata family (Parsis being the group of some 62,000 people who migrated from Persia three centuries ago), the forefathers of Air India, with large interests in most things including steel. With some 25 and 21 hotels apiece, the rivals appear to be continually fighting over the 'Golden Triangle': the lucrative tourist circuit of Delhi-Agra-Jaipur (the pink city).

In Delhi the competition is just about as close as it could get, geographically, between the Welcomgroup's **Maurya Sheraton** (Sardar Patel Marg; tel: 370 271; telex: 03161447), with whom there is a marketing and reservations agreement with Sheraton, and the **Taj Palace** (Sardar Patel Marg; tel: 344 900; telex: 315151) which, of the two, is six acres nearer the airport – the six acres being the size of the Palace's grounds. Proximity to the airport, from an area known as the Diplomatic Enclave, is the best thing they both have going for them in view of the fact that most of Delhi's arriving/departing flights do so in the small hours.

There was no-one around during my time at the Palace, which contributed to a sense of being lost in a vast, marble mausoleum. Though this was counteracted somewhat by the gallant attentions of the 'hospitality desk' who frequently rang my room to ask if I had enjoyed my breakfast and to invite me to *"have a nice day"*. The hotel has all the usual amenities, including executive offices rentable by the hour, and all in good order. It also has the extraordinary Orient Express restaurant whose menu traces the great train's journey with specialities from each region. Single Rs 750; double Rs 850; suite Rs 1,250-1,875.

The Maurya Sheraton, with about the same number of rooms, around 500, was a busier place – especially around the 'all-weather, solar-heated' pool, a favourite with airline crews, and around its executive areas – 40 rooms, a separate tower and very large (1,200-seated) banqueting hall. The efficiency of this hotel is best attested to by the fact that though it lies some eight kilometres from the New Delhi railway station, it checked me out and delivered me to the *Taj Express* in 25 minutes very early indeed one morning. Well done. Single Rs 900; double Rs 1,000; suite Rs 1,000-2,500.

The battle continues apace with the Taj's **Taj Mahal** (Mansingh Road; tel: 386 162; telex: 313604) which, like the Palace, is bookable through the HRI group. More established than its sister, the Taj Mahal follows the same lines of ornate *jali* screens of hand-carved marble and truly imposing staircases – less a hotel than an impeccably-kept national art gallery. This hotel is centrally-located and has a reputedly fine Italian/French restaurant in its rooftop Casa Medici. The only problem I had here was the difficulty of making pool-side contact for service – the pool, like the public areas in general being well-patronised by locals. Single Rs 800; double Rs 900; suite Rs 2,000-3,000.

For those who have become addicted to the 'hotel within a hotel' concept, the **Hyatt Regency** (Bhikaiji Cama Place, Ring Road; tel: 609 911; telex: 0314579) should fit the bill. On the sixth floor is the Regency Club (own elevator key, personalised stationery, bath robes and people who remember your name etc) where the lounge is convivial and the conference room has large desks. This is an entirely pleasant place to stay and with complimentary cocktails during a 'happy-hour' which lasts for two, useful for making contacts, given that Delhi has no pubs and hotel bars are usually of daunting dimensions. Elsewhere, the hotel has a notably large shopping centre – an arcade with space for 76 shops – a worthwhile Chinese restaurant called Pearls and a lively piano bar. Regency club rooms (single occupancy) Rs 1,150; double 1,300. Standard single Rs 850-950; suite Rs 1,150-1,300.

From what I saw and heard, few people would *choose* to stay at the government-run **Ashok Hotel** (Chanakyapuri; tel: 600 121; telex: 312567) though, of course, 'official' guests might not get that choice. As Delhi's oldest and largest hotel, at 30 years and 589 rooms, there is said to be trouble on all fronts in view of the excellence of the competition. One outstanding success this hotel does have though, is its alleged rapid turnover in the duty free store with which the diplomatic community does a steady trade. And should you for whatever reason desire Cypriot food, then the hotel's Taverna Cyprus is the only place in town you'll get it. Single Rs 750; double Rs 850; suite Rs 1,400.

The new **Meridien** (Windsor Place, Janpath; tel: 381 550; telex: 5566) is destined to put the cat very much among the pigeons as it has this prime site (virtually on Connaught Place) to itself. It is a 450-room property with a popular restaurant, La Brasserie. Single Rs 500; double Rs 600; suite prices on request.

Among the bonuses on the Delhi hotel scene are that it represents good value for money, the government having abolished a hefty 15 per cent total-receipts tax in 1982, also most properties do not include a service charge. The going rate for tips, which are not asked for, but are nonetheless evidently appreciated, is 10 per cent on restaurant bills and five per cent for other services. Finally, an insider's tip: though you must pay your hotel bill in foreign currency, incidental restaurant and bar bills can be settled on the spot in rupees. This allows a saving of seven per cent off 'luxury' tax levied on the final hotel bill.

# WHERE TO EAT

The 'Indian' food popularised in all manner of 'authentic' back street flock-wallpapered emporiums from Cork in the Irish Republic to Christchurch in New Zealand tends to be the non-vegetarian *tandoori* cuisine that originated in the Mughal courts. And Delhi being the seat of the Mughal dynasty for more than two centuries, this is where you'll find the real 'juicy kebab' thing. And one more indigestible misconception that cries out for clarification – Indian food has nothing to do with 'curry', that yellowish, bilish mess used by lazy Europeans to jazz up mince and, even worse, eggs.

The principal that guides Indian cuisine, be it the *idlis* (steamed rice cakes) and *dosas* (rice flour pancakes) of the southern dishes or the fish and pork-based cuisine of Goa, is that it must blend six essential flavours in various strengths to make wet, dry, savoury and pickled dishes with each region zealously guarding the secrets of its own. The short-cut to sampling the widest possible range of such cuisines at one sitting is the *thali,* literally a platter, which is what I was assured you would find in most Indian homes.

Besides the 'curry' factor, there are two other popular misconceptions about dining out in Delhi – that it automatically results in a 'Delhi belly' stomach upset and that prohibition is practised. Regarding the former, according to a consensus of hotel doctors most foreigners eat too much of what they are not used to too soon thus sending their stomachs into a state of shock. The other aspect of this problem is, of course, that which is too dreary to go into . . . the list of dos and don'ts: *"never buy anything off a hawker or roadside stall, never drink water unless it has been freshly boiled, never eat uncooked foods and cold dishes."* Regarding 'dry' days as they are known in the Union Territory of Delhi, these fall on the first and the seventh of each month and on gazetted holidays. Then, officially, alcohol is out of the question, except for hotel guests choosing to consume it in their room – but my experience on two such 'dry' occasions was satisfactorily wet in hotel restaurants.

Which leads to the vexing question of what alcohol to accompany your meal with. Imported alcohol comes dear and if you have had your fill of Kingfisher and Black Label beers, I propose that Indian wine isn't as unpalatable as some people suggest. The Bosca (rosé) comes a bit sweet for me but the Riesling didn't hurt (tasting not dissimilar to Retsina). One might, of course, care to look at the ridiculously cheap prices of the food and settle on imported wine to round the bill off to the sort of sum one would pay at home, thus balancing things out rather nicely. Nor, as some people insist, is dining *only* a rewarding and 'safe' proposition on the five-star circuit. There are other possibilities, notably a growing choice of fast food outlets – Wimpy hamburgers, McDowells' Pizzakings and a chain called Nirula, credited with popularising the concept in Delhi, specialising in ice cream – rum-raisin, butterscotch and chocolate chip being the favourites.

All the top hotels have at least one ethnic restaurant offering 'purist' menus from different parts of the subcontinent, like the Maurya Sheraton's **Mayur** (tel: 301 0101) where the speciality is *Dum Pusht,* which means the 'maturing' of a prepared dish sealed in its pot and steamed over a gentle heat. It has been suggested that this ancient cooking style is the Indian counterpart of *nouvelle cuisine,* the emphasis being on lightness, naturalness and delicacy of flavour. At the Mayur one sits amid burnished copper under a ceiling of white clouds on a blue sky: special executive lunch costs Rs 125. The Maurya's other speciality Indian restaurant is the **Bukhara** (on the same phone number) where they serve north-west frontier cuisine – largely from the *tandoor,* non-vegetarian and 'fatless'.

The Taj Mahal's **Haveli** (tel: 386 162) specialises in Peshawari dishes and the likes of the Hyderabadi vegetarian 'special' – tomatoes, whole green chillies and curry leaves, piquant indeed, and around Rs 110 for two. At the other Taj, the Palace, the **Orient Express** (tel: 301 0404) rates as one of the most up-market restaurants in town. Here one passes along a gas-lit 'platform' to 'din-

*Street vendors' fare could lead to Delhi belly*

ing cars' which are said to faithfully mirror the elegance of the world's most gracious train – finely-etched glass, table brackets etc. – while the menu charts the real train's run from London to Venice starting with a gin-based Cliffs of Dover cocktail. The table d'hote menu, three courses for lunch, four for dinner, runs to the likes of Hercule Poirot bisque, camembert stuffed steak, spinach soufflé and follows the cardinal principles of *nouvelle cuisine.* Staff are astonishingly attentive and wear Victorian costumes. A buffet lunch/dinner costs Rs 300.

European food also appears prominently on the menu at **Pickwicks** (tel: 301 0211), the coffee shop at Claridges Hotel (Aurangzeb Road) where antique English sideboards and displays of china with Mr Pickwick on sepia tablemats complete the *"corner of the foreign field forever England"* picture. Here you can try grandma's broth, pork chops Robert and a 'sizzler'.

The Taj Mahal's **Casa Medici** (tel: 386 162) does a lunchtime buffet between 1 and 3p.m. for Rs 130, dinner from 8p.m. to midnight for around Rs 200, and offers a fairly convincing Mediterranean atmosphere – lots of white arches and trailing greenery and a larger than usual wine list, French/Italian and Indian. For top-notch French cuisine though, the recommended places are the **Auberge** (tel: 252 5464) at the Oberoi Maidens and the **Burgundy** (tel: 600 121 ext. 2842) at the Ashok Hotel – lunch 1-2.45p.m., dinner 7.30-11p.m. Here the decor runs to pin-striped burgundy fabric on the walls, suede chairs and much use of the *fleur-de-lis* motif.

Those favouring Chinese and Eastern food will be pleased to hear that there are at least a dozen reasonably-priced and remarkably 'authentic' restaurants to choose from with Japanese, Cantonese, Manchurian, Pekinese and Szechuan cuisines all being in the running. At this point it is also worth noting that because Delhi is not Bombay, nor Calcutta, obtaining fresh fish isn't a particularly straightforward business. Even more interesting is the 300 per cent 'tax' on some of the more exotic ingredients such cuisines require. One Chinese chef told me he pays *"the equivalent of US$8 for a standard-sized bottle of oyster sauce, 150 per cent duty and 150 per cent fine".* I was also told that for restaurants, and necessarily hotel restaurants in particular, foreign exchange spending is directly related to foreign exchange earnings. In the light of this information the opinion that the Oberoi Inter-Continental's **Taipan** (tel: 699 571) has the best Chinese food in town comes as no surprise.

On inspection the Taipan shows every outward sign of deserving such a reputation: walls graced by fine 19th century Chinese watercolours with the *Taipan* (the supreme leader in the Chinese hierarchy) himself gazing down at you from a priceless creation on silk. And the Oberoi's overseas buying power is clearly reflected in a menu which includes the last word in the exotic (at least in Delhi) namely, abalone braised with sea slugs, broccoli with black mushrooms and steamed chicken lotus leaves. Dining is on the roof (a landscaped garden on the surrounding balcony) 12.30-3p.m. for lunch, dinner 8p.m.-midnight.

For reliably good and varied Szechuanese, Cantonese and Hakka cuisine at a significant notch cheaper than the Taipan, the place to head is where the diplomats go, **Pearls** (tel: 609 911) at the Hyatt Regency, lunch 12-2.45p.m., dinner 3-11.45p.m., and around Rs 150 for two. Here the helpful chef, Mr K.S. Wong, confided that the hotel, as a whole, consumes some 350 chickens a day and that *halal* is not a factor that has to be taken into consideration in the kitchen. He also explained the mysterious absence of duck from most menus *"the Indians don't like it much, they consider it too tough".* With the menu running to such savoury delights as shredded lamb with hot garlic sauce and minced pork with bean curd, to be consumed in restful, silk-panelled surroundings to the attendance of swift and unobtrusive staff, dining at Pearls is altogether a good bet. There is also a vegetarian menu and, for that matter, a selection of no fewer than 21 salads at another Hyatt restaurant, the 24-hour **Café Promenade** (tel: 609 911). This restaurant also serves fairly elaborate Indian meals and has a 'Food Festival' once a month with a buffet menu and a live band, both of which are said to be worth watching out for.

Indicative of how popular eating out has become in Delhi is the fact that **La Brasserie** (tel: 381 550) in the Meridien was pretty full on all its three levels most evenings before the hotel itself was anywhere near opening. The downtown location may have something to do with this or, of course, the appetising menu: classic French specialities like the excellent French onion soup and stuffed chicken supreme with a delicate mushroom sauce, not to forget meringue chantilly with cognac-flavoured chocolate sauce.

The most popular venue for non-hotel cuisine is the **Village Complex,** built to house the Asiad athletics, and running to four restaurants – **Chopsticks** (tel: 662 448), **Angeethi, Ankur** and **American Pie** (all on 666 230). Angeethi is an informal, barbecue-style restaurant (with dining outdoors) and ludicrously inexpensive – around Rs 50 for two but possible only in the evenings 7.30-11.30p.m. Ankur goes for classical cuisine – Mughlai dishes high on aroma and flavoured with dried fruits. Open for lunch and dinner 12.30-3p.m. and 7.30-11.45p.m. at around Rs 60 for two, Sunday buffet lunch Rs 70 for two. Chopsticks is closer to gourmet standards than its name would imply with Szechuan fare predominating (watch out for the rice noodle soup cooked with rice wine). American Pie does very fast burgers, pizzas, fish-'n'chips and all manner of western confectionery.

The **El Arab** (tel: 311 444) in the Regal Building in Connaught Place makes a welcome retreat from a chaotic area and serves reasonably good Lebanese/Egyptian dishes for around Rs 75 from 11a.m. to 11p.m. Also in Connaught Place is the **Mughlai** (tel: 351 101) – opposite the fire station – which also serves the fare its name suggests, between 11a.m. and midnight.

Finally, for those out early to avoid some of the heat and much of the congestion, the place to stop for breakfast is the **Kwality** (tel: 320 875) in the Regal Building in Parliament Street, between 8.30 and 11a.m.

# NIGHTLIFE

Outside the rim of five-star hotels, standing like beckoning bottles on the outskirts of a dust bowl, Delhi has no desirable watering holes at all; pubs and even bars do not exist except within hotel premises. Once this shock settles in, the visitor inevitably finds himself enquiring what the locals do of an evening? Surely they can't all be content to watch the official *Doordarshan* television channel (details of which can be found on the local page of the morning newspapers)? Or are business travellers supposed to be content to watch reruns of British and American soaps and 'comedies' offered by the hotels in-house? Not that the sheer availability of television sets is anything to be dismissive about with colour sets only being *in situ* since the 1983 Asian Games – and on the streets a 20-inch set still goes for an astronomical Rs9,000.

There are a few restaurants with decent wine cellars, but locals are more likely to belong to a club, or to attend some cultural event. Of the clubs, the most-acclaimed is the **Gymkhana,** a rajish, many-pillared and splendid building near the Ashok Hotel. However, on the Tuesday night I went along, it was deserted but for a few squash-playing youths and an elderly lady in a pale blue silk saree with a large diamond in the side of her nose. As I was beating a sad retreat she enquired, in perfectly annunciated English, whether I would like a lift. I was quite stupid to have declined the offer and to have gone instead, and with excessive optimism, to that last bastion of noisy behaviour in any town, the **Press Club.** Here two crumpled-looking photographers sharing a lime and soda under the lurching ceiling fan were the only occupants.

Of the five-star bars, the most sophisticated tend to be in the chains – the Maurya Sheraton, which has a piano bar, the Hyatt, with a disco, and the Oberoi Inter-Continental where there's dancing, as opposed to what happens in a disco, as well. If you should be so unlucky as to arrive on a dry day, the first, seventh and public holidays in each month, hotels are happy to serve alcoholic drinks in your room. Even then though, there's no escaping the grim warning inscribed on the bottom of even humble, bottled beer: *"alcohol can seriously injure your health"*.

Given that the consumption of alcohol is so actively discouraged, it is surprising to occasionally see small, warehouse-like shops announcing *"English wine sold here."* I wonder if this is what they really sell. More than occasionally the 'change money' men infesting Connaught Place will, in a way that seems quite excessive, offer Rs250 for your duty free bottle of whisky. If nothing else, this is a good measure of the effect of a 27 per cent tax on the price of imported liquor. Of the local spirits, Diplomat and Peter Scott are the recommended whiskies, Tsar the top vodka and Old Monk – the most palatable of the lot – the best rum. Beware, though, of the soft drink called G Spot.

Culture, I was told, *"tends to be seasonal but on during winter"* (November to February) with summer seeing an exodus to London, Switzerland, the

US and the hill stations. The most consistently 'on' events appear to be those that take place in the cultural centres attached to the various embassies – seminars on Japanese management techniques and their application to Indian industry, for example.

Perusal of the classified ads – in-between the matrimonials and the slimming clinics, which indicate that rolls of waistline fat are no longer uniformly desirable – will confirm that India truly is home to the Big Screen.

The Hindi epics sometimes carry English sub-titles and are said to be worth making the effort to see. There also appear to be several cinemas showing exclusively English-language films, among them **Archa** (Greater Kailash; tel: 641 4559). For details see the weekly *Delhi Diary* (Rs 1.50, available from your hotel) or contact the tourist office (88 Janpath; tel: 320 005). What are described as *"all time events"* – films on wildlife, ecology and conservation – are shown at the National Museum of Natural History (tel: 385 549) while the **Our India Pavilion** (Pragati Maidan) gives audio-visual shows, the **Red Fort** hosts the dreaded Sound and Light Show in English 9-10 p.m. (tel: 600 121) and the **Teen Murti House** (tel: 301 5026) does something similar in English 8.15-9.15 p.m. daily. Classical, folk and tribal dances can also be attended daily at the **Parsi Anjuman Hall,** Bahadur Shah Zafar Marg (tel: 331 7831 or 331 7228) from 7 p.m.

Finally, to other visitors who find themselves stranded in vast and deliciously cold hotel lobbies of an evening, I would like to explain the mysteries of the groups of 10-20 women who frequently gather there. They are not, as their flashy jewellery and smart attire might suggest, waiting to be picked up. They are rich Punjabi wives showing off their latest jewels and clothes while eating chocolate ice cream and drinking cold, iced-coffee at what are institutionally known as 'kitty parties'.

# GETTING AROUND

Getting from the airport presents a straightforward two-option choice: by taxi (between Rs 40 and 90, depending on your distance) and by the EATS (ex-servicemen's Air Transport Service) bus which stops at all the major hotels on the way to Connaught Place. The service runs 24-hours and, though it doesn't come air-conditioned, it is ludicrously inexpensive at some Rs 10. The hotels say the reason they have not yet been able to lay on air-conditioned airport transfer cars is that the taxi union is very strong.

Delhi's indigenous forms of transport, auto-rickshaws, horse-drawn *tongas* and pedal trishaws are not recommended because of the generally hazardous road conditions, as stated elsewhere. Those who cannot bear the non-air-conditioned and lumbering Ambassador taxis can hire chauffeur-driven cars from the travel desks in all the five-star hotels. There are no self-drive cars for hire in Delhi.

Internal flights departing from Delhi represent good value, especially since the introduction of the recent 'Wonderfare' offer from Indian Airlines. These allow travel within any one of the four groups in the northern, eastern, western and southern regions for US$200 for a seven-day period. As far as India's far-flung rail network is concerned, there is a 90-day Indrail Pass with fares varying between US$35 to $600 according to the class of travel and the period of validity.

*Oxen and cart add to the traffic congestion*

# Frankfurt

Frankfurt is a city of ersatz post-war reconstruction whose natives appear to enjoy its reputation as the brusque, international Head Office of Germany. But there is more to the place than self-deprecation, banking and the Rothschilds.

By Michael Scott

One eventually tires of hearing Frankfurters expound their creed: *"This city is not as bad as you've heard."* Frequent and diverse encounters with this phrase, along with many and varied arguments in support, at first seem revealing, since generations of repetition have lent the litany a kind of wry, self-deprecating, altogether un-*German* humour. This is, however, only on loan.

Truth is, the Frankfurters are proud of their bad reputation. The reasons for feeling unjustly tarnished vary – one senior woman journalist is tired of it being cast as *"the Chicago of Germany,"* the place where German gangster films are set; an efficient marketing manager carefully illustrates by anecdote how brusque manners conceal a helpful heart. But they all miss the essential: that the Frankfurters' bad name is for being smug, not rough and tough, and that assuming a *different* bad reputation is part of this smugness.

Then again, perhaps this is too harsh. Perhaps a more sympathetic view will finally settle on the frequent visitor. Frankfurt is a city where 500,000 people work, and 300,000 of them pile into their company cars and drive away as fast as they can at 5p.m. each day, commuting along good roads to pleasantly-wooded suburbs along the Main river or in the nearby Taunus mountains. Inevitably, what is a lively and industrious city by day dies by night, and echoing empty streets result in a lack of identity that leaves the Frankfurters anxious to grab hold of any kind of character that they can call their own.

Frankfurt's chief sin, in a chauvinistic country, lies in being an international rather than German city . . . the complete antithesis of (for example) Münich. And it is Münich against which all Frankfurters rail the most persistently – dismissing its jolly beer-swilling image as concealing a honey-lipped insincerity, and a narrow-minded outlook.

On the other hand, even the nearby industrial wastelands of the Rhine have a more identifiable national character – albeit unpleasant – than this modern city, where even the antiques are *ersatz*. Frankfurt was all but flattened by Allied bombers, and as such the historic Römer town hall, dating back to 1405, and the *Alte Oper* (Old Opera – now a high level conference centre) are post-war reconstructions, using in the first case authentic materials and techniques. Very nice, but where are all the people? I wondered recently, en route to investigate whether the recently-opened and equally deserted Press Club bar had begun to attract any custom. But no, and it was back to the international hotels to seek company that wouldn't tell me that *"Frankfurt is not as bad as you have heard."*

You might think that an international outlook would be a benefit to a visiting businessman. And indeed it is, as long as he wishes to do business. English is widely spoken, and Frankfurt has some right to the claim to be the Head Office of Germany. Conference and meeting facilities are abundant (and expensive) in the international hotels, as are the lunch-time restaurants where the executives from these head offices like to discuss deals over the rich and meaty local diet.

It is at night, when those restaurants are closed and the same streets empty, save for the streetwalkers and police patrols down by the station, that the visiting businessman might wish himself somewhere a little more personal.

Frankfurt-am-Main (to distinguish it from the *other* Frankfurt . . . -am-Oder, now in East Germany) owes its livelihood and existence to a ford over the Main river, conveniently sited to become a prehistoric trade crossroads, linking northern Europe with the Mediterranean countries, and East with West.

Thus from earliest times it has been a cosmopolitan and pragmatic settlement that has put trade before the niceties of discourse. Celts, Romans, Germans, Saxons and the Franks who gave the city its modern name have all taken a turn at controlling this crucial junction, and the trade went on. Frankfurt grew in importance, and took a turn as a capital city, and in the 16th century came an event of much significance: the right to mint money.

It was Frankfurt's first step to becoming the modern banking and financial centre that spreads its influence far beyond Germany. When, in the 18th century, the Rothschilds founded their banking dynasty here, they first exploited and later enhanced the city's position as a focus of world banking. Today, there are still Rothschilds in Frankfurt, and there are many more banks, more than 247 by one count, commercial and mercantile, public and private, local and international.

Indeed, it is the banks which dominate the modern skyline, engaged in a private competition to justify the tourist office's excruciating pun: *"Main-hattan"*. In the autumn of 1984 the twin glass towers of the new Deutscherbank building relegated the silver flanked Dresdnerbank headquarters to the status of last year's model, and the

*The Deutscherbank building adds to the 'Main hattan' skyline*

gleaming white Canadian Pacific hotel, at 44 storeys Europe's tallest residential building, was joined by another giant alongside.

All this has rather dismayed some of the locals, fresh from loving reconstruction of the Römer, and, not convinced that the modern German style is attractive, with its rounded corners, reflective glass, and metal-clad walls, they have dubbed the buildings 'Iron Age'. I cannot agree with their disapproval. The view of the setting sun from the Ober-Main Bridge (if only homeward commuters to Neue Isenberg and the southern dormitory towns would look) has been much enhanced by the latest well-spaced gleaming towers; while the equally splendid morning panorama from the top floors of the Canadian-Pacific on the outskirts of the city centre was available previously only to aviators.

The city you see from such a vantage point is compact, defined by the river Main, a tranquil waterway plied by a small but steady number of barges, as befits a backwater of the Rhine-Danube system. The central area is immediately north of the river, with the Römer at its hub, and containing both major churches, the main shopping area, and several of the tall buildings. This business-pleasure-tourist zone is small enough to be comfortably negotiable on foot, within an area defined by a belt of grass, trees and public gardens, following the ancient city walls.

The waterfront is almost continuous garden, and is a pleasant enough spot to take the air, unless you are disturbed by the faceless stare of the blank buildings above. One can be, particularly if already feeling oppressed by the rather clinical atmosphere of the remade city, and the air with which the very lawns seem to say: *"Keep off the grass."*

Directly across the river lies the Sachsenhausen, the prime night-time leisure area, with the extensive *Stadtwald* (City wood) beyond, ending the urban sprawl with natural forest.

To the north, outside the ring of green, the city spills out into less distinguished business areas, followed soon afterwards by the city suburbs. It is here that a small revival is gaining force, propelled by fashion and economic need. Apartment houses that had become seedy are now refurbished and repainted, for the new inhabitants who line the streets outside with fuel-injected Golfs, small BMWs and Mercedes-Benzes. Of course, some people never left the city, but a sharp rise in property values in recent years confirms the trend to move back.

Beyond the obvious business-orientated facilities of the hotels, and the sex-shops and illicit pleasures of the Kaiserstrasse and Münchnerstrasse, running between the banking districts from the main station, the business or holiday visitor will inevitably find himself in the Sachsenhausen, prime recreational area for foreigners and even some Frankfurters. This is one of the few parts of old Frankfurt to escape destruction in the Second World War, and narrow, twisting cobbled streets run among higgledy-piggledy half-timbered buildings. There are some good restaurants here, but the decline over the past 10 years has been sad to see, with burger joints playing loud rock music proliferating at the expense of more authentically-flavoured cafés and bars.

Away from Sachsenhausen's centre, tradition has survived. The drink of the region is *ebbelwei* (literally apple wine), an acidic and alcoholically-mild thin cider that shocks the palate. I have always

*What little remains of pre-war Frankfurt sits uneasily beside the new*

taken this as evidence that Frankfurters have a sense of humour, yet they seem serious with their assurances that it is possible to develop a taste for this unpleasant libation, served in countless small pubs, distinguished by a funereal wreath of green leaves. Certainly, you can tell the locals from the outsiders . . . the locals order a second glass.

With theatre almost invariably in German, and many city-centre restaurants closed at night, it is hardly surprising that much of a visitor's social life will be centred on his hotel (nor that at least some of that social life will be spent watching the US Forces TV channel . . . you have to take your friends where you find them). In spite of a large US military presence here, this is the only cultural impression they have made. The Frankfurters prefer to ignore the US military, and they in turn keep themselves to themselves, beyond the occasional visit to the Sachsenhausen.

Because of the insularity of its suburban dwellers, and the large numbers of commuters, Frankfurt is a daytime city, cheerful and bustling, and dedicated to conspicuous consumption. This is enshrined in the *Fressgasse,* which would translate literally into the 'street of gluttony', were it not that eating too much rich food is not in this context considered sinful, or even unusual. Centred round Grosse Bockenheimerstrasse, this ancient food market has been turned into a pedestrian area, and the traditional small shops selling bewildering varieties of sausages and other comestibles are today surrounded by restaurants of every type – trendy and expensive boutiques, and a few smaller department stores. Handy for the commercial areas, the number of daytime shoppers here is considerably swelled by the executive lunchers, for whom this is the main social meal of the day, albeit combined with business.

Should you be there over a weekend, you will discover that the nightly exodus of workers is much augmented on Fridays, and that many of the negative aspects of the city's nightlife are redoubled on Sundays. Now is the time to search the suburbs for suitable *weinstubbe.* Jazz-lovers, however, are in luck. In this respect at least, Frankfurt does resemble Chicago. In the Sachsenhausen and in the old city (especially Berlinerstrasse), scores of jazz bands play at lunchtime and in the evening, in the cafés and restaurants, and the surrounding gloom is forgotten.

Frankfurt is a city that exists for trade and commerce, and as a result is free from heavy industry .... the biggest factory is Hoecht's pharmaceutical plant. The city has kept pace with the changing world, so as to remain as central to modern trade as it was when the Franks used to assist traders' caravans across the Main, for a fee, of course.

The Rothschilds were not the only influential Jewish family among the bankers of Frankfurt before the war, and Hitler's persecution of the Jews left many scars on Frankfurt. Indeed, older Frankfurters will tell tales of how some Jews were protected by German families, as well as how mixed families were split during the reign of the Third Reich.

They prefer to talk about the speedy recovery, and how rapidly the rebirth of trade and commerce was accomplished. Historically cosmopolitan, and relatively free from the chauvinism that infects other German cities, Frankfurt has a tradition of accepting anyone who is prepared to work hard, and respecting people for their achievements rather than their accent or family background. This is a sound approach for such projects as rebuilding a shattered economy.

Loudest in praise of this attitude are the *Wahl-Frankfurters,* people who live in the city by choice rather than by birth. And not surprisingly, for they have gained the most. They are glad to assert that this is the least snobbish German city, and to deny that it is cold-hearted. It may *seem* so, they say, and they agree that Frankfurt changes people who come here, *"even Austrians"*, by teaching them that a minute is a minute, and time wasted in niceties is time lost. But this is part of the city's charm, they argue, a refreshing matter-of-fact approach that conceals an open-minded attitude.

Frankfurt, they say, is *"love at second sight"*, a very touchable city, where everyone gets a chance. Yet even those who have made it agree it is not for the faint-hearted. *"You must show your strength in business, otherwise you are lost. It is a hard city, this hidden capital of Germany."*

All of which would be easier to believe if most of them didn't hasten to leave the city as soon as their work is done.

For those visitors unable to do so, there is just one final message. The aforegoing is not intended to give an entirely negative picture . . . and Frankfurt is not nearly as bad as its reputation might lead you to expect.

# WHERE TO STAY

Frankfurt hotels tend to fall into one category . . . expensive, well-equipped, and booked-out during fair-time. But it is exceedingly difficult to find more moderately priced accommodation suitable for the business traveller so he has the choice of paying up or going outside the city.

Nor are the hoteliers – both international and German chains are represented – compelled to tout for business. Even the relatively recent arrival of the 44-storey, 1,182-bed **Canadian-Pacific** hotel near the city centre has not created a surplus, nor has the Airport Sheraton's 240-room extension put a glut on the market. Indeed, when the *Messe* is in full swing with exhibitions, especially during April and May, some hotel rooms are booked no less than two years in advance.

However, the choice of 'type' of hotel is rather better, ranging from the American-style impersonality and efficiency of the Canadian-Pacific, the Inter-Continental and the Sheraton Airport, to some really grand European-style hotels, and a few pleasantly rural properties as well.

If you fly in (and most people do), you will be disgorged almost into the foyer of the **Frankfurt-Sheraton,** (Flughaven, Terminal Mitte, D-6000 Frankfurt/Main 75; tel: 69770; telex: 4189 294). It is connected to the arrivals/departures lounge by a short walkway, and rooms on one side of the building (all heavily sound-proofed) give a fine view of the maze of runways. The station, with quick connections to Frankfurt's main station, is in the basement, and the A3 autobahn runs right past the back door. This unique location means that visiting businessmen often never need to leave the airport, and the underground city beneath the terminal has supermarkets, boutiques, cinemas, jewellers and an exclusive discotheque. Three restaurants, including the **Papillion,** serve international gourmet cuisine. Sauna, swimming-pool and solarium complete the ensemble, which lacks character, but scores on convenience. Prices: single from Dm215-315; double Dm235-345; suites Dm550-1,800.

The nearby **Steigenberger-Airport Hotel** (Unterschweinstiege 16, D-6000 Frankfurt/Main 75; tel: 69851; telex: 413112) offers a German alternative. Unprepossessing from outside, it is quiet and spacious within, and its woodland setting belies its closeness to the airport. 350 rooms all with colour TV, minibars and autovalets; 14 conference rooms can take up to 650 at once. But if it matches the American hotels for facilities, it exceeds them all for atmosphere, not least because of the 200-year-old farmhouse restaurant that is attached, the **Unterschweinsteiger,** a rendezvous outstanding for ambience as well as the hearty local food. Price: single Dm169-249; double Dm240-310; double suites Dm410-490.

The **Frankfurter Hof,** (Kaiserplatz, D-6000 Frankfurt 16; tel: 20251; telex: 411806) is the only major hotel within the old town, close to both river and Römer, and itself a reconstruction. In its original 1876 form, Thomas Mann wrote that it was *"a genuine grand hotel"*, and indeed it still is, filled with fine tapestries and paintings, a sweeping main staircase, an elegant mirrored bar, and a tinkling pianist on duty in the reception lounge. 400 rooms decorated in modern style, usual complement of restaurants, from the highly recommended but pricey *nouvelle cuisine* **Restaurant Français** to the cheerful but not cheap **Frankfurter Stubbe,** serving exemplary regional German food. Price: single from Dm290; double from Dm320; suites from Dm750.

But it has a formidable and cheaper (if less outwardly imposing) rival for elegance in the **Hessischer Hof** (Friedrich-Ebert-Anlage 40; tel: 475 400; telex: 411776) a former town house of the Hessen royal family (still the owners). Museum-piece antiques everywhere, each room its own safe, and personal service that knows what to do if you leave a pair of shoes outside your bedroom door. Prices: single Dm179-339; double Dm250-370; suites Dm460-1,025.

Less distinguished but in similar mode is the **Park Hotel** (Wiesenhütten Platz 28-38; tel: 26970; telex: 412808) with simpler old furniture scattered about, and over-decoration in the Casablanca Bar – trying a bit *too* hard to be 'the small grand hotel'. It is close to the station, has 280 rooms, with those in the old wing more spacious. Prices: single Dm160-260; double Dm230-360; suites from Dm310-1,200.

Then there are the American-style hotels. Canadian-Pacific call their hotel **Frankfurt Plaza**

*Frankfurt Plaza hotel*

(Hamburger Allee 2-10; tel: 770 721; telex: 416 745). Be warned, the taxi drivers don't, and are likely to take you to an older hotel of the same name out of spite. It is Europe's tallest residential building, with offices below, and 591 double rooms starting on the 26th floor. A typical American-style hotel, the Canadian-Pacific has one major asset – it's right across the road from the *Messe.* Also popular with US air crews and military personnel. Three restaurants include the **Geheimratsstube,** serving interesting if heavy-handed *nouvelle cuisine;* and one attached to a 24-hour bakery, with a zillion-course breakfast buffet that is a paragon of its type. It also has the only in-hotel nightclub, the **Blue Infinitum.** Prices: single Dm160-290; double Dm210-340; suites Dm400-1,500.

Until the completion of the Sheraton's new wing, the **Frankfurt Inter-Continental** (Wilhelm-Leuschner-Str 43, 6000 Frankfurt; tel: 230 561; telex: 413639) was the largest – 814 double rooms, not counting two 64-room balcony suites, and the showpiece presidential suite. Prices: single Dm250; double Dm340; suites from Dm800.

# WHERE TO EAT

The Hessen region is not noted for refined cuisine, leaning rather to strong meats and cheeses served with spicy sauces, or hearty but pungent country fare. For carnivores of good appetite, this is no bad news, and traditional restaurants specialising in game and seafoods guarantee that glutted feeling for Dm40 to 50. Gourmet restaurants, and there are many, cost a bit more . . . anything up to Dm80 before wine.

There is more emphasis on lunch than dinner, with the afternoon break (when all but the Asian restaurants are closed) being filled with coffee and rich pastries at the numerous cafés in the city centre.

Like everything here,it all works to a timetable, and if you haven't lunched by 3 p.m., forget it until 5.30 p.m. or 6 p.m. However, if you behave yourself, and lunch at the correct time, you can take advantage of the common business lunch set menus, running anywhere between Dm30 and 50 for a three-course meal, and reliably good value for money.

With life for foreign visitors centred on the international hotels, all of these have restaurants, generally to a very high standard. Those in the hotel guide can drum up anything from a burger to *haute* or *nouvelle cuisine.* Specially good of their type are the Frankfurter Hof's **Restaurant Francais;** the **Frankfurter Stubbe** in the same hotel, lower down the price range; and the Inter-Continental's elegant riverside **Rotisserie.** The C-P Plaza's **Geheimratsstube** has an inventive chef, recommended for unusually strong-flavoured *nouvelle cuisine,* and the Park Hotel's **La Truffe** restaurant specialises in delicate truffle dishes.

The most atmospheric of all major hotel restaurants is the Steigenberger Airport Hotel's historic woodland **Unterschweinstiege.** Stone floors and genuine roof-beams of a 200-year-old farmhouse, and a generous line in roast boar dishes, are a powerful draw to Frankfurters, and it is usually essential to book here (and recommended at most other places, come to that).

In general, though, hotels can't beat the atmosphere of the small traditional restaurants, with smoked pork, venison, and wild boar on the menu, and hapless trout and lobster swimming their last in display tanks. The **Altänchen** (Gr Rittergasse 112; tel: 618 540), is a find among the bustle of the Sachsenhausen. Don't make my mistake, though, and go overly local, with *ribbchen mit kraut,* an ultimately overpowering smoked pork chop with sauerkraut, or you'll end up as I did drooling over your companion's venison. Dinner for two – Dm90, plus wine.

The **Humperdinck** (corner Liebigstr and Grünebergweg; tel: 722 122), is another find, somewhat off the beaten track, though popular with US staff officers from the nearby army HQ. Set in an old house, you can specify a smaller more private room if you book in advance. Rich sauces, trout, seafood and rich puddings.

Other goodies in the local line are the **Brückenkeller** (Schützenstr 6; tel: 284 238); **Heyland's Weinstuben** (Kaiserhofstr 7; tel: 284 840), off the Fressegasse; **Börsenkeller** (Schillerstr 11; tel: 281 115), handy for the banking district, and the **Dippegucker** (tel: 551 965), corner Eschenheimer Anglage and Oderweg just a little further out. These central restaurants are especially busy at lunchtime.

French and Alsatian cuisine with local modifications (mainly heartier portions) are also abundant. **Erno's Bistro** (Liebigstr 15; tel: 721 997), is a paragon of the breed, but small, so you need to book. On the other side of the river, in the south of the Sachsenhausen, **Bistro M** (Wendelsweg 79; tel: 627 192), offers similar variations.

For the late eaters (those who missed lunch), the **Schildkröte** (Gr Eschenheimerstr 41; tel: 281 036), serves French food until 4 a.m.; while **Tadiana's Grill** (Kirchnerstr 7; tel: 505 955), offers plainer grills of steak and rib (often a relief after days of aromatic gravy) until 3.30 a.m. The C-P Plaza Hotel's **Backerei,** which really is a bakery, is open 24 hours . . . though if you're that late you might as well wait until their feast of a breakfast is served.

Finally, as an international city, Frankfurt has its share of Asian restaurants. The Japanese **Juchheim's** (Am Salzhaus 1; tel: 280 262), next to the Göethehaus, and **Mikuni** (Fahrgasse 93; tel: 283 627), are authentic and excellent. And the **Bangkok** (Sandweg 17; tel: 491 360), serves genuine Thai specialities, while **Tse Yang** (Kaiserstr 67; tel: 232 541), is reckoned hard to beat among numerous Chinese restaurants.

For those who like to eat Italian, again a wide choice, of which **La Galleria** (corner Münchnerstr and Neue Mainzerstr; tel: 235 680), serves the bankers at packed lunchtime sessions; while **Da Bruno** (corner Elbest and Münchnerstr; tel: 233 416), overcomes its location uncomfortably close to the sex shops with an enviable menu.

Plenty of other choices, from Russian and Hungarian to American. Frankfurt's nightlife may be limited, but its inhabitants do like to eat well, and so can you.

# NIGHTLIFE

The 'excitement' of Frankfurt's red light district is summed up by lonely men with disgruntled expressions heading back across the road towards the railway station. Behind them, street-corner tarts trade insults with their costlier counterparts cruising the blocks between Kaiserstrasse and Münchnerstrasse in Porsche or Mercedes coupés; touts accost you whether or not you loiter, drumming up business for 'sex club' clip joints; and the sex shops and peep shows are the only lights this side of the darkened city centre.

In a city where expensive tastes are not merely catered for but positively encouraged, there are more decorous ways of enjoying the mercantile sex, but far be it from me (an innocent abroad) to usurp the role of the hotel hall porter, who will indubitably have his own recommendations.

More convivial pursuits are to be found in Frankfurt, even on weekends, but you have to know where to look. Two good starting points are **Jimmy's Bar** (Friedr-Ebert-Anlager 40) and **Fidelio** (Bockenheimer Landstr 1) just off the Opernplatz. The former has a pipe-smoking atmosphere, with chess at the tables, but a more lively set at the bar; the second is a haunt of the advertising crowd, who try and impress one another to a background of classical music.

When feeling jolly, the usual thing to do after that is to repair to the Sachsenhausen district, where the very homesick might even look into the **Irish Pub,** in the noisiest square off the Kleine Rittergasse. I'd sooner recommend the more German and old-fashioned **Aprikösie** (Wallstr) as a choice example of the traditional apple-wine cellar that abounds here or either **Zum grauen Bock** (Rittergasse) or the **Bavarian Kutsch** (Kleine Rittergasse) for snacks and live music with your liquor. **Palais des Bières** (corner Schweizerstr and Textorstr) is a rendezvous for knowledgeable lager drinkers.

In summer, however, the Sachsenhausen district is noisy and full of tourists, and the hot tip is to

*The Alte Oper for highbrow evenings*

*Gothic inn sign in the Romerberg*

avoid it altogether (as do many Frankfurters) and instead take advantage of the improving suburban life in the Bornheim district, back across the river and a little to the east. Earlier on, from 5 p.m. until 9 p.m. only, local wine-tasting and light meals at the **Dünker** (Burgerstr 265); apple-wine at **Solzer** (Burgerstr 260) and **Zur Eulenberg** (Eulengasse 46) later into the night.

If it's culture you're after, it's always worth checking what's on at the **Alte Oper** (Opernplatz) or the trio of opera, concert and chamber-music venues **(Oper, Schauspiel** and **Kammerspiel),** while English-language plays are the fare of the **Café Theatre** (Hamburger-Allee 45).

And from then on, it's discos or jazz. Frankfurters are big on swing . . . oompah jazz, if you like, and the Fressegasse is the main place for the clubs, mainly small and invariably chokingly hot and smoky. Open variously until night or as late as 2 a.m.

# GETTING AROUND

Frankfurt is small, the public transport is efficient, and reasonably easy to understand, and city journeys too long to walk are served by a choice from street-cars to taxis.

Public transport is on an integrated ticket system, sold by automatic dispensers at pick-up points that (in the case of train fares at least) need a helpful German guide if not a degree in juke boxes to understand when you first see them. These serve for underground and overground trains, buses and streetcars (soon to disappear).

Your first encounter with the ticket machines is likely to be in the basement of the airport, to pick up one of the frequent rapid S-bahn trains direct to the central station in 12 minutes. Depending on the time, this will cost between Dm2.80 and 3.10. Just pay what the machine says.

It's worth persevering, because the same ride in a taxi will take several minutes longer, and cost Dm25. Frankfurt cabbies are a breed almost as dour as the Mercedes diesels they drive, and it costs you Dm3.60 just to climb in, with the meter clicking up rapidly in 30 pfennig jumps. The average cross-town journey ends up between seven and 10 marks.

Four underground lines serve the city-centre and suburbs, and are cheap and simple to use.

Naturally, all major car hire companies are at the airport, and driving in Frankfurt is less intimidating than the aggressive sounds of the numerous Porsches would suggest, once you master the one-way streets. Since it's a compact town, this doesn't take long. Good roads clear the rush hour quickly, and there are numerous parking garages, but the number of commuters means that these can fill up fast under any extra pressure. Beware of what seem like the world's longest red traffic lights, they haven't broken down.

# A very exalted brand of Swiss chocolate, generally found at an altitude of 12,000 meters.

We're not exaggerating: our *chocolatiers* make a hundred different chocolates for our First Class passengers – even if you think that's overdoing things and if there's unlikely to be anyone who'll try them all at one go. But there is one conclusion you can draw from this: an airline which takes so much trouble does a little bit more for all its guests than it needs to. At an altitude of 12,000 meters as well as on the ground. From inflight service to aircraft maintenance. Something which even those people who don't like chocolate won't regard as an exaggeration.

**swissair**

# Geneva

**Life in Geneva, that most blameless of cities, revolves around sticking to the rules and getting on with the job in hand. Its prosperity, location, neutrality and reputation for fair play make it a veritable paradise for the business traveller.**

**By David Owen**

Some local businessmen rave about Geneva's red light district. "*You'll find it between Maxim's and the Ramada Hotel,*" they told me, "*Berne and Monthoux are the rues chaudes.*" Perhaps I picked a bad night. Or perhaps I was rejected as impecunious or 'just looking'. Whatever the case, I can only report I have seen more flesh on a broiler chicken.

Those who bemoan the city's tame but improving nightlife often forget that Geneva is tiny by international standards. Barely 350,000 people inhabit the entire canton, of whom fewer than 150,000 populate the city itself. This makes its considerable international renown all the harder to fathom. Just as pharmaceuticals firms have flocked to Lausanne, bankers to Zurich and metal traders to Zug, so Geneva has come to house a plethora of international prestige organisations. Why?

Regular visitors attribute this to a combination of four factors: its prosperity, its neutrality, its situation (within easy reach of the Alps in winter and not too far from the Mediterranean in summer) and the simple fact that it is a disarmingly pleasant place in which to live and work. Come to Geneva to find all the tranquil stability you could ever wish for.

But don't be deceived by the relaxed, provincial atmosphere. The Genevois have perfected the art (which I used to think was exclusive preserve of Oxbridge economics students) of appearing laid back when actually working very hard indeed. You will find most businessmen in their offices by 8.30 a.m. and lunch breaks, when clients aren't being entertained, tend to be perfunctory. Nor will you be expected to take part in time-consuming customs and preliminaries before getting down to business – an attitude which should enable the visiting businessman to keep his appointments-per-day ratio to a maximum. But be warned, punctuality is of the essence.

No real business etiquette can be said to exist in Geneva, although those dealing with Swiss bankers should take care not to rush their customary somewhat 'stuffed shirt' approach. Even here,as one much-travelled US software rep told me, you should not be cowed into keeping your best side to yourself. "*The Swiss may be dogmatic,*" he explained, "*but they do listen.*" The main reason for the lack of formalities is that you are more likely to be dealing with an expatriate working in Geneva than a native Genevois. The city is a melting pot for various nationalities the like of which is seldom encountered outside North America. While the majority are businessmen, Geneva has also become a celebrated refuge for political fugitives. Lenin spent a number of years here before the revolution and, more recently, Iranians fleeing from Khomeini have settled in Geneva in their thousands.

Outside the business of finance (interest rates are the lowest in the world, prompting Japan to take as much as 75 per cent of its worldwide borrowing requirements from Switzerland in 1984) change happens slowly. When faced with a decision likely to impact significantly on their lifestyle, the Swiss way is to hold a referendum. As a confederation of cantons, regional power is very strong in Switzerland, with individual cantons holding sway over the whole gamut of public affairs from local transport to most police matters. Accordingly, the referenda are predominently local, with the populace balloted on everything from proposals for a new motorway to the accordance of Swiss nationality to foreigners. While many people point to the system as a model democracy, it is expensive to run and a poll-weary electorate tends to produce low turnouts on all but the most pressing issues.

This conservatism has doubtless contributed to the wealth of the country. However, its consequences cannot be said to be uniformly positive – women achieved the vote in Switzerland only within the last decade. In addition, few can remember the last shift in the balance of power of the seven-member council which nominally rules the country (its powers reside mainly in the international sphere). While the socialists are widely considered to be losing popularity in Switzerland at present, their two-man presence on the federal council is assured.

"*Switzerland is a police state,*" one Californian who settled in Geneva four years ago informed me. "*A very pleasant police state but a police state nonetheless,*" he added. It is hard to disagree. Foreign businessmen are most welcome provided they play unquestioningly by the rules. Those living locally are generally careful not to exceed the limits on meat imports from nearby France, for example, despite large price incentives to slip through with an extra pound or two. By the same token, everything from prostitution to the family pet appears to be licenced, while anyone wishing to set up in the lucrative Geneva restaurant business has, I am told, first to make his peace with the perfectly legitimate syndicates who oversee the business.

On a local level, a number of 'burning issues' ripple the surface of contemporary Genevan political and economic life. There is a hard drugs problem, worsened by the number of bored teenagers in the city, but seldom reported in the press. The papers say the city's prime concern (apart from minor niggles such as whether or not to extend the airport and the way in which rents are inflated by the large international business population) is its lack of an industrial base to sustain the economy should its unparalleled reputation for services ever go sour. The Swiss are unspeakably proud of their annual inflation rate: I remember a news broadcast some years ago which spoke of little else and featured a table with Switzerland perched proudly above the likes of West Germany, the USA and even Japan. Be that as it may, and despite last year's high increase in prices of 3.9 per cent, there is little sign of the Swiss franc collapsing just yet. Recent comparatively steep hikes have pushed the national index (1966 = 100) to 226.2. Furthermore, Switzerland maintains a healthy third position in the world GDP per capita table for 1984 – tucked in neatly behind United Arab Emirates and Kuwait and just ahead of Saudi Arabia.

This is not to say Geneva is outrageously expensive. It isn't. While nothing is cheap or nasty, good quality comes reasonably priced – even in the international hotels. It is no doubt possible to get ripped off in Geneva, but a sense of fair play and value for money has lingered longer here than in many cities where vulnerable and loaded business travellers tend to congregate.

Geneva has not always been so middle-of-the-road. Having passed through the hands of a succession of empires (Roman, Burgundian, German . . .), Geneva was a fiercely independent protestant state in the 16th century, with the uncompromising religious theorist Jean Calvin its most renowned inhabitant. During most of this period, the tiny state was coveted by the Dukes of Savoy. The crunch came in 1602 when the aggressors were firmly and decisively beaten back. With neutrality starving them of significant military success since then, the Genevois have turned this victory into an annual festival, The Escalade, which they celebrate on December 11 and 12. Legend has it that a certain 'Mère Royaume' fought back the invading hordes by the simple expedient of pouring her pot of boiling soup over them. However dubious the authenticity of this heroic deed, today's children are loathe to quibble, since they can thank the Mère for the chocolate saucepan and marzipan vegetables they traditionally receive.

Geneva did not join the Swiss confederation until 1815, after a spell as part of France following annexation by Napoleon. It was already wealthy having enjoyed a profitable 18th century during which it provided a peaceful haven for Voltaire and Rousseau to work in. (Contrary to popular belief, the major Genevois contribution to French culture is not the retention of the archaic 'nonante' to mean 90, instead of the clumsy, modern 'quatre-vingt-dix'.)

Many people seem to forget that beneath its carefully-nurtured facade of neutrality, Switzerland boasts what is arguably the best prepared 'defence' force outside Israel and Vietnam. After the initial military service period, every able-bodied Swiss male spends from one to three weeks per year in uniform, depending on his age. All have their kitbags perpetually at the ready at home and tales of hollowed out mountains hiding vast caches of arms and even tanks are substantially true. The Vatican knows a thing or two about this and continues to entrust its defence to the Swiss Guard.

A glance at Geneva's geographical position does much to reveal why it has acquired more of an international outlook than even other Swiss cities. Bordered on three sides by France, its main connection to the rest of Switzerland is submerged beneath the waters of Lac Léman. This may explain why the French-speaking Genevois tend to be more relaxed, refined and imaginative than the caricature of their German-speaking countrymen. But remnants of the disciplined, sullen Swiss stereotype remain. Jaywalking is banned on pain of an on-the-spot fine, while the streets are not exactly overflowing with happy smiling faces. Nonetheless, the mood is infinitely more cosmopolitan than even in Lausanne, a mere 35 miles up the road.

If Genevois seem cagey, it is because the rapid turnover of foreign businessmen passing through the city encourages them to look on foreigners as parvenus. Those who have chosen to settle in Geneva (and have taken the trouble to learn French – highly recommended) report the locals to be friendly, if initially withdrawn, with a penchant for cracking jokes at their own expense.

Despite the international HQs and the dominant silhouette of Saint Pierre's Cathedral, the focal point of the city remains its irrepressible Jet d'Eau. While some would say the 470-foot fountain is no more than a wildly extravagant weather vane, its reappearance in March after its winter break is an annual sign to most Genevois that spring has arrived, as unmistakable as Wordsworth's lakeside daffodils. As my Californian friend explained, "*The first time in the year you see the fountain, it sounds kind of trite, but you really do get a lift.*" It sounds kind of trite but that is a view I can wholeheartedly endorse.

*Life revolves round the lake in Geneva*

# WHERE TO STAY

Geneva boasts over 15,000 hotel beds – about one for every ten of the city's inhabitants. The bulk are situated relatively close together, in an area bounded by the lake, rue de Lausanne and the railway station. Perhaps it is the atmosphere of competition, which both of these facts must help to engender, that has kept prices down. I was certainly surprised by the value for money represented by even the city's luxury hotels in a country which has a reputation for being expensive. Most rates quoted are inclusive of service, tax and sometimes continental breakfast. Tipping is not usually expected.

Four-star hotels – often de-luxe by normal European standards – can be particularly good value in Geneva and offer welcome savings if your expenses are calculated per diem. Air-conditioning and 24-hour service is not unusual in three-star establishments, while even some two-star hotels have private bath and telephone and mini-bars in their rooms.

Of the clutch of five-star establishments overlooking the lake, the **Noga Hilton** (Quai du Mont Blanc; tel: 319 811; telex 289704), equipped with swimming pool, fitness club, discotheque, three restaurants, casino (the only one in Geneva – maximum roulette stake SF5, hardened gamblers take note) and shopping centre, is the most modern. Rooms are comfortable and well-appointed (the bathroom speaker is a good idea) and service discreetly efficient. The views are arguably the best in Geneva. The Noga Hilton also boasts a fine, traditional-style French restaurant, Le Cygne, endowed with an exceptional wine list. Single SF220-320; double SF300-410; suite SF1400.

Handily-placed for the United Nations, the recently-refurbished **Inter-Continental** (Chemin du Petit-Saconnx; tel: 346091; telex: 23130), is a favourite with Americans and Arabs. Though the building itelf is rather unprepossessing in appearance regulars regard the service as exemplary. There is an open-air swimming pool. Single SF200; double SF260; suites SF750-4000.

If you prefer something smaller and older, the 30-room **Les Armures** (rue du Puits; tel: 289 172; telex 421129), near the cathedral in the old town, is highly recommended – although these days it is usually booked up far in advance.

Should this indeed be the case during your visit, you might have better luck at its sister property **L'Arbalète** (Tour-Maîtresse; tel: 284 155; telex 427293), on the left bank. Both are repositaries of the traditional art of Swiss hotel keeping, incorporating personalised service and sumptuous, original decor. The restaurant in Les Armures is probably the best in the city for local cuisine. Single SF180; double SF230.

Three names which together constitute the old guard of the city's hotels are the **President** (Quai Wilson; tel: 310 000; telex 22780), **Hotel des Bergues,** (Quai des Bergues; tel: 315 050; telex 23383), and the **Hotel du Rhone** (Quai Turrettini; tel: 319 831; telex 22213). While all maintain high standards of comfort and service, they lack on the one hand the superb facilities of the Noga Hilton and the Inter-Continental and on the other the sheer luxury and elegance of Les Armures. I am informed that the rooms in the President are also rather small, although you might find yourself rubbing shoulders with a visiting statesman or two. President: single SF215; double SF315. Bergues: single SF210; double SF265-310. Rhone: single SF185; double SF265-295.

In the four-star category, two of the best are the Manotel-owned **Hotel Rex** (Avenue Wendt; tel: 457 150; telex: 23387), and the **Hotel Royal** (rue de Lausanne; tel: 313 600; telex 27631). The Rex is as convenient as the Inter-Continental for the United Nations and service is well above average. One snag: the hotel is not situated in the most vibrant of areas. The Royal is simple, inexpensive and convenient, situated little more than a stone's throw from the station. Though it generally adopts a 'no frills' approach, it boasts features such as rooms with kitchenettes and parking facilities which make it stand out from the run-of-the-mill four-star hotel. Rex: single SF109; double SF155. Royal: single SF117; double SF161.

Pick of the airport hotels is the **Penta** (Avenue Louis Casai; tel: 984 700; telex 27044), particularly if you manage to sidestep the frequent conferences. While rates are reckoned by some to be expensive, the Penta adopts a flexible policy to pricing which means that discounts are frequently obtainable – particularly in the November to

*The Noga Hilton hotel*

February low season. Single SF125; double SF170.

Finally, a new addition to the Geneva luxury hotel scene has recently surfaced in the form of the **Metropole** (Quai Général Guisan; tel: 211 344; telex: 421550). The hotel boasts ultra-modern fittings housed in a period building, although visitors report that the designers saw fit not to install air-conditioning. This leaves summer occupants an occasionally uncomfortable choice between sweating it out or opening a window onto frequently congested nearby roads.

# WHERE TO EAT

Outside La Pax, Bolivia, where the best restaurant in town is Swiss, the country is not reputed for its culinary excellence – chocolate and fondue, of course, excepted. But Geneva is outstandingly imbued with fine restaurants which, in turn, are well-patronised by the sizeable international business contingent. Apart from the quality of the food itself, the balmy, relaxed atmosphere of a spring or summer's evening in the old town or by the lake is most conducive to lingering over a bottle of wine and an excellent meal. Particularly if you are accustomed to the eccentricities of certain Swiss waiters.

It is not at all unusual to sit for 20 minutes at a Genevan restaurant without hearing a peep from the waiters studiously avoiding your glance. Eventually, however, one of them will sidle up to your table and ask what you would like to eat, sometimes in a tone of voice which suggests he genuinely believes you have only come to listen to the background music or study the wallpaper. From then on, there is no turning back, although those unfamiliar with Swiss dining etiquette and feeling aggrieved at the paucity of the main course which has been set before them, should note that at traditional restaurants it is still the norm to serve two helpings.

While it is advisable to reserve well in advance when eating at many Genevan restaurants, there are usually tables free at the **Restaurant du Parc des Eaux-vives** (tel: 354 140 or 354 148), one of several overlooking the lake. Food is rich and traditional and the setting is mansion-style. Similar but slightly cheaper and more classically romantic (particularly if you ask for a terrace table with a view of Mont Blanc) is the **Perle du Lac** (tel: 317 935). Expect to pay around SF100 a head including wine. Closed Mondays.

There are plenty of opportunities in Geneva for Italian food aficionados to indulge. Pick of the bunch in the eyes of many is **Chez Valentino** (tel: 521 440), on the outskirts of town at Vesenaz, although it is not recommended for those who prefer to avoid crowds. Service can suffer as a result but the standard dishes are all well worth waiting for. It's cheap too, at SF30-40 a head, plus wine. If you just want a pizza or a snack, the atmosphere at **San Marco** (tel: 369 598), is friendly and authentic. You can spend anything from SF7-40.

For an inexpensive business lunch, a carbonnade of beef at **Le Bouchon** (12, rue Blavignac, tel: 428 498), is ideal. Particularly recommended for those with large appetites.

Two of Geneva's finest gourmet restaurants are the **Olivier de Provence** (tel: 420 450), at Carouge and the well-known **Lion D'Or** (tel: 364 432 or 365 447), at Cologny – the suburb inhabited by many of the better-heeled expatriates. The Olivier, whose ambience can be best equated with an upmarket Hampstead wine bar, is in the middle price bracket, with à la carte around SF 60-70 plus wine, while the Lion D'Or is more snobbish and more expensive. There is a choice of two menus, one at SF95, one at SF110, plus wine.

For Chinese food, the restaurant at the **La Réserve Hotel** (tel: 741 741), on the Lausanne road, enjoys a matchless reputation. But at SF50-85 a head, it is not cheap. A sister restaurant, the **Tse Yang** (tel: 325 081), has recently opened up near the Noga Hilton. The newcomer has received generally favourable initial reports and shrewdly offers a business lunch at SF38.

You have to drive half an hour to Crissier to eat at the best restaurant in the area, however. A visit to **Girardet** (tel: 021 341 514), is always an unmitigated pleasure, as many a guidebook will attest. Reserve a table. The return journey can seem very long if you fail to get in. The bill should come to around SF130 a head, including wine.

*La Réserve Hotel*

# NIGHTLIFE

While vice is no doubt a low priority of most travelling businessmen, Geneva is not one of the world's most sinful cities. Indeed, the near moribund state of the city's supposedly infamous *rues chaudes* does nothing to contradict Geneva's reputation as a city whose populace likes to be tucked up in bed well before midnight.

In fact, things are improving. No longer does Genevan nightlife have the doomed aspect of the alpine health resorts described by the likes of André Gide and Llewellyn Powys, where TB sufferers congregated to frolic away the twilight of their lives in the crisp alpine air.

Ironically, no sooner does the city develop an area where the nightlife is vibrant, agreeable and original – the old quarter – than it comes under threat from residents complaining about the noise. Admittedly, what hangs over the head of the likes of the trendy **La Tour** nightclub (tel: 210 033), the student hangout **La Clémence** (tel: 201 096), and the numerous cafés and bars in the area is a penknife rather than a sword of Damocles. But rents are high, which inevitably lends weight to the residents' case. One rather hackneyed establishment with a predominantly young and rowdy clientele which rejoices in the name **The Old Town Pub** (tel: 216 387), bans terrace drinking after 10p.m. as a compromise measure. In the meantime,there is no pleasanter way of spending an evening in Geneva than dawdling in the narrow, cobbled streets, pausing intermittently in one of the many bars and perhaps taking your time over an inexpensive but hearty supper. At least the future of the plethora of antique shops in the area looks secure.

For other would-be revellers, the chic **Griffin's Club** (tel: 351 218), is the place to be seen. Elsewhere, **Régine's** (tel: 315 735), and **Maxim's** (tel: 329 900), are much as you would expect, while my taxi driver recommended the newish **Whisky Bar** (tel: 281 428), in rue du Prince. Others told me it was the sort of place taxi drivers frequent. Geneva's concert and theatre circuits are tolerable (despite a preponderance of bad translations of hammed English classics), café-theatre is in vogue and jazz aficionados will note the presence of **New Morning** (tel: 280 641) – such a success in Paris – amongst the favourite European venues of big names like Jaco Pastorius and the late Kenny Clarke. Only the young still complain there is nothing to do in Geneva as they mope disconsolately beside the lake or speed past you on their roller skates and motorbikes.

# GETTING AROUND

Transport from the airport to downtown Geneva is plentiful and efficient but can be time-consuming when traffic is bad. Allow 15-20 minutes outside rush hours for the taxi journey. Geneva cabs are sumptuous and expensive. Expect to pay SF20-30 from the airport to the centre of town. If you opt for the bus, you can save money by taking a number 33 to the city's central railway station. This covers precisely the same route as the official airport bus and costs SF1.20 as opposed to SF5.

Public transport throughout the city runs punctually and is extremely clean, as you would expect in Switzerland. Most destinations can be reached on the bus/tram network and tickets, valid for one hour on any route, cost a flat rate SF1.20.

All major car hire firms are represented at the airport and in central Geneva – but costs are high. Expect to pay around SF45 a day plus SF0.60 per km for a mid-range model and there's often a surcharge for collision insurance.

On the whole, it is better to stick to taxis or public transport – unless you need to travel well out of town, especially in view of the traffic – which can be nightmarish. Geneva is a small town with more than its fair share of commuters, all of them channelled across a handful of bridges. Resultant congestion can at times be extremely frustrating, particularly when punctuality is of the essence.

Alternatively, if your appointments are clustered around the centre of town and weather permits, the best and most agreeable way to get around is on foot. Geneva is so small, you can walk most distances with ease and without losing time.

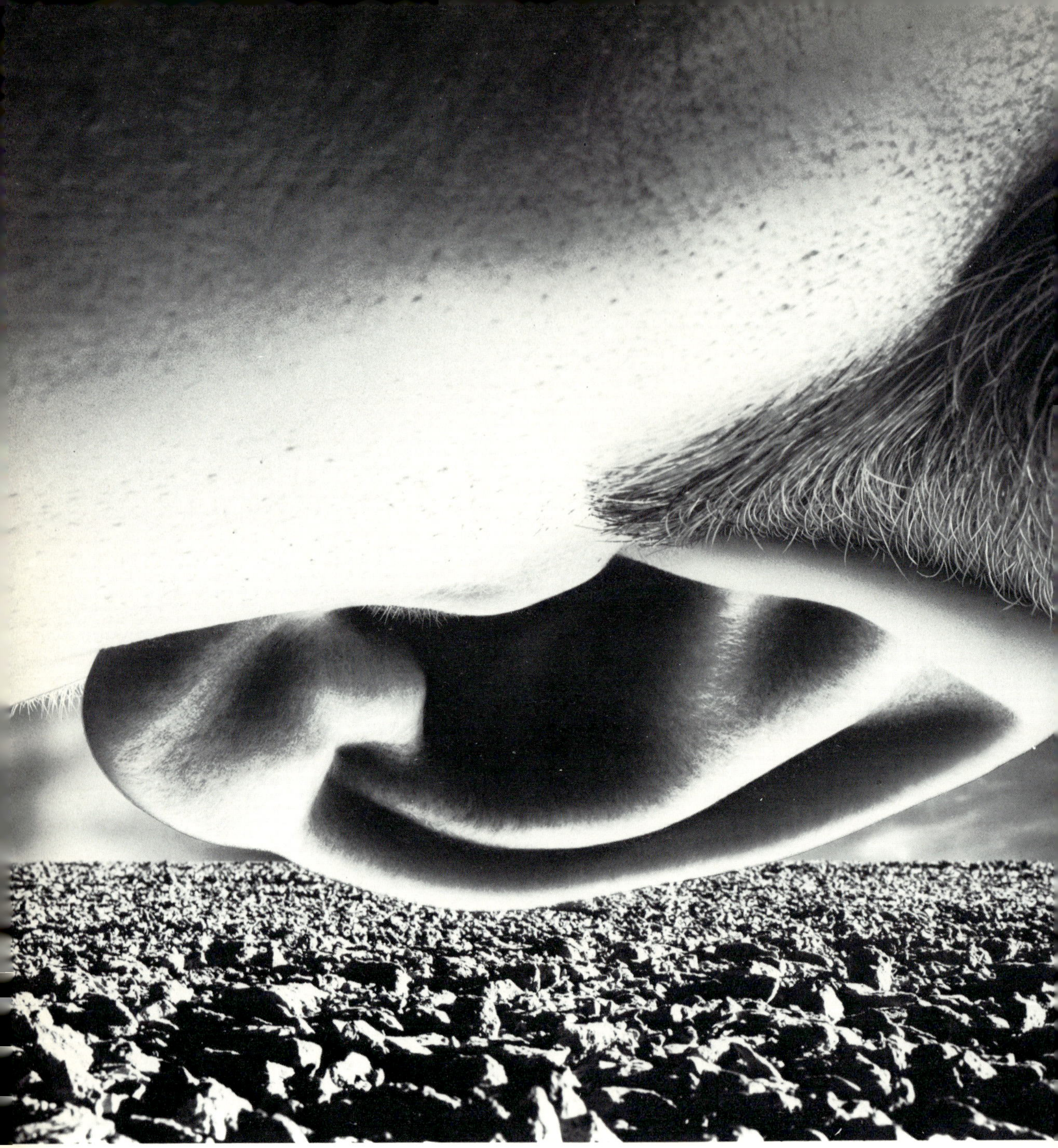

# What gives us better intelligence than the world's most advanced travel computer?

Hundreds of computer terminals whisper urgently to each other night and day. They're gathering intelligence on hotel vacancies, flight times and fare reductions for TRIPS.

TRIPS, our computer network, allows us to plan the most intricate international itineraries from an office near you.

It helps us to see crises before they can even happen.

And it's placed at the exclusive service of the customers of American Express Travel.

Nevertheless, our intelligence does not stop with computers. (Unlike companies of more limited intelligence.)

An unrivalled network of personal contacts – from restaurateurs to police chiefs – has been cultivated by our Travel Consultants in over 1,200 local offices.

Funnily enough, what these Consultants hear through the grapevine often proves more helpful to our customers than all the electronic gadgetry in the world. For further intelligence, write to: Travel Management Services, American Express Europe Ltd., Windsor House, 50 Victoria Street, London SW1H 0NH. Tel: 01-222 7966.

AMERICAN EXPRESS

**Travel Management Services**

*American Express Europe Limited, incorporated with limited liability in the State of Delaware, U.S.A.*

# Glasgow

The violent, despairing image that has long been associated with the Glasgow of the Gorbals is slowly being replaced by a flourishing, civilised and motivated society that appears to be superbly confident of its future.

By Simon Inglis

At the risk of sounding like a publicity hand-out, surely no-one who has visited Glasgow recently can fail to be impressed by the city's resurgent sense of purpose and optimism.

Glasgow reminds me of Sydney. So many people have their preconceived ideas about the place and yet all who experience the city first-hand come back with nothing but praise.

Glasgow, the dirty, grimy, self-pitying derelict city cast under a permanent haze of alcohol and drenched in polluted rain . . . that city is no more, if indeed it ever existed.

Scots who used to avoid Glasgow like the plague now speak of their conversion. Even my father, a staunch Edinburgh man, has had to admit that Glasgow is, just as the city's promotions people put it, 'Miles Better'.

Many Glaswegians are, in fact, almost sickeningly optimistic. They take you to ultra-civilised café-bars where you can drink coffee at lunchtime and have a beer in the afternoon. They show off the recently cleaned-up sandstone tenements which may so easily be home to unemployed dockers or advertising executives. Then of course there are all those theatres, operas, ballets and restaurants and wine bars (though no decent pubs and too few cinemas) and the Burrell Collection, which has now become Scotland's most popular tourist attraction, surpassing even Edinburgh Castle.

And if you are a well-paid Yuppie life in Glasgow is just dandy. Skiing at Aviemore, yachting on Loch Lomond, swimming on the coast (with perhaps a second home there or in the Highlands), glorious scenery all around, and it only takes ten minutes to drive along a usually empty motorway from the city centre to Glasgow airport, where a shuttle flight is a mere hour away from Heathrow.

*"Glasgow is the biggest village in the world,"* one young executive told me. *"You soon get to know people and start bumping into them on the streets and in bars. And yet there's a million people here."*

Older ones recall a very different city; a more uncomfortable place where people were huddled into small areas and the working population would travel out of the centre to work in shipyards and factories. The docks thrived. There were regular passenger ships to all corners of the globe and goods poured in until the container revolution shifted the work to Greenock. Everyone else seemed to be in heavy industry, whereas nowadays barely a third work in any sort of manufacturing.

Older Glaswegians remember consumption, pollution, poverty, political radicalism and, until about 1970, some of the worst unemployment and child death rate figures of any British region. And yet throughout the discomfort of the inter-war era there was always that sense, in the words of Will Fyffe (who was, incidentally, from Dundee), that *"I belong to Glasgow, dear old Glasgow town."*

Indeed, perhaps it is because of the city's transformation, whether perceived or real, that the younger generation is now so proud to echo Fyffe's song. They even have research to show how improved life and work is in their city. For instance, there are surveys showing that American and European firms, about 55 of them in Glasgow alone, are delighted with their Scottish workers. Glasgow graduates are now staying in greater numbers than ever before, and numerous ex-patriot graduates are returning from their so-called havens in America and Europe.

Did I also know that office space in Greenock (along the Clyde from Glasgow) where IBM have their headquarters, is ten times cheaper than in London and that even the very finest office space in central Glasgow – which nowadays means a hi-tech interior set in a restored Victorian block – costs only £8 per square foot as opposed to about £30 per square foot in London's West End or the City?

There is another sparkle in the Glaswegian's eye as he turns to the future. On the formerly derelict banks of the Clyde (whose shipyards at their peak just before the First World War produced approximately 75 per cent of the world's total tonnage) a vast new £36 million Scottish Exhibition and Conference Centre has recently been completed, with 19,000 square metres of flexible floor space.

Alongside this centre in April 1988 Glasgow plans its own Liverpool-style Garden Festival, which will fill another 120 acres of derelict dockland. The Clyde promises to be resplendent with marinas, riverside entertainments and cafés. Even the fish, which have been sighted as close as two miles from the city, along what was once described as an open sewer, may be tempted to return to Glasgow.

All this endeavour is expensive, especially for a city which receives less grant aid than London and has so much urban blight to rectify.

But the Scottish are nothing if not canny. In fact their whole cosmopolitan approach to life, and the environment they have created, are in many

*The docks which brought prosperity to the city now stand derelict*

ways as foreign to the English as would be Vienna or Boston. I mention those two cities because the parallels are strong. Two other examples: Glasgow's grid pattern layout is very American, and its cafés have a distinctly European ambience. Scotland is most definitely not England, even down to its different banknotes.

Furthermore, in its overt display of technology Glasgow is streets ahead of most comparable English cities. Almost every bank branch has an automatic teller machine outside, and most good shops and restaurants sport the latest computerised goodies served up by the surrounding electronics companies.

But Glasgow is also an easy city for the stranger to manage. Distances are short, taxis and public transport are excellent, and walking in the city centre is a pleasure because of the street layout.

Enough of the commercial. Now you know that I like the place, some facts. One pioneering scheme is particularly worthy of note. Begun in 1976 and known as Gear, the Glasgow Eastern Area Renewal aims to improve the East End, one of Europe's most deprived urban areas, with low employment, appalling housing and little hope for its increasingly alienated communities. Torn by the depression in the 1920s and 30s, those people who had not managed to escape to the post-war new towns then found their grim but familiar surroundings torn down by the planners in the 1960s.

Gear began to alleviate those problems, with help from a variety of public and private bodies, including the Government, the Strathclyde Regional Council, Glasgow District Council and the Scottish Development Agency. Because the project began to work and the community responded well, Glaswegians were gradually made to see their city not so much as a burden to be borne as an asset to be exploited.

The 'Glasgow's Miles Better' campaign, symbolised by a round, yellow, smiling face, was the first outward expression of this renewed confidence, but the real issues were only pinpointed by the American strategic management consultants McKinsey and Co. Their study concluded that Glasgow's manufacturing base had declined as much as anywhere in the British Isles, but that Glasgow had failed badly to encourage any compensating growth in the service sector.

Taking into account the old saying, *"Edinburgh is the capital but Glasgow has the capital"*, the study recommended that Glasgow develop various sectors, especially in the financial world. One strategy in particular was recommended: that Glasgow try to attact the headquarters of big companies, with Britoil serving as an example of how advantageous such a move could be.

Britoil was ordered to relocate in Glasgow by central government, as was a section of the Ministry of Defence, but as David Macdonald, an official of the Scottish Development Agency points out, the staff soon began to appreciate their new surroundings. *"In almost every case the reality has proved better than those people's perception. Even immigration of English people to Glasgow has become common."*

Americans, Japanese and Europeans are already there, the greatest number being involved in Scotland's expanding electronics industry. Scots call their best of hi-technology factories 'Silicon Glen', in the centre of which lies Glasgow, with roughly a fifth of the total Scottish population of five million.

Compared with its Californian model, Silicon Glen is tiny. Approximately 230 companies employ 40,000 staff, and as recent redundancies at National Semi-Conductor in Greenock proved, no-one's future is guaranteed.

Nevertheless, Glasgow plans ahead with quite breathtaking enthusiasm. One plan is to make it the first non-smoking city in the world by the year 2000. Another, and perhaps the most crucial part of the city's rejuvenation, is the setting up of a group called Glasgow Action.

Chaired by a self-made Glaswegian millionaire, Sir Norman MacFarlane, this group of politicans, financiers, businessmen and academics plan, rather in the manner of medieval city elders, to give Glasgow city centre a more comprehensive face-lift than any previously attempted in Europe.

Basing their aims on the studies of McKinsey and Co and Dr Gordon Cullen, an eminent Scottish planner, Glasgow Action's programme is quite startling. Just a few of its details are the transportation of an entire church, designed by Alexander 'Greek' Thomson (one of Glasgow's favourite sons, after Rennie Mackintosh) from the Gorbals to the city centre, where it will form one side of a vast new square.

There is to be an 'urban village' where St Enoch's railway station once stood, a huge canopy covering part of it, and a chain of differing environments – craft villages, entertainment areas and so on – to be built alongside the Clyde.

When I viewed these plans I was both flabbergasted and sceptical. Where would the money come from? Would there be the demand? Both questions were answered calmly. Private investment would pay for most of the redevelopment and, if the success of Gear is anything to go by, the response will be forthcoming.

But my third doubt was the strongest. Glasgow is, for me, two cities. There is the rough, hard-drinking and down-to-earth Glasgow, centred on areas where shops are boarded up, graffiti is com-

*East End Glasgow: real Jimmys and aspiring Yuppies share the same patch*

mon, especially that aimed at the hated 'polis', and where football loyalists of Celtic and Rangers fight out their supposed Catholic and Protestant differences in freezing weather wearing T-shirts and ragged silk scarves.

One English businesswoman living in Glasgow told me how she always feels an undercurrent of crime. There is, she says, a constant stream of people offering to sell stolen goods. Everyone seems to have a friend 'inside' or someone who had committed a recent act of violence.

Then there is the almost idyllic calm of suburbs like Broomhill and Pollokshields, where freshly scrubbed tenements are full of potted plants and have BMWs parked outside. This is the Glasgow I recognise when I'm told that the city has more parkland per head of the population than any other British city.

One factor does unite the Glaswegian character, I was told. They will be friendly on a superficial level, but underneath know exactly what they want and will not take long to come to the point. I met several immigrants who loved Glasgow but found its people niggardly or brusque. Otherwise, the suburban stone mansions and the leafy, quiet streets are components of another city, a million miles away from the dreadful Basil Spence highrise blocks in the Gorbals and the barren 1960s estates where sparrows cough and the grass bristles with broken glass.

So what will Glasgow Action's multi-million pound programme do for the under-privileged of the city? Will Jimmy (as every Glasgow man is called) really give a hoot for some arty-crafty, synthesised world where wine replaces his favourite 'heavy' and the infamous Paddy's Market is transformed into a gentrified bazaar?

Again there came a good answer. *"We are definitely not trying to be twee,"* says David Macdonald. Dr Cullen says that Glasgow is not pretentious: *"It is tough and it rains a lot. It is like a car without an ignition, suffering from implosion."*

Glasgow Action, it is suggested, will restore Jimmy's pride in the city, and it may even help towards finding him a job, perhaps by attracting more tourists (a major failing recently), perhaps by succeeding in its business aims.

*"This is a campaign for a real city,"* says Dr Cullen.

So I am impressed. Very impressed. And what is more I think Glasgow really will carry out its grandiose plans. Everyone I met was so convinced,

*The infamous Gorbals*

so thoughtful. And they all love the place. In David Daiches' excellent history of Glasgow there is a quote from an American who described Glasgow at the turn of the century as *"the most aggressively efficient city in Great Britain."*

I believe that with the success of Gear and the determination of Glasgow Action, that description may well be appropriate today. It is certainly the most aggressively optimistic city I have ever visited, and this is the nearest I have ever come to writing a publicity handout.

## WHERE TO STAY

Although I cannot profess to ever having received that oft-quoted Scottish form of welcome: *"You'll have had your tea?"*, I can say that my experience of Glasgow hotels has led me to believe that some of them do need a bit of stirring.

I could find no fault with the rooms or standards at the Trust House Forte **Albany** (Bothwell Street; tel: 041 248 2656; telex: 77440, until one night I waited for two hours for a very simple room service order. Added to the fact that my usual lifeline was absent – there were no local telephone directories in the room – I harboured a very slight sense of aggravation, alleviated only as I departed by the efficiency of a young hall porter.

I should point out, however, that the Albany does possess a fine restaurant and carvery, which for ten years after its opening in 1973 was the only four-star establishment in the centre. Its only inconvenience as far as I could tell was its limited parking facilities. Single £46; double £56; suites £120 to £160.

Since 1982, though, the Albany has been eclipsed by the nearby **Holiday Inn** (Argyle Street; tel: 226 5577; telex: 77734), Glasgow's most up-to-date city centre hotel. Just off the M8 turnoff, the Holiday Inn costs marginally more than the Albany, but there is ample parking, a sauna, four squash courts, a gym, an indoor pool, free in-house films and two good restaurants. Surprising as it may seem, it is also Glasgow's most sophisticated hotel, and that is to cast neither a slur upon the city nor the rest of the Holiday Inns. Single £52; double £57; suites £80-£143, not including VAT.

If the Holiday Inn leads the field because it is the newest purpose-built hotel in Glasgow, the newly-refurbished and confusingly tiled **Hospitality Inn** (Cambridge Street; tel: 332 3311; telex: 77334) merits a mention if only for attempting the same level of pseudo-transatlantic luxury on a slightly smaller scale.

Formerly the Skeandhu, the Hospitality Inn actually has more rooms than any other Scottish hotel, but its public areas are relatively compressed. With good parking facilities and a central location – a few yards from Sauchiehall Street – at £39.50 for a single room I would rate this as the best deal in the city. However, this is no secret and the hotel is very popular, so book well ahead. Double £50; suites £100.

Two other central hotels have a more traditional ambience commanding different loyalties. The **Central Hotel** (Gordon Street; tel: 221 9680; telex: 777771) is one of the few surviving Victorian railway hotels, and despite slipping behind the field in recent years – its once opulent Malmaison restaurant is now closed – with its sweeping staircase and imposing exterior it is still my favourite British station hotel. Singles are from £37.50 with bath; double £46; suites £56-£70.

The **Diplomat** (George Square; tel: 332 6711; telex: 777334), formerly the North British, has the finest setting (if you have a room at the front) and has been extensively remodelled. There is a lively café-bar with an unusually imaginative carvery adjacent. Single £42; double £46, including VAT and service.

Scotland's biggest hotel chain, though, is Stakis, who run six establishments in Glasgow alone. The **Stakis Ingram** (Ingram Street; tel: 248 4401; telex: 776470) is small and efficient, but I prefer their hotels just out of the city centre. Single £45; double £52, including breakfast, VAT and service.

The **Grosvenor** (Great Western Road; tel: 339 8811; telex: 776277) is the most impressive, set in a restored Victorian terrace opposite Paxton's Botanic Gardens, a two-minute drive from the centre. The hotel was badly damaged in a fire several years ago but thankfully the refurbishment has not masked some of the building's more elegant proportions. It is in many ways a typical Glasgow establishment. Old values are preserved up front, but the business at the back is all modern. Single £51; double £60. Weekend prices are cheaper and include breakfast.

The **Stakis Pond** (Great Western Road; tel: 334 8161), has much to recommend it, including a light and tastefully finished indoor pool (tailor-made rather than a basement afterthought), good parking and simple, but adequate, rooms from £42 for a single. And if I may make a personal note: pleasure of pleasures, the decor has not been selected by a colour blind consultant with a fetish for florid fabrics.

This, sadly was the fate of the **Stakis Normandy** (Inchinnan Road, Renfrew; tel: 886 4100; telex: 778897), an otherwise reliable hotel near Glasgow airport. But if painful interiors do not bother you, and you need to be close to the airport, I would opt for the Normandy and its quieter setting at £42 per night including breakfast, rather than the Trust House Forte **Excelsior** (tel: 887 1212; telex: 777733) which is a matter of 30 yards from the airport's arrivals terminal.

Sound is not a major problem at the Excelsior, however, and facilities are fine, but you pay another £5 or so to stay there and the parking is limited. Some may call it a bed factory for use of aircrews and unimaginative businessmen, but if you have a 7a.m. shuttle flight to catch, the Excelsior has obvious attractions. And I know of no other airport hotel so close to the check-in desk.

Otherwise, Glasgow is so small and the airport so close to the centre – ten minutes in a fast taxi – that unless timing, or business in Renfrew, Paisley and westwards dictates otherwise, I would recommend leaving the airport area.

Finally, my two favourite Glasgow gems. In the fashionable West End, the **White House** (Cleveden Crescent; tel: 339 9375; telex: 777582) is a truly independent establishment in a quiet,

*George Square: hub of municipal munificence*

dignified, Adam-style Georgian terrace. Among the 32 suites, mostly traditional, is one hi-tech suite of ample dimensions complete with kitchen, video, stereo and bathroom for a mere £51 a night. Some of the suites are large enough to hold decent-sized business meetings. Although there is no restaurant or bar, each suite has full room service and the hotel, which was Glasgow's only entry in the two most recent *Good Hotel Guides,* has a reciprocal arrangement with the Rogano and Buttery restaurants. Single £35; double £42; suites £51-£65.

I conclude, one eye on the reddening sunset, the other on a warming bottle of Glenmorangie, with a hotel which at first glance may appear to attract honeymooners more than serious businessmen. It overlooks the Clyde and the Lomond Hills, has rooms named after birds, and it is a good 20 minute drive from the centre of Glasgow. **Gleddoch House** (Langbank; tel: 047 554 711; telex: 779801) in Langbank was originally the 1927 mansion of the Lithgow shipbuilding family. It has 20 rooms and an outstanding restaurant. Outdoor enthusiasts should be delighted to hear that there is an 18-hole golf course and country club with stables, sauna, snooker and squash facilities within the hotel grounds. Single £51-£58; double £73; suites £89. Prices include VAT, service and breakfast. There are also weekend reductions.

Although taxis into Glasgow add another £8 per trip, personally I would put up with the inconvenience. Gleddoch House is exactly how some Americans must idealise their picture of Scotland; a warm retreat set in a rolling landscape. One spirited jaunt out into the surrounding hills and you'll have earned your tea indeed.

# WHERE TO EAT

"*Glaswegians just love to eat out,*" I was informed by a local Foodie, after trying unsuccessfully to find a table at three different restaurants on a Friday night. I was also told that when the Holiday Inn hotel opened in 1982 the management were somewhat taken aback by the number of Glaswegians coming in to try the hotel café and restaurant. In the end they had to expand their facilities to cope with the unexpected demand.

Part of this tradition for eating out must surely go back to the numerous tea houses which flourished under a certain Miss Cranston's inspiration in Glasgow during early 20th century. Her **Willow Tea Room** (217 Sauchiehall Street; tel: 332 0521), designed by Rennie Mackintosh, is about the only survivor of this boom, but its successors are the trendy café-bars which, thanks to Scotland's reform of the licensing laws a few years ago, now stay open all day.

My favourite café-bar is the **Café Noir** on Queen Street. It is unashamedly synthetic and full of poseurs, but is always thriving and full of attractive Yuppies. **Café Zazou** (tel: 248 3553) on the corner of York and Argyle is favoured more by after hours businessmen. I would also recommend **Café Gandolfi** (tel: 552 6813) in Albion Street.

Some Glasgow restaurants have won me over simply for their setting and decor. For example, drinks on the terrace at **Gleddoch House** (Langbank; tel: 047 554 711) overlooking the Clyde, followed by lunch or dinner, is a rare Glasgow indulgence. It takes about 15 minutes to drive out there from the centre, but it's just the place to win over foreign clients, even if the *Good Food Guide* did drop it from their latest list because of a change in the kitchen.

Gleddoch House, in common with several reputed Glasgow restaurants, has learnt the marketability of pure Scottish cuisine: Argyle salmon, Aberdeen beef, Highland deer, atholl brose, woodland pigeon, cock-a-leekie and so on. This is all immensely gratifying for a Londoner tired of the usual conceits, even if the names of some dishes are only meant to enliven essentially home-cooked old favourites.

In fact, I found several Glasgow restaurants to be very inventive, not altogether surprising in a city which claims to have invented the now ubiquitous sandwich bar in the mid-19th century. At the awkwardly titled **Ubiquitous Chip** (Ashton Lane; tel: 334 5007) – chips used to be served with everything in Glasgow but never at this place – almost every dish was the chef's own invention, and I can testify to the freshness of their produce. Fish and seafood figure prominently – I enjoyed monkfish from Oban in a lightly curried sauterne sauce – but you can also indulge in other local feasties such as haggis (well at least I can say that I've tried it), Ayrshire roe deer or Scotch Lamb.

The Chip is indeed a most unusual restaurant, most of it being in the covered courtyard of an old joinery workshop, now disguised with greenery and fountains. The effect is not a bit chichi, and customers do linger under the influence of all those negative ions, helped no doubt by a colossal wine list which includes 101 different types of Scotch. The record for indulgence, I'm told, belongs to three businessmen who came for lunch and departed at 9.30p.m.

The Chip's local rival is **Poachers** (Ruthven Lane, tel: 339 0932), situated in a converted 1870 farmhouse off Byres Road. Some reports put Poachers ahead of the Chip nowadays, but, except to say that I prefer the desserts at Poachers, I'm going to duck out of a judgement. I like both restaurants enormously, and I can even forgive Poachers its blue plastic table covers.

Faced with a decision, I might prefer the Chip at lunchtime and Poachers in the evening. The **Buttery** (Argyle Street; tel: 221 8188), alternatively, is somehow a moodier place: much more serious (and expensive, at around £25 a head), with the accent on French cuisine.

Also set in a restored Victorian building, the Buttery's only drawback is its location, stranded at the end of Argyle Street, on the wrong side of the motorway. And, unless you are staying at the nearby Holiday Inn, a taxi is definitely called for.

Downstairs at the Buttery is the very dark and compact **Belfry,** where the food is simpler – but no less good – and the low ceilings and scattered artefacts seem to have been soaked in a century of rich cooking juices. With jazz in the background it is hard to believe one is slap bang in the middle of a 1960s concrete jungle.

I was overjoyed with the interior of **Rogano's** (Exchange Place; tel: 248 4055), possibly Glasgow's best-loved institution. Before its demise in the 1970s, Rogano's was a family-run bar and restaurant specialising in seafood. Every middle-class Glasgow kid went there. Recently restored to its full art deco glory – the outside is perfectly understated, while inside is plush and intricate – Rogano's has two thoroughly modern menus, one being eclectic enough to satisfy half the Northern hemisphere.

More traditional, more formal, but to my mind infinitely less interesting, is the **Ambassador** (Blythswood Square; tel: 221 2034) which has a predictably 'fine' Continental menu and fine prices to match.

For the more formal occasion I would choose instead either the Albany Hotel's **Four Season's** restaurant (tel: 248 2656) or the Stakis **Grosvenor Hotel** (tel: 339 8811). I have also heard favourable comments on **La Provençale** (Royal Exchange; tel: 221 0798).

For Indian food, all roads lead to Gibson Street, where a mixture of students and directors appear to prefer the **Shish Mahal** among several others. Nearby **Jo's Garage** is good for hearty breakfasts, while at the Charing Cross end of Sauchiehall Street there are a few good Chinese Restaurants, the **Lun Fung** (tel: 221 4205) being favoured for its dim sum.

But try the taste of Scotland first, if only because that is the course most of Glasgow's top restaurants are following and therefore competition has raised standards to a high level. Whether this is maintained depends, I fear, not so much on future demand as the management's abilities to cope with the recent crushing rates revaluation. One Glasgow restaurant discovered that its annual rates bill was to rise from £9,000 per annum to £22,000. No matter how fine their chefs may be, I cannot foresee Glasgow's restaurants surviving this blow unscathed.

# NIGHT LIFE

A joke: one Glaswegian trips over a man lying prostrate on the pavement. *"Is he drunk?"* asks a passer-by. *"No"*, comes the reply, *"I just saw him move."*

It was like that for years, I was told by a lifelong Glaswegian resident. Drunks and vagrants were everywhere. In one survey a century ago it was discovered that within one area of a few hundred square yards in central Glasgow there were approximately 200 brothels and 150 shebeens, or illegal drinking houses.

Nowadays Glasgow is a different place. The reformed licensing laws have discarded the 1915 restrictions on afternoon drinking so that licensed premises in Scotland now stay open from morning till night. Thus a dilemma: the breweries say that alcoholism has decreased, since customers no longer have to cram in their boozing to limited hours. Conversely, the medical profession cites figures to show that alcohol abuse has increased since 1980. But whoever is right, one consequence of the law reform has been a decrease in the number of drunks on Glasgow's streets. They can sit all day and pickle themselves without ever having to wander onto the streets before midnight.

I dislike Glasgow pubs a great deal. Those that had any old world charm have either been cocooned in formica and cheap carpets or transformed into pretentious-sounding wine bars. Compared with some of Edinburgh's treasures, Glasgow pubs tend to be dark, almost windowless, and in most cases tatty. Those that were recommended to me by locals were no better.

And so to the nightlife. Glasgow, in the words of one club owner, is a very brash city in which everyone likes to pose. For sure I saw more stylish boutiques there than I can recall in any other British city apart from London.

The sunshine boys and glam girls frequent a number of discos and clubs, the two most recommended being **Pzazz** (Royal Exchange Square), above Charlie Parkers, and for an older crowd (ie over 21) **Cardinal Folly,** which is in a converted Alexander 'Greek' Thompson church on Pitt Street.

The newest poseur's spot is **Fouquet's Wine Bar** (Renfield Street), set in an old shop basement where over the years apparently most Glasgow children were taken to be fitted up with new school uniforms. I would not eat there (too noisy) but it's a good bar.

The same applies to **Harvey's,** a slick joint on Park Terrace in the West End. The setting is charming and the atmosphere friendly.

Other bars worth a try are **The Nile** (West Nile Street), the **Centre Court** and **Nicos,** both on Sauchiehall Street (where all the discos are centred) and **Carruthers** (Hope Street), where a media crowd gathers after hours.

Theatre life in Glasgow is thriving and forever growing in the shadows of neighbouring Edinburgh, and I would strongly recommend checking out the **Tron Theatre** (Trongate), where, apart from some interesting plays and shows, there is an informal and welcoming bar and café. And, like several favourite haunts of Glasgow's young professional middle-classes, the Tron has live jazz on a Sunday.

Live floor shows, however, you won't find. Apart from a few sauna/massage parlours and the shivering, statuesque figures of prostitutes on many a city centre street corner, Glasgow is a puritanical city. Apart from wining and dining the only other vice significantly catered for is gambling. There are several smart casinos: **Chevalier** (Hope Street) the **Regency,** (Waterloo Street) and the **Princes** (Sauchiehall Street), for instance.

# GETTING AROUND

For such a relatively compact city Glasgow can be geographically confusing. It used to be simply a question of whether you were on the North or South side of the River Clyde, which flows diagonally across the city from North West to South East.

Then in 1973 the central Clydeside Expressway opened cutting through the city from East to West and linking with the M8 motorway, which runs in the same direction but cuts across the Clyde at the impressive Kingston Bridge.

Once you get the hang of these divides, Glasgow is a doddle. The city centre is in most parts organised on an orderly grid system, and is small enough to be able to walk from end to end in a leisurely half hour.

Unless your visit takes you beyond the centre, car-hire would be pointless. Taxis are plentiful – although I found private mini-cabs booked from hotels to be erratic – and cheap. A cab to the airport costs about £6 and takes 10-15 minutes.

For quick journeys around the centre you should try the Glasgow subway, known locally as the Clockwork Orange. It runs in a circle and each train has only two small carriages. It used to be antiquated, dirty but cute. A £54 million modernisation programme now puts it on par with any of Europe's subway systems.

To see what it was like on the subway before 1977, take the excellent city bus tour for £3 from Enoch Square, included in which is a stop-off at the fascinating transport museum. And going over the Kingston Bridge on the top of a double decker bus, incidentally, rates as a spectacular and heart-stopping experience.

*The Clyde: once written off as an open sewer but now the fish are coming back*

# Hamburg

**West Germany's largest city has sloughed off the infamy of the 60s when it was all vice, violence and ugly excitement. Hamburg has regained control of its image and is once again a green, pleasant and prosperous place.**

**By Michael Scott**

The worst thing that happened to Hamburg since the war was when a struggling British pop group called the Beatles came to town in 1961.

They were just cheap labour to keep the beat going on the Reeperbahn . . . the sleazy street for the sailors and low-lifers of Germany's biggest port.

As the Beatles' fame proceeded to transcend anybody's wildest imaginings, so too did the reputation of the Reeperbahn transcend everything else about Hamburg. Compressed by the popular press into a few words, Hamburg became a big bad city of vice and violence, prostitutes and pill-poppers, and ugly, exciting streets.

An easy image for the world to assimilate, and constantly reinforced in every language. Also grossly distorted.

It's a bit like taking a Time Square tart to represent all New York womanhood; or seeing only Soho, and then imagining that you know London.

For Hamburg could hardly be more unlike its grimy image. It is calm, self-possessed, and indeed a green and beautiful city, whose prosperous and conservative inhabitants are rather smug about their strong sense of history and identity.

There is even a word for it: *'Hanseatic'*, which is used both as an official title (the Free and Hanseatic City of Hamburg); and, less formally, to sum up a way of thinking that includes extreme bourgeois conservatism, patrician protectionism, a rare respect for gentlemanly conduct; and – rather incongruously – tremendous tolerance. Hence the open sinfulness of the Reeperbahn – and the distinctly left-of-centre politics.

At root Hanseatic implies a rather sober-sided philosophy, that dates back to the Hanseatic League. This was an alliance of north German towns, formed to protect and control trade. It was at its most powerful in the 15th century, numbering among its chores the elimination of North Sea pirates, some of whom were brought back to Hamburg to be executed. A very Hanseatic act, perhaps.

Through the succeeding centuries, Hamburg bought off a challenge from the Danes and sought alliances with the Prussians and Saxons, all the while retaining their republican city-state independence, and continuing to grow fat on the fruits of the port. Also very Hanseatic.

And so it is too that these steadfast and rather dour burgers, with high cheekbones and an air of reserve, should have retained their republican independence right through to modern times. Along with nearby Bremen, Hamburg is one of a pair of West German city-states represented in the federal parliament (West Berlin makes a trio, but is regarded rather as an involuntary off-shore island).

It is Hanseatic to be trustworthy in business, it is Hanseatic to be standoffish with strangers. It is even Hanseatic to claim that Hamburgers are more like the English than any other nation – an oft-repeated assertion that would have some validity but for the local lack of a sense of the absurd. (Unless this claim itself is an abstruse example of Hanseatic humour?) And it is certainly Hanseatic to be prosperous, to be proud of the beauty of Hamburg, and to live a well-ordered middle-class life in a green and pleasant suburb.

But today's Hamburg faces not exactly a crisis, but certainly unaccustomed financial discomfort. At around ten per cent, unemployment is roughly two per cent higher than the German national average, and a lethargic city government seems unable to halt the decline.

With real reason now to look glum, the people of Hamburg seem bewildered at the price they're paying for generations of accumulated Hanseatic complacency.

Their very real prosperity was built on ships, shipping, and the resulting trade and commerce (Hamburg is not, contrary to another popular misconception, an industrial city). And their deep-rooted resistance to change left them ill-prepared when maritime decline saw first the passenger liners disappear, then the dockers thrown out of work by containerisation, and finally the ship-building contracts dwindle in the face of Far Eastern competition.

A further blow is the result of the city-state's inevitably compact dimensions . . . 25 miles across at its broadest, Hamburg borders Schleswig Holstein to the north and Nedersachsen to the south.

*Lone Gothic spire amid the concrete*

Both of these rural areas enjoy lower rates and taxes as well as government subsidies which have attracted most of the region's new industry, and tempted a fair number of Hamburg concerns (including printing works) to move the short distance out of town . . . still enjoying the amenities and labour pool, but not contributing to the city's covers.

(It is entirely Hanseatic that people who do move out are mildly despised. *"If I moved 500 metres to the west,"* a senior executive told me, *"I would be out of Hamburg and into Pinneberg, and I would save 50 per cent on my rates and car tax."* So why didn't he move? He laughed. *"Because then instead of HH (Hansestadt Hamburg), my car numberplate would be PI. Ha! We call them 'Provincial Idiots'."*)

Not that any of the above should imply a port brought to its knees, in the manner of Liverpool. Hamburg is still full of shiny cars and expensive shops, and all but a few of the suburbs are smartly painted.

But the reason for concern is that there is no easy way out. *"Electronics? Everyone in the world is looking to electronics to lead the revival. Unless we can find some new application or technique of our own, I believe we have to look for something different,"* the

*Shoppers take a coffee break*

same executive said.

Maybe that's where the city's future lies. A very relevant and instructive example came at the roof-wetting ceremony for a Hamburg hotel. The Elysée is a modern luxury-class 300-bedder which has come into existence through the entrepreneurial spirit of one Eugene Block.

Now Herr Block is a millionaire, self-made due to the success of his Block House chain of steak-houses. As it is also very unHanseatic to be a self-made man to Hamburg's establishment the whole venture was tinged with suspicion. The hotel was bulldozed through with unseemly haste, and what is more, Herr Block plucked the management from his steak-house chain, instead of drawing from the existing pool of hotel talent. Heresy!

At the roof-wetting ceremony – all oompah-band and beer for the builders – the hotel's backer, Mr Robert Vogel, made an impassioned speech complaining at the delays imposed between planning the hotel and obtaining permission to build it. The dragging feet of bureaucracy, he said, were keeping new investment out of Hamburg.

A slightly nonplussed city senator was left to reply to the speech, and was forced to agree that forward planning was perhaps just a little bit inert.

Mr Block may be well ahead of the game, here, even though the Hanseatic reaction to a self-made man is to wait for him to 'run his head through the wall' (no German ever seems without a proverb for every eventuality). The reason is that one of the only real areas of growth immediately obvious is in tourism and increased business travel. For while it has been languishing without attempting to change its tarnished and inaccurate international image, Hamburg has nevertheless remained the only 'mainland' German city with charm, character, tradition and beauty intact enough to compare with Munich. Something, indeed, of a sleeping beauty.

Which is where you come in. Hamburg has already missed opportunities by promoting its excellent exhibition facilities poorly – too many local shows, not enough international ones. Now a new push has begun, not only as an incentive destination, especially in the United States.

Hamburg is on the junction between the Elbe and Alster rivers. The former loops its way down from Czechoslovakia, past Prague, and then into East Germany via Dresden. By the time it reaches its tidal reaches at Hamburg, it has become the most polluted river in Europe. The Hanseatic view of this is to blame the East German's dirty industrial habits. *"They want us to pay for anti-pollution equipment,"* a spokesman for the information bureau told me. Dr Rudolf Leonhardt, a senior journalist on *Die Zeit*, one of Hamburg's influential national Sunday papers, takes a less self-satisfied attitude. *"People like to blame the DDR, but that's an excuse. We contribute plenty to the pollution."*

The Alster, on the other hand, is a short stream with its source in the fresh countryside north of Hamburg, and it meanders prettily through the smart suburbs before making the Alster lake – principal and central feature of Hamburg.

The foot of the Alster lake defines the northern limits of the city centre, and it stretches northwards for two miles, lined on both sides by boulevards of imposing buildings – superbly traditional old hotels, embassies (Hamburg has more than any other European city), exclusive clubs, restaurants, parks and generous town houses that reek of old maritime money.

In the summer, the Alster is dotted with the sails of yachts and wind-surfers, while ferries and tourist boats make their way along the shores. And in the colder winters it freezes over, and energetic Hamburgers can skate to work. The Alster is a landmark, a beauty spot, a thoroughfare, and the heart of Hamburg.

The city runs south from the foot of the lake: first the shopping area, with its glassed-in walkways and boulevards, bulging with luxury goods; then the Rathaus square – said by the Hamburgers to rival St Mark's square in Venice; then the central business district, and finally the Gothic warehouses of the old spice and coffee trade.

The Royal Navy have a parking lot on the north side of the Elbe: the main industrial container port is on the south side, with bleak warehouses stretching away out of site.

Some surprising facts: the central area of Hamburg is built on piles, like Venice, and is criss-crossed by canals; and though these waterways are less numerous than in Venice, Hamburg does however have more bridges than the jewel of the Adriatic. Then again, it's much bigger than Venice, so unless you stray into the southern marshlands, stay in the port or near the Alster, you don't actually feel the presence of so much water.

Except, of course, in the Hanseatic mode of speech. Maritime metaphors crop up continually: *"The Haerlin family are the owners of the ship, Herr Prantner is the captain, I am the chief engineer,"* (a director of the *Vier Jahreszeiten Hotel,* explaining how the private ownership was arranged); *"There is only one captain, but he has many lieutenants,"* (Mr Leonhardt, with the reason why so staunchly conservative a town should have socialist politics); *"You don't put up your sails until you've smelt the wind,"* (a passing comment about the precipitate planning of the Elysée hotel).

The business quarter comprises not only the old shipping, commercial and insurance interests upon which the city's prosperity was founded, but also the newspaper and magazine offices that make Hamburg the media centre of Germany. This pre-eminence in communication dates from after the war. It started when the British forces of occupation were quick to grant licences to print newspapers (an operation carefully controlled by the Psychological Warfare Unit), was reinforced when the film studios that had formerly been in Berlin moved across, and strengthened further by the establishment of the first TV centre (Hamburg still provides the national TV news).

Today, scores of publishing houses include such giants as Axel Springer, Gruner + Jahr, Heinrich Bauer and Jahreszeiten Verlag; and Hamburg accounts for roughly 40 per cent of the audited circulation of Germany's daily and weekly newspapers. Big dailies include *Die Welt* and *Bild-Zeitung.* Illustrated newsy weeklies in Germany exceed newspaper circulations with titles such as *Stern, Der Spiegel* and *Hörzu* published in Hamburg.

The city centre is compact, meaner streets and plush suburbs alternately radiating outwards. St Pauli, home of the Reeperbahn, is next west, followed by Altona, an old Danish town that is still a centre of residential and visiting Danes. Furthest west is the fashionable suburb of Blankenese, whose quaint winding streets run up a hill overlooking the big ships passing up the Elbe.

Another arm of the city extends north, through the fashionable suburbs of Eppendorf and Poppenbüttel, past the airport and towards the recent industrial development.

The city doesn't stop at its borders, however, but sprawls out to the countryside beyond, conurbation having swallowed up villages to give much of Hamburg the sort of village character of London.

Thus, although you never really need to leave the area around the Alster and St Pauli to find every kind of entertainment, there are some very excellent restaurants and innumerable rather English pubs out in the suburbs.

This of course serves to reinforce the Hanseatic belief that they are like the English. So too does their mentality of holding home as castle. You are unlikely to be invited into a business colleague's domestic life: their entertaining will be done in one of the many restaurants. No cause for complaint, though, for generations of a high standard of living have left the Hamburgers with high criteria, and the standard is excellent.

The same thing applies to the hundreds of foreign restaurants, from Algerian to Vietnamese – the long way round. This mixture of sub-cultures is only to be expected in an ancient port, but of course the foreign population has been much swelled in recent years by the arrival of the families of the *Gastarbeiter.*

As Hamburg has rather more than the national average share of imported foreign labour, it would seem likely that – at a time of rising unemployment – the Germans would look awry at the problem they had created. Some do, but Hanseatic tolerance has left room for the other point of view: as expressed by Dr Leonhardt: *"When Germans speak of* Gastarbeiter, *they mean Turks. And because Ger-*

*Despite its saucy image Hamburg has its sedate side*

*many has no colonial or commonwealth past, they are not accustomed to such numbers of foreigners. But the truth is that there are plenty of dirty jobs that the Germans would never do for themselves – so it is a fallacy to blame the* Gastarbeiter *for unemployment."*

The Hamburgers like to think of themselves as cold and reserved, but it is not a view shared by those who came to the city as adults. *"I found it harder to make friends in southern Germany than I did here,"* said one businessman's wife, happily settled after only three years in Eppendorf. *"The people are quiet and courteous, but very warm underneath it."* She was not the only person to repeat the same view.

And there is certainly warmth towards English speaking people. A high proportion of the citizens, especially the younger Hamburgers, speak excellent English; trade and press links are also strong. There is even an Anglo-German club, members only, near the US Embassy.

A surprising city, then, closer geographically, in appearance, and in many aspects of character to Amsterdam and Copenhagen than to Stuttgart and Munich. And a city so steeped in living tradition that when its image gets out of control it is too reserved to do anything about it.

After all, even the notorious Reeperbahn is a street with a history. As another Hamburg information office spokesman put it to me: *"Prostitutes have been in the St Pauli district for more than 150 years."* I immediately began to look for an opportunity to add: *"Yes, and some of them look like it."* But since most of the flesh for hire in the streets and car-park-like Kontakthalle of the world's most sinful street look as though they should be doing their homework instead, the chance did not present itself.

Finally, lest that mention of the Reeperbahn should reawaken the image of a city where anything goes, a cameo at a pedestrian crossing on a busy Saturday morning. There were no cars on the intersection, but the horde of pedestrians obediently awaited a green light before crossing the road. People behave like that in Germany, and you are advised to do the same, to avoid the chance of an on the spot fine.

Suddenly, a youth, a pubescent punk, broke ranks, and darted across the road.

He was met on the other side by an irate elderly gentleman in a leather overcoat who embarked on a violent torrent of abuse, looking round from time to time as if to quell any other possible breaches of discipline. And the youth hung his half-shaven head and took his punishment like a man. So *that's* what Hanseatic means.

# WHERE TO STAY

Hamburg is generously supplied with hotels both ancient and modern, many dating back to the days when the great passenger liners plied the Atlantic, depositing loads of leisured passengers, and their retinue of servants. There is also the usual complement of upstart US-style hotels.

With rather less seasonal variation than the fair city of Frankfurt and the tourist centre of Munich, availability is relatively good, and it is not usually necessary to book more than a week or two in advance.

Reflecting the predominance of business travellers, the old-fashioned hotels that offer a choice tend to have more single rooms than doubles, and have a quick turnover, with an average stay of about 1.2 nights. And it is extremely rare to find a hotel employee of any level who does not speak English.

Hamburg's top hotel is reckoned by some guides as the best hotel in the world, and certainly the best in Europe. It is the family-owned **Vier Jahreszeiten** (Four Seasons – Neuer Jungfernstieg 9-14; tel: 34941; telex: 211629). Dating back to 1895, and owned by the Haerlin shipping family, it is commandingly placed alongside the shopping district overlooking the foot of the Binnenalster lake, a distinctly non-crumbling monument to the best of the good old days.

Certainly grand, it is also – well not exactly personal, but with the easy formality and polish of an exclusive club. Antique furniture, a tinkling pianist in the lobby lounge (where the dowagers of other old shipping families come to eat too much cake of a winter afternoon), and it has a policy of *decreasing* the present number of 295 beds to 250, so as to improve the service still further.

In such a pre-eminent position, the Four Seasons does not feel threatened by the rising tide of Ramadas etc. There will always be a Rolls-Royce market, and they have first call on it.

They score by providing service forgotten elsewhere, with 350 staff for a possible maximum of 290 guests. And they mean Service. For instance, minibars are not provided – but there are bells in each room that will summon room service (or a maid, or a porter) at once.

It also has one of the best restaurants in town. Single Dm195-280; twin Dm295-390; alcove double Dm400-495; suites from Dm495; breakfast – served all day – extra. Be warned that both the restaurant and grill close at 10p.m., with only the 'late-supper room' left open.

In some ways, its only real rival is a nicer hotel. The 75-year-old **Atlantic Hotel** (An der Alster, 72-79; tel: 248 001; telex: 2163297) is across the Alster, on the shore of the main lake. Recently sold to Lufthansa in partnership with Arab interests and with a ballroom big enough for 1,100 people, conference facilities for up to 450, and enormous carpeted corridors strewn about with fine furniture, it takes a close and worthy second place.

The rooms overlooking the lake which have quadruple glazing to muffle traffic noise fall short of the standard of the Four Seasons. But the hotel's character means that other parts are a bit pokey. The back rooms were for the retinue of domestic servants brought by the passengers from across the Atlantic. And though small rooms have been connected up to make entirely charming alcove bedrooms, the corridors remain narrow. Nor is the service up to the exceptional standards of the Four Seasons – a bit slower in every way. Full complement of restaurants, however, plus an extremely elegant pillared courtyard where on summer Friday nights there's a popular buffet at Dm65 all in. Single from Dm234 to 284; double from Dm309 to 369; suites from Dm380.

Next comes the chains, most of which are familiar and predictable (not that this is necessarily a bad thing).

The **Inter-Continental** (Fontenay 10; tel: 414 150; telex: 211099/217073) has one unique feature – Hamburg's only casino on its ninth floor. It has a fitness centre with a pool on a verandah, enclosed in winter; fine views over the Alster to the Atlantic Hotel, especially from the roof top gourmet restaurant. Single Dm225-275; double Dm270-320; suites from Dm640; breakfast extra.

The **C-P Pacific Plaza** (Hamburg Plaza-Marseillerstrasse 2; tel: 35 020; telex: 214 400) is the tallest and (at 570 rooms) the biggest hotel in Hamburg. It has the foremost hotel disco, on the 26th floor, and is directly across the Planten und Blomen park from the Congress and Trade Fair (Messe) centres. Its modern architecture imposes on the skyline and still, after more than 13 years,

*The Atlantic hotel overlooks the Alster lake*

some Hamburgers look askance. Single Dm188 to 258; double Dm246-316; suites from Dm400, (and good deals available in July/August and December/January, low seasons).

By far the most aggressive of the chains is the new **Ramada Renaissance** (Grosse Bleichen; tel: 349 180; telex: 2162983) in a prime (if not picturesque) site in the middle of town, and backing onto the Hansa Viertel arcade. Creative and aggressive marketing has won it the respect of its established rivals as well as awards within the group. Features include an award-winning **Neue Deutsche Küchen** restaurant; an airline-style Club class, with a wing of its own, special reception, houris to unpack for you and perform other less intimate wifely services, and free drinks – all for a Dm40 supplement; and 'VI Lady', which caters for the much-neglected female business traveller.

It's also housed behind the authentic-looking but partly reconstructed facade of an historic building, so it escapes from looking as thrusting and aggressive as it in fact is. Single Dm295-380; double Dm195-240; suites from Dm750.

One small step down the scale of rate and quality, there are a number of traditional hotels, many family-owned, and usually reflecting Hamburg's past as a passenger port.

A line of these faces the main station, along Kirchenallee: Phönix, Kronprinz and Continental are larger than Fürst Bismarck and Baumann's. The Big **Europäischer Hof** (Kirchenallee 45; tel: 248 171; telex: 2162493) is popular with British business visitors, with rates from Dm85 upwards.

But the newly refurbished **Reichshof** (Kirchenallee 34-36; tel: 248 330; telex: 2163396) is something of a special case. Until the arrival of the chains some 15 years ago, its 500 beds (now 320) made it the biggest hotel in Germany. It is family-owned, and independent even to the extent of having its own water supply, from a borehole beneath the basement. Also a splendid restaurant in the style of a cruise liner, a cocktail barman with over 50 years in the same bar, and a string of balcony rooms in the restaurant that can be closed off for small business meals and meetings. Single from Dm128 to 175; double from Dm186 to 228; suites from Dm250.

Final choice in this well-supported category is the **Prem** (An der Alster 9; tel: 241 726-28; telex 2163115). It is another big old hotel, and its lakeside position is as good as that of the Atlantic, while a new chef at the French restaurant has improved its local reputation. Single Dm 110-175; double Dm150-200.

Finally, the so-called 'hidden hotels' of Hamburg . . .and there are many such small but luxurious and elegant properties.

Best in town must be the **Garden Hotel,** (Magdalenenstrasse 60; tel: 449 959; telex: 212 621). It is among (indeed, was once one of) the fashionable town-houses in the exclusive suburb of Pöseldorf, behind the Inter-Continental. The rooms are small but luxurious: the conservatory/breakfast room is beautiful, and it attracts a lot of models and media people, despite having no restaurant. Single Dm120 to 180; double Dm160 to 280.

And the best out of town, in the expensive western suburb of Blakenese, is an absolute jewel. The **Strand Hotel Blankenese** (Strandweg 13; tel: 860 993/861 651; no telex) is a fully restored showpiece of *Jugendstiel* or (if you prefer) *art nouveau* architecture and furnishings. Owned by a couple, and with only 13 rooms, it is personal to the point of being intimate. The restaurant has a small but frequently changing menu, and the view from the very shores of the Elbe, to the great merchant ships steaming past, is splendid. It is about 20 to 30 minutes (and about Dm35) by taxi into town, along a busy commuter route, but there is also an efficient train service, or you could always choose to go by ferry, which takes about 30 minutes. Single Dm100-280; double Dm175-325.

Other names to look for in the same category are: **Thiele** (Sophienterrasse 10; tel: 455 054; single from Dm40), **Alsterblick** (Schwanewik 14; tel: 220 5592; from Dm42 single), **Am Nonnenstieg** (Nonnenstieg 11; tel: 479 066; from Dm70 single), **York** (Hofweg 19; tel: 220 2653; from Dm45 single), **Hase Heimhude** (Heimhuder strasse 16; tel: 442 721; from Dm55 single), and **Bellevue** (An der Alster 14; tel: 248 011; telex: 2162929; from Dm94 single), to name but a few.

The brand-new maverick **Elysée** (Rothenbaumchaussee 10; tel: 414 120; telex 17403202), an independent luxury class hotel with 300 rooms, is priced from Dm 170 per room, and Dm40 extra for double occupancy, suites cost from Dm400 to Dm1,200, depending on size. Situated between the Inter-Continental and the CP Plaza, it can hardly fail to make an impact on the hotel scene.

The Marriott group are also planning a big Hamburg property.

# WHERE TO EAT

German 'foodies' will be glad to tell you about *"das neue Deutsche Kochen"* - the new German cooking. Or, to give it its full title, the New North German Cooking Miracle.

Hamburg is the centre of this Teutonic *nouvelle cuisine,* and I advise you to try it at once. It derives its decorative two-tone sauces and mixture of flavours from the French version, but adds one very German element . . . big portions.

Hamburg also offers old German cooking, and plenty of it; a dab hand with rich tea cakes; a number of really excellent fish restaurants and no less than 800 foreign restaurants, including a number of French and Italian, as well as every other national cuisine you could imagine.

Quality and standards of service are tip-top, and prices not out of the way. Dm60 to 70 a head will buy you a superlative meal (without wine), and a small sacrifice in the standard of the restaurant will knock 25 or 30 per cent off the price.

One of the best *neue kochen* meals I've had was in the unlikely-seeming venue of the Ramada Renaissance restaurant, the **Noblesse,** where a green-leaf salad with lobster preceded a fillet of salmon couched in prawn meat and a two-tone chocolate mousse, made a meal to remember.

Other recommended hotel restaurants are the **Haerlin** restaurant at the Vier Jahreszeiten, the **Fontenay Grille** at the Inter-Continental, the **Reichshof** restaurant, and the French **La Mer** at the Prem, while out of town the small but perfectly formed *art nouveau* Blankenese Strand Hotel has an à la carte restaurant with a short but interesting *neue kochen* menu that changes frequently according to the fresh ingredients available.

Even some of the traditional restaurants mix elements of the new cooking with traditional hearty dishes. Try *Hasenrückenfilet* (fillet of hare's back), a strong, gamey meat usually served slightly bloody with a sweet sauce; or goose breast or leg, with red cabbage *(rotkraut)*. Flavoursome fare.

In town, **Peter Lembke** (tel: 243 290) (near the station) is quiet and very traditional; **Zum alten Rathaus** (243 290) is a popular lunch spot, mixing old with new. On the Elbe shores towards Blankenese, **Landhaus Scherrer** (tel: 880 1325), is excellent.

But one of the best things about Hamburg cuisine is the respect they show for the same North Sea fish that in England are turned to textureless pulp in batter.

Of the many fish restaurants a personal best is **Sellmer** (tel: 473 057) in Eppendorf, where dedication to quick service of freshly-cooked ingredients elevates the humble flatfish to a place in heaven.

As well as noble fish like pike-perch *(zander)* and salmon *(lachs)*, Sellmer also serves *labskaus* (or in Liverpool, simply 'scouse') – a sailor's hash of preserved ingredients made on becalmed sailing ships: salt beef, pickled herring, pickled beetroot and gherkins, mashed into a paste, and topped with a fried egg. Sellmer even debunks a local myth, that *aalsuppe* – a curious sweet-sour broth of pears, bacon fat and fish – is eel soup, which is the way it is usually translated. In fact, says the owner Herr Pauly, *"aal"* is Hamburg dialect for *"all"*, meaning a soup containing everything. Even so, he puts a slice of eel in to satisfy the customers.

Other notable fish venues include the **Überseebrück** (tel: 313 333), and the **Fischereihafen-Restaurant** (tel: 381 816), the former on the Elbe close to the city centre, the latter further west. And grandest of them all, **Schumann's Austernkeller** on the Alster (tel: 345 328), where the food is served in private rooms, richly decorated in various antique styles, and taking between two and 16 people. Discretion assured.

Talking of grand, the historic **Süllberg** restaurant (tel: 861 686) is in a turreted castle atop Hamburg's highest hill, overlooking Blankenese and the shipping on the Elbe. Several mahogany-panelled rooms cater for up to 380 people, with very good fish and traditional meats, and a sensational view.

Top French choices are **Le Canard** (tel: 460 4830) and **Le Délice** (tel: 327 727), afternoon coffee with ridiculously rich cakes is an experience at the **Vier Jahreszeiten** hotel's Bedemeier-style **Cafe Condi;** cheaper traditional food is good at the **Ratsweinkeller** (tel: 364 153) off the Rathaus square; and a pleasant bohemian beer-and-sausages atmosphere prevails at **Max & Consorten,** on Kirchenallee near the station.

Finally, amid all this rich food, who would expect to find the world's oldest vegetarian restaurant? Closed in the evening, the **Vegetarische Gaststätte & Cafe** (tel: 344 702) overlooks the Rathaus square, and offers an economical, refreshing and healthy lunch break from the pungent flavours and creamy sauces of both old and new German cooking.

*The world's oldest vegetarian restaurant*

# NIGHT LIFE

Rare indeed is the visiting businessman who doesn't take at least a look down the Reeperbahn. This is mainstreet Sin City and the shop window of the sex market of St Pauli that the locals call 'the human zoo'.

It is not a particularly pretty sight, and Hamburgers will try to direct you to the Hanseplatz in the St Georg area near the main station, where less commercialised and gang-ridden red-light delights are available.

Nevertheless, there can be few places in the world that offer the variety of the St Pauli district, so almost everyone ignores this advice.

The Reeperbahn has changed a lot since those well-reported Beatle days. The **Star Club** and the **Top Ten Club** are both now discos; the sailors have to a large extent disappeared, since turnround time in the container port is often only a few hours. Now sex kinos and video booths line the pavement. A number of bars offer a 'live show', but inevitably turn out to be clip joints: instead, you are advised to visit the cabarets on **Grosse Freiheit,** a street running off the Reeperbahn (like **Tabu, Salombo, Safari** and **Regina),** where prices from drinks are advertised.

The actual shows will either shock or disappoint you, depending on your pre-disposition. I can do no better than quote an advertising guide book on the transvestite show of the **Pulverfass Cabaret:** *"To this confusing performance with masks and costumes belongs such a dragging program, so that every minute will be enjoyed."*

More intimate sex shows are to be seen: **Amphore, Pompadour** and **Jockeyclub.**

And so to contact, or, in the obscure local dialect, *Kontakt.* This is prearranged with the usual disciplined efficiency. If you escape being picked up by the glamorous hoydens in their flashy cars on the street, you can choose from several different ways of meeting the girl with your name on her.

Reeperbahn *Kontakthallen* are provided by the **Eros-Centre** and the **Palais d'Amour.** Walk in to an echoing, softly-lit car-park atmosphere and girls of quite astonishing youth, vigour and naked-

*The notorious Reeperbahn*

ness will converge on you with expressions of fondness (they don't really mean it though). DM50 is the official price of a quick trip upstairs, with extras arranged on site.

More traditionally, **Herbertstrasse** on the other side of the Reeperbahn, sealed from those under 18 by wooden boards, has *les girls* posing in windows.

For a more exclusive atmosphere, there are *kontaktcafes.* **Mehrer** and **Lausen** are names recommended in the guide books.

And of course the most exclusive of the lot is in Blankenese, a sex club called **Hotel Blankenese,** which is a handy title to have on receipts or credit-card debits.

Replete with debauchery, you may then turn your attention to Hamburg's other late-night pursuits.

Dixieland jazz with an oompah beat is big here. **Onkel Pö's Carnegie Hall** is a crowded, smoky bar in Eppendorf that has presented such as Al Jarreau, Chick Corea and Chet Baker. There's the **Cotton Club** in the centre of town, and also **Markthalle** and **Fabrik** in Altona – good late-night connections to keep you going until the nearby Fish Market opens at 6a.m. every Sunday.

Grand opera has an impressive setting in the **Staatsoper,** while the two top concert venues are the **Musikhalle** (in Karl-Muck-Platz – who he?), and the hall of the **Congress Centrum.**

Lively theatre scene includes what they call the smallest theatre in the world, the **Kammerspiele,** and the last surviving true music hall variety theatre, the **Hansa-Theatre** near the Alster.

There's only one casino in town, on the ninth floor of the Inter-Continental Hotel; and for more innocent gyrations, the **Dom** is a world-famous funfair that visits Hamburg twice yearly.

# GETTING AROUND

While not a large city, Hamburg sprawls a bit to the north of the Alster, and to the west, along the north bank of the Elbe. Yet the city centre is fairly compact, and it is possible to walk to most places from the major hotels – often a matter of a pleasant stroll along the banks of the Alster lake.

The airport is within the greater city, and linked by a shuttle bus, dropping off at the main hotels, but departing only from the main station, which costs Dm6.50, and takes less than 30 minutes. The same journey in a taxi may save a few minutes but will cost more than Dm20.

In town, taxis are numerous. There's a standing charge of Dm3, and most journeys average out at about Dm8 to 12, though the meter clicks up alarmingly if you get caught in the morning and evening rush hour – large numbers of commuters head for the motorways and the countryside nearby every evening. Even then the traffic moves fairly freely and at other times of the day road transport is generally quick and efficient.

The public transport is an efficient integrated system, including buses, U-bahn underground, and S-bahn suburban trains. The combination of three underground and many more overground lines is easy to follow, and tickets are dispensed by machine at stations and bus stops. Press the button next to your destination, and the screen shows you the fare (Dm1.80 for inner-city trips); put in your coins, and you get ticket and change – there's no autoticket nonsense about having to have the right cash.

The same ticket services if you have to change from U-to-S-Bahn, or from bus to train.

To the dismay of the citizens, the Alster boat was recently removed from the integrated system. But the boats still run in summer, and there are few pleasanter ways of getting round the city, especially useful if you are in one of the hotels higher up the lake.

# Helsinki

An impenetrable language and a reputation for reserve conspire to make Helsinki appear one of the world's toughest business capitals. But behind the reserve is a city of efficiency, intimacy and stylish flair.

By Philip Jacobson

On the plane from Stockholm to Helsinki, a Finnish businessman, learning that I was making my first visit to his country, kindly gave me a crash-course in getting by in what he described as "*a rather odd place*". It was essential, he said, not to confuse the Finns' supposed reserve with a certain shyness which appears in the presence of foreigners. "*You may have to make the first approach,*" he observed,"*but after that, watch out, because when we take it into our minds to look after someone it can be an exhausting business.*"

This turned out to be a self-fulfilling prophesy. On landing, I was bundled into the car with his waiting family, driven to my hotel, bought my first bottle of Finland's remarkable 'IV A' beer (of which more later) and given several introductions to people who might be helpful with the research I was undertaking. The charming wife of my new acquaintance tut-tutted about my lack of proper headgear – the temperature was then sliding into the minus 15 degrees range – and promised to look out a woolly ski hat.

A few days later, still attempting to pay for a drink or a meal in the company of what was now a sizeable circle of Finnish friends, I came across a magazine article by a former British ambassador in Helsinki, Mr Andrew Stuart. He also leant towards the shy as opposed to reserved assessment of Finns, shrewdly pointing out that they are quick to respond to 'triggers' to help them relax and have, accordingly, provided themselves with an impressive variety of reasons for having a good time. These range from name days to May day, Christmas day to mid-summer day (with something called Little Christmas thrown in), opening of the season for crayfish, closing of same and, it is rumoured, homage to the noble Finnish potato.

Mr Stuart had some other observations, too, which struck me, on the basis of a short visit, as extremely perceptive. Until independence was achieved in 1917 Finnish history was one of more or less unrelieved occupation by powerful neighbours in, successively, Sweden and Russia. Most of the frequent wars in the Baltic sucked in Finland, sometimes as combatants, more often as a battlefield for others. No sooner had they obtained their cherished freedom than a bloody civil war rent the nation. Yet just two decades later, the Finns came together with such unity and intensity of purpose that the country's hugely outnumbered and outgunned army was able to inflict some of the most staggering military defeats of the 20th century on the invading Soviet Red Army.

The Winter War of 1939-40 remains, understandably, a page of history of which today's Finns, practising their highly successful brand of neutralism, are still intensely proud. If you want to understand better why, visit the Military Museum of the Defence Ministry on Maurin Katu. Among other things it will give you a slightly better grasp of the meaning of *sisu,* which every Finn I met defined differently, but which is broadly synonymous with the qualities of toughness and endurance, mental as well as physical. (I would observe, in passing, that this is one of the shorter words in the Finnish language, which I'm told, bears no relation whatsoever to any major group of languages, past or present. It may help you get the picture to know that the word for cheese is, deep breath, *juustotarjottimen.)*

Anyway, *sisu* and the Finnish national character are inextricably linked, together with a very striking sense of identity with their beautiful country. The elegant wife of Finland's President, Mrs Rellervo Koivisto, explains it thus: "*In a large country like ours there is a lot of nature per head of the population, so to speak, and moreover we have not dissociated ourselves from nature.*" Foreigners who know Finland well say that the practical effect of this admirable trait is that in the short (but sunny) summer, the bulk of the population heads for the plentiful woods to walk, run, swim, sail, fish and relax in the family sauna.

Since it is impossible to say anything profound about Finns and their sauna at less than doctoral thesis length, I will merely observe that this is a national institution of near-mystic significance, about which one does not make jokes. It certainly has nothing whatsoever in common with establishments trading under the name in the sleazier fringes of cities from Bangkok to Birmingham. Most hotels in Finland have one, in which it is not unusual, of a morning, to find fellows sweating out a hangover.

This leads me to that IV A beer, and to Finnish vodka, and to the curiously ambivalent approach to drinking in Finland. There are any number of laws about buying, transporting and consuming alcohol, but none which would appear to cramp the style of thirsty foreigners too much. As for the Finns, one has to observe that many certainly like a drink and more than a few can't handle it. The classic rubber-legged drunk is no stranger to the streets of Helsinki, which may explain why most pubs/clubs/

dancehalls etc. have largish doormen in attendance at night. Having also seen Finns letting their hair down in Leningrad and on the ferry between Helsinki and Stockholm, I would conclude that although there is probably more sound than fury, they are best given a wide berth.

Finnish beers are graded I, III or IV in ascending order of strength (nobody can explain what happened to II). In practical terms, this ranges from virtually non-alcoholic to very potent indeed. Your correspondent fancied he knew a bit about strong lager, but Karjala Export IV A is an altogether different proposition. I complained to a local journalist that I found it sometimes gave me a slight headache the morning after. "*Only a little headache?*" he said. "*They must be watering the stuff.*"

Where vodka is concerned, no true Finn will concede that Koskenkorva or Finlandia (slightly the stronger) is bettered anywhere in the world. I noticed that young women often took their vodka with exotic-looking juices: I was offered a taste of something called Vodka Polar, which turned out to be a mix using cranberry juice. Frankly, I'd stick to *snapsi,* i.e. schnapps, especially with the many variations on the theme of Baltic herring which appear on restaurant menus. It appears to be illegal to serve this splendid fish (*silakka* in Finnish) without boiled potato; other treats from Finland's long, fecund coastline and 62,000 lakes include the roe of *muikka,* served Russian-style with chopped onions, pepper and sour cream, Finnish salmon (often eaten raw) and the local crayfish. By contrast, I found reindeer meat rather tough and gamey: Finns swear by it, however, especially cold smoked, which sounds a bit like *biltong* – which is to say, definitely an acquired taste.

Female readers may be interested to know that it is considered perfectly normal for women to go into bars and restaurants on their own: I never saw any sign of them being pestered by male customers. Finnish women I met consider that they have achieved a considerable degree of equality in most aspects of everyday life over the past couple of decades (although a law which would have permitted them to retain maiden names after marriage was recently rejected by parliament).

Male readers, on the other hand, may be interested to know that Helsinki appears to have an unusually large number of handsome, well-dressed and self-assured women. Finns seem to be great dancers, which provides a good way of opening contacts, though proficiency in the waltz, polka and tango (rose optional) rates somewhat above that of disco dancing. It is quite usual for women to ask men onto the floor – there are even afternoon dances catering specifically for ladies leaving the office, at which the men sit around nervously hoping that they won't be wallflowers. Friday night is traditionally the most popular for going out, which usually means queues at the best places.

Helsinki struck me as an exceptional city, combining a high degree of efficiency and sound planning with an intimacy and stylish flair which other larger capitals (the population is around 500,000) find very difficult to achieve these days. Architecturally it is a constant delight, a striking building, it seems, around every corner. Every style is represented: Neo-Classical, Victorian, National Romantic, Space Age, you name it. The excellent *Berlitz travel guide to Helsinki* suggests a walking tour that takes in many of the outstanding buildings, among them, for those who share my weakness for the monumental, the vast Byzantine Uspensky cathedral and the central railway station, designed by Eliel Saarinen along eye-catching 1930s heroic lines.

I have long held that main stations are a reliable guide to the nature of the city they serve. Helsinki's is spotless, sensibly laid out, well warmed in winter and full of useful information in foreign languages. Beneath it is a remarkable centre containing a fine squash club, supermarkets, cinemas, fashion shops and a glassed-in tropical garden (well, something along those lines).

*Helsinki's striking railway station*

*The impressive Uspensky cathedral*

Getting around the central zone of Helsinki, where a basic grid system exists, is a piece of cake, even with street names in Finnish (and Swedish, the official minority language). Multi-lingual information about tram, bus and metro services is easily obtained from tourist bureaux, and more easily from exceedingly helpful fellow passengers. In summer, the 3T and 3B trams travel on a leisurely figure of eight route which takes in the heart of the city, with multi-lingual commentary on the main sights thrown in. I didn't travel on the metro, but to judge from the bright, clean and warm stations, it should be a pleasure to ride.

Walking in temperatures of minus 20 degrees is perfectly feasible, I concluded, as long as one is well wrapped up and properly hatted, with protection for the ears. A set of thermal insoles for shoes is a better bet than thermal underwear if you are going to be in and out of super-heated offices. Finns seem to be very protective towards foreigners where their winter is concerned. I lost count of the times I was advised – sensibly – not to walk too quickly when thawing snow was freezing over again, not to breath in too deeply when the air temperature is really low (it does the lungs no good at all) and not to forget to take a hearty breakfast when it is cold outside, to say nothing of a decent lunch and then a bowl of pea soup.

Mrs Koivisto, the president's wife, coined a nice phrase recently when she described the Finns as "*an in-between people*", isolated by their weird language and pulled back and forth between powerful Slav and Scandinavian neighbours for so much of their turbulent history. An outsider might expect this to produce a somewhat schizoid society, searching endlessly for its real identity. Not a bit of it. You'd have to go a long way to find a country with a stronger sense of national identity and values – a totally different thing, incidentally, from jingoism. No wonder Finns are touchy about being written off as some sort of Arctic outpost or an obscure offshoot of Scandinavia.

## WHERE TO STAY

Helsinki, like most capitals, offers a high standard of accommodation with price brackets to suit most pockets.

One of the city's premier hotels is the **Hotel Kalastajatorppa** (Kalastajatorparrie 1; tel: 488 011; telex: 121571) or, more simply, Fisherman's Cottage. The hotel's overwhelming attraction is that it is located by the sea, yet is mere minutes from the city centre.

Most rooms have superb sea views; they cost between 610-1350 FM exclusive of meals. Elsewhere the accommodation scene is dominated by Helsinki Hotels, a chain of three to five star properties and 20 restaurants in the Greater Helsinki area. The group is significant because it has a total of 1,065 rooms and a 30 per cent share of Helsinki's total room capacity. Among its properties are:

**Hotel Hesperia** (Manneheimintie 50; tel: 441 311; telex 122177), a modern, multi-storey de-luxe hotel popular with businessmen. The 286 room hotel is next to Hesperia Park by the city air terminal and within walking distance of the Finlandia House congress and concert hall, Olympic Stadium, National Museum and the Töölö market place.

The hotel's restaurant has a sumptuous lunchtime smorgasbord and there is also a steak house, a lobby bar, a Latin-style club and a nightclub with underwater decor and live entertainment. Rooms cost between FM 582-1,600.

**Hotel Vaakuna** (Asema-aukio 2; tel: 171 811; telex: 121381), is a distinguished four-star property opposite the main railway station. It has 290 handsomely appointed rooms equipped down to a trouser press. Single rooms start at FM 390, doubles at FM 530, including breakfast and service.

The ninth floor restaurant with a roof-top terrace is open in summer, and justly famous for its cuisine, particularly the crayfish. The hotel also has a grill restaurant with fish and seafood specialities, and the Sky Bar, with soft music and dancing, is very popular.

**Hotel Torni** (Yrjönkatu 26; tel: 644 611; telex: 125153), is an attractive four-star hotel (158 rooms) in the centre of town, which served as the headquarters of the Occupation Army during the Winter War. It was completely renovated in 1981.

There are three restaurants – Parilla Espanola, The Balkan Room and O'Malley's, the only genuine Irish Pub (but with no Guinness) in Helsinki – offering a wide choice of bar food. The American Bar and the Atelier Bar are admirable meeting places.

**Hotel Helsinki** (Hallistuskatu 12; tel: 171 401; telex: 121022), is a 130-room hotel located in the centre, near the historic Old City and the business and shopping areas.

The hotel's Helsinki Dining Rooms, seating 120, features a lavish buffet for lunch and à la carte dining in the evening. Also in the evening, the Helsinki Club, with its stylish interior and latest disco, is one of the liveliest dance spots in town. Rooms cost between FM 340-440.

The **Marski Hotel's** location (Mannerheimintie 10; tel: 641 717; telex 121240) is ideal for anyone wishing to see and experience as much as possible in Helsinki. The Aulabaari, the hotel's lobby bar, is a popular meeting place. Hotel guests are admitted to the members-only M-Club nightclub, which closes its doors at 3 a.m. Rates: single FM 450-495; double FM 580.

The **Hotel Rivoli Jardin** (Kasarminkatu 40; tel: 177 880; telex 125881), set in a courtyard near the south harbour, is one of Helsinki's newest hotels. The 53-room hotel doesn't have a restaurant, but serves a good breakfast. Rates: single FM 400; double FM 480-1,400.

## WHERE TO EAT

Finland's geographical position has, not surprisingly, left its mark on the country's traditional food. Salmon, crayfish, reindeer and pasties are probably the best known Finnish foods abroad. But other dishes, like Karelian meat stew, made of pork, beef and mutton, or casseroled reindeer, served with mashed potatoes and lingon berries, are also widely available. Some more typically

Finnish dishes may prove too heavy for the visitor, but they are worth trying.

The top four Helsinki restaurants, and the most expensive, are reckoned to be **Havis Amanda** (Unioninkatu 23; tel: 666 882), **Restaurant Karl König** (Mikonkatu 4; tel: 171 271), **The Palace Hotel Restaurant** (Eteläranta 10; tel: 171 114) and **The Savoy Restaurant** (Eteläesplanadi 14; tel: 176 571), all in the city centre.

Havis Amanda, situated in the south harbour market place, is a first class restaurant serving a bewildering variety of dishes. Although the accent is on seafood the restaurant also serves some meat dishes, and it offers a daily lunch (about 70 FIM per person) and a more costly à la carte menu.

Restaurant Karl König, which opened in 1892, has a reputation as a meeting place for the famous, like poet Eino Leino, Jean Sibelius and Marshal Mannerheim.

Facing the south harbour, The Palace Hotel Restaurant is noted for its breathtaking harbour view. It serves a good selection of Finnish and French delicacies.

The Savoy, a high-priced but excellent restaurant, is mainly used by businessmen. They say that the *vorschmack* is the best in town and the *nouvelle cuisine* has many admirers.

For a really different meal try the Russian specialities at **Bellevue** (Rahapajankatu 3; tel: 179 560). Another Russian style restaurant specialising in Georgian food is **Kazbek** (Läntinen Brahenkatu 2; tel: 763 848).

Other noted Helsinki restaurants include the **Hesperia Hotel** (tel: 441 311), **The Torni** (644 717), **Motti** (tel: 494 918), **Hotelli Kalastajatorppa** (tel: 488 011), the celebrated and historic **Seurahuone Socis Hotel** (tel: 170 441), and the **Säkkipilli Restaurant** (The Bagpipe) (tel: 605 607).

If you really feel like going mad, go to **Kreisi** (Crazy) (tel: 611 081). There you can eat your meal in a prison, sauna, Indian or surfing setting.

Helsinki has a number of outdoor summer restaurants which are well worth visiting. **Mestaritalli** (tel: 440 274) is set in a delightful park close to the sea just a short ride from the centre. **Pikkuparlamentti** (The Little Parliament) overlooked by the real parliament building, right in the centre, is also a very popular haunt. The address is Arkadian puisto (tel: 694 0360).

*The south harbour market place has several good places to eat*

# NIGHT LIFE

It comes as something of a cultural shock for the restaurant-going foreign businessman to be invited to dance by a lady, and later escorted back to his seat. But that's precisely what happens if the visitor goes to one of Helsinki's famed dance-restaurants.

On certain dance nights, it's the rule that the lady does the asking. The man accepts or otherwise, although it's considered very ill-mannered to say no.

The special lady dances usually start around 4p.m. and continue until 1a.m. On the night I visited Restaurant **Vanha Maestro** (Fredrikinkatu 51-53; tel: 644 303), some 800 people crowded the dance floor, restaurant and bars. And the ladies are not shy when it comes to asking and language usually poses no problem if you speak English.

Other noted dance-restaurants, often open seven nights a week, are **Fenniea** (Mikonkatu 17; tel: 175 433) and **Botnia Club** (Museokatu 10; tel: 446 940). The entry fee is about 20 FIM.

It's best to telephone for details as programmes vary at different times of the year. Remember that July is very quiet as it's the traditional holiday month.

The **Groovy Restaurant** (Ruoholahdenkatu 4; tel: 694 5118), is reckoned by many to be the best jazz club in Scandinavia. Top flight musicians perform six nights a week, everything from Dixieland or New Orleans through to swing and bebop. **Kaivohuone** (The Well Room) (Kaivopuisto Park; tel: 177 881), near the centre, is about the best-known nightclub in the city. In the 1830s, the czar and high-ranking Russian officers came here to take the mineral waters. Nowadays, it's a place to eat, drink and dance and the management has recently made great strides to improve overall quality. There's no entrance fee, but drinks are costly.

But for the rhythmically inept, the Hesparia Hotel organises a yearly Samba Carnival where dancing of a gratifyingly unprincipalled nature is positively encouraged. The carnival, which, says the hotel, is intended to break up the monotony of the long dark winter, is a four-day riot of bright colours and loud music. Some 200 dancers and musicians from Brazil, Spain, Italy, Cuba, US and Scandinavia perform on three separate floors from 7p.m. to 3a.m. every night of the carnival and guests and spectators are invited to join in.

# GETTING AROUND

Finland suffers from many misconceptions but the one that alarms and infuriates Finns most is that the country is part of the Soviet Union. The SF sign on the rear of cars doesn't stand for Soviet Finland but *Suomi*, Finnish for Finland.

Finland does share a 700 mile border with the Soviet Union, in the east, and trips can be arranged by plane, bus or train. But a Russian visa should be obtained in your own country at least three weeks before departure.

Helsinki-Vantaa Airport is 12 miles to the north of the city. A city bus leaves the airport every 20 minutes for the City Air Terminal (Töölönkatu 21) and costs about FM 12. The same journey by taxi will cost FM 80-90.

A convenient amenity is the Helsinki Card, available from the Helsinki City Tourist Office, (Pohjoisesplanadi 19; tel: 174 088), for one, two or three days, (70 FIM for three days). This gives free travel on city buses, trams and the metro, free sightseeing trips and boat trips, and entrance to museums, among other things.

Probably the best saunas in the Helsinki region are at the Finnish Sauna Society (Suomen Sauna-Seura), at Lauttasaari, a short bus or taxi ride from the city centre. Four genuine sauna baths, heated with firewood, two savusaunas (smoke saunas) and two others, which let the smoke out during heating, can be used. Founded in 1937, the society has 1,800 members and foreigners are eligible to join. The cost is about 50 FIM per visit (tel: 678 677).

The business traveller really wanting to get away from it all should try a Finnair trip to Lapland. This wilderness in Finland's far north is probably the only remaining wilderness in Europe. Various short journeys are arranged by Finnair (Töölönkatu 21; tel: 410 411).

# Hong Kong

Still more than a decade away from the Chinese handover, Hong Kong is enjoying a revival of confidence that is in keeping with its entrepreneurial enthusiasm. Being in a city that exists almost exclusively as a business centre it also provides the visiting executive with the most modern, efficient and sumptuous facilities of any business capital in the world.

By Graham Boynton

When the new Financial Secretary of Hong Kong, Sir David Akers-Jones, was officiating recently at the roll-out of a new Cathay Pacific jumbo jet, he took time out to stroll across to a gaggle of British journalists and confide somewhat emphatically that he hoped the world would regard Hong Kong as an Asian capital in its own right rather than as a gateway to China. As admirable as the notion may sound, and one would expect nothing less from the colony's top Brit, it is clearly not in keeping with the realities of the situation.

Already, Hong Kong is mainland China's most important trading partner after the United States and, whatever Sir David wishes people to think, its future must surely be as the major gateway between China and the West. There is clearly a special relationship between the two business communities (I was reminded on a number of occasions in China recently that these were the only capitalists they really understood), and any Western businessman who travels frequently to the mainland will tell you that without Hong Kong as a staging post, business prospects, and life in general, would be infinitely bleaker.

One has to come from a couple of weeks on the mainland to fully appreciate this over-crowded, clattering city in perpetual motion. After the grinding inefficiencies, appalling service and mediocre facilities of the Chinese capitals, Hong Kong is a veritable jewel, a haven of high standards and slick modernity. Critics claim it has no soul, that it has no real culture and that its temples are the race tracks at Happy Valley and Shatin. But after doing business in China such aesthetic considerations become secondary to the pleasures of a juicy steak and a full-blooded Australian cabernet at the Foreign Correspondents' Club and regular updates of the Test match scores at Lords.

I must confess my first impressions of Hong Kong, some ten years ago, were quite unfavourable. I found the climate oppressive in the extreme, the sheer mass of humanity crammed into such a small space overwhelming, and the round-the-clock rush hour anything but exciting. It seemed like New York at twice the speed but with nowhere to go, a continuous human loop threading its way from one high-rise to the next without once pausing to reflect. Then there were the ex-pats, many bearing a striking resemblance to the worst of the nouveau colonials one encountered in Salisbury, Nairobi and even Durban.

Quite soon I became acclimatised to the terrible humidity (the only really pleasant months are in the autumn), then to the wall-to-wall people on the pavements, and finally reason returned and I discovered, as was the case in Africa, that there are ex-pats and ex-pats.

Today, I am able to view Hong Kong as a familiar acquaintance and feel a surge of adrenalin every time the 747 loops over the city and I see that bank of glittering skyscrapers for the first time. Although convinced that it no longer has the pazazz it did in the 60s and 70s, I can now understand what the old hands mean when they say that Hong Kong was once a very exciting place to be. It was far enough away from Hampstead for one to commit social indiscretions and get away with them and there was a wild frontier atmosphere about the place, where today there is order, restraint and comparative self-discipline.

The most recent recovery of confidence coincides approximately with Hong Kong pegging its dollar to the American dollar at the end of 1983. Until then the prospect of the Red Army marching down Nathan Road had caused property prices to plummet and the currency to fall alarmingly. By the middle of 1984 the prospect of a satisfactory Sino-British agreement further bolstered confidence and by the time it was signed in September Hong Kong was downright bullish.

Apart from a brief hiccup as a result of the Overseas Trust Bank scandal early in 1985, that optimism has persisted and at the time of writing there is relative euphoria on the Hong Kong Stock Exchange, interest rates have halved in the space of 12 months and land prices continue to recover, albeit turgidly. Such a volatile market – Hong Kong has always thrived on short-term risks – will no doubt provide a number of spectacular leaps and dramatic freefalls on the Hang Seng Index over the next ten years. What it also means is that 1997 and all the accompanying convulsions are a long way off indeed.

On the surface at least the recovery of confidence (and subsequent troughs and peaks) seems to have had little effect on the daily life. It has always had a sense of, in the words of Chinese author Han Su-yin, *"borrowed time, borrowed place"*. As it has no raw materials it survives by trading, by its wits. This is probably why the Hong Kong Chinese are the ones so virulently opposed to the 1997 Agreement, for they fear that Chinese bureaucracy will stifle the creative flair that is the lifeblood of Hong Kong. They also say it is easy for the *gweilos* (the ex-pats) because they can always move off and find another arena within which they can pit wits – the Hong Kong Chinese do not have the necessary travel documents.

If there is no open resentment between the *gweilos* and the Chinese there is certainly an undercurrent of mutual mistrust. The word *gweilo* means ghost person and is not used fondly, rather like referring to someone as a wog, wop or spick. The ex-pats are equally disparaging – one of the common phrases in their repertoire, usually introduced after a visitor has been ripped off, is *"well, you know what the Chinese are like. . ."* Nobody in their right mind admits to knowing what the Chinese are like.

Socially, too, the lives of the 60,000-odd Westerners and 5½ million Chinese are poles apart. You will find the whites, and perhaps a handful of wealthy Chinese, at the Captain's Bar, Landau's or Gaddi's, and the Chinese cramming into any of the 30,000 eating places Hong Kong is said to have. The whites will go home to air-conditioned apartments up the hill to Victoria Park and the Chinese will jostle their way home to those overcrowded tower blocks that so dominate Kowloon. More than 50 per cent of Hong Kong's population is housed in the squalid blocks that make such a vivid impression on the first-time visitor on the road from Kai Tak Airport to one of the most luxurious hotels in the world.

I am assured that the Chinese are quite stoical about their overcrowded living conditions and regard themselves better off than many Chinese communities elsewhere in Asia. They are certainly better off than their relatives in mainland China and are the first to jeer at the backwardness of their communist kin. In fact, in China the fiercest critics of the country's leaden bureaucracy and general inefficiency are Hong Kong Chinese, usually reluctantly posted to regional offices in Shanghai and Peking and rather regarding it as one of the most unpleasant prices one has to pay for advancement in the company. They are the ones who fear 1997 more than most and are even now looking into ways of moving on.

On a day-to-day basis however neither the politics nor ideologies nor great causes cut any ice, they're all in there making money. From the little old lady who sells wrinkled, cut-price international newspapers at the Star Ferry (apparently removed from the cabins of incoming jets at Kai Tak airport and then ironed flat again) through to the chairmen of Swire or Jardine Matheson, they seem to survive only to make money. That they have built around

*The spectacular sweep of Hong Kong's waterfront*

them arguably the most efficient business city in the world makes life a great deal simpler for the visiting executive.

From the moment he is picked up at the airport by an air-conditioned hotel limousine and spirited through the mayhem of the congested streets to one of the world's best hotels, the business traveller will realise he is one of a pampered and revered species. In Latin America football players are the true VIPs, in Europe and America it is the film stars and pop idols who receive unquestioning five-star treatment . . . and in Hong Kong it is the businessman, especially the expense account marque from out of town.

He is the prize customer for the luxury hotels, the big spender in the restaurants, and in theory the customer least likely to haggle in the Nathan Road electronics and camera emporiums. He is also likely to buy a tailor-made suit, buy his family an armful of presents and tip generously. In exchange for his largesse he will receive the best treatment that money can buy – a personal valet in the top hotels, unquestionably the best food in the Far East, certainly the best Chinese cuisine in the world, and if he is very lucky he might even come away from Hong Kong with a bargain buy, although these are becoming increasingly rare.

Communications, both international and local, are of the highest standards, something one would expect, I suppose, in the world's third most important financial centre, and one is constantly in contact with international events, something European businessmen find quite frustrating about America, not to mention Third World and Iron Curtain countries. In Hong Kong one really does feel like a member of the international community, while local matters are covered expertly by publications like the *South China Morning Post* and the highly respected *Far Eastern Economic Review.* (Whatever else, the *gweilos* must be credited with establishing a high standard in the media.)

And it is these basics of comfort, cuisine and communications that make Hong Kong the very pearl that it is. If it has no time for sentiment or the finer virtues in life, then it compensates for all that with well-oiled efficiency and an infectiously entrepreneurial and flexible approach to the day-to-day matters of 20th century life. The best example of this returns us rather neatly to the question of whether or not Hong Kong will become the main gateway to China or an Asian capital in its own right. To the Hong Kong business community such concepts are no more than esoteric niceties. The fact that in the first quarter of 1985 its exports to China increased by 150 per cent, that it is involved in an enormous number of joint ventures with the Chinese, and that it is currently the Chinese businessman's best capitalist ally is enough. Like the city itself, its residents prefer to leave the rhetoric to others.

## WHERE TO STAY

Superlatives have been heaped on Hong Kong's top hotels for decades now and in that time their own competitiveness has driven them on to higher things. There remain few hotels outside the Far East that can compare with the likes of the Mandarin, Peninsula, Regent and Shangri-La. They have all been at the top of survey listings and continually attract glowing praise from the international travelling community... and the only problem is they are becoming frighteningly expensive.

The Business Traveller readers' Hotel of The Year for two years running has been the **Mandarin Hotel** (5 Connaught Road, Central; tel: 522 0111; telex: 73653), probably the least prepossessing architecturally but the most impressive in terms of sheer class. The staff remember your name, your foibles and your preferences from one year to the next, and they share with the Peninsula staff a sense of discretion that is no longer commonplace in Far Eastern hotels. The lobby is rather plain and the rooms similarly so, but the decor throughout is impeccable and it truly has the air of a great hotel about it.

The Mandarin Grill lives up to its reputation and is, not unexpectedly, rather expensive. One can expect to play around H.K. $240 for lobster thermidor, H.K. $160 for fresh salmon and H.K. $190 for a 16-ounce T-bone steak. Room rates are also high and rising: for the lowest-price studio room one pays around H.K. $1,000 a night; a medium room costs H.K. $1,500; and a superior H.K. $1,650; suites range from H.K. $2,700 to almost H.K. $10,000 for the Mandarin Suite. According to the Mandarin one can expect to pay between H.K. $65 and H.K. $85 for breakfast,

*Tucked behind the Post Office, the Mandarin is unsurpassed inside*

H.K. $250 for *à la carte* lunch and H.K. $300 for dinner. When you add 10 per cent tax for the food and 15 per cent for rooms it is clear that the Mandarin has to be superb.

The 200-room **Peninsula** (Salisbury Road, Kowloon; tel: 366 6251; telex: 43821) is the grand dame of Hong Kong's luxury hotels and its elegant atmosphere and superb service are matched only by the Mandarin. When you arrive you are spirited to your room where your personal room attendant pours a welcoming cup of Chinese tea and offers you a selection of toiletries while offering to draw your bath. After a 17-hour journey from Europe this is most welcome pampering.

There has been debate for some time over the future of the Peninsula, which is too small by modern Hong Kong standards. The question is whether to add a new wing to the existing hotel or to pull the whole thing down and start all over again. It is true that the rooms are somewhat antiquated and dowdy compared with the Regent over the road, but a lot of regular travellers to the Far East would consider its demolition sheer barbarism.

Some complain that the Pen's famous restaurant, Gaddi's, is overpriced and not as good as it once was, but the Hong Kong food critic Willie Marc and a number of hoteliers all confirmed to me that it remains one of the finest European restaurants in the region.

The cheapest rooms at the Pen cost around H.K. $1,050, the harbour view deluxe rooms cost H.K. $1,350 and harbour view suites cost between H.K. $2,500 and H.K. $3,650. Food prices are similar to the Mandarin's.

Just 500 yards away and commanding the most spectacular view of Hong Kong harbour, is **The Regent** (Salisbury Road, Kowloon; tel: 369 2282; telex: 49794), and its glittering modernity is one of the reasons the Peninsula Group feel obliged to do something about their flagship. Ironically, The Regent is on the site that was originally earmarked for the new Peninsula.

Those who have been regular clients of the Pen or the Mandarin will not be overwhelmed by The Regent – it has an enormous (and to my mind very attractive) foyer, there are always masses of people flowing one way and the other and there is a general clamour about the place that would not appeal to more conservative guests. What it does have, above all else, is one of the best views in the world – in the harbourside rooms, in the foyer (through gigantic sheets of glass), and at a table in the hotel's elegant Plume Restaurant.

If you can afford The Regent then you can certainly afford H.K. $250 for what it somewhat coyly calls the Total Environment Treatment. In simple English this is an hour-long indulgence in the hotel's health centre, involving a jacuzzi, a steam sauna, a sunbathe and a Chinese massage in the privacy of your own cubicle. I would rate it as one of the best buys in Hong Kong.

The Regent's prices are: from H.K.$980 for an ordinary room without a harbour view, H.K. $1,280 for a room with a harbour or plaza view, H.K. $1,450 for deluxe and up to H.K. $2,000 for an ordinary suite. Then again you could pay H.K. $9,000 a day for the splendid Regent Suite.

The **Shangri-La** (64 Mody Road, Tsimshatsui, Kowloon; tel: 372 12111; telex: 36718) is the last of the Big Four. It is located on the waterfront a few hundred yards from The Regent and boasts a spectacular foyer and almost the unparalleled standards of service set by the Mandarin and Peninsula. Particularly recommended is Club 21, the executive floor at the top of the hotel, which throws a limousine service to and from Kai Tak (as do all the other hotels for VIP guests), complimentary continental breakfast, free cocktails between 5 and 7 p.m. and has a special lounge. Also recommended is the excellent Japanese restaurant.

Standard rooms (without a harbour view) start at H.K. $750, deluxe rooms cost H.K. $1,700 with a harbour view and H.K. $1,300 without, and suites go all the way up to H.K. $8,000 a day.

Although the aforementioned hotels set the standards there are many other hotels that come highly recommended, and were they situated in another capital in the world would certainly be placed among the best. The **Royal Garden** (69 Mody Road, East Tsimshatsui, Kowloon; tel: 372 15215; telex: 39539) is just behind the Shangri-La and doesn't quite have the view but it is a fine hotel and at H.K. $750-H.K. $900 for a double room and H.K. $1,400-H.K. $4,000 for suite it is somewhat cheaper than the others.

In Causeway Bay, the **Lee Gardens Hotel** (Hysan Avenue, Causeway Bay, Hong Kong Island; tel: 527 0721; telex: 75601) comes highly recommended and with single occupancy starting at H.K. $580 and double at H.K. $630, it is clearly far more economical than the luxury hotels. So too the **Harbour View Holiday Inn** (70 Mody Road, East Tsimshatsui, Kowloon; tel: 372 15161; telex: 38670) near the Shangri-La which starts at H.K. $660 for single occupancy; and the Peninsula Group's **Hong Kong Hotel** (3 Canton Road, Kowloon; tel: 367 6011; telex: 43838) which does a reasonable impersonation of a top Hong Kong hotel. Single occupancy starts at H.K. $500.

# WHERE TO EAT

There are either 8,000, 17,500 or 30,000 eating places in Hong Kong – it all depends on which source you believe. Even if you take the lowest estimate it is a formidable number for a city with a population of five and a half million. And when you consider that the city is widely regarded as the modern home of Cantonese cuisine, it becomes quite clear that the visiting businessman will find himself spoilt for choice.

*Junks in the harbour*

Faced with such daunting numbers one can only capitulate to the experience of a local expert – and one such expert is Willie Marc, the region's top restaurant critic and an internationally acclaimed authority on Chinese dishes. After we had emerged from a short trip to Canton, throughout which he had seemed quite restrained and withdrawn, Willie Marc suddenly became expansive over several long glasses of decadent Western nourishment in the Hong Kong Hotel's Gun Bar, and indulged in one of the food critic's favourite pastimes – naming his favourite local restaurants.

Not surprisingly the Canton trip had confirmed Hong Kong's culinary superiority and Marc named five restaurants that he believes are among the best of their kind on the planet: the **Sun Tung Cok Shark's Fin Restaurant** (Harbour City, 25-27 Canton Rd; tel: 372 20288;), the **Flower Lounge** at the Royal Garden Hotel (East Tsimshatsui, Kowloon; tel: 372 15215), the **King Heung Peking Restaurant,** (59-65 Patterson Street, Causeway Bay; tel: 557 71035), the **Cleveland Szechuan Restaurant** (6 Cleveland St, Causeway Bay; tel: 576 3876) and **City Chiuchow Restaurant** (East Ocean Centre, 98 Granville Road, Tsimshatsui East; tel: 372 45383).

The Sun Tung Cok is Kowloon's top place for southern Chinese cooking and apart from the frighteningly expensive shark's fin soup (the best costs up to H.K.$150 per person), it specialises in game in season and snake in winter. Without such extravagances as shark's fin soup one would expect to pay around H.K.$200 a head. The City Chiuchow is Kowloon's other top restaurant and is famous for its goose dishes and other specialities from the Chiuchow region (you may also wish to try the beef satay done in a creamy sauce). It is slightly cheaper than the Sun Tung Cok.

Just 10 minutes from Hong Kong's International Airport, The Royal Garden Hotel is

situated at the centre of the city's busiest shopping, dining and nightlife districts.

# Images of Excellence

A central 110 ft landscaped Garden Atrium makes it unique among Hong Kong's top hotels.

Glass-sided lifts rise through the Atrium to 34 luxury suites and 399 rooms.

5 top class restaurants and bars offer wide variety. Restaurant Lalique is renowned for its Continental cuisine, and The Flower Lounge for its Cantonese. The Greenery and The Balcony are set in the elegant Atrium, and The Falcon is both a Victorian pub and a popular discotheque.

The Royal Garden also offers 4 floors of shops, a full service Business Centre, and excellent Banqueting facilities.

The Royal Garden

For Reservations, please contact the Leading Hotels of the World (HRI); Utell International (U.I.); Odner Hotel Representative Ltd (O.H.R.); your travel agent or the hotel direct.

For further information contact The Royal Garden direct at Tsimshatsui East, Kowloon, Hong Kong. P.O. Box 95366 Tsimshatsui. Phone: 3-7215215, Telex:39539 RGHTL HX, Cable: ROYALHOTEL.

A member of The Leading Hotels of the World®

The King Heung, not surprisingly, specialises in Peking duck (better than any you'll find in Peking) and also features delicious hot and sour soup; and the Cleveland in Causeway Bay offers the spiciest of China's regional cuisines – Szechuan. The dishes are steamed, smoked and often marinated for up to 24 hours and are laced with garlic, fennel, coriander and pepper.

Given that Willie Marc has probably eaten at several hundred top Hong Kong restaurants over the years you couldn't really argue with his choice of the top five Chinese establishments, although he is first to add there are many more that he would recommend. My own personal favourite is the most expensive Chinese restaurant in the city – the Regent Hotel's **Lai Ching Heen.** An exquisite meal there included suckling pig, braised snake skin, deep fried fresh pears with scallops, Peking duck, crispy walnut cake and fresh milk tartlettes and cost around H.K.$600 a head including wine, and remains the most memorable Chinese meal I have had. The expensive but tasteful decor of the room and the jade and ivory table furniture add to the sheer elegance of the Lai Ching Heen and if you are looking to impress, there is no better place to entertain.

Understandably, European restaurants are not quite in the same class although Willie Marc offers three outstanding exceptions to the rule – the Peninsula Hotel's famous (and very expensive) **Gaddi's,** the **Au Trou Normand,** (6 Carnarvon Rd, Tsimshatsui, Kowloon; tel: 366 8754) and **Landau's** (Harbour View Mansions, 257 Gloucester Rd, Causeway Bay; tel: 579 05867).

Gaddi's is discussed elsewhere in these pages and suffice to say it comes recommended even by rival hoteliers as the best of its kind, although I have heard complaints from businessmen of late that it is not as good as it was. (One should bear in mind here that this has been said about every restaurant around the world that ever established a reputation.) The Au Trou Normand, run by Bernard Vigneau, offers French provincial cuisine to a good European standard, and Landau's, run by the eponymous family that also owns Jimmy's Kitchen, is described by Marc as serving top quality pub grub, although one would expect the proprietors to make more extravagant claims. **Jimmy's Kitchen** (Wyndham Street, Central; tel: 526 5293) serves similar plain western food that can often taste like *haute cuisine* after a couple of weeks of nothing but Chinese meals.

# NIGHT LIFE

Hong Kong nights are not what they were . . . then again perhaps they weren't that good in the first place. The Suzie Wong world of the Wanchai District in the 60s and even early 70s is no more or at most it is a shadow of its former self. During the Vietnam War American GIs roamed the Wanchai streets with fire and booze in their bellies, and the girls and the mama-sans got very rich indeed. Today, the nightspots are still there but they seem to have lost that passion; there is a sleazy listlessness where there was once raw excitement.

On the other side of the cultural fence Hong Kong has a symphony orchestra of some merit, but there is little in the way of theatre, bar the occasional touring West End hit with a second division cast or caterwauling Cantonese opera that tends to pall after the first half hour; and the legitimate nightclubs are little more than the faceless, uniform discotheques one finds in cities all over the world. The foreign devils tend to hold dinner parties at exclusive clubs while the Chinese fill those enormous eating places with noise and exuberance. No doubt the visiting businessman will be entertained in the former and thoroughly enjoy the graceful surrounds of the clubs, but he would be wise to spend a night out at one of the Chinese eateries – it is infinitely more entertaining than a cheerless night out at one of the Lockhart Road topless bars.

The topless bars provide hostesses who charge the regulation outrageous prices for their company, usually in the form of watered-down drinks at H.K. $60 or $70 a shot. The bill at the end of an evening can be quite frightening and if they think you are a push-over, you could leave without your shirt. Then again it's no different to the sleazy dives in New York or London, only more oriental and therefore more difficult to work out how they're ripping you off.

The discotheques in the neighbouring Central district are a great deal safer and quite sterile. If you've seen one discotheque you've seen them all – the same monotonous beat, the same blindingly

*The world of Suzie Wong is dead*

boring light shows, and an appalling exhibitionist in the middle of it all, delivering unintelligible inanities in a fake mid-Atlantic accent. Far better are the restaurant bars like **California Bar and Grill** (tel: 211 345) in Lan Kwai Fong, which is a good quality hamburger joint with unobtrusive music, videos and a better class of popular music than the discos. The other good one is **1997** (tel: 260 303) which is a private club (that isn't too difficult to get into), a restaurant and a bar.

Over the water in Kowloon is one of my favourite Hong Kong nightspots, **Rick's Café** (tel: 672 939) on Hart Avenue. Despite the Casablanca theme that is becoming almost as common as the discotheque in capitals worldwide (including, I hasten to add, in Casablanca itself), it is a very good club and often has excellent jazz bands playing. **Ned Kelly's Last Stand** (tel: 660 562) also provides a good atmosphere and some hot jazz, while **Red Lips** (tel: 684 511) is distinctly raunchy and is worth a visit if only to see the juke box.

If you don't expect too much from a night out on the town, and you have convivial company, you'll probably enjoy Hong Kong. One thing is certain, even after a moderately entertaining night out, a ride across the harbour on the Star Ferry or a walk along the waterfront on the Kowloon side provides the most enjoyable conclusion to an evening I can think of anywhere in the world.

## GETTING AROUND

There are allegedly around 350,000 vehicles cluttering up the roads of Hong Kong, which means that progress by taxi (the most sensible way for visiting businessmen to travel from one appointment to the next) can often be frustrating and slow. The short distances involved in such travel make up to some extent for the pedestrian crawl.

All Hong Kong taxis are metered and with a H.K.$5 flagfall, local fares seldom exceed H.K.$30. The most expensive ride is the one in from the airport to the centre, and if the centre means the Central district the fare will run at around H.K.$35, which includes H.K.$10 toll at the cross-harbour tunnel.

Public transport in the form of the Mass Transit Railway (MTR) and the Star Ferry can be used in tandem with taxis and both are cheaper than crossing the harbour through the tunnel. There are taxi ranks on either side of the harbour, and generally there is no problem picking up a cab.

Probably the most important tip pertains to departing travellers taking a cab out to Kai Tak – remember to have enough Hong Kong dollars in reserve to pay for the cab and the $120 airport departure tax.

For the rest, the best way of getting around Hong Kong is on foot.

# Houston

Hi-tech Houston reflects the futuristic aspirations of nearby NASA headquarters and for visiting businessmen probably offers a foretaste of the shape of things to come. Thus executives can expect to find an efficient city finely tuned to their requirements but not necessarily their tastes.

By Simon Inglis

I am standing in what they call, for want of a more convincing word, an atrium, a polished and tinted version of Paxton's 1851 Great Exhibition glasshouse. There are tubular fountains, immaculate plants and in the air the sweet odour of perfume someone has added to the air-conditioning. A few yards away is McDonald's, and next to it an electric indicator telling me the current Wall Street prices. I am in a temple of capitalism.

I am in Houston again, and two years ago this McDonald's and this germ-free shopping mall was a car lot. And all the other car lots I remember are now office blocks and condominiums and hotels and McDonald's. Houston is not bigger, it is fuller.

With 560 square miles of flat land, compared, for example, with Greater London's 610 square miles, Houston has a mere three million inhabitants. Only half the land is developed. Ten minutes out of downtown and you are in the country, but it's an illusion. Or you are in a suburb but there's an office block, in a shopping centre and there's a skyscraper, in a sleazy bar but there's a school.

There are no rules in Houston, only building, expanding, developing. There are no zones. You can do it where you want – if you have the money. In Houston they have the money.

*Tranquility Park*

It is perhaps the largest unzoned city in the world, the sign of American cities to come. Out on the edges the new Energy Corridor swells out into a city of its own, with half a million inhabitants scheduled by 1990. By the 21st century Houston's population will double, and there will still be room.

Houston does not conform. It is a jar upon the sensibilities of the old world which liked its cities a certain way. The pavements are deserted, except for the minority – those without cars. The underground tunnels are carpeted, smart, insulated from harm. Cameras watch you, security men root out the undesirables. You need never see the poor.

*"The meek shall never inherit Houston,"* I was told by respected writer Douglas Milburn. But would they want to?

Petro Metro, Space City, Tomorrow City, a developer's dream, call Houston what you will – some call it a mess – but people are still flocking to its call. It is the fastest growing American city, from 14th to the fourth largest in just 35 years, and is possibly the last frontier. It was also the last place to catch the recession, but so buoyant was the spirit, despite the oil glut and the collapse of the Mexican peso, that it blusters on, almost undaunted.

Hotels that were planned during the boom have just been finished and sit half empty. Whole housing and office blocks are unoccupied, but if anyone is worrying they hardly show it.

More people will come, just as in the late 70s workers from the north flocked into Houston in search of sun and work. They found humidity and grind, but with plenteous rewards, and they added an astonishing 1,000 new cars onto the Houston roads every week. Some couldn't take it and left, but more still came, so that those born in Texas are outnumbered three to one.

Foreign businessmen pour in seeking Texas money for their own projects. Foreign businesses buy up Houston properties as a sound investment – the car parks belong to Hong Kong, an office block to the British postal workers' pension fund, another to West German workers.

Houston's smooth, clipped tone is borrowed from NASA, just down the road (all visitors should find time to sit in Mission Control). It is polite but very firm. Inverted machismo I call it. *"Excuse me sir, may I help you,"* say the security men who see my incredulous face doesn't fit. They could kill with kindness, whereas in Dallas, 300 miles away, the tone is unashamedly Texan. Houston is Texas, but not of it. Too cosmopolitan, too sophisticated. Hellfire! There's even a large gay community around the Montrose area.

But Houston is not that far ahead. The Chamber of Commerce and the Economic Development Council try to wean the city off oil and gas dependency and into high technology. Out in Galveston there are vast stocks of unwanted oil pipes waiting for foreign buyers.

A large pharmaceuticals industry helps, but then Houston has the largest medical centre in the world, and that helps a lot in a nation dependent on private medicine.

In one field Houston does lead – modern architecture. Like an architect's model with sprayed on grass and model trees, the newer developments defy human intrusion. Philip Johnson has run riot on Houston money. His Pennzoil Place broke the rectangular mould of skyscrapers, his Republic Bank Center is a fairytale Gothic cathedral, stretched into the sky in red granite. At the Transco Tower, a 64-storey suburban office block, he fulfilled Frank Lloyd Wright's dream of building a skyscraper set entirely on its own. Then he tacked a monumental stone entrance onto the glass front.

Only in Houston.

It is the largest exhibition of buildings in the world. Some work, some don't. Some beg the question, who is kidding whom? But it's art, and Houston wants art like a teenage girl wants make-up, as a sign of growing up. Remember, less than 75 years ago Houston was tiny. A hurricane destroyed neighbouring Galveston so they built a ship canal to Houston where it was safer and now Houston is the largest international port in North America.

And so it needed to catch up, to acquire all the hallmarks of a great city. All the performing arts are now installed, while corporations and hotels buy up art work as fast as artists can produce it. Artistic value is measured in dollars by many Houstonians – a Texan trait.

In the downtown area, where no one goes at night – because it is dead rather than dangerous – there are massive, playful sculptures by Miro and Dubuffet. Because there is enough space, and because there is enough money.

Sometimes it is painful for the visitor from Manhattan or Europe – so much excellence yet how much appreciation? So many willing purchasers yet how much taste? So much to see and yet so difficult to see it all through the car windshield.

*"But I want to take the bus,"* I insisted at times, and not just because taxis are horrendously expensive. To unclog the freeways city authorities want more commuters to join the blacks, hispanics, students and poor whites on the buses, so they introduced smart air-conditioned coaches and even tinted the windows so your friends in their cars might not see you aboard. But who could tell me which bus to take? *"Take a cab!"* they all said.

*"I'll walk,"* I said. *"You're crazy,"* they told me. But I walked, even where there were no pavements. I met one man who drives 200 yards to his office every day then jogs at lunchtime. There are special jogging routes everywhere, even an entire avenue lit at night at the expense of affluent local joggers.

People work hard and play hard. Many of them were lured from their home towns by the promise of high salaries and the good life. Those that stayed were surprised at the challenge, surprised at how much the city could offer, albeit spread around.

*"It's a melting pot,"* I am told, and I am served, smiled at and spoken to in broken English by a multitude of races.

*Capital National Bank Building*

*"It's a dustbin,"* says a Chicago cabby who hates Houston but admires its anti-union posture and lack of state income tax.

*"It's a very macho city,"* a woman tells me. *"Look at all those tall, thin skyscrapers."* Houston still likes its women in the more traditional Texan role.

*"It's a greenhouse,"* says a new immigrant in the oil industry. *"I never go out of doors except in the fall or to swim."* I see his point as I sweat in the second or two of humidity which chokes me in between the air-conditioned limousine and the air-conditioned lobby.

It is all these things. It is the embodiment of that definition of capitalism which says that you have complete freedom; the freedom to be rich and the freedom to be poor. In Houston the rich are all around you, gliding through padded tunnels, across walkways, along freeways, consuming energy, creating energy; lounging in sumptuous bars sipping cocktails, dining where *nouvelle cuisine* and European wines are served. The strain of keeping up does not show, but in private moments it is there.

I stand in a space age hotel lobby next to a clean-cut but frantic businessman trying to phone London, Paris and New York. *"This phone is a lesbian phone link,"* he tries to convince me. *"I tell you, this city is crazy. It is not the world you or I grew up in."*

I smell the sweetened air and watch illuminated glass elevators dart up and down to the sound of a grand piano and tinkling cocktail glasses.

You might not like Houston but if it fails to fascinate you then beware of the 21st century.

# WHERE TO STAY

Overbuilt and overdone, that is the current state of Houston hotels. There are far too many, they range from the luxurious to the sumptuous, with little to choose from in the moderate bracket and they are desperately difficult to choose between. That's the bad news.

The good news is that competition is now so high that widespread undercutting has made the top hotels at least very tempting. *"Slap your passport down on the desk and ask for a reduction,"* was one instruction I received. It works too, so be prepared to bargain hard. Occupancy rates average at around 50-55 per cent, therefore you are unlikely to be turned away. But beware the big conventions, as in the first week of May and late February/early March annually.

It is vital to choose your location carefully, since a cheaper hotel on the wrong side of town can cost you dearly in taxis. Every major business area has its own set of hotels.

Taking the city in sections, in the downtown area there is the **Hyatt Regency** (1200 Louisiana; tel: 654 1234; telex: 767118) which is the largest in town and was the tallest building when it went up in 1972. Now overshadowed by its neighbours, it has lost a fraction of its glittering modernity, but the vast open atrium with illuminated glass elevators still gives me a thrill, as does the revolving restaurant. This is the most convenient hotel for the direct airport bus. Singles from around $85.

Close by is the only hotel I know which closes at weekends and thus has cheaper rates for businessmen. The **Whitehall** (1700 Smith; tel: 659 5000; telex: 775256) seems dowdy and strangely dated in such a polished city, but don't be fooled. It probably has the highest occupancy rate in town (75 per cent) and is renowned for personal service. Good free limousines are very useful too. Rates from around $70.

Two new hotels downtown are the **Meridien** (400 Dallas; tel: 759 0202; telex 762544), the only one run by Europeans, with an excellent French restaurant and corporate rates negotiable around $90; and the **Four Seasons** (1300 Lamar; tel: 650 1300; telex 794653) at the same rates, in which art deco meets the modernists and gets a bit tangled up in an effort to be luxurious. But the open-air pool and whirlpool are very pleasant and the Park shopping mall next door is convenient for short-stay shoppers. The Four Seasons is the most exclusive downtown. Rates from $105.

The smallest downtown hotel gets away from the predictable American line in tasteless luxury by copying British styles but not, thankfully, British service. Opened in 1983, the **Lancaster** (701 Texas; tel: 228 9500; telex: 790506) has only 93 rooms with a preferred corporate rate of $115. The restaurant serves quite the best English food I've had for ages, and the rooms make a welcome change from multinational boredom. Singles start from $125; doubles from $150; suites from $275.

Clean, no frills accommodation downtown but still with pool and limousine service is cheapest at the **Rodeway Inn** (1015 Texas; tel: 224 4511; telex: 791753). Single rooms at $35 or $169 weekly are better than higher priced names like the Sheraton Houston.

A few miles out in the Galleria area are two hotels built as part of the shopping mall, the **Westin Oaks** (tel: 623 4300; telex: 792096) and **Westin Galleria** (tel: 960 8100; telex: 4990983), both around $120, both reliable and probably the best locations for shopping.

Holiday Inn's improved **Crowne Plaza** (2222 West Loop; tel: 961 7272; telex 792761) is superb value at $69 for a single and an example of how H.I. are updating their prime locations. Stay two nights or more and the first night is free. Also modern, fresh and nicely uncluttered in the Galleria area is the **Grand Hotel** (2525 West Loop; tel: 961 3000; telex 7920) at similar prices.

The **Warwick Post Oak** (2001 Post Oak Bvd; tel: 961 9500; telex 762590) is new, architecturally breathtaking and probably the best of the Galleria group. Push hard for singles from $80. Nearer downtown is its sister hotel, stuffed with rich furniture, paintings and tapestries and revered in the city almost as a palace. Overlooking Hermann Park, it has a central position and the service is impeccable, as is the catering. Again, worth pressing for $80.

Newer is the **Inn on the Park** (Riverway; tel: 871 8181; telex 794510) set in a spotless landscaped park development barely stained by human frailty. Black swans glide across the lake, swimmers listen to stereo under water; all is health club and happiness. Starts from about $120 and it's worth it. At a similar price but in a very different mould, the **Remington on Post Oak,** good for the Galleria area (1919 Briars Oaks Drive; tel: 845 7600; telex: 765535 or 765536 reservations), is a study in elegance; an art gallery and private club in such tasteful decor that it cannot hope to pay for itself.

The proprietors, Rosewood Hotels (also Mansions on Turtle Creek, Dallas and Bel Air, L.A.) are backed by the daughter of H.L. Hunt, Caroline Hunt Schoellkopf, who apparently sees hotels as a hobby. She is reputedly the fifth richest person in the USA and it shows. The art and sculpture are worthy of any fine gallery – the staff all look and behave like law graduates. If budgets are no problem stay here, at around $135 upwards. Otherwise come for a look and a cocktail.

At the Greenway Plaza business district **Stoufer's Hotel** (6 Greenway Plaza East; tel: 629 1200; telex: 62821924) stands out, both physically and in service, especially since an expensive refit. Guests can use the exclusive Houston City Club, a considerable plus point for fitness enthusiasts. With the excellent City Lights roof-top lounge, Stouffer's singles start around $110, but are as low as $59 at the weekend.

*Sculpture by Miró enlivens the banking district*

At the Medical Center area the **Shamrock Hilton** (6900 South Main; tel: 668 9211; telex: 775853) is solid, reliable, unspectacular and when built in 1949 was in the middle of nowhere. It has large rooms and the largest hotel swimming pool in the world. The high occupancy rate is indicative of popularity among businessmen, golfers and rich patients using the Medical Center. Rooms from $70 are very good value.

Most guidebooks omit Houston's, and perhaps the world's, smallest luxury hotel, the five suite **Colombe d'Or** (3410 Montrose; tel: 524 7999; no telex), because it doesn't conform. A converted mansion built by oilman Walter J. Fondren in 1923, it is a rich man's guesthouse where each guest is pampered. Houstonians hold it in awe – it's so small, so old – but owner Steve Zimmerman (of

Zimm's wine bar), who based it on an *auberge* in Provence, will budge from his set $150-400 rate if you have a good bargaining ploy. With breakfast and free limousine and secretarial service thrown in, the price is competitive.

Far West is a Hyatt look-alike, **Adam's Mark Hotel** (2900 Briarpark; tel: 978 7400; telex: 91088/5497), personally a great favourite for its friendly service with good indoor pool and Quincy's disco. Singles from $80.

Close by is the **Westchase Hilton** (9999 Westheimer;tel:974 1000), popular with businessmen; spectacular outside, predictable inside. Prices as for its neighbour.

And so the list goes on: then beyond these areas is yet another new cluster around the expanding Energy Corridor, plus those hotels near the Astrodome, NASA, Galveston and the Inter-Continental Airport.

Anyone wanting a complete directory could write to the Greater Houston's Convention and Visitors' Council for their *Travel Planners Guide* and *Accommodations Directory* at: 3300 Main, Houston, Texas 77002; tel: 523 5050.

# WHERE TO EAT

There will be times in Houston when you ask yourself if anyone ever eats at home. Several years ago I had the impression there were more car lots than anything else, but now I'd estimate that food lots have the edge.

Any drive along any freeway rarely puts you more than a few hundred yards away from a franchise outlet, while in the shopping areas eating space easily matches retail areas. Oral consumption is everywhere, and in almost every form to match the 99 different ethnic groups in Houston.

Always book whenever possible, go where your contacts would go, taking into account location, price (what they call cheap is often quite dear for visitors) and your hunger. Ridiculously large servings at high prices are hard to resist when so much of the food is excellent, but with a busy schedule they can be disastrous. You will notice how carefully your hosts eat: not only are they unimpressed with quantity but they also spend a fortune on health clubs.

The best Mexican food in the world is made in Texas because some of the best Mexican caterers went there. From a wide choice I would plump for **Pappasito's** (6445 Richmond; tel: 784 5253), with its frontier-decor and sumptuous portions (even for Houston). For Tex-Mex variations with noise graffiti and barnyard decor the incongruously-titled **Cadillac Bar** (1802 Shepherd; tel: 862 2020) is popular for its roasted quail and Ramos Gin Fizzes. **The Cortes** (2404 W. Alabama; tel: 522 7771) in the Montrose area is small, genuine and great value except that it does not accept credit cards, which is quite rare.

Of course there are excellent Indian, Japanese and Chinese restaurants, but what is outstanding is some of the Hunan-style Chinese cuisine. The most expensive such dinner, costing around $100 for two, is at **Uncle Tai's** (1890 S. Post Oak; tel: 960 8000), recently moved from New York, as is so much else in Houston. I have never tasted crispier more succulent water chestnuts in my life.

However, as an introduction to Hunan cooking in slightly brighter surroundings at a lesser price, though still not cheap, I would go for **Dong Ting** (2727 Fondren; tel: 789 6920) and put yourself in the hands of owner San Hwang, who took me through some 10 delicate courses with explanations and folk tales in between. The penultimate dish of dried and crushed chestnuts with cream is indescribably good.

No one should go to Houston, or indeed anywhere in Texas, without having a steak. Lately, Houston restaurants are coming round to the fact that good steak doesn't have to be just slapped down on a barbecue. Locals will argue which is the best; I would go to either **Brenner's** (10911 Katy Freeway; tel: 465 2901), a family venture in a homely setting – try the German fried potatoes with caramelized onions – or **Ruth's Chris Steakhouse** (6213 Richmond; tel: 789 2333) where one steak will feed two. Many people ask for doggy bags, a custom which I find somewhat distasteful but at this place it is only sensible. Similarly the **Palm** (6100 Westheimer; tel: 977 2544) is good for steaks but just ridiculous for lobsters. You order these by weight and struggle to eat the lot just to protect your investment.

Slightly cheaper and a lot of raucous fun is the **Hofbrau** (1803 Shepherd; tel: 869 7074), popular with students but with a fairly limited menu.

Away from steak but still on the American theme (or what Americans have taken to be so) the chains of restaurants called **Chilli's, Black-Eyed Pea** and **Bennigan's** are worth a try if you are near one. The latter have long happy hours and are designed to look like English pubs (and are therefore much nicer than English pubs), the major difference being that the service is so sickeningly good.

For the best hamburger in Houston I recommend the **Fuddrucker's** chain where you queue up past the baker making the buns, the butcher chopping up the meat, and then make your own burger up with fresh salads. They each have bars, gardens and buildings which look like one-off renovations but of course are just instant Texana.

Just as Houston has embraced the arts at any cost, so have the restaurants striven to adopt French and particularly *nouvelle cuisine.* Not all of them get it right, and none of them are cheap. I liked **Brennan's** (3300 Smith Street; tel: 522 8711) the best because it was set in a restored New Orleans-style building and had few airs and graces. Entrées at around $29 are merely a small part of the story, so perhaps try the cheaper lunch menu. It's hardly French but I did enjoy a mixed grill cooked over mesquite, the most commonly found wood in Texas, which gives the meat a slightly scented, almost bitter taste.

Despite its name, **Tony's** (1801 Post Oak Boulevard; tel: 622 6778) is widely held to be the best French restaurant in town, although the regular attendance of local celebrities adds greatly to its lustre. It is showy, spectacular and with wine you can easily spend more than $80 a head.

In close competition is the relatively new **Restaurant de France** at the Meridien Hotel (400 Dallas, downtown; tel: 759 0202) where I revelled in some Wisconsin pigeon poached in red wine on a base of pears. There is a good prix fixe for $20 plus tax and service (which is generally 15 per cent in Houston). Also recommended is the very intimate **Colombe d'Or** (tel: 977 9524) where, unlike the two aforementioned places, it is possible to dispense with a tie.

Less French, more international, is the **Rivoli** (5636 Richmond; tel: 780 7464) and the new superb **La Cave des Rois** (1220 Augusta; tel: 953 1000) which is all bricks and pastel shades hidden cunningly in a hi-tech glass office block. The interior is refreshingly understated and the food is unfussy yet original. *"American transcendant,"* my escort called it, meaning, I think, American food cooked with European sensitivity. La Cave also has pleasant evening entertainment with a complimentary buffet with cocktails.

Most Houston restaurants serve excellent seafood, but for the real seafront atmosphere it is worth asking someone to take you to one of the seafood cafés on the Gulf of Mexico at Galveston (50 minutes drive from Houston).

Otherwise the best specialist seafood house in Houston is **Don's Seafood Restaurant** (3009 Post Oake; tel: 629 5380), for atmosphere and Cajun-style gumbos, bisque and fried catfish.

Finally, on Sunday lunchtime the **Warwick Hotel's** (5701 Main; tel: 526 1991) Sunday Brunch is a new Houston fad, perhaps because it is a challenge of greed over good sense. Do not arrange anything for the afternoon.

*Cowboy cuisine is only one of the delights on offer in Houston*

If your idea of a Saturday night out is sitting on a wooden bleacher, a plastic cup of beer in one hand and a paper bucketful of popcorn in the other, while before your very eyes an assortment of Marlboro men chase after bewildered calves or try to sit on various animals who don't wish to be sat upon, with the sickly sweet aroma of dung wafting about your nostrils, then you might wish to seek out a few of the last vestiges of cowboy culture still surviving in Houston.

Make no mistake, Houston ain't no cow-town, unlike Dallas-Fort Worth, but it does have one or two notable watering holes for the curious visitor and nostalgia buff. Snobbery or delicacy are certainly not excuses for giving them a miss.

**Gilley's** (4500 Spencer Highway, Pasadena – 40 mins drive from downtown; tel: 941 7990) is the most famous because it was once the biggest nightclub in the world, until Billy Bob's opened in Fort Worth, and there was a film made there called *Urban Cowboy*.

First impressions are that it is a vast warehouse full of uncouth beer swillers, second impressions are that it is a vast warehouse full of music-loving, friendly beer swillers. On Saturday nights there is a rodeo in an adjoining and equally vast warehouse. You can also ride a mechanical bull, or be taken for a ride in the large souvenir shop, where I saw what was surely one of the world's cheekiest bits of commercialism. At the bar a can of Gilley's beer poured into a plastic cup costs around $1.50; in the souvenir shop you can then purchase an empty Gilley's beer can for $2.25.

If you can't get to Gilley's try **Dancetown USA** (7214 Airline Drive; tel: 697 2083; open on Wednesday, Friday and Saturday only), one of Houston's best 'downtown honky-tonks' where you can bring your own bottle of liquor and they will provide glasses and ice. This is called a set-up, and is a great deal, though beer and wine are also available. Personally I would not go to a honky-tonk on my own, since all the tables and drinking seems to be organised for groups, but they are by no means daunting or unsafe. You are more likely to meet someone's grandmother on the dance floor than someone's younger sister. Look out for Mr Stolarski, the owner. He's very hospitable to foreign visitors.

But if you really want to get some earthier Western grit into your boots try the Saturday night **Round-Up Rodeo** in Simonton, 36 miles out (tel: 499 1479), air-conditioned but somehow wilder in spirit than the Gilley's version. Ten miles away is **Papa Blakely's** (21602 Farm Road 1093; tel: 342 9641) for wooden frame decor, sawdust and barbecued steaks.

With all these Western joints probably the best policy is to go where your contacts will take you – taxis would cost a great deal – and don't be put off by the Dolly Parton/Nashville image: live C&W played well can liven up the deadest of feet and Houston attracts all the best musicians.

If you are in Houston mid-week and don't want to go far, the best C&W disco bar is **San Antone Rose** (Voss Road at San Felipe; tel: 977 7116),designed for the drugstore cowboy with full bar service.

I could not imagine friendship or romance forming at Gilley's or a steak bar, but **Cody's Jazz Bar** (3400 Montrose; tel: 522 9747) is a perfect setting and probably my favourite bar in Houston. Set on the top of an office block, but some way from the built-up areas, you can see all of Houston's remarkable skyline from here; islands of skyscrapers amid a surprisingly luxuriant sea of greenery.

But *the* place is the **Remington Hotel** bar on Post Oak Park (1919 Briar Oaks Lane; tel: 845 7600), popular for early evening business drinks and with late night high-class singles.

Back in the Montrose area **Birdwatchers Jazz Club** (907 Westheimer) is unusually intimate and European for Houston. Nearby is **Zimm's** (4319 Montrose, tel: 529 4600), an excellent wine bar and one of the few places where you can imagine that the locals may actually have walked from their homes.

For watching young Houstonians at play, which effectively means over 25s since everything costs so much, I would choose **Studebaker's** (Augusta Drive; tel: 783 4142). It is a brash, neon-lit, chrome and polish poser's paradise, full of boppers and great records from the 60s.

When I first went there the politely macho bouncers would not let me in because they classified my expensive white shoes as sneakers.

Dress code can be a problem in Houston; some clubs enforce it rigidly, others do not. To be on the safe side, always take a jacket and a tie in your pocket just in case. Only wear jeans for honky-tonkying.

Even clubs that sound as if they are very informal can prove to be quite upmarket. In this category are Houston's **Comedy Workshop** (2105 San Felipe; tel: 524 7333), the best of the revue and cabaret venues with stand-up comics in the annexe next door, the **Laff Stop** (1952 W. Gray, River Oaks; tel: 524 4333) and **Cabaret West** (2639 Winrock; tel: 974 3867), popular among students of anatomy, with a touch more refinement but no less flesh at the **Windsor Plaza Shopping Centre** where you'll find a lively disco, swinging singles bars and a couple of strip joints.

Unashamedly, however, I admit that the best night I had in Houston was at the indoor **Summit Arena** (Greenway Plaza; tel: 627 0600) in a 16,000 all-seated all-hysterical crowd, watching the newly-resurgent Houston Rockets basketball team. For an all-American night out it can't be surpassed (but arrange to eat before or after because the Summit catering is abysmal). Equally good, I'm sure, would be a baseball (Astros) or football (Oilers) game both at the Astrodome, Houston's very own wonder of the world.

None of these places are downtown, incidentally. Your best bets there are **La Carafe** (813 Congress; tel: 229 9399), the revolving roof top bar at the **Hyatt Regency** or a quick taxi out of the place.

# GETTING AROUND

Houston is car city, and unless you are familiar with driving in the States, or are staying a long time, avoid hiring a car. But the taxis are unpredictable, and it's odds on that after a few days you might know your way around some areas better than the driver.

Always, therefore, carry a map and familiarise yourself with the main routes and names. Keep a check on where the driver is taking you. I took the same journey three times and the fare varied between $6 and $12.

From the airport a taxi will cost at least $25. In preference take the Northline bus ($6) and get off at the appropriate terminal (ask the driver), from where courtesy cars will pick you up. This is not only cheaper but quicker, since the bus uses a rapid contraflow route which taxis cannot.

To cut costs, check out where free limousines can take you from your hotel. For example, most go to the Galleria, and from there you could get a taxi.

For a faster getaway helicopters link various parts of the city with the airport. Contact Air Link on 230 1254 for scheduled flights (around $45 one way) or Armadillo Airways on 975 8989.

*Petro Metro's futuristic skyline*

# Jakarta

**With years of turbulence to look back on, the Indonesian capital appears determined to settle down to a period of stability and prosperity. And the signs of a sturdy infrastructure in its infancy are already there for the visitor to see.**

**By Carol Weingott**

The strongest single image you come away from Jakarta with is its open Dutch drainage canal system: a fetid legacy of 330-odd years of Dutch colonialism that seems omnipresent, a cruel parody of the River Of Life theme that one subconsciously equates with water.

There is life along this 'river', 7.3 million specimens of it packed into a flat coastal plain of sprawling, unsanitized kampongs, industrial estates and some affluent suburbs. The kampongs keep springing up as the *orang gelandangan,* people from all over the Republic, continue seeking their fortunes in the *Ibu Kota,* Mother Town. With television now having reached the furthest outposts of the implosion of 13,677 atolls and islands that constitute Indonesia, so have pictures of modern life in Jakarta. And however effective the current official 're-settlement' plans end up being, Jakarta is already overcrowded with its population set to hit 16 million by the turn of the century.

It is immediately apparent to a visitor that most people seem to be under 20. If anyone needs further convincing, a vigorous family planning department is happy to oblige by handing out merit awards to be stuck on the outside of dwellings proclaiming which method is being used in that household.

The fact also remains that there is nowhere for people to go, though according to official figures slum dwellers are 26 per cent – negligible compared to Calcutta's 67 per cent. But what constitutes a slum? West Jakarta's Mayor, H. Eddy Ruchijat Soheh, puts the problem in perspective when he says that of the 1.3 million people in his patch, only 28 per cent of homes have access to piped water.

The situation's most outspoken critic though, was former Vice President, the late Adam Malik, who frequently deplored *"the large numbers of Indonesian people still living in destitution".* Beyond the eight-lane business district of Jalan Thamrin, Malik's destitute can be seen literally clinging for their lives under the narrow bridges that cross the refuse-filled canals – their worldly possessions, bundles of dirty rags, floating about them in buckets.

When Malik was 'replaced' as Vice President in March 1983 by Umar Wirahadiksumah, after five years in office, he also deplored the so-called death squads, made up of the military and police, at whose hands several thousand people have died since President Sukarno took office in 1968. (The President is now in his fourth five year term and rivals Singapore's Lee Kuan Yew for years in office.)

Curiously enough, the killings provoked little public outcry, the most voluble reaction coming from tattooed men (many of the victims were thus identified), and there was said to be an understandable rush to get tattoos removed. But then it has long been a bloody place: the conservative estimate of those slaughtered in a frenzy of retribution following the failed communist coup on September 30, 1965, is half a million.

The most recent bloody outbreaks in what rates as the world's largest Islamic nation (as well as its fifth most populous country) concern clashes between the state ideology, *Pancasila,* and Moslem fundamentalists. The first large-scale opposition came in the depressed port area of Tanjung Priok on September 12, 1984, when 1,500 people armed with sickles and knives marched on a police station demanding the release of four men. The army was brought in, shops and cars burnt and 18 people died. The incident had its origins a week earlier when 'emotive posters fanning religious, racial and ethnic differences' were found at a mosque in Tanjung Priok. An official attempting to remove the posters was beaten up and had his motorcycle set alight – it was this that led to the detention of the four men.

The irony is that *Pancasila* is intended to eliminate conflicts based on ideological differences, but to the Moslem extremists it is seen as intruding on their belief that state and religion can't be separated. All students now receive a 'civic education' on the ideology whose five principles are: faith in God, humanitarianism, social justice, democracy and national unity.

Other signs that national unity is in trouble concern the 4-6 million Indonesian Chinese who, here as elsewhere in the region, wield considerable economic power. The country's biggest private bank, Bank Central Asia, is, for instance, controlled by Indonesian-Chinese tycoon Liem Sioe Liong – several of its offices were, for the first time, the targets of a series of bomb attacks late in 1984.

Despite the volatile political climate and the evident poverty, life has improved vastly during the past decade, at least according to the ex-pats. They cite *"dynamic pace of development"* which has seen exports climb to US$20 billion annually – more jobs for an exceedingly willing labour force, *"they make the Australians look half-asleep"*, and the successful lowering of the inflation rate from several hundred per cent to Western-style levels.

Indonesia undoubtedly is a rich country – it is the world's largest exporter of liquified natural gas and plywood – and intends to become a major exporter of coal with reserves estimated at 22.5 billion tons. As is evident from the large number of Japanese restaurants in town, influence from this quarter is highly significant as is that of American oil money. This has been successfully attracted through production-sharing contracts where the development costs are shared and oil production, rather than profit, is split 85:15 – with the state oil company, Pertamina, taking the larger share.

The ex-pats say it's easier to live in Jakarta these days: among the ubiquitous sprawl of red-tiled roofs theirs are the larger properties bedecked with handsome gardens, swimming pools and tennis courts. And although there remains a horrifying level of official red tape, old hands say that while you can't get around it, you can learn the ropes and devise ways to cut down on delays. Prime tips for doing just this include getting yourself a good driver who knows office addresses and can calculate travel times, and having a healthy respect for bargaining. This, apparently, is a serious part of business – consider it a mere preamble and you're lost – shrewdness is appreciated and quick concessions are seen as stupidity.

Politeness in Indonesia also involves asking a lot of personal questions about family and local customs – visitors are not only expected to answer, but to ask the same questions in return. In the same vein, visitors should also be aware that the command of the English language won't necessarily be as good as, say, in Singapore or Hong Kong. Although English is widely used in business circles, its use is not always automatic. This can mean that you may find yourself negotiating with someone chosen for his or her language ability rather than their position in the company – and while Indonesians are generally far better linguists than Westerners, misunderstandings can have serious consequences.

*The red-tiled roof tops of Jakarta*

One of the most rewarding aspects of doing business in Jakarta is that its nightlife is still interestingly unregulated – that side of things which is being wiped off the map in Singapore, such as open-air food stalls, cabarets, massage parlours and the notorious transvestites, is very much alive.

Whatever becomes of such things in Jakarta's future, it is unlikely that the city will lose its other distinguishing characteristics – its canals flanked by broad avenues and squares bearing the names of its heroes: the missionary warrior Fatahillah who drove the Portuguese out in 1527; Hyam Wuruk, the great king of the Mojopahit dynasty. Nor is it likely to lose its ugly public monuments concentrated thickly around Merdeka (Freedom) Square and an extremely enervating climate with relative humidity a high 75 per cent.

Jakarta's monuments may speak rather too dutifully of nationalistic aspirations but its museums identify it as a place where the evolutionary scale can be measured from orangutans to jewels of Eastern art like the great temple at Borobudur. Especially recommended is the National Museum which has an outstanding collection of Chinese porcelain and a peaceful central courtyard where free-standing statues from the Hindu and Buddhist periods gaze out, sublimely unconscious of what has since come to pass.

## WHERE TO STAY

For a city so keen on the statuesque, or monuments *ad infinitum,* it is ironic that a height restriction governs the rise of the hotel industry in Jakarta: nothing, it appears, is permitted to outstrip the 30-storey ascendancy of the midtown government offices. For all this, the main business street, Jalan Thamrin, is fast taking on the appearance of a baby Grand Canyon – offices, banks and hotels being marshalled along its borders.

This gulch aspect is best appreciated from the maverick 29th floor of the Mandarin : from here it is fascinating to watch the traffic police whirring past in helicopters, vainly attempting to disentangle the *bemo* discord down below. It is also from this vantage point that you'll observe the chief idiosyncrasy of the Welcome Statue in a dish on the constipated roundabout on Jalan Thamrin immediately outside. This 5½ tons of male and female bronze atop vast concrete pillars and waving, actually faces

*Jalan Thamrin*

the wrong way to welcome visitors arriving from Halim airport. Never mind. This about-faced behaviour is exhibited only to visiting dignitaries and members of the Armed Forces – Halim being culled especially for their use. Undistinguished visitors now arrive at the new Cengkareng airport and are spared the rear view.

All things considered, wet-blanket humidity and not much that's uplifting to look at, short-stay visitors might derive the greatest degree of comfort from a few days at the **Mandarin** (Jalan M. H. Thamrin; tel: 321 307; telex: 45755). This gleaming, white marble godsend is sister to the Mandarin Hong Kong, and to the Oriental Bangkok.

Besides having some of the tastiest restaurants in town and a finely-tuned staff who are experts at operating the radio-paging service in the most dulcet of tones – the Mandarin is wrapped in more luxury than anywhere else. There are 504 spacious rooms, 19 of them highly desirable suites: anyone who can think of a way to wangle their way into one, is strenuously advised to do so.

An aura of teak, polish, thickness, silence and silkiness pervades the guest rooms: the beds and baths all appear to be extra wide/large and handbasins come in pairs. Elsewhere, the hotel is also faultlessly interesting. The lobby is one of the very few it is possible for women to sit in on their own without creating suspicious overtones: its trio of stone Sumatran statues and a couple of four-headed sculptures are guaranteed to repay close attention.

The impecunious might like to note that discounts are available, otherwise prices are among the least attractive in town. Singles Rp114,400; doubles Rp144,800; suites Rp312,000-754,000; all inclusive of 15½ per cent service charge and government tax.

Among the city's most attractive prices are those of the **Indonesia** (Jalan M. H. Thamrin; tel: 320 008; telex: 44233), on the opposite lip of the Welcome Statue's saucer. This place is just about as monumental as the statue, at least historically. When construction began in 1959, it was out of a budget from the Japanese Government's War Compensation fund. When it was completed, three years later, it was in time for Jakarta to host the 1962 Asian Games.

The Indonesia spent the next decade in the glorious position of being the only international hotel in town – for visitors, however, this meant drastic measures such as bumping whenever the government held a conference. The arrival of the 1974 PATA bandwagon saw a spate of hotel development with the second piece of international property being the Boroburdur Inter-Continental. Inter-Continental had previously managed the Indonesia, as Sheraton were later to do; the property is now firmly in the control of the hotel group of the same name who operate a chain throughout the country.

The 666-room Indonesia is undergoing a necessary facial – its wrinkles and outright cracks being covered up with a Rp13 million beauty treatment. There is a pleasant informality and a good dash of the ethnic. There are Japanese and Chinese (Cantonese) restaurants and a Scandinavian-style lunch on Fridays. For insistent entertainment from the Vocal Group le Roy and Western cabaret imports, try the Nirvana Supper Club (which also does lunch) on the 15th floor. The hotel has pleasant grounds, a large pool and two well-located tennis courts. It also serves its fare at State banquets. Singles Rp60,800; doubles Rp78,000; suites Rp88,400-119,600; all inclusive of service and tax.

Just beyond the shadow of the Welcome Statue but still in the heart of the business district is the flashy **Sari Pacific** (Jalan M. H. Thamrin; tel: 323 707; telex: 44514), of the Pan Pacific Group. Despite a healthy 87 per cent occupancy, this establishment thrusts forth the specials at an amazing rate. Magic Noodle Week had just departed while I was there, and on trotted Here Comes America: Statue of Liberty in lard; Texas-size portions and a Dancing Buffalo Saloon. Fine if you like places that wear their heart so prominently on their sleeve. Here, under your pillow, on all bathroom accessories, guests are repeatedly told that this is 'the hotel with a heart'. Other vital organs include an international Pitstop disco, swimming pool brimming with activity and a lift service that is cunningly designed to appear as an appendage to Singapore Airlines. The lift floor mats are changed at midnight to announce the coming day just in case, amid so much fun, guests should forget what day it is. Singles Rp93,600; doubles from Rp134,400; suites Rp218,400-416,100.

Getting away from the centre of things is **Hilton International's** largest resort development worldwide (Jalan Jenderal Gatot Suroto; tel: 583 051; telex: 46673). Most of the tropical/ethnic excesses have been applied rather thickly here: open-air theatre, man-made lagoon, full-scale bazaar to name but a few. What it all adds up to is 32 acres of lush Luna Park. Businessmen who find that they have to extend their stay recommend the Hilton because of its general extensiveness – this runs to bowling alley, golf course, gymnasium, two swimming pools and plenty of squash and tennis courts.

The recent extension has added a 17-storey garden tower with 224 rooms to the existing 396. Of the new tower, the showcase is the Penthouse Suite with its own swimming pool and helipad. Long-stay executives can join the Private Executive Club which gives privileged access to the second swimming pool. Short-stay guests can wander round the grounds and crick their necks while peering at the curious stilted Batak houses – palm-thatched, pointed-roof dwellings which list forward like the prows of ships – or at the massive Dwarapala, stone Gods guarding the hotel gates, whose job it is to prevent the forces of discord and evil from entering the Kingdom of Heaven.

The Hilton's lobby does have Kingdomly qualities, namely its beautifully carved wooden pillars and gold-leaf ceiling modelled on the Royal Palace at Jogyakarta. All very stunning, very formal, mildly intimidating.

Anyone who wants to spend their time in Jakarta pretending that they are not really there at all would be quite happy in this verdant environment, but anyone with business on Jalan Thamrin might find the journeying to and fro a little tedious. Singles Rp134,000; doubles Rp176,800; suites Rp197,600-618,800; apartments Rp197,600-384,800.

*The lobby of the Hilton International*

James N. Hart,
Export Manager,
Wallace and Tiernan Pty Ltd. Syd
Flew 70,000 kms in 1984.

# "It's a winner. A real gem. Garuda have really done their homework on their new Executive Class."

GARUDA
EXECUTIVE
CLASS

Garuda has provided the traveller with a business class that really does cater to his needs.

In every way, Garuda's new Executive Class puts the businessman first.

Upon boarding, passengers are escorted to their seats in the nose of the aircraft. This section, previously reserved for first class passengers, combines a spacious environment with a secluded, intimate atmosphere.

The unique location allows greater freedom of movement and provides wider, deep-cushion easy-seats. The perfect combination for a comfortable flight.

But it is Garuda's exclusive services that truly set their Executive Class apart.

To facilitate the 'working' passenger, Garuda provides a stationery portfolio with desk pad,

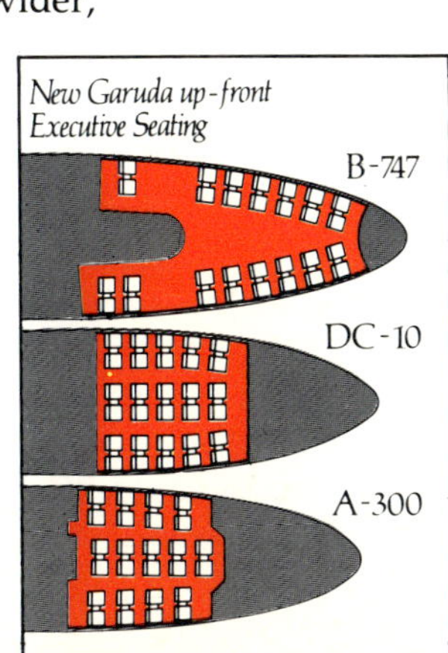

letter paper, and colourful postcards to keep you in touch with loved ones left behind.

Of course, cocktails and drinks are complimentary throughout the flight, as are the specially chosen wines.

There is a choice of 2 menus, Asian or European, each dish prepared to seduce the most discerning palate.

No airline has understood and fulfilled executives' needs better than Garuda.

Garuda's new Executive Class is the beginning of a new era of business travel.

Where executives come first.

The **Boroburdur Inter-Continental** (Lapangan Banteng Selatan; tel: 370 108; telex: 44156) has the same country-club attributes as the Hilton, with less lavishness, plus the advantage of being centrally located. Also in the market for longer staying guests, it has recently added a 140-suite annex to top up its existing 866 rooms. The gardens are attractive, all 23 acres of them, with pride of place given to an olympic-sized swimming pool.

A great deal of money has recently been spent on a fire protection programme which, rather unfortunately from the aesthetic point of view, has involved the replacement of wooden ceiling and doors with metal and fibreglass ones. The public areas are informal and there's no hint of pretentiousness. Singles Rp114,400; doubles Rp124,400; suites Rp93,600-176,800.

Of the other main chains, Hyatt is represented by the **Aryaduta Hyatt** (J. L. Prapatan; tel: 376 008; telex: 46220) close to the Presidential Palace. Anyone with dealings at that level might like to stay here, but I can think of no other good reason for doing so. This property is not up the usual Hyatt standards – one way and another it fails to be impressive, a failing which an extremely ugly exterior contributes much to. Singles Rp88,400; doubles Rp119,600; suites Rp124,800.

# WHERE TO EAT

Jakarta being the capital of the erstwhile Spice Islands, timid palates and sensitive stomachs will no doubt be extremely wary about what they let themselves in for. Such caution is not really necessary however, once the ground rules of eating Indonesian have been understood. Nor, because the food is an amalgam of influences of the cuisines of Arabia, China, India and Holland, does it necessarily contain the outlandishly exotic.

Where the formidable reputation for spice really comes in is in Sumatran food – barely bearable dishes like *nasi padang* are the sort to recommend only to those whose tongues you may wish to scorch evermore. Where the spicy reputation does come in unfairly, is in relation to the *sambals,* side dishes of almost any kind of sauce or relish – fermented fish paste, coconut, aubergine, soya sauce – all with varying amounts of chilli. Because the *sambal* is usually self-administered, it doesn't have to leave you alone and dying at a foreign foodstall. If you do go too far with it the best remedy is rice, bread or banana, *not* liquid.

Not surprisingly, there is always plenty of rice, usually steamed and sometimes done up in small packages stapled in banana leaves when it is known as *lontong.* Another speciality for those whose intimacy with Indonesian food is confined to the universally acknowledged *nasi goreng* (fried rice and fried egg), is *ikan asem,* sweet and sour fish. Jakarta's seafood, whether smoked, salted, dried or fresh, usually repays investigation – the vegetables do too, they are always fresh and used liberally.

When it comes to stall food, the official line is that it sits well with the accustomed stomach but visitors are generally advised to resist the temptation. This is a shame. I had pancakes, *murthaba,* from the stalls by the **Merdeka Bioskop** with no ill-effects and considerable delight – and my stomach is the usual, feeble, Western sort.

Glodock and the rumbling port area, Tanjung Priok, are renowned for the excellence of their seafood – be it at a huge noisy Cantonese hall or a more modest four-table establishment. These may appear to lack sophistication, but if it's the food you came for, you're unlikely to go away disappointed. Among the innumerably good, two outstanding places are the **Jun Nyan** (tel: 364 063), small, simple with excellent frog's legs and the bigger, more central **Furama.** (72 Jalan Hayam Wuruk; tel: 632 599).

Elsewhere, the formal restaurants and hotels compete fiercely as the 'ideal venue for that intimate dinner or that business lunch' – and the thing to remember is that such places don't come cheap. At the top end of the scale, dinner for two with wine and liqueurs will cost about Rp126,880. It's worth remembering that wine is not a good buy in Jakarta: even in the smaller restaurants a bottle of *vin ordinaire* will set you back about Rp15,000. For those who don't mind splashing out, the grill rooms at the Sari Pacific, Hotel Sahid Jaya and the Borobodur Inter-Continental have extensive wine lists.

**Le Bistro** (Jalan Wahid Hasyim; tel: 327 580), is one of Jakarta's best restaurants – small, seating only 44 people, and expensive. The well-balanced menu includes *carré d'agneau provençale* (traditional baby lamb), chicken livers *flambés* with cream sherry *demi-glacé,* and a delicious selection of desserts, most of them steeped in cognac.

*A taste of the exotic*

**The Oasis,** (Jalan Raden Saleh; tel: 327 818), is rated as the most glamorous and oldest of the city's Western restaurants. It occupies the ground floor of a large Dutch villa with a long and colourful history and opens into a garden. While the food is good, rather than excellent, the atmosphere more than makes up for any culinary inadequacies.

The Mandarin's **Spice Garden** (tel: 321 307 ext. 2843) was the first Sichuan restaurant in Jakarta and, with a range of 167 dishes, it probably remains the most comprehensive. Taiwanese chefs supervise the menu which includes the likes of hot smoked duck marinated with camphor and stewed fish heads prepared in a sand pot. The Spice Garden is resplendent in crimson, cream and gold with intimate booths around the perimeter for those who may not be adept at handling fish heads. The Mandarin's other justly famous restaurant is the **Club Room** done out in charcoal grey and black leather upholstery. It has a large French à la carte menu with specialities like *filet de pomfret* "Nelson", and *soufflé d 'aubergines.*

Anyone interested in navigating a steamboat should trek out to the Hilton's **Sriwedari Gardens** (tel: 583 051 ext. 283) especially on Friday when dining is accompanied by live jazz. This restaurant is outdoors by the main pool, and goes in for Indonesian favourites, *satay, kakap* (which is like the North American grouper) and barbecues on Sunday evenings.

The Hyatt Aryaduta's **Shima** (tel: 376 008) is widely thought to serve the best Japanese food in town, with specialities like *teppanyaki, yakiniku* and *shabu-shabu.* The same hotel's **Le Parisien** is known for such delicate menus as: poached goose liver, quail broth and Beluga caviar in curry cream.

Of a more proletarian nature is the **Front Page** (Wisma Antara; tel: 348 045) near the Sari Pacific where a lot of journalists, foreign and local, eat and drink against a backdrop of walls covered with front pages from around the world.

Anyone who finds the gastronomic delights of Jakarta getting to them can head for the **American Hamburger** (tel: 350 888) in Glodock Plaza where this is just what they'll get.

The most unpleasant aspects of being in Jakarta disappear promptly at 6 p.m. when night comes rushing down: this total eclipse happens in a merciful five minutes. Wake up and the dilapidated houses, the eternity of crumbling red tile roofs, the noise and dirt, will have been swept away. You are left with a *bir pilsener Bintang* – bottled in Indonesia with 'technical assistance' from Heineken Holland – in hand, your head wreathed in smoke from clove-impregnated *(kretek)* cigarettes.

As in any large Eastern city, there is plenty of the seedy stuff: swarms of massage parlours (300 including the sauna and steam baths), hordes of *bancis* (transvestites) and euphemistic 'coffee' bars check by jowl on Jalan Mangga Besar. Best known of the massage parlours are **Monggo Mas** (Please Sir), **Cemoro Sewu** (Thousand Pines) and **Dolly,** all around Chinatown's Jalan Hayam Wuruk. Rates are between Rp4,000 and Rp8,000 an hour (tips Rp2,000-Rp5,000), and, if you have extras, the expected tip is between Rp15,000 and Rp25,000.

Jakarta also has South East Asia's biggest hostess club, the **Palace Nightclub** (Gajah Mada Plaza Lantai; tel: 357 725), with seats enough for 2,500 punters. This is a heavily-lacquered cavern where Rp7,500 buys a table from which to watch artistes like Taiwan's Chou Chou Mei supported by Miss Tien Nui. In the advent of more alluring 'international' artistes appearing, the cover charge escalates to Rp25,000. Hostesses will dance for prices in the range of Rp6,000 an hour (minimum two hours), but that's all you'll get – it is not possible here, as it is in other Asian cities, to buy a girl out of a bar. All arrangements must be made after working hours. Other Chinatown clubs/cabarets (average cover charge Rp7,500) include **Valentino's, Sim Yan** and the **Hayam Wuruk Theatre,** Jakarta's only live strip show.

Until a few years ago Chinatown was rivalled as the centre of nightlife by Ancol Dreamland, in northeast Jakarta, on the coast. Just as Ancol started to boom – its casino beloved by planeloads of Singaporeans – and its accoutrements of red lights and striptease starting to become legendary, the government bowed to pressure from the extreme Right and all the games and most of the fun were extinguished. What remains at Ancol in this particular vein are striptease artistes flitting against the red lights in some futility: the area is widely regarded as being hygienically off-limits.

The strongest element in nocturnal Jakarta however, is none of the sex industry spin-offs. It is local hawkers and whole extended families out for incidental street entertainment which they appear to greatly enjoy. One of probably many places presenting a comprehensive version of such things is **Loksari** where Rp100 at the gate lets you into a large open-air collection of stalls – food and merchandise – quoit and coconut-shy sideshows and revelatory street theatre.

Amid the candy floss, fun-fair atmosphere – *papier mâché* tigers, horses, elephants and roosters dancing in the street – there are attractions of a more startling nature: Kung Fu kings imitating machine-guns by firing chopsticks in rapid succession into innocent pieces of plywood; jugglers tossing giant rats perilously close to enthralled crowds of small boys. There are also plenty of contented-looking diners gnawing their way through 'special' menus: *sedia binyawak goreng* (crocodile); *monyet* (monkey meat); *ular sanca* (cobra); *pioh* (tortoise) while their relatives show evident signs of alarm scrabbling away in assorted cages nearby.

The ultimate in skilled traditions and sedentary participation comes in the form of shadow plays, *wayang kulit,* and plays without shadows, *wayang golek.* These involve exquisite leather or wooden puppets and narrations from the Hindu epics *Mahabharata* and the *Ramayana* which can go on all night. Insomniacs or anyone up to catching a 9p.m.-5a.m. session can obtain details from: the **Wayang Museum** (Jalan Pintu Besar Utara).

This is a city which excels in its performing arts: dance/drama and *gamelan* orchestras (xylophones, drums, gongs, string instruments and flutes). The **Visitor Information Services** at the Jakarta Theatre (tel: 354 094) and Halim airport (tel: 801 817) will supply details of venues.

# GETTING AROUND

After taking a hotel limousine or taxi from the airport to your hotel, around a 25-minute ride, the way to get around Jakarta is to fork out Rp20,800 a day for an air-conditioned hotel hire car with a driver who speaks basic English. Then, once you have your bearings, there exists a colourful range of public transport buses, *betchaks, bemos* and Colt minibuses.

Buses are cheap at Rp100, but in peak hours you'll find yourself prey to pick-pockets and jammed amid scores of passengers, some hanging perilously out the doors. Not recommended, except on a Sunday in a quiet location.

*Betchaks* (pedicabs) – a sort of trishaw in reverse – are a joy after 8p.m. when they defy government regulations banning them from main roads. No engine, no fumes – only the soft hissing of tyres, good conversation and a plastic canopy if it rains.

*Bemos* – olive-shaped three-wheelers or motorised pedicabs – are quick, cheap and efficient for short hops and a favourite with the locals. They are also a quick way to rattle the teeth out of your head and are at exactly the right height for the passenger to be asphixiated by exhaust fumes. Settle on the price before you board.

Colts take eight or so people knee-to-knee in the back of a small pick-up. They are cheap and uncomfortable but accommodating if they happen to be going your way.

There are about 8,000 taxis in Jakarta, so it's easy to find a cab when you want one. Fares are reasonable at Rp400 for the first kilometre and Rp20 for each additional 100 metres.

*Betchacks are fun if you've got the time*

Of course, you get what you pay for, and many taxis are in a very dilapidated state. One overweight foreigner recently put both feet right through the rusty floor . . . and the driver expected him to pay for the damage. Some residents swear by Bluebird cabs, which have a radio call service, others by the yellow President taxis. Make sure the meter is on; if it's not, get out and take another cab.

For a short trip costing less than Rp1,000 or after midnight a tip will be expected. Don't expect drivers always to know the way and don't assume they can speak English (hotel doormen can always help). If a cab breaks down, drivers traditionally consider it their duty to waive the fair and find you another cab. It's worth carrying plenty of low-denomination notes: a favourite game is *"sorry, no change."*

Driving oneself is not recommended. The traffic isn't as kamikaze-like as that of Bangkok, but it can be baffling. In accidents the driver behind is automatically wrong and foreigners are fair prey for 'instant insurance claims'. In side streets, often without pavements, watch out for children, *betchaks* and minibuses. Parking attendants ask for Rp100 minimum and the police, especially after midnight, are more inclined to stop you for a few thousand Rupiah tea-money than for a traffic violation.

# SHOPPING

Unless you are fond of *batik*, the ubiquitous local cloth, shopping in Jakarta is a rather lacklustre affair although it is possible to find quality *wayang* figures, *kris* daggers and wood-carvings if you are prepared to look hard.

For *batik* and a view of the range of handicrafts available, best bet is the **Sarinah** department store on Jalan Thamrin – apparently the shirts made by Irwan Tirta are the best quality. There is also a 250-strong cooperative of batik-makers known as **Batik G.K.B.** on Jalan Jend Sudirman close to the Hilton.

Visitors are often sent to the 'flea market' at **Jalan Surabaya** to sort through piles of bric-à-brac and 'antiques' in the hope of finding something original. What they will find is a regular stop for the tourist buses and an overrated collection of 'Chinese' porcelain, much of which comes from a Bandung factory, and hot out-of-the-mould brassware. Anyone wanting to bargain for these items is advised to get the price down to half the asking rate.

There also appears to be a busy tailoring industry with prices which compete with those of Singapore and Hong Kong – labour costs are lower here, but duty is paid on imported cloth. Good for made-to-measure safari suits is **Fuji Original Tailor** (Jalan Mangga Besar Raya; tel: 355 133 or 364 975). Many similar establishments can be found on Jalan Hayam Wuruk going towards Old Batavia.

Indonesia mines diamonds and opals – with the black opals being a snip compared to the Australian sort. The places to ask to see some are **Kevin Jewellery** (tel: 583 051 ext. 318) and **P.D. Pelangi** (tel: 587 981 ext. 426).

# Johannesburg

As South Africa braces itself for an era of dramatic social change, the African continent's major business capital continues to function with relative efficiency in the eye of the storm. And for the moment its white inhabitants soak up the last days of an affluent era.

By Graham Boynton

*"Ag man, it's not as bad as it looks from overseas. The blacks will quieten down and then the government will give them a bit more. That's how things change in this country, slow and orderly."* – Afrikaans-speaking Johannesburg businessman.

*"It's not that bad really – we see the troubles on television like you do. We reckon there'll be another mini-boom and maybe after that we'll start looking to Australia or Canada, or at worst, the UK."* – English-speaking Johannesburg businessman.

The two voices from within the white laager that is now Johannesburg, sound at once quite hollow and irrelevant; as if the tide of history is about to engulf them and they are left merely regurgitating familiar old lines. Suddenly it is difficult to look at Africa's most powerful city and imagine what it will be like in ten, even five years. Oliver Tambo, president of the African National Council, says they are aiming for majority rule in less than a decade; the South African government insists there will never be majority rule.

How then can one see the Johannesburg of the near future? Will it be run under martial law? Would its businesses continue to operate internationally under an uneasy multi-racial alliance like the Muzorewa-Smith partnership in the last decade? Will the cream of the business community have already fled with their families?

Or will it be like Salisbury in the 70s, in the epicentre of a violent struggle for power, and yet seldom touched by that violence? White South Africans had always said that you could not compare the fate of Rhodesia with their own country . . . too powerful, too rich, too important strategically for the West to allow it to fall apart. But as each month passes it becomes increasingly evident that the Rhodesian experience was a foretaste of what was to come in the south. The details may differ slightly, but the overall picture is very similar.

After the economic boom and loosening of the apartheid noose in the late 70s and early 80s, Johannesburg became an optimistic and rather thrusting city. That changed in 1984 when a slump coincided with the worst internal uprising since the 1976 Soweto riots, and today Johannesburg has lost its swagger, its illusions of impregnability and grandeur. Its citizens, both black and white, go about their daily business as usual but at the dinner tables in Parktown and Soweto there is talk of great upheaval ahead.

Ironically, it is the Randlords, the Johannesburg business leaders, who have over the past decade been warning the government that it had to speed up reforms. Now it is this highly pragmatic group who are discussing the future of South Africa with exiled African National Congress leaders in black African capitals, while the government and its *sjambok*-wielding police force are attempting to shore up the defences at home.

That this curious shift in political power has taken place is evidence not only of the power and influence of Johannesburg's Randlords but also of the seriousness of the matter. Yet, apart from the dinner-table conversations, you wouldn't know that something quite monumental was taking place just a few tree-lined avenues away. In the northern suburbs it's G & Ts around the swimming pool as usual, and later a dinner party and perhaps videos of British television programmes. The flash young executives and their mates are soaking up the final days of an affluent and leisured era, the last luxuries of a very privileged lifestyle.

The city itself provides a most unusual backdrop to this developing drama. Built literally on top of a gold mine, encircled by yellow mine dumps, Johannesburg is the richest city in Africa and at the same time one of the most soulless. The victim of sustained international boycotts since the late 60s, it has not kept up with the other frontier towns of the old Empire like Sydney or Montreal or even Nairobi. Western culture is imported secondhand and then sold off in random job-lots at highly inflated prices. The resultant mishmash of American (increasingly prevalent as it is in Australia), British and African influences leave one with the feeling that had Paul Kruger or Chaka lived to see their people in the late 20th century they would have joined together in mutual horror.

From America, Johannesburg has imported the concept of decentralised shopping malls at just about the time that cities like Dallas and Houston have realised their blunder and are attempting to breathe life back into their deserted city centres. Johannesburg is currently sprawling, suburban mall by surburban mall, towards Pretoria, which in turn is sprawling towards Johannesburg. As businesses move out of the city into the suburbs, so it becomes more like Los Angeles – just a series of suburban satellites with no perceptible focal point. (It must be said here, however, that the city fathers are clearly aware of this problem and recently employed the Chicago architect Helmut Jahn to design a spectacular glass skyscraper which recently

*The American influence on South Africa shows in the city skyline*

reached completion and will liven up the rather plain cityscape.)

From Britain, Johannesburg has inherited an unwieldly bureaucracy which, when grafted onto home-grown political idiosyncracies and the inefficiencies endemic in Third World countries, leaves one wondering how the city has gained a reputation for brisk efficiency over the years. The whole clumsy business of defining what is a black person (Japanese businessmen, West Indian cricket teams and visiting dignitaries of every hue are deemed honorary whites) and where he can eat and drink (all races can eat and drink at hotels the government declares 'international' but some races can't always dance there) is just one example of a city in the throes of British bureaucracy gone bananas.

What Johannesburg has in common with other Third World cities, and African cities in particular, is its volatile nature. Violence, which incidentally transcends the colour bar, is part and parcel of daily life here, so much so that the Carlton Hotel, for example, issues a warning to every foreign guest about wandering around the surrounding streets after dark – not even New York's hotels do that. And one local journalist told me that he had long since given up going to nightclubs, particularly with an attractive woman, because they are full of mean *ous*, all bored and drunk and looking for a fight. This certainly doesn't apply to the up-market supper clubs and the like (or indeed the suburban mall nighteries), but it does take the atmosphere away from a city if the more colourful street clubs are no-go areas.

Liberal sociologists view all this as a predictable consequence of legislative differentiation and segregation. I would suggest that it is also to do with Johannesburg, through cultural isolation, retaining many of the raw qualities of a Wild West town: hard drinking, obsessive camaraderie and masculinity are qualities held in high esteem by the rugby, beer and *braaivleis* set. Not unlike the less civilised Australians, tough white South Africans are not broad-minded enough to see debate and argument as healthy, but view it rather with deep suspicion. If you talk *skeef* they'll *klap* you.

Not that the visiting businessman is likely to encounter this raw-boned species in his day-to-day dealings. His contacts will more probably be variations of Johannesburg's mink-and-manure set, the prosperous and travelled élite who were student activists in bygone days, now mellowed with age and seduced by easy living. Ten years ago they protested rather lamely but said there was little they could do about the political system. . . . today their loyalties are divided. They are heartened by what they see as P.W. Botha's orderly crawl towards some form of integration and appalled at the thought of it all being a case of too little too late.

It is within this community that one finds the most graphic evidence of Johannesburg's First and Third World dichotomy. They are aware of their cultural remoteness from touchstones like London, New York and Paris and go to extraordinary lengths to secure symbols of Western elegance. They say that the most sought-after commodity here after gold is style, and they go after it with the grim determination of frontierfolk in the misguided belief that this is something one purchases rather than acquires. Every weekday the wealthy women of the northern suburbs carefully don their latest Dior creations, decorate themselves with matching Gucci accessories and then head for Sandton City in their Porsche 924s, whereupon they spend the better part of the day sitting around the tea shops and nattering among themselves. Like much of Johannesburg, all dressed up with nowhere to go.

This remoteness is reflected in every aspect of the city's life. In the hotels one finds third-rate cabaret acts, who couldn't get work in their home countries, lured through the boycott net by easy pickings. In the theatre, minor celebrities from English provincial theatres are given star billing in inept interpretations of last year's West End hits. At the glorious Wanderers cricket ground, a country that not too long ago produced one of the greatest teams of all time is reduced to watching hotch-potch West Indian or Australian pick-up teams playing out 'test matches' the rest of the world doesn't acknowledge.

This is not to say that the citizens are not aware of such paucity – hoteliers are beginning to abandon cabaret rather than import no-hopers at great expense, and recent cricket tours attracted neither the ballyhoo nor the crowds of the earlier ones. It is simply that they can do little about it.

Significantly, Johannesburg's financial press is the only arm of the local media that retains an international reputation. For the most part the newspapers, magazines, television and radio vary from poor to downright insulting.

Throughout the 60s and early 70s the government resisted the introduction of television, believing that it would unleash all manner of unacceptable ideas on its innocent citizens. When they finally capitulated they bestowed upon the nation a

*Johannesburg Stock Exchange*

service that exudes servile enthusiasm, gross naiveté and monstrous incompetence. As an instrument of education it is virtually worthless and, in fact, further distances an already isolated people from the outside world.

The wider implications of all this clearly struck a chord with journalist Anthony Lejeune who, on a visit to Johannesburg, said that the main difference between South Africa and other countries 'is that it is the last nation in the world without television.' Then again, that was the government's intention all along.

Johannesburg's English language press remains independent but, apart from occasional sallies, seems to have lost its appetite for a scrap. When you see national dailies that were once the scourge of the Nationalist government carrying headlines like *"Magnum Back In TV Reshuffle"* you begin to think that even the serious newspapers have been infected by SATV's dreadful mediocrity. The Sundays confirm this by pitching themselves downmarket of *The News Of The World* and sometimes even *The National Enquirer.* The three English language Sundays, the *Times, The Sunday Star* and the *Tribune,* take all of 15 minutes to read and one emerges at the end no wiser than when one began.

Sadly, all of this mediocrity is the price Johannesburg, and South Africa as a whole, has had to pay for rigid state control of almost everything and growing international isolation from almost everyone. As it has become more of a social and cultural island so Johannesburg and its people have become more parochial and more likely to support policies that ten years ago they would have abhorred . . . it is spoken of in South Africa as the 'laager mentality' and it is the inevitable hardening of attitudes in the face of great adversity, something that the Rhodesians perfected in the early 70s.

For all that the White tribe retain a warmth and a generous nature that belies their reputation as lantern-jawed bigots whose main mission in life is to exploit and oppress pathetic starving blacks. They are a deeply worried people who have inherited a wretched legacy and this has made them defensive and suspicious, used to foreigners flying in for a short time, pronouncing judgement and then disappearing back to their own worlds.

They will shrug and then look to the north, to the appalling massacres in Zimbabwe, to the endless coups and counter-coups further north, to the starvation and poverty on their east and west flanks – and remain convinced that, given these alternatives, what they are doing is better in the long run for white and black. Neatly sidestepping decent democratic norms – and they may not agree with past ideology or present methodology – they will continue to echo the *cri de coeur* of the white man in Africa: the alternative is too terrible to contemplate.

For the time being Johannesburg will remain this embattled enclave of great power and wealth. In the long term (five, ten, 15 years?) much depends on whether the Nationalist government chooses, in Jan Morris's words, to submit to history or defy it. If it is to be the former then both the country and its business capital will leap into the late 20th century with great confidence and a sense of purpose. If they choose the latter course I can see Johannesburg becoming like the Salisbury of the late 70s – filled with the deepest suspicion, hope abandoned altogether, and left only with fond reminiscences of an inglorious but pleasant past.

## WHERE TO STAY

Johannesburg's position at the crossroads of First and Third Worlds is no more graphically illustrated than in the standards of hostelry. While they are not in the same class as better European and American hotels (and nowhere near the Far East), neither do they suffer from the vagaries and horrors one can expect to encounter in some African and Asian capitals.

Certainly the city's top hotel, **The Carlton** (Main Street; tel: 331 8911; telex: 95486130) would be considered average by European and American standards but at the same time good value for money. Situated within close proximity of the Johannesburg Stock Exchange, the 600-room main hotel is set in the middle of a shopping complex and the foyer is a bit like London's King's Cross Station at rush hour. The rooms are plain, the service adequate, and there is a swimming pool. Rooms range from R112 to R143 for single or double occupancy and suites cost between R220 and R385.

*The Carlton hotel*

Discreetly set apart from all the hubbub is the Carlton Court, the 63-room executive annexe, which at R170 for a room and around R340 for a suite, provides a different class of service. Each *en suite* bathroom has a jacuzzi, fresh fruit is supplied daily, prompt 24-hour room service is available and all the added extras one normally associates with executive floors are apparent. The excellent Club Room Restaurant, mentioned elsewhere, is open only to clients and their guests. My only complaint is that the rooms are rather small, although I was assured by an eager marketing lady that a survey they had conducted proved conclusively that businessmen *"did not like rattling around in large rooms"*. I should like to meet these people.

There is not much else in the city centre worth noting. The once prestigious President is only a shadow of its former self, **The Landdrost** (Plein Street; tel: 281 770; telex: 84092) is clean, ordinary and quite cheap (between R98 and R102 a night), and that's just about it in the centre of town. In the nearby suburbs, **The Sunnyside Park** (2 York Road, Parktown; tel: 643 7226; telex: 484092) should be mentioned because of its pleasant location and its modest tariffs (between R87 and R104 a night), as should the **Hotel Braamfontein** (120 De Korte Street, Braamfontein; tel: 725 4110; telex: 430620), which is aiming at the business traveller and promising to provide all the relevant amenities. Its rates are R89 for a single room and R95 for a double.

In fact, the most interesting hotels are situated in Sandton City, some 15 miles from downtown Johannesburg. The most established is the **Holiday Inn** (Cnr, Rivonia and North, Sandton; tel: 783 5262; telex: 427002) which although a rather horrid squat building from the outside, is light, airy and attractive inside. Regarded as the best Holiday Inn in the country it is also reasonably priced at R81 for a single and from R94 for a double.

The most dazzling and indeed most controversial hotel is the **Sandton Sun** (Fifth Street, Sandhurst; tel: 783 8701; telex: 430338), modelled along the lines of the new American properties with regulation spectacular atrium, waterfalls all over the place, glittering public areas, and dramatic lifts. One could be in Dallas but for the inefficiencies of the staff, who provide the have-a-nice-day willingness of their US counterparts but don't actually deliver the goods. It is a young hotel and staff are still in training and the service should improve considerably, so for those who prefer this type of hotel it's almost as good as the real thing. Single from R115; double from R134; suites R220 to 400.

For those who prefer to be reminded that they *are* in Africa, the third Sandton City hotel worth noting is undoubtedly the most unusual. **The Balalaika,** (Maud Street, Sandown; tel: 784 0400; telex: 424962) has the distinction of being the largest thatched roof hotel in southern Africa and is set in peaceful gardens around a large swimming pool. The main building and the *rondavels* (cottages) have the best rooms and one should stipulate a preference to avoid being placed in the new unthatched annexe.

The country atmosphere is only disrupted at sundowner time (particularly Fridays) when the locals descend on the lovely beer garden as if it were the only watering hole in the area, and during the international grands prix when the racing fraternity move in. (It should be said, however, that family men like former motorcycle world champion Marco Luchinelli stay at the Balalaika with wife and children to avoid the crowds and the clamour.) The restaurant, Thatches, has a marvellous atmosphere and, I am reliably informed, above average food (including kudu and ostrich steaks). Room rates are between R50 and R90 a night.

# WHERE TO EAT

Peter Devereux is Johannesburg's most respected food and wine critic, a man who wears a row of gastronomic titles like a war veteran wears campaign medals – Member of the South African Chefs' Association, Chairman of the International Food and Wine Society, Member of the Cookery and Food Association and so on. In a city that is not known for its culinary eminence, he is a man whose opinions should be taken seriously.

According to Devereux, South Africa has only five restaurants that would rate Michelin Two star status, and three of them are in the Johannesburg area. He cites The Lombardy near Pretoria, Le Marquis in Sandton and the Zoo Lake Restaurant.

**The Lombardy** (tel: 012 87 1284) is the best known restaurant in the country (a decade ago probably the only international restaurant), being the frequent haunt of Cabinet Ministers, captains of industry and visiting dignitaries. Run by Mario and Maria Moggia, it is a big house set in beautiful grounds and has the style to afford such pretensions as to serve *filet mignon* rare, very rare or not at all. The Lombardy also has the biggest cellar in the country with more than 70,000 bottles.

**Le Marquis** (tel: 783 8947) is a rather chic restaurant run by Germain Marquis, formerly of the top class St Germain. Pink and blue decor, three top Parisian chefs, French waiters, very good food, highly intelligent wine list . . . and all this for around R70 a head with wine.

His third choice **The Zoo Lake Restaurant** (tel: 646 8807) serves more conventional but nevertheless excellent food. Its superb setting and outstanding wine list (allegedly the biggest range of champagnes in the country) set it apart from most others.

By South African standards these three are expensive restaurants and one can expect to pay around R45 a head excluding wine. Europeans will see this as quite reasonable compared to equivalent establishments at home, and will rightly conclude that wining and dining in Johannesburg is not expensive.

The best bargain in town used to be **The Blue Room** (tel: 713 2761) at Johannesburg Station but there have been reports that it has become inconsistent – it still might be worth trying. Formerly specialising in huge portions of anything for its clientele of South African Railways middle management, the restaurant is now partly owned and run by Kurt Ammann, once proprietor of the TV Tower Restaurant. At around R25 a head excluding wine the predominantly French-style cuisine is good value, although apparently Ammann is under siege from the old regulars because the portions are too small. Ammann is a wine connoisseur and the list is extensive.

In the centre of town there are four restaurants worth recommending, each for different reasons. **The Fisherman's Grotto** (tel: 834 3800) in Plein Street specialises in Japanese cuisine and has 15,000 bottles of wine on display. It is informal, scruffy and yet populated by the city's more discerning businessmen. Fresh fish is flown up from the coast daily and average price of a meal is between R40 and R45 per head. **The Dragon Tower** (tel: 725 1719) in Twist Street is one of several excellent Taiwanese restaurants opened since South Africa and Taiwan publicly embraced back in the late 70s. The Peking duck (at R45 apiece) is apparently superb and the Mongolian Firepot has the seal of approval of no less vaunted a gastronome than Tony Lord.

The other two central city restaurants are mentioned because they serve outstanding food round the clock. **Late Night Al's** in Pretorius Street, Hillbrow, is licenced and offers excellent steak, while **The Club Room** at the Carlton Court serves the best *filet mignon* I have eaten at three o'clock in the morning. The Club Room is only open to Carlton Court clients and their guests.

For readers with a view to experimental dining there are two top class ethnic (Cape Malay and Cape Dutch that is) restaurants, **Gramadoelas** (tel: 643 1923) in Bok Street, Joubert Park, and **Leipoldt's** in Juta Street, Braamfontein. The former specialises in such unpronouncable delicacies as *Swart Buur, Waterblommetjie Bredie, Denningvlies* and *Koeksisters,* while the latter tends towards traditional Cape Malay, which is not unlike Indonesian food.

Slightly out of town at Halfway House is the marvellous **L'Orient Express,** four railway carriages run, so to speak, by one of South Africa's most influential chefs, Marc Guebert. A *maître chef de France,* Guebert allegedly introduced *nouvelle cuisine* to South Africa and does unquestionably operate a most unusual, if expensive, restaurant.

Finally, it should be mentioned that the city's much vaunted Dino's is no longer the great restaurant it once was. The departure of former British Chef of The Year, Bill Stafford, has reduced a legendary venue to mortality. Although it is still quite worthwhile, reports suggest it has lost the artistry of the Stafford era.

# NIGHT LIFE

It has been suggested that the best way to enjoy a night out in Washington is to catch an early evening flight to New York. There is no such nocturnal oasis within easy reach of Johannesburg (unless you count Sun City), so one is forced to examine the rather limited alternatives that are on offer.

The city's residents sum it up by admitting that their nights out are taken up largely with eating and drinking, sometimes at restaurants, sometimes at one another's homes. Occasionally they sally forth to Sun City (2½ hours away by road) to see a major show and do a bit of gambling. Once in a while a decent play, usually home-grown, passes through, less frequently musicians and entertainers of international stature.

However, like most locals, Johannesburgers tend to take their own artists for granted, bewailing the fact that they are outside the international circuit and often subjected to visits from yesterday's heroes out to make a fast buck before they're put out to stud. My advice to visiting businessmen is to seek out the indigenous entertainers and to ignore the imports.

The London successes of *Woza Albert, Saturday Night At The Palace* and *Harold and The Boys* have confirmed the importance of the Market Theatre (cnr Bree and Wolhter; tel: 832 1641) as a major platform for South African theatre, and both the main theatre and the Laager Theatre present mainly local plays. In a strict disciplinarian society it is doubly rewarding to witness such exuberant writing and performing, and be it reworkings of old Athol Fugard plays or brave new works from the young emerging playwrights, a visit to The Market is most worthwhile.

There are also one or two satirists around, a fact that surprises many visitors who are led to expect a Special Branch raid at the merest hint of an anti-Botha joke. Pieter-Dirk Uys is the most prolific and vivid, in a camp way, and any one of his plays or revues are worth looking out for.

Local music is not as consistently well represented and one has to be lucky to catch the good artists live. Dollar Brand occasionally passes through on a tour, the great Hugh Masakela is currently domiciled in neighbouring Botswana, and most of the country's major jazz exponents seem to live abroad. There are two African influenced pop-oriented bands worth seeing – Juluka and Via Afrika. They're both based in Johannesburg and play sporadically at local clubs.

For the rest it's the usual round of dining-'n'dancing, discos and cabaret that one finds in every major business city. The loudest, brashest part of the city is Hillbrow which is dotted with late-night bars and clubs, often populated by brawling drunks and raving lunatics. One should approach Hillbrow with a certain caution as it can be a trifle Wild Westish for the European with a delicate constitution. The other night-time gathering place is Rockey Street in Yeoville, which attracts a more arty crowd and is consequently far more benign.

As one local said, you simply can't build a culture around swimming pools and shopping centres. So too the nightlife.

# GETTING AROUND

There is only one practical way of getting around the city – and that is by car, and in the visitor's case, hire car. There is a paucity of public transport other than taxis. Given the large distances to be covered, however, taxis become uneconomical and at night they, too, disappear into the suburbs.

Hertz, Avis and Budget all have rental locations at the airport and in town and their rates are, not surprisingly, almost identical. Remembering that the frequent traveller can expect a discount, below are examples of published rates to give some idea of rental costs in South Africa: the smallest car like a VW Golf would cost R25 plus 28 cents per kilometre on a daily rate or R203 a week with unlimited mileage (five-day minimum rental) if you rent from Avis, and R21 plus 32 cents per kilometre on a daily rate or R78 for three days unlimited mileage, if you book one week in advance with Hertz. CDW costs R8 a day but again the wise traveller should have already made his own insurance arrangements.

Visitors should be warned that despite the modest 100 kilometre an hour speed limit (strictly enforced by the not altogether charming local police), driving on Johannesburg's roads, particularly the freeways, is unnerving to say the least. The driving methods teeter between crazed and downright anarchic, and many of the drivers are not only without licences but have been deemed by the courts to be unfit to hold them. Invariably, the latter category will be at the wheel of the pantechnicon that thunders past you on your left-hand side just as you're moving across to the off-ramp. It should also be mentioned that the authorities are particularly harsh on drinking and driving offenders and patrol the streets zealously. Hence, the success of surburban restaurants and watering holes which seem to be strategically placed only a few side streets away from home.

*Student rag entertains shoppers*

# Kuala Lumpur

Malaysia's riverside capital is undergoing strenuous upheaval in an attempt to make its mark as the conference and incentive capital of South East Asia. The evidence is in the half-finished buildings that dominate the city and the air of determined optimism that pervades its people.

By Carol Weingott

You're flying into Kuala Lumpur over the snakey, silt-filled beige of the Gombak and Klang rivers and it seems unlikely that they could be leading anywhere. Around them stretches the hugging jungle of legends like the *orang minyak* (oily man), who molests young girls, and the sub-human 'Big Foot', whose 45 centimetre footprint was found by a couple of Americans a few years ago. There are patchy interruptions of crooked lines of rubber trees, thatches of sticky-looking oil palms and tidy tucked-away *kampongs* (villages) where whole settlements live with the profound fear of elephants rampaging through their vegetable gardens. Somewhere, too, are a few thousand outlawed Chinese communists.

When you land at the junction of the Klang and Gombak at shiny new Subang International Airport you'll find a small facsimile of Singapore's airport, your first clue to how serious this place is about catching up with its breakaway 'state'. Although things run smoothly at Subang there's an idle moment's irrational consternation about when there'll be another flight out – this is the aftershock of exposure to that inhospitable jungle. The run into town takes half an hour, is smooth, sophisticated and fringed by strong evidence that this is indeed the Garden City.

That it is also officially Muslim means one has certain fundamental expections: the early morning blast of static from the loudspeaker as the *meuzzin* prepares to divide the day into five, prostrate bodies devotedly blocking your path. But this rich young Federal capital doesn't in any way strongly exhibit such tendencies. Kuala Lumpur has just two significant mosques, Masjid Negara (National Mosque) and the Jame Mosque. The Jame has the essential prerequisites for a good Arabian fantasy: red brick and a courtyard with a bathing pool for the faithful. It also has age, circa 1897, which places it among this town's pioneers. Masjid Negara, on the other hand, was conceived for the people only in 1965. It is a vast (13½ acre) extravaganza of pink marble, tiled walks, reflecting pools, multiple minarets and palm fringes. A nation's showpiece, its first baby carefully presented in a frilly pram. That both these places are open to *all* comers should be seized on by female business travellers, as it is in KL that you'll find the exception that breaks the general Islamic rule.

Nor is there much point in a protracted search for many architectural aspects of colonial rule: Kuala Lumpur never really was in the now extinguished Singapore tradition. Its infancy sounds mostly wretched with bloodied gang wars among the Chinese over tin mining claims. In the state of Perak at Larut in 1874 a thousand miners were killed by rival gangs in a single day: this led to a peace treaty and the start of direct British intervention. KL was also unhealthily overcrowded in *atap* shacks which were filled with the pervading pall of opium – and according to André Gide, *Kouala l'impure,* because of its brothels (of which more elsewhere).

*The Masjid Negara*

Evidence of colonial rule is reposited in such hallowed institutions as the Tudor-styled Selangor Club, where adventurous misfits who made it big after supervising the hacking out of rubber plantations (hacking done by Indians) liked to go to look at one another's wives. And there are colonial names: Templer Park, a tract of zoo-cum-jungle ten miles north of KL, named in honour of Sir Gerald Templer who played a vital role in the formation of the Federation of Malaya, which is what the place became known as in 1948 after it embraced north Borneo and Sarawak, those other pieces that make up the country's crescent shape 1,000 kilometres away across the South China Sea.

Malaysia, as it became in 1963 to the confusion of geography textbook publishers all over the world, continues, however it is spelt, to lie beyond the boundaries of the European mind. Kuala Lumpur travel agents recently asserted that no one in Europe knew where it was and described the Tourist Development Corporation's budget for publicising it as 'chicken feed'. The same can't be said of the Chinese port of Penang. Early Malays, intent on getting it right, decided to call the offshore island 'Single Island' before bravely switching to 'Island of the Betel Nut Tree'. Then the British, keen as ever, stuck it firmly in their crown as 'Prince of Wales' island'. But it was really put on the map, and lasciviously, by the GI's who used it as an R&R base from Vietnam. Since then it has been *the* tourist destination but is now in a crisis of pollution.

There appears to be no other crisis, as such, but there is the perennial struggle of the Malays to not only get into the mainstream but to dominate the life of the country: they certainly do the latter politically. Thus the Malays, *bumiputras,* (which also takes in other indigenous races, the Ibans and Land Dyaks of Sarawak, the Muruts of Sabah: there are 900,000 of these indigenous jungle dwellers) have imposed their religion, Islam, and their language, *Bahasa* Malaysia, on the Chinese and Indians.

Officially, *bumiputras* are deemed to constitute a small majority of the 14½ million population. The Chinese, however, say the balance is in their favour (officially – they're given 35 per cent), and the divisive Indians, at about 11 per cent, can't say anything. None of this will matter very much if the current population drive hits its 70 million target by the end of the century. By then the *bumiputras* really will be the majority: the family-loving Chinese are already having fewer children because of the expense of sending them abroad for a 'proper' education, which means university.

The bumiputrisation of Malaysia is best seen in a change in the constitution which made *Bahasa* Malaysia the official tongue in government offices and schools *and* universities, replacing English. The turning point was the post-election bloodbath in 1969 when the politically dominant Malays and economically dominant Chinese clashed in the streets of KL leaving hundreds dead. After this it was decided to *"reduce the importance of English in the interests of national unity"*.

*Citibank building*

The surprising thing is that national unity is doing so well, though the term seems absurd in relation to those 900,000 jungle dwellers, despite contentious issues like the government's repeated refusal to build a Chinese university. It was suggested that in some circles the thinking is that such an institution could lead to the dreaded 'left wing tendencies' which in turn seems to be too tenuous a link with the communist subversives hiding in the jungle. But it is definitely this lot who are responsible for the continuing existence of the death penalty for carrying explosives and unlicensed arms.

None of this affects the business community: the Chinese, who still largely run it, simply continue to use English as the business language. Business travellers shouldn't have to worry too much about *Bahasa* either except on the road where the equivalents of *"Stop, caution and drive slowly"* appear in that multi-syllabled language. The mysteries of this *Kampong* tongue are seen in the likes of *barbeku, bakteria, elektron* not to mention *insuran brokar.* The merest raised eyebrow over the logic of such spellings brings the weary rebuke: *"As an independent country we have to have our own language".*

It is statements like that, a general elusiveness, the sense of a half-made country, that will ultimately send the visitor out from his hotel early in the morning to trust the judgement of his own eyes. Mornings are fresh with exhalations of a jungly flavour, and there is still *some* jungle in central KL mainly tidied away in small parks; the humidity hasn't begun to close in and there's a briskness about the place. If you are up early enough you can watch Indonesian labourers squatting round on building sites, towels about their necks, as they spend 15 minutes cleaning their teeth with sticks. Out here the real jungle is one of cranes, twisted wasp-waisted superstructures for hotels, shopping complexes, banks, conference centres and Islamic foundations.

The animals are a hungry zoo of bulldozers pawing the ground and riding roughshod over 1930s frail wooden bungalows, which, while they survive, express an ineffable charm. Some of this rapidly-rising massively-erect Malay modern architecture, like Prime Minister Datuk Seri Dr Mahathir Mohamad's pet Dayabumi Project, is carefully Islamic and staggeringly beautiful. Some of it is complementary to the 'dreaming spires' of the wonderful Moorish railway station and its administrative building.

This structural upheaval that is KL bares a gappy grin to any suggestion that in all this haste there's the risk of increasingly diminished charm: with great self-confidence it announces itself as *"tomorrow's conference and seminar centre for the whole of South East Asia".* And they're very sensitive to criticism, these *bumiputras.* It is all too easily imagined that you are somehow challenging the nation's right to progress.

That you *are* walking on a goldmine, albeit one whose infrastructure is just going up, seems to be what most people think. Such optimism appears to be fuelled by the belief that Malaysia is economically and politically stable and full of unexploited wealth.

As is generally appreciated, Malaysia ranks as the world's largest exporter of rubber (gloves, tyres and contraceptives), tin, timber, palm oil and pepper, with the new glamour crop, cocoa, fast on the move. The new wealth is coming in pipelines like the one being built from Trengganu to Singapore to carry natural gas: there are also significant finds of off-shore oil on the East Coast.

What the current investor's market does indicate is massive confidence in the Prime Minister, a former rebel who was once thrown out of the party for writing the highly polemical *Malay Dilemma* (banned until he regained office in 1982). Mahathir has ploughed on with the Tun Razak government implemented New Economic Policy, NEP, a grand scheme for four five-year development plans designed to promote *bumiputras* into the socio-economic mainstream; to bring them out of the *kampongs.* These days it is obligatory that there is a *bumiputra* on every board of directors and you'll see them in all the front jobs.

To those who object to this positive discrimination, this spoon feeding, I would suggest perusal of the government figures for the economy as of 1971. Then, 14 years after independence, foreigners (the British) held 63.3 per cent of the corporate share capital, the Chinese had the bulk of the 34.3 per cent in non-Malay Malaysian hands and the *bumiputras* were left the crumbs, or precisely 2.4 per cent of their own economy. Since then foreign banks and rubber plantations have been forced to sell up or restructure according to NEP guidelines. The last of the British giants Harrisons and Crosfield held out until June 1982 when it was forced to put its Malaysian assets into one company of which it now holds about 30 per cent. It also got a £150 million cash reward. An embittered employee with a score of years in the industry informed me that the process by which this nationalisation happens is known as *'gazetting',* whereby industries are bought through government-dominated holding companies.

Mahathir expanded the NEP by introducing his 1982 'Look East' policy hard on the heels of the withdrawal of the 'Buy British Last' policy which he also imposed. When Britain joined the EEC Malaysia felt neglected and very upset indeed about the subsequent increased fees for its, mainly Chinese, students at British universities. In looking East Mahathir urged that Japan and South Korea be taken as exemplary models, slamming the West as soft and decadent. He suggested that were Malaysia to emulate the West *"it would land itself in the quagmire they are in without ever passing through the golden period they went through".* This has resulted in extremely stiff competition for European businessmen. An English engineer told me that the government contracts all go to the *bumiputras* who then sub-contract out to the expats and the Chinese. The same source was extremely cynical about the way the government's Pioneer Status programme to attract investors has been abused. (The scheme allows a two to five year tax holiday for an investment of $250,000 to $100,000.) According to him: *"The locals get the land and the Japanese bring in second-hand machinery, labour is dirt cheap so they make fat profits and all for next to nothing."*

Whatever the machinations of big business, physically Kuala Lumpur is a clean city: there are massive fines for littering, as in Singapore, and smoking in public is strongly discouraged. What you do have to watch out for are the deep open drains along the sides of the roads: when the rain comes it is torrential.

The city is growing by the minute too, additions like Petaling Jaya, a former swamp become satellite business town 20 minutes away, where Volvos are assembled, are happening on all fronts. Five or six years ago the population was around half a million, now it's doubled. Quite where these people live is difficult to determine but as you speed by on one of the main macadamised roads (here they've used opulent quantities of rubber) you may glimpse the red rust roofs of shacks closely assembled amid sheaves of banana palms.

And back to the political minefield of religion; avoid writing the word *pig* if at all possible. It is said, with alarm, that there are some government officers who refuse to handle documents which contain the word which, incidentally, is *babi*.

When the Malaysian government tabled legislation that would give it sweeping powers to ban any publication considered to be against the national interest. Opposition figures called the move a further gag on the press and an attempt to intimidate both foreign and local journalists. As far as foreign publications are concerned, they now have to place a deposit with the government to be forfeited if the publication falls foul of the law or if the publisher fails to appear in court to face any subsequent charge. The government also has wide powers of control under the Official Secrets Act and the Internal Security Act. An amendment to the Official Secrets Act in 1983 made it an offence for any citizen not to report anyone seeking official information. I have no idea if I was reported.

*The railway station dates from colonial days*

Anyone who went to Kuala Lumpur's Golden Triangle, which is the equivalent of Singapore's Orchard Road, before 1986, could expect to be showered with fallout from construction sites, and have their path blocked by lorry loads of hotel fitments. They could expect to be utterly perplexed by what the Tourist Development Corporation describes as a 'Typhoon' in the hotel building trade.

Kuala Lumpur already had at least half a dozen international hotels, or, including all its hotels, around 7,000 rooms, so how is it that a further 3,000 or 4,000 were deemed necessary within the relatively short space of three years?

Part of the answer lies in the government's Investments Incentives Act which, among other things, made hotel development a particularly attractive idea. Under the Act, hotels that opened before 1986 received special concessions including the exemption from income and development tax for five to eight years.

The other reason for the hotel boom is the widely voiced intention to turn Kuala Lumpur into South East Asia's conference and seminar centre and to develop it as the springboard for tourism elsewhere in the country.

First of the new hotels is the 447-room **Ming Court** (tel: 482 566; telex: 32621) which lies in the heart of embassy territory on Jalan Ampang and claims to be among the first hotels in the country to have computerised check-in and a no-smoking floor. It has cultivated a continental atmosphere by way of a French provincial restaurant and is aiming itself at FITs and businessmen. Rates are pegged slightly below the Hilton and Regent with most rooms going for between $200 and $220.

Almost as new is the **PJ Hilton** (tel: 553 533; telex 36008) at Petaling Jaya, the country's first satellite town 20 minutes from central KL. This is convenient as a first night stopover as it lies midway between KL and the airport. It is also convenient for anyone intending to do business in the adjacent industrial estate. As far as Hiltons go this one is not particularly lavish. It is a functional hotel with good direct dial facilities, a business centre, executive floors and is considerably less expensive than its KL namesake. Among its special features is the Uniqey – a card that replaces the conventional key. Singles $150-$180; doubles $170-$200.

The Kuala Lumpur **Hilton,** (Jalan Sultan Ismail; tel: 422 122; telex: 309495) is imposing in most senses of the word. It rises 36 storeys, has 593 rooms, and overlooks most of the city but specifically the Selangor Turf Club Race Course. It has six restaurants and a nightclub, the Tin Mine. Service is exemplary as is security with the Uniqey backed up by butlers at the elevator landings on all floors. Traditionally the Hilton and the Regent have been neck and neck as the top hotels in KL, a situation which will be worth watching with the up and coming Shangri-La and Oriental. Rooms from $195 to $1,250.

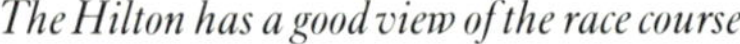
*The Hilton has a good view of the race course*

The **Regent** (tel: 425 588; telex: 30486) has 400 rooms and sits slightly off-centre from the golden triangle on Jalan Imbi. This is the most 'ethnic' of KL's grand hotels and uses generous amounts of native timber in both public and private areas. It also has what is widely considered the best French restaurant in town, the elegant Suasa.

Another strong point for this hotel is that its spacious bathrooms actually have baths that *are* kingsize. There is an executive centre and an interesting bar, the Library Bar, which functions as such. Rooms from $205 to $235; suites $500 to $1,500.

The **Equatorial** (Jalan Sultan Ismail; tel:422 022; telex: 30263) is in the centre of the golden triangle and has 300 refurbished rooms. The only real drawback to this comfortable hotel is that it has just two lifts. The biggest plus, on the other hand, is that it has three first class restaurants. Singles $175; doubles $195; suites $300 upwards.

The **Federal** (tel: 489 166; telex: 30429) is the most central of KL's hotels and has the only revolving lounge on its 18th floor. There are 450 smartly done up rooms and suites, an 18-lane bowling alley and two large convention halls. Holders of American Express can expect to get a sizeable chunk off the usual tariff as can monthly and long-term guests. Rates are among the best in town with singles from $145, doubles $160 and suites $310.

# WHERE TO EAT

Anyone who goes to Malaysia thinking that if it's not *satays* – the ubiquitous barbeque on a stick – it's curries, has got it wrong. It is perfectly true to say that the much-touted *satay*, mutton, beef or chicken marinated and served with peanut sauce, cucumber and onion, abounds, and also that it won't satisfy a serious gastronome for long. But the designation 'curry' is quite misleading.

The Malay 'curry' breakfast *nasi lemak* is actually rice cooked in coconut milk (to make it rich) and served with meat, eggs and vegetables or chilli prawns and crunchy anchovies. Like most food in this country it is eaten with a spoon and fork. Also extremely popular in the Malay kitchen is *sambal udang* which is prawns, chillies, turmeric and candlenuts; and *nasi padang,* rice with a small flotilla of spiced side dishes of meat, fish and vegetables.

For the hot stuff there's both northern and southern Indian cuisine. There's a salad called *rojak* made from cuttlefish, shrimp paste, chillies and balachan and *murtabak* (also known as *murthaba)* which belongs to the omelette family except that it is stuffed with meat, fish or vegetables and wrapped in paper-thin pastry and served with turmeric gravy.

Chinese food is what is most widely available: Cantonese, Hong Kong style and by popular consensus best of all, *nonya.* The latter is the food that's evolved from the Straits-born Chinese. It gets its name from their word for females (the word for males is *babas)* and is characterised by meticulous preparation, slow cooking and spices. It is a variation of this which is most commonly sold at the 'stalls', the proliferation of street shacks everywhere in KL whose proprietors are known as 'hawkers'.

Besides being the best food going, stall food is incredibly inexpensive. Don't let the unsavoury appearance of these places put you off: the food has a reputation for being hygienic as well as delicious.

The big surprise about K L's eating habits is that its Kentucky Fried Chicken outlets have the highest turnover anywhere. The Colonel's diners get the opportunity to win videos and even a crack at a $5,000 cash prize. Local boss Loo Cheng Ghee is not, however, as finger licking happy as he could be. He has taken to suing the Commodities Trading Council for libel after noises were made about the *halal* content of his menu. One of the requirements of Muslim law is that to be *halal* the animal must have been prayed for at the moment its throat was slit, another, of course, is the ban on pork. (The Indians too have rules, about not eating beef, in accordance with the Hindu beliefs – but then there are Muslim Indians).

In the light of the government's declared Islamisation Policy the *halal* question has interesting implications. One hotel source suggests that there's legislation coming up that will insist on hotels having at least one *halal* kitchen. Another source is saying that it is rather a matter of restaurants receiving grades, with Grade One going to porkless kitchens. Officials at the TDC didn't seem to know anything about it.

There is some evidence in the absence of bacon and sausages from the breakfast menus of top hotels. But more can be deduced from the fact that the newly-opened Petaling Jaya (or PJ) Hilton takes pains to point out that it has the only *halal* Chinese restaurant (the **Toh Yuen** or Peach Garden) in the country. It also has a fine Japanese restaurant, the **Nippon-Kan** (tel: 554 190), an affiliate of the famous Tokyo chain, which brings its own tuna and shellfish in twice a week from Japan because *"the local shellfish isn't so good".*

By European standards hotel food isn't expensive, and this despite the 10 per cent government tax and 10 per cent service charge automatically added to the bill. Then there's the wine. Cheap Australian whites are just about affordable at two to three times their usual cost but anything French can go sky high.

In the top league of hotel restaurants is the Regent's lineal **Suasa** (tel: 425 588) where Yves Leberon, schooled under Anton Mosimann, experiments with subtle French and Malay cuisines. Visually this is a superb place heavy with the Malaccan touch: lots of warm wood, and elegant furniture.

The **Equatorial** deserves a mention for accomplishing the feat of having three first class restaurants under one roof. For continental food go to its **Chalet** where the beef or cheese fondue at around $40 for two is excellent, and authentic – there are three Swiss chefs. Or you could have New Zealand oysters at $21 a half a dozen and charcoal prime rib of beef off the wagon at $70 for two. At the Japanese **Kampachi** if you're very brave you'll try the live little crabs; if you're not so brave there's the set lunch box at $12, and set dinner at $25. The other excellent restaurant is the **Golden Phoenix** where the speciality is Cantonese smoked duck at $35 a plate. All three restaurants are bookable (tel: 422 022).

If you want to eat Malaysian and absorb a bit of 'culture' as well, the place that's usually recommended is **Sri Yazmin Restaurant** in the Ampang Park shopping complex (tel: 487 377 or 487 490). Apparently there's a strobe lit stage where native folk dances are performed to a background of resounding gongs. They also do something called the *joget* dance with audience participation. You have been warned. The other Malaysian place that's frequently mentioned is **The Pines** at Jalan Brickfields (tel: 441 194).

Anyone invited to the **Selangor Club** should request their *steamboat,* a stock in which you get to cook your own selection of meat, fish, noodles and vegetables before drinking the soup. This is a bit like a barbeque, interestingly informal, and thus a useful way of doing away with the tedious side of dining with little-known business acquaintances.

# NIGHTLIFE

On the way to KL a heavy-bottomed Englishman, who has sweated it out there 20 years, suggested there wasn't any nightlife in KL. *"How can you build entertainment around tops and kites?"* There were kites, the traditional *Wau Bulan* used by the national carrier MAS. There was nightlife: clean, questionable and sporty.

I first embraced the clean, as practised at the highly visible and central **Selangor Club** (tel: 428 433) known as 'the Dog' after the Dalmation a former lady guest used to tie up outside in the days when it was *the* society stronghold. Cricket is still played on the *padang* (pitch) before its correct Tudor portals.

This is as comfortable a place as any, especially the low-slung verandah bar, from which to watch a parade of Indian doctors and lawyers, Chinese businessmen, a few ex-pats. It was a Tamil doctor who broke the ice: *"How are the Pakis getting on over there these days?"*

There's subsidised eating and drinking (Anchors $2) and you can play cricket, lawn tennis and squash. Temporary membership costs a refundable $1,000 deposit plus $150 a month for a maximum of six months.

The same graciousness goes on with less drinking at the newish and more salubrious **Raintree Club** in the garden suburb of Jalan Wickham (tel: 479 066) where 2,000 people wasted no time in forking out $50,000 to join as soon as it opened its doors. This club is heavily Chinese and sophisticated to the extent of having two blind masseurs – one for each sex. Temporary membership is available but there are all manner of restrictions. This is the only place in KL where you can play indoor tennis when the changeable sky decides to open up.

You may be told that the Hilton's **Tin Mine** (free to ladies sometimes, otherwise a $30 to $35 cover charge) is the best disco in town. It isn't. This is the 'gem of a disco' **Sapphire** (tel: 438 450) in Plaza Yow Chuan at which both temporary and corporate membership are available.

All is blue velvet and lasers: four million *ringgit* of sheer effects for the benefit of rich young things in Japanese designer clothes who like to shake themselves with an abandon not commonly seen among the coy disco-goers of KL. They have fashion shows here, and free admission for ladies wearing leotards or tights (?), otherwise the cover charge is $25 with drinks around $10 to $15.

Unless you're a Malay Muslim you can go up to the **Genting Highlands Casino,** an hour's drive away, and join hundreds or even thousands of fervoured Chinese at blackjack, baccarat, French bull, Tai Sai, Keno and a thousand one-arm bandits. The government has banned Malay Muslims and apparently 'inspections' are made to ensure the ruling is being adhered to.

For those who feel incorrigibiy drawn to the low life I recommend the area north of Jalan Tunku Abdul Rahman towards the **Coliseum Café** and the **Rex Hotel.** This is the sort of place where people of indeterminate sex slide by waving slices of watermelon (perhaps they are beckoning) before withdrawing into shadowy doorways to recline on cane chairs. Around midnight you may find traffic jams as punters and pickpockets come to look at the transvestites (they also drape themselves over the Mercedes and Volvos around the corner from the Selangor Club at the same hour). To me they called out *"Johnny, Johnny":* I don't know what they say to men.

In **Jalan Chow Kit** there are numerous *Korek Kopi* shops the direct translation of which is 'coffee scratch' bars. Here there are social escorts like Jessica, a beautiful Indian girl with an interesting history involving two Polish husbands. I'm told there are also Australians. And Filipinos, who pass themselves off as Mexicans, the lighter their skin the more they cost. The going rate is alleged to be between $80 to $150 an hour. The red light district proper is around **Jalan Hicks.** There is by no means a lot of this sort of thing. I was advised: *"This is not Bangkok".*

The gay pub is a place called the **Blue Boy** off Jalan Bukit Bintang where there's a large dance floor and a $6 cover charge. The helpful Indian lawyer who showed me most of these places explained the situation thus: *"Perversion is not well-marketed here".*

*Nightlife in KL is a low key affair*

# GETTING AROUND

Unless you're being met, you'll probably leave Subang International Airport in an air-conditioned Nissan, Volvo or Mercedes clutching a coupon. These are issued from a prominent stand outside the airport and are the *only* currency for getting a taxi. To Petaling Jaya, the 20-year-old satellite 'business' town, the fare is about $18 and to KL itself about $40 depending on your exact location. The fare is calculated by the taxi coupon booth in advance and you hand over the coupon at your destination.

To KL it's about a half hour ride (unless you're in the rush hour) which for the exhausted *arrivée* wanting to sit back and luxuriate *and* smoke is too long not to do so: but they don't like you doing so. In taxis, as in lifts, and what are deemed 'public' places, smoking is actively discouraged by signs like *"by all means smoke if you have to, but don't expel"*. Within the city itself taxis are easily hailed (they're black and yellow and battered, atopped by the word teksi) and cheap: 70 *sens* (cents) for the first mile with a 50 per cent surcharge between midnight and 6 a.m. The limousines (mainly un-battered Volvos and Mercedes) run by the big hotels cost about three times as much as the generally either un-air-conditioned or leakily air-conditioned *teksis.*

Buses, known as *bas minis,* abound, some would say recklessly. A $110 million light rapid transport Aerobus system is due for completion in 1987.

Cars can be rented through the offices of Avis (tel: 443 085), Hertz (tel: 433 014), National Car Rental (tel: 489 188), City Car Rentals (tel: 420 240) and through outlets at the big hotels. Rates are competitive and from what I heard discounts are available. A 1.3 Toyota Corolla costs $47 a day, $282 weekly and 0.47 cents per km: unlimited mileage costs $121 a day and $726 weekly. A top range automatic Volvo 240 costs $112 a day, $627 weekly, 1.12 cents per km: unlimited daily $280, weekly $1,680.

An international licence is required (you can get your licence re-endorsed in KL but because of queues this is not recommended). Driving is on the left and front seat passengers must wear safety belts or pay a large fine. A recently introduced demerit system may contribute towards safer roads in the future but at present driving is hair-raising: there are plagues of weaving Hondas. Road signs are seldom seen in English but the international code is in evidence – watch out for the skull at a driving wheel. All this aside, KL's roads are severely congested, a situation which it is hoped that planned inner and outer ring roads will alleviate.

The most persuasive argument against driving yourself around, however, is the high incidence of staged 'accidents' whereby passing motorists are rather horribly taken for a ride by being robbed and sometimes beaten.

Pedestrians have a difficult time competing with the Hondas: don't mistake generous-looking paths for footpaths, these are for the Hondas; footpaths don't really exist. For getting out of the country there are trains to Singapore and Thailand (tel: 284 132, 281 861, 287 297, 287 296, 287 721).

For gimmickry's sake, a few trishaws have been thrown in, mainly around Chinatown. Anyone peculiar enough to choose this form of transport should be prepared to bargain.

# Lisbon

**Lisbon wears the scars of its socialist revolution like other cities display their public monuments – proudly and loudly. For all this, the Portuguese capital is an extremely pleasant place in which to do business.**

**By Carol Weingott**

The residue of Portugal's 1974 revolution and its left-wing armed forces takeover bid a year later is still evident on the streets of Lisbon. And it is unlikely that the capital's *rosa*-coloured walls will succumb to any whitewash. There certainly appears to be no money for paint.

Leaving aside the enduring quotations to *vota, vota,* some of the graffiti qualifies as Socialist art – especially that at the central railway station, near the Quarter of Carmo, where the then Prime Minister was imprisoned during the revolution. The hapless, curious visitor should be careful though, in expressing admiration for this bold revolutionary symbolism; muscular labourers with rolled up sleeves poised to get the country going again.

*"It is good to remember your history, the revolution,"* one might venture.

*"No. It is good to remember the 17th century when we were rich. Now we're just . . ."*

The driver of this particularly shiny mercedes taxi wasn't a socialist. To him the revolutionary etchings covering the seven hills of his city are an affront. (He reckons they're there to stay though, at least until the next substantial earthquake.)

*"After the revolution they put all their friends in, but all their friends were incompetent. Now we've got 30 per cent inflation and the people are getting poorer from year to year."*

One way and another the man in the street appears to be feeling the pinch: in 1972, 20 escudos made up a dollar, in 1985 it took 185 to do so. Add to this significant unemployment (11 per cent in mid-1985), high interest rates and inflexible labour laws, and one begins to understand the sentiments expressed by the likes of my taxi driver. The taxis, incidentally, are the cheapest in Europe. But then so is labour, with an hourly rate of US$1.63 compared to $6.47 in Britain – real wages are said to have fallen by 20 per cent since 1977.

The effects of the economic crisis can be seen all over the capital – halted construction, holes in the roads, dilapidated schools and hospitals. And not even the optimists are expecting Portugal's troubled entry to the EEC to change this one jot. (The critics were voluble in saying that the US, Brazil and the former colonies were more apposite trading partners, especially given this once great seafaring nation's Atlantic geography.)

It is the same Atlantic/Algarvian geography that pulls in today's tourist dollar, and the Brits' not-so-sterling stuff. The English have always loved the place, fondly calling it their 'oldest ally' – or as some wit put it: *"They are the best of friends with the English, because we can't get no port wine nowhere else."*

In 1984 the tourist market showed a healthy 10 per cent increase, with the visitor total up to ten million and for the first time equalling the Portuguese population – allowing the exception of three million Portuguese working abroad. Regarding the latter, it is worth noting that tourism is the country's second largest source of foreign exchange after emigrants' remittances. The punishing factor in the tourism stakes, as far as the locals go, is that the majority of visitors are Spaniards: *"They're just day-trippers, and they earn twice our wages."*

The acrimony between the Portuguese and Spanish is, of course, legendary, or proverbial: *"Strip a Spaniard of his virtues and you've got a Portuguese."* There appears to be though, a school of thought that decrees the Portuguese less flamboyant than the Spaniards – their bullfights are held only on Sundays and the bulls survive. It is the Latin link, and assumptions made about the Spanish and Portuguese tongues, that steer visitors off course. I was told: *"We can understand them, but they can get just a few words of ours."* The explanation went something like: *"As Spanish is to Mexican, Portugese is to Brazilian."*

The linguistic dialects shouldn't worry anyone who speaks English, however – the Portuguese are enthusiastic about it. Taxis, hotels, restaurants and the sports field certainly present no obstacle to making yourself understood. (A recent tourism drive dubbed the country Sportugal in homage, no doubt, to the year-round sunshine and the abundance of facilities for tennis, riding, watersports and golf – Lisbon has seven courses).

The capital also has a rich assortment of architecture, rich enough for people to want to argue about it. One camp insists that it is impure, that the famous *azulejos,* the painted tiles bedecking exteriors, were adopted from the Arabs and subjected to Dutch influence. The devastating earthquake of 1755 pretty much wiped out the evidence of what was really going on – though you'll find your strongest Moorish clues around the Castle of St George, the city's oldest monument crowning the Alfama district. Alfama itelf should be negotiated but not by self-drivers: not only is parking next to impossible, but the streets are rather alleys, shudderingly cobbled etc . . . From here, on a good day, the view is spectacular and it is

*Europe's longest suspension bridge straddles the River Tagus*

possible to make out the famous seven hills. The southern aspect is dominated by the 25th of April Bridge (a suspension construction said to be the longest in Europe) straddling the steamy Tagus and leading to the Setúbal peninsula.

Adjacent to the bridge is a massive Jesus, a 60s apparition whose arms are outstretched to the city. You can take the lift in the statue's centre and gaze back at the huddle of tiled roofs, churches and miniature Eiffel Tower. The tower is in fact the Santa Justa elevator (and it was built by Eiffel), leading to the Quarter of Carmo. It is well worth the ride,if only for another aspect of this city of tucked away vestibules and shadowy *travessas* – what they call the short, narrow streets in many of which your outspread arms can touch the buildings on either side.

The capital is walkable, the heart of it being laid open after an hour's stroll. It is very pleasant indeed, bathed in sea air and basically constituting a couple of squares. These are the Praca do Comercio (Black Horse Square) with the commercial centre, banks, shops and offices directly to the north and Praco do Rossio, all pigeons and flower-sellers and where the favourite occupation is drinking small, sweet cups of coffee and eating cakes at 11a.m. precisely. Another landmark worth seeking out requires a diversion to the north of town: here you'll *"look on my works ye mighty and despair"* at the 18th century Aguas Livres Aqueduct – 11 miles of it – which still brings in the capital's fresh water.

Nocturnally, the most rewarding pastimes are undoubtedly eating and drinking, although there are options. You may be persuaded that you'd enjoy a night in a *Fado* house – *Fado* being the business of melancholic and emotional folk-singing. From what I saw, *Fado* is strictly for the 'tourist'. Business travellers might prefer the attractions of Estoril, 'the seaside garden of Lisbon', 25 kilometres to the west. Here it is suggested one might visit the casino: *"A magnet for international society, a glittering glass contemporary building housing a cinema, restaurant, nightclub with international floorshows and a dance orchestra and, of course, the gaming rooms for the adventurous."*

Or, then again, one might not.

Back to eating and drinking: the seafood is fresh, inexpensive and varied. Besides the ubiquitous national dish, *bacalhau,* dried, salted codfish, the menu should run to swordfish, oysters, clams, mussels, black grouper, sea bass, salmon, turbot and prawns. If you don't like seafood, the recommended meat is pork, roast, *à la nortenha* (herbs and port wine).

Portugal claims to be the world's fourth largest wine producer, being responsible for more than a hundred different types. Among the best respected are *Dao,* Terras Altas, red and white, Branco Seco Especial, a dry white special, Periquita, an excellent aged red wine with body, Camarate, a well-aged claret and Lancers or Faisca, the two rosé and white wines known the world over. The opportunity to sample the wine and, of course, the seafood, is refreshingly inexpensive in Lisbon.

Afterwards, if you feel particularly restless, you could inspect the port area where the sailors appear very serious indeed about having a good time. There are all manner of seedy-looking bars here and all manner of national brandies being knocked back – something like 26 at the last count, I was assured.

# WHERE TO STAY

Presumably, and not unreasonably, Portugal's entry to the EEC was taken by some hoteliers to herald the start of a steady influx of business clients. The Meridien group certainly appears to have expressed such confidence, with the completion of two properties, in Lisbon and Oporto, the former, in December 1984, in record time. *"It went up in something like a year,"* said a still-stunned observer. Something of a record indeed in a capital blighted by half-completed and wholly forgotten-looking structures.

The 331-room, 18 storey **Meridien** hotel (Rua Rodrigo da Fonseca; tel: 690 400; telex 64315) was clearly constructed with the pyramids in mind, and rises awkwardly behind the shady Parque Eduardo VII. Service is efficient and brisk, the rooms are a good size, have desks and are soundproofed, but they tend to be bland. There is nothing bland about the lofty atrium, though – all massive white girders and glass. Waiting there one half-expects tamed birds to come bursting through the abundant foliage and perch on one's shoulders. Single Esc 9,750-13,000; double Esc 12,500-15,100; suite Esc 17,000-20,000.

Nothing so frivolous could be said about the neighbouring **Ritz Inter-Continental** (Rua Rodrigo da Fonseca; tel: 684 131; telex: 12589), which formerly enjoyed a reputation as the most respected address in town. These days, despite the alarmingly close competition from Meridien, it still merits a name for its faded but refined decor and the discreet service so efficiently metered out by the Inter-Continental management. The main bar is pleasantly large and dim and the grill room is said to serve superior meat, something of an achievement in Lisbon. Single Esc 9,759-10,954; double Esc 11,950-13,145; suite Esc 19,519-24,499.

The **Sheraton** (Rua Latino Coelho; tel: 575 575; telex: 12774) has a sterling reputation among business visitors who cite its location near the business centre and its effective telex service and switchboard as plenty of reason to book in. It is a little worse for the wear it has had since it opened in 1972, when the travel trade named it 'Hotel of the Year', but being geared to the 'international' market does, of course, mean that the trimmings are all present, including a heated outdoor pool and well equipped health club. There also appears to be a

*Lisbon offers accommodation to suit every pocket*

steady stream of taxis marshalled at the door. Single Esc 10,000-12,000; double Esc 12,500-14,500; suite Esc 22,700-34,900.

The **Tivoli** (Avenida da Liberdade; tel: 530 181; telex 12588) is also handy for the business centre plus some of the capital's 50-odd cinemas and is reasonably modern. It flags slightly on the service side, though there is certainly nothing deliberately off-hand about the place. The property provides good conference facilities and has a worthwhile Tivoli Club – located in the garden – which gives access to a heated swimming pool and tennis courts. This is a lobby you can sit in without fear of anything as exotic as a tamed bird landing on your shoulders. Single Esc 6,312; double Esc 8,173; suite Esc 12,500.

The **Atlis** hotel (Rua Castilho; tel: 560 071; telex 13314) shares the Tivoli's excellent location but retains something of the Sheraton's plastic efficiency. Among its amenities, the Grill Dom Fernado (on the ninth floor overlooking the city) is recommended. There's also the Restaurant Girassol, which serves an appealing Portuguese lunchtime buffet. Single from Esc 6,500; double Esc 11,500; suite 17,000-22,000.

Of smaller hotels the best are the **Hotel Diplomatico** (Rua Castilho; tel: 562 041), single Esc 4,900; double Esc 5,800; suites from Esc 7,000; the **Hotel Lutecia** (Avenida Frei Miguel Contreiras; tel: 803 121) with a rooftop bar and restaurant and the **Hotel Avenida Palace** (Rua 1 de Dezembro; tel: 360 151), an 1894-built property neighbouring the Rossio railway station. This establishment gets my vote for sticking to tradition with heavy, highly-polished furniture and an especially lovely staircase. Single Esc 2,285; double Esc 2,793; suite Esc 5,841.

The Penta chain is represented by the 592-room **Lisboa Penta** (Avenida dos Combatentes; tel: 725 050), whose main advantage is its proximity to the airport. Single Esc 5,975; double Esc 7,967; suite Esc 11,751.

Lisbon also offers plenty of other accommodation – *albergaria* or *residencia* – which are grouped together as inns, and various *pensao-residencia,* classified as boarding houses. The State owns and runs an interesting collection of some 26 *pousadas,* which provide accommodation in historic buildings, castles, palaces and mansions. Almost always set in superb locations, a number are accessible from the capital. Details from the Empresa Nacional de Turismo (tel: 881 221). It is worth noting that during the low season, November 1 to March 31, prices can be as much as 15 per cent lower than for the rest of the year. Visitors in possession of one of the strong currencies find five-star luxury comes cheaply. Most double rooms cost between Esc 10,895 and Esc 13,663. As with restaurants, bills include service and taxes. Tips are always appreciated, Esc 10 being the minimum for a small service. Season and currency fluctuations aside, Lisbon's hoteliers generally run tight ships with amicable service.

# WHERE TO EAT

Portugal's colonial past in Macao, Goa, Brazil and Timor has not inflamed the imaginations of the nation's chefs as much as one might have hoped, but Portuguese food is relatively straightforward and hard to beat for good old-fashioned value for money. It is also hard to beat for freshness, particularly where seafood is concerned. The Portuguese housewife would not, one imagines, dream of buying a fish without first checking it over and ideally would like to see it still twitching.

The fish you can expect to encounter include sole, sea bream, whiting, stone bass, mackerel, red mullet, shad, sardines, octopus, squid, tuna, eel and the ubiquitous *bacalhau* (salted codfish). And this is not to begin to enumerate the seafood proper – lobster, shrimp, crawfish, oysters, mussels, prawns, crab. . .

Carnivores will possibly have a tough time of it. For them, especially, the recommendation is pork, especially the Ritz's *leitao* (suckling pig); rabbit *(coelho),* or the Portuguese stew *(cozido a Portuguese).*

At luxury establishments heavy on old-world charm, plus decor and devoted waiters, expect to pay around Esc 9,616 for dinner, plus wine, for two. In this category belongs **Aviz** (Rua Serpha Pinto; tel: 328 391), just off the Chiado, in the panelled rooms of an elegant building. Here you can discover the delights of smoked duck's breast, smoked swordfish, gratinéed black grouper with cream and onions, and partridge alcantara (marin-

*The beautifully laid out Park Eduardo VII.*

ated in red wine and served with *foie gras*). Closed on Sundays and for lunch on Saturdays.

In the same class is **Tavares** (Rua da Misericordia; tel: 321 112), which can evidently afford rather restricted opening hours: 1p.m.-2p.m. and 8p.m.-10p.m. closed Saturdays. This rates as one of Lisbon's most famous *fin de siècle* restaurants, with lots of plush and huge gilded mirrors. The roast pork *(à la nortenha,* with port wine and herbs) is especially recommended here, with *toucinho do ceu* (literally fat of the Gods), made of crushed almonds and lots of egg yolks and sugar, to follow.

For dinner with a view try **Tagide** (Largo da Biblioteca Publica; tel: 320 720), where you can sample the likes of salmon pâté, veal escalopes baked with cheese and hot or cold fruit-filled pancakes while gazing over the Tagus, the Town Hall and the Cathedral. Closed Saturdays for dinner and all day Sunday; reservations recommended.

At what are called first class restaurants, as opposed to the luxury establishments mentioned above, the bill will be something like a third less – inexpensive into the bargain. Such restaurants include **Gambrinus** (Rua das Portas de Santo Antao; tel: 321 466) open daily 11a.m.-2p.m. and renowned for speedy counter service and excellent shellfish; **Escorial** (Rua das Portas de Santo Antao; tel: 363 758), a modern establishment with Spanish overtones, open daily from noon till 2a.m.; and **Cervejaria da Trinidade** (Rua Nova da Trinidade; tel: 323 506), where there are three sizeable dining rooms and an outdoor garden. This is a well-established, family run restaurant with somewhat idiosyncratic opening hours.

Bargain restaurants are abundant in Lisbon, and among the best are **Sua Excelencia** (Rua do Conde; tel: 603 614); **Belcanto** (Largoa de S. Carlos; tel: 320 607) and **Passos Perdidos** (Rua Miguel Lupi; tel: 664 152), which is a favourite with senior politicians.

The best thing about eating out in Lisbon, though, is that you can drink just about anywhere, anytime, for there are no restrictive licensing laws. Even cafeterias, snack bars and tea houses serve alcoholic drinks. For cocktails stick to the plusher bars, but remember,as you prowl the *tascas* tasting their immense variety of regional food, that Portuguese beer is light, dry and very good.

# NIGHT LIFE

Lisbon's tourist literature would have you believe that every Lisbonite adores spending his evenings listening to *Fado*. In fact most *Fado* houses appear to make their living off the need of tourists for folkloric nourishment but, unless you speak Portuguese, there seems to be little point in the exercise. Anyone interested in pursuing this further might like to try **O Forcado** (tel: 368 579) which appears to be as 'authentic' as the fundaments of this business allow.

The capital does, of course, have 'international' nightlife: top people apparently head for the **Banana Power Disco** (tel: 631 815); **Whispers** (tel: 575 489) and **Charlie's Place** (tel: 760 157). Or **Maxim's.** (tel: 365 366).

The choice of live entertainment does range beyond *Fado*, from piano bars to jazz bars and music halls. The following establishments do not require membership: **B'Arte** (tel: 324 266) closed Sundays; **Bar Concerto** (tel: 862 508) also closed Sundays; **Hot Clube de Portugal** (tel: 367 369) reputedly a jazz venue) **Skylab** (tel: 658 955) exotic cocktails and dancing; and **Nina** (tel: 364 859) with a live show.

The places the locals go are referred to as *tascas* or *tabernas*, typical working men's cafes where simple meals and glasses of wine are the order of the day. For 'atmosphere', these are hard to beat.

The places the sailors go are largely in the Barrio Alto district which gets deadly serious in the small hours – not for the faint-hearted nor female business travellers out on their own. Pubs in the European sense are a little thin on the ground but approximations of the same exist at: **Bela Bar Toque** (tel: 657 548); **Bora-Bora** (tel: 805 873); **Chez'i** (tel: 671 856) and **Foxtrot** (tel: 670 697).

Outside Lisbon there is some nocturnal activity at Estoril and Cascais – at the latter bullfights are held on summer Sundays at the Praca de Tour. Estoril's main attraction is undoubtedly the casino which is more of a vast amusement arcade designed to dazzle the holidaymaker. Besides gambling, the casino offers the opportunity to go to the cinema, dine, watch an 'international floorshow' or look at the handiwork of local artists.

# GETTING AROUND

The most elevating way to see Lisbon is surely from a tram: turn-of-the-century but solid, these make no complaint about twisting up the sides of this riverside city's seven hills. Because they are electric, they more than outwit the congestion, and the buses. Tickets for both are interchangeable and available from kiosks in Cais do Sodré or beside the Santa Justa elevator: trams cost between Esc 16.50-32.50; buses Esc 22.50-50.

With taxis running on a basic rate of Esc 50, the same as the bus fare, plus Esc 3 for each additional 180 yards, visitors may wish to forget about public transport altogether. On trips outside Lisbon, however, the driver is entitled to charge the return fare. A 10 per cent tip will be appreciated and up to 50 per cent more than the total charge may be added on for luggage weighing in excess of 30kgs. By law you must get in and out of taxis on the pavement side.

The city's Metropolitan (Underground) is fast and frequent but limited in the area it spans. The most central stations are Rossio and Restauradores which, like all entrance points, are designated by a large red 'M' above ground – city fare: Esc 27.50. Commuters use the trains, from Cais do Sodré for the coastal trip to Estoril, and from Rossio for Cascais, Sintra and Azambuja.

For crossing the Tagus for fun, the best means is a ferry: these depart from Terreiro do Paço and Cais do Sodré wharfs. Via the 25th of April Bridge (pedestrians banned), the toll ranges from Esc 30 to 40.

TAP-AIR Portugal operates several daily flights from Lisbon International (about 20 minutes from the city centre) to the international airports of Faro (Algarve), Funchal (Madeira), Oporto and the Azores. The major car hire companies are represented by Avis (tel: 361 170), Hertz (tel: 579 027), Europcar (tel: 524 558), and InterRent (tel: 690 391).

# London

London is no longer the threatening, soot-covered city of Dickensian lore, nor is it the garishly swinging pop capital of the 60s. Yet the essence of London, as captured in the Ealing comedies, remains intact through the 80s.

By Michael Leapman

A city's image often lingers longer than the reality. There are some who still see London as the setting for those atmospheric black-and-white film dramas made 30 or 40 years ago: the sooty buildings, the pea-souper fogs, the stranger in trilby and raincoat appearing from the murk to proffer a light.

It is more than 30 years since London suffered regularly from those thick fogs that sometimes were as truly romantic as the films depicted them. I remember one or two occasions when I walked the four miles home from work because transport was at a standstill. On the way I would drop into pubs, those oases of light and warmth, striking up casual acquaintances based on shared adventure.

Since coal-burning in central London was banned, such traffic-halting fogs no longer occur. At the same time, Londoners have grown out of the belief that layers of grime, plastered on historic buildings, are an integral part of the city's character. Now they wash their monuments with spectacularly revealing results.

Yet having said all that, it does seem to me that London absorbs change better than many other major cities. Its character and spirit have been less compromised by new physical developments than those of, say, Paris. A surprising number of Dickensian alleys and Georgian terraces survive. So do bespoke tailors, hand-made shoe shops and the old street markets, many on their original sites. And though the pubs change to accommodate fleeting fashions (they are just emerging from a brown, fake Victorian stage) they are still the cheery and informal places of refreshment they always were.

Some of London's changes have actually enhanced its traditional character. Take Covent Garden. In 1974 the wholesale vegetable market moved from there to Nine Elms, south of Vauxhall Bridge, and there was talk of pulling down the market buildings, with their elegant iron pillars and

*Covent Garden is the fashionable place to shop*

arches and their glass roofs. Instead, the area has been converted into a street market and shopping precinct.

Part of it, you might think, is a bit tatty – optimistic 'craftspeople' trying to sell hand-carved bookmarks and tie-dyed yashmaks. But the permanent shops mostly sell high quality goods that a visitor might want to take home, and there are some handy eating places. (The quality of snacking in London has greatly improved in the last few years, under the pressure of competition from American hamburger and pizza chains).

Many regretted it when the fruit and vegetable market moved away, but by the 1970s the huge refrigerated lorries squeezing incongruously through the narrow streets had robbed Covent Garden of the romance it exuded before the invention of motor vehicles.

Now much of that romance has returned and pedestrians have resumed control. Thousands of them are lured by the shops and other attractions: there are museums of transport and holography and perhaps soon a theatre museum. And Inigo Jones's fine 17th century Church of St. Paul's, once almost hidden behind the market paraphernalia, is now better visible and accessible, again the hub of a thriving neighbourhood.

Walking a little north and west from here, past the famous outfitting firm of Moss Brothers and then the prestigious Garrick Club, we reach a street with an equally romantic past but a less certain future. Charing Cross Road was once lined with shops selling old and new books of every stamp. Book lovers still head there to visit Foyle's, London's largest and most bewildering bookshop, but part of the west side of the street has been pulled down and on the east side the number of second-hand bookshops is dwindling, while the few that remain are doubtful about their long-term survival. But for the time being it is still a place to browse for an old book or an engraving.

Moving further west we penetrate Soho, a district famous for more lurid pleasures. From time to time plans are announced to 'clean up' this traditional den of vice but there is scant evidence of their success. Sex shops and strip clubs abound, as do grubby cards announcing *"French model – walk up"* or more discreet bell-pushes coyly marked *"Michelle"*.

Despite such manifestations Soho has remained a thriving residential area with an active residents' association that does its best to remind us that other things are sold there besides sex. Berwick Street has an open-air food market, there are first-rate continental food and wine shops and still some decent restaurants.

Legitimate theatre survives in the West End, despite constant cries of impending doom from impresarios. Shaftesbury Avenue is still filled, shoulder-to-shoulder, at curtain-up time and again when the performances end – not so vast a sea of humanity as on Broadway at the same hours but still enough to persuade us that there is one part of London alive at night.

Continuing north and west, the area around Carnaby Street has become a fading monument to the 1960s, when for a time it was the centre of youthful fashion. Now most of the shops lining the narrow, traffic-free streets sell souvenirs and tacky tourist items. But close at hand is Liberty's, a traditionally swank department store, to restore our faith in a London where an emphasis on quality outlasts ephemeral trends.

At the southern end of Regent Street, Piccadilly Circus has for so long been the subject of redevelopment schemes that it is hard at any particular time to be precise about what the current blueprint for the future contains. I suspect it will in the end stay much as it is, with the historic Eros statue providing a venue for the almost equally historic drug addicts who lounge around its base, the historic neon advertisements flashing above them.

The old Trocadero dance hall has been transformed into a new leisure complex complete with numerous shops and amusement arcades. Despite the complaints about the new Trocadero's garishness, the shops thrive. Several other buildings in the area are covered with scaffolding or tarpaulin. South of here, St. James's and Westminster are much as they have always been, quite recognisable to the stars of those old movies, assuming they ever saw them without a pall of fog.

Yet if those districts are effectively unchanged the City, the heart of old London and now the nation's commercial hub, has changed almost beyond recognition. St. Paul's Cathedral, once easily the tallest building, is now hemmed in by skyscraper office towers. Here again, though, the changes are not all for the worse: the Barbican development, a little north of St. Paul's, has brought a residential and arts complex into what had effectively become a dead area after 6p.m., when the last office workers went home.

You could argue that if there is a single attri-

*Hyde Park, the largest of London's many parks*

bute of a city that determines its character, it is its parks. Central Park in New York, on a summer weekend, contains all the energy, enterprise and ethnic variety – as well as the danger – of the city itself. The parks of Paris are classically graceful, orderly and well-groomed. London's parks contain elements from both those models. St. James's, effectively the front garden of Buckingham Palace, is as carefully landscaped and planted as those in Paris, if less formal. Hyde Park and Regents Park, like Central Park, are devoted primarily to allowing the citizen to let off steam, with horse riding, boating, open-air theatre and music at the bandstands. Jealously preserved from encroachment by surrounding buildings, they remain constant backdrops to the changing city.

A visitor, waking early on a brisk winter morning, could do worse than make for Hyde Park before breakfast. The mist may still linger beneath the trees and in the distance the riders of Rotten Row will be no more than dim shapes, like ghostly horsemen. From across Green Park and St. James's the muffled chime of Big Ben might be heard. Not many men in trilbies, perhaps, but our dawn wanderer may feel that the essence of London, as portrayed in those black-and-white films, has remained intact.

# WHERE TO STAY

At about four in the afternoon London's legendary hotels become showcases for conspicuous idlers: Americans, and others, plant themselves amid the potted palms and the clotted cream to take part in a beloved English afternoon tea party. Quite how close these gracious proceedings are to the Real Buckingham Palace Thing in the minds of tradition-starved foreigners the hotels can never know. What they must know is that their Amazonian flowers, marble furniture and live music are a wonderful success; you'll be lucky if there's room to stir your tea.

This particular slice of the high life at London's top hotels isn't expensive or exclusive; it belongs to anyone (guest or not) with the inclination for an £8 feast of fancy. For the uninitiated it also provides a useful indicator of just how grand that particular hotel is. But even if your lobby isn't positively slippery with polished hospitality at four o'clock, the chances are you're still in good hands.

London's hoteliers cherish a reputation for keeping their houses in good order and their guests happy, if only as an apology for the VAT and service charges that add 30 per cent to the bill. And with 150,000-plus beds it's difficult to imagine that there isn't a roost for every bird.

Strangely it is *only* the business traveller who might have cause for complaint when it comes to choosing an ideal location; it is difficult indeed to stay in the City. London's financial district has a dearth of hotels, a situation only slightly alleviated by the newish **Tower Hotel** (St. Katherine's Way, E1; tel: 481 2575; telex: 885934. Single £58; double £69; suites £164-£275) at Tower Bridge from where, I'm informed, access to the rest of the capital presents a problem.

What the business traveller will find is that segregation from the bedlam of tourists, trade shows and conventions is easily done. All he need do, expense account in hand, is head for the grand hotels slung like careless pearls around the thick and prosperous neck of Oxford Street, Piccadilly, Regent Street and Hyde Park. A pretty parallelogram this, and tidy too, but for its omission of the Savoy which shines in splendid isolation on an S-bend in the Thames half way along the Strand. But for all of London's wealth of hotels there are only a few (large ones) with true patrician origins, and three of these belong in the diadem of the Savoy Group.

The **Ritz** (Piccadilly, W1; tel: 493 8181; telex: 267200), the Great Dame of Piccadilly, quickly becomes a landmark to visitors by virtue of being adjacent to Green Park and the lights that spell out its name at night. Palatial grandeur is the well-worn phrase most often used to describe its splendid pink dining room whose cerulean ceiling is more of a sea tossed with wood nymphs and cherubs.

When Trafalgar House bought the hotel they poured unspeakable amounts of cash into refurbishing the entire edifice – paying particular attention to the plumbing, something which formerly led even the most polite of guests to gurgle with discontent. The over-riding impression at the Ritz is one of hospitable good taste open to allcomers. Single £100; double £125; suites £300-£525.

Then there is **Claridge's** (Brook Street, W1; tel: 629 8860; telex: 21872). The best known fact about this carefully screened hotel used to be that it had no official tariff. When this changed the surprise was that many rooms cost less than at other hotels owned by the Savoy Group. Claridge's is the only known great hotel not to have a bar, which is utterly in keeping with its dignified country house atmosphere.

I am left with an impression of slightly shabby gentility: the carpets aren't all spotless, nor the paintwork all fresh and spruce, not that such minor imperfections are likely to alter Claridge's standing as *the* resort of kings and princes. Single £95 to £130; double £140 to £165; suites £250 to 500.

*The Ritz hotel*

**The Connaught** (Carlos Place, Mayfair, W1; tel: 499 7070) is a mannerly little hideaway with neither a telex (because such impersonal machinery doesn't belong in the world of gentlemen), nor so much as a rate card, which just about sums things up. Even less than Claridge's, this hotel does *not* want publicity. (Even through its owners, the Savoy Group, I failed to get permission to inspect its rooms.) An incognito visit, however, confirmed all I had been told: the hotel *is* run along the lines of a private country mansion, there's no noise, no bustle and no frippery. Single £79, double £100-£125; suites from £200. All prices exclusive of 15 per cent VAT.

At the **Savoy** (The Strand, WC2; tel: 836 4343; telex: 24234) the first indication that this is something special comes as you dive off the roaring Strand into a tiny tucked away street where the cars are all on the 'wrong' side, something you *shouldn't* see elsewhere in England.

This Queen Mother of hotels has won global recognition as an innovator and standard-bearer and has sent scores of world class hoteliers from its ranks to the very farthest outposts. Top people have passed good and bad days in its all-embalming comfort: Winston Churchill spent the worst days of the last war there and today it's where Mick Jagger goes when he wants the publicity.

Anyone lucky enough to bag a room overlooking the Thames can rest assured that the view of the 10 bridges is the finest the city has. The Savoy provides the best access to the City and to theatreland while some of the capital's top shopping can be done at the revamped Covent Garden just a step away. Single £105; double £130; suites £270-400.

The **Dorchester** (Park Lane, W1; tel: 629 8888; telex: 887704) was the first of the great London hotels to be sold to the Arabs, something which clearly didn't sit well with some sectors of the community and to which some people attributed a decline in its popularity. When the hotel wasn't subsequently submerged by Gulf magnates and when it again changed hands, a further two times, the Dorchester returned to its heyday.

This is a large, rambling and curiously E-shaped hotel with miles of corridors in vividly-coloured hand-knotted Filipino carpets. Some of its suites have flower-lined balconies while many rooms have broad views over Hyde Park, all of which adds to its stately-home ambience.

Serious eating is done in the famous 1930s Grill Room (recently accorded Restaurant of the Year status by Egon Ronay) and in the Terrace Restaurant where the one and only Anton Mosimann presides over 70 chefs. Single £130; double £160; suites £250-£700, including VAT and service. There is a corporate rate available to companies which gives substantial reductions.

*The Dorchester hotel*

Not far from the Savoy is the **Waldorf** (Aldwych, WC2; tel: 836 2400; telex: 24574). In the hierarchy of London's first-class establishments, the Waldorf rates a paltry four stars. The turn of the century building is more imposing than grand, while the Palm Court Lounge is quietly dignified in the best manner of things British. To Londoners, the Waldorf is known for its *thé dansants* – tea dances – complete with live orchestra. Single £63; double £80; suites £155 to £310.

**Brown's** (Albemarle Street, W1; tel: 493 6020; telex: 28686) is graced with a lovely Georgian facade – giving it the air of a comfortable family home. Sitting in the heart of Mayfair, Brown's location is one of the most pleasant in London. Single £90 to 98; double £115 to 120; suites £230 to 260.

Two hotels deserve special mention as being representative of the best of the contemporary scene. The **Inn on the Park** (Hamilton Place, Park Lane, W1; tel: 499 0888; telex: 22771) belongs to the Canadian Four Seasons Group (also responsible for the famed Pierre in New York) and is the first choice of many of London's American visitors. When it opened in 1970 Egon Ronay christened it *Hotel of the Year* and by any reckoning it is still going strong. It is a commodious place with handsome furniture and efficient service. Single £119-130; double £150; suites £235-555. Prices do not include 15 per cent VAT.

**The Howard** (Temple Place, WC2; tel: 836 3555; telex: 268047), just along from the Savoy is another good bet for anyone needing to get to the City. This is a relatively new hotel whose office-like exterior belies a sumptuous interior: Adam-style ceilings and lots of Italian marble. Japanese businessmen have staked their claim here in significant numbers which is hardly surprising given that the Howard does the city's only Japanese breakfast. Many rooms and suites have balconies with wide river views. Single £122; double £138; suites £147-270.

For small, efficient and pleasant hotels at prices substantially lower than their better-known peers London is exceptionally well off. These include the **Hallam Hotel** (12 Hallam Street, W1; tel: 580 1166) just behind Broadcasting House: central, quiet and with an NCP (National Car Park) just around the corner. Prices include breakfast from £20 to £24. The **Elizabeth Hotel** (37 Eccleston Square; tel: 828 6812) is within walking distance of Victoria Station and overlooks well-kept gardens. This modest establishment has an NCP garage for 400 cars nearby and costs £20 to £44. Winner of the first César's Awards given by the *Good Hotel Guide* in 1984 for the best bed and breakfast in town is **Number Sixteen** (16 Sumner Place, SW7; tel: 589 5232; telex: 266638). Single £29 to £38; double £55 to £70. Service charges are discretionary at most of London's less expensive hotels.

# WHERE TO EAT

Confronted by a list of London's restaurants, many and varied as they are, and asked to make a preference for an evening out or a business lunch, even the *au fait* foodie would be tempted to play it safe and plump for one presided over by one of the great French chefs, whose reputations tend to dominate the London restaurant scene. And since London's eateries have not escaped the taunts of aggrieved visitors, whose over-riding impression is one of flavourless and over-priced meals, disagreeably served in dreary surroundings, it's probably the most sensible course of action.

So it is refreshing to learn that English chefs and English food are coming into their own these days: less fodder, more cuisine – in fact, a general realisation that our cold to middling climate does not necessarily demand enormous dollops of filler at the expense of culinary imagination. People can now come to London and eat local, instead of feeling if it's not French it's not worth bothering with.

That said, some of London's French restaurants deserve all the accolades they have been collecting over the years. **Chez Nico** (129 Queenstown Road, SW8; tel: 720 6960) is the proud possessor of two Michelin stars, and the chef, Nico Laden, is determined to acquire another, although that may mean moving to larger premises north of the river. Next door, **L'Arlequin** (123 Queenstown Road, SW8; tel: 622 0555), is quickly gaining on its neighbour in reputation: famed particularly for its delightfully textured and presented food and intricate desserts, the sorbets being especially delicious. These restaurants are making this rather grimy road in South London a gourmet's paradise. Koffman, the chef at **La Tante Claire** (68 Royal Hospital Road, SW3; tel: 352 6045) has been called *"a culinary artist"*. Fish is his speciality, and a set lunch of £12 a head makes his artistry accessible even to the most impecunious.

**Le Gavroche** (44 Upper Brook St, W1; tel: 408 0881) has made the running over the last few years. It is usually possible to get in at lunch but you have to wear a tie. You eat in turn-of-the-century luxury in an atmosphere that is not unlike a top class speakeasy. Albert Roux's cooking has a peasant feel to it and his *pot au feu sauce Albert* will keep you going until Tuesday week, but he has a perceptive touch with more delicate dishes too – his shrimp bisque has been particularly fine and the pastry is always superb. But it is a place to eat rather than drink though the wine cellar is among the best in London. Aperitifs, cognacs and cigars have doubled some people's bills.

Not long ago it was nigh on impossible to find a restaurant with sufficient confidence in the British culinary tradition to actually call itself an English restaurant. Now such places abound and many of

London's streets are filled with names like Bates, Rules, Porters and School Dinners, which bring to mind images of that other great British institution, the public school.

For solid and dependable old favourites, the bastions of London eating are still the best. The **Dorchester Grill** (Dorchester Hotel, Park Lane, W1; tel: 629 8888), under the all-knowing eye of the fabled Anton Mosimann, specialises in regional dishes, bringing a whole new meaning to boiled beef and carrots. The **Savoy Grill** (The Savoy Hotel, The Strand, WC2; tel: 836 4343) where the game is always hung to perfection, is as formal as it is expensive, but delights those who have been brought up on tales of English superiority, taste and class, and fail to see it in action anywhere else.

**The Connaught** (Carlos Place, W1; tel: 499 7070) has been a reliable stalwart of London eating for some time. It pays to be adventurous from the big menu,which includes such traditional specialities as bread and butter pudding and mince pies alongside some superlative soups and patés. Trying to find somewhere to eat English food reminds one of how much of a seafaring and trading nation England has become – there are very few genuinely English menus in London. The atmosphere, at least, at **Boulestin's** (Henrietta St, WC2) tel: 836 7061) in Covent Garden is as English as the ante room of Windsor Palace and the room itself is magnificent. The food has French parents and can be quite ineffective but the wines are superb and it is a good place for a celebration.

More authentic English cooking is to be found at the **English House** (3 Milner Street, SW3; tel: 584 3002) in Kensington, which is a restaurant imposed on a private house with a reputation for good game, or else the smartly executive **Leith's** (92 Kensington Park Road; tel: 229 4481) in Holland Park where duck is the house speciality.

Indian cooking is now so prevalent (with even the smallest of villages having an Indian restaurant) that it is in danger of being considered indigenous. Indian food connoisseurs should be well satisfied with **Lal Qila** (117 Tottenham Court Road, W1, tel: 387 4570) or with the **Bombay Brasserie** (140 Gloucester Road, SW7; tel: 370 4040) where the Sunday brunch is miraculous.

Chinatown, situated between Soho and Leicester Square, offers some cheap and good cooking (though not as good as say Chinatown in San Francisco, Toronto or Hong Kong) if the surroundings are a bit rough and ready. **Poons** (4 Leicester St, WC2; tel: 437 1528) has excellent wind dried foods and the massive **Chuen Cheng Ku** (17 Wardour St, W1; tel: 437 1398) has first rate dim sum. More elegant, is **Tiger Lee** (251 Old Brompton Rd, SW7; tel: 370 2323) where Cantonese seafood cooking is handled with *nouvelle cuisine* style elegance. This is the only Chinese restaurant in London with a Michelin Rosette.

Fashionable London still goes to **Langan's Brasserie** (Stratton House, Stratton Street, W1; tel: 493 6437) where the food is remarkably good and famous people enjoy looking at each other. The theatre world heads for **Joe Allen** (13 Exeter Street, WC2; tel: 836 0651) in Covent Garden where the salads and cocktails go down well with people on diets.

But if you really want to make an impression then **Blakes Hotel** (33 Roland Gardens, SW7; tel: 370 6701) in South Kensington combines a strikingly Eastern decor with some splendid cooking, again much in the modern European style. It is run by actress Anoushka Hempel and has yet to be fully discovered.

Perhaps the best value for money for a set dinner in the capital at the moment is at **Gavvers** (61-63 Lower Sloane Street, SW1; tel: 730 5983), near Sloane Square, which is an offshoot of Le Gavroche. The set price (£38 will cover two people) includes a glass of kir to start and half a bottle of wine and some slightly unpolished but promising French cooking in a relaxed but swish setting.

Good fish restaurants are hard to find and perhaps the best is **Le Suquet** (104 Draycott Avenue, SW3; tel: 581 1785) in Kensington where the fish is flown in from Brittany each week and if you don't feel like a full meal you can have a huge plate of crab, whelks, oysters, mussels, langoustines and winkles and a bottle of Muscadet at the bar downstairs.

A personal favourite is **Anna's Place** (90 Mildmay Park, N1; tel: 249 9379) in Islington, which has recently expanded from a handful of tables in the front room of a private house in a street that has seen better days. Anna herself explains all the dishes on the menu in sensual detail and her gravlax and lamb nuggets with pear butter are delicious; finish with a spectacular plate of mixed fruits and sorbets.

For a business lunch in the city, the best (and practically only) place to go is **Le Gamin** (32 Old Bailey EC4; tel: 236 7931), Le Gavroche's younger brother. The food is excellent, of course, and

*Wherever you look there's a pub*

the price is particularly good – £16.50 for a 3-course set menu which includes a multitude of choices, wine, service and 15 per cent VAT.

If your luncheon requirements are more modest, one simple way to track down a bargain lunch is to arm yourself with a copy of the *British Relais Routier Guide* and eat in the places recommended in the London section. A Routier lunch costs around £7.00, excluding drinks and service charges, and culinary standards – although easily surpassed by those of its French counterparts – are reasonably high.

Wine bars, pubs and sandwich shops are the best bets for a quick bite to eat. However, food is not of prime importance for a true English business lunch, which consists of six pints of beer (at least – and bitter has more street-cred. than lager).

Who once claimed that anyone tired of London was tired of life? Actually, it was Dr Samuel Johnson and he wasn't wrong. With its myriad theatres, opera houses and concert halls, not to mention a multitude of watering holes – many of them survivors of Dr Johnson's own era – London is surely one of the foremost entertainment capitals of the world.

Not that things have not changed radically since Dr Johnson's time or, indeed, since the glorious days of *Hair* and *Oh, Calcutta.* Certainly, the bright lights of London are not what they were in the Swinging 60s. Gone are the expresso bars, the smoke-filled speakeasies and the shrines to popular music. Gone, too, are the psychedelic and the hirsute, replaced by endless waves of Yuppies and Yappies undulating from wine bar to wine bar. And yet, after the cultural and social dearth that was the 70s, London nightlife is as lively as ever it was. Despite the savage cuts which have long threatened to erode British theatre, the theatres themselves are full again and London is even exporting some of its top musicals and dramas to Broadway.

Theatre, of course, is what London does best after dark and in any given week choice ranges from Shakespeare to Alan Ayckbourn to Sam Shepard to the latest Tom Stoppard. The Royal Shakespeare Company, or RSC, predictably enough, is the principal purveyor of Shakespeare although it does throw in the occasional classic or modern drama. Based at the **Barbican** (tel: 628 8795) the RSC is a subsidised theatre company with two theatres, one of which shows the more traditional dramas while the other, **The Pit,** provides theatre of a more experimental nature.

The only other nationally subsidised theatre in London is run by the **National Theatre Company** (tel: 928 2252) on the South Bank, although recent cuts have endangered one of its present three theatres. Shakespeare is not a main feature of the National, which tends to produce English drama and foreign plays with additional talks, poetry recitals and play readings as well as exhibitions and chamber music.

Otherwise, most of the commercial theatres tend to cluster around the Shaftesbury Avenue, St Martin's Lane and Strand area, providing several square miles of farce, light comedy and serious drama. Further out, fringe theatre is making something of a comeback on the so-called alternative scene and places like the **Lyric Studio** (King Street, W6; tel: 741 2311), the **Gate Theatre Club,** above the Prince Albert Pub (11 Pembridge Road, W11; tel: 229 0706), also the **Donmar Warehouse** (41 Earlham Street, WC2; tel: 836 3028) and the **Tricycle Theatre** (26a Kilburn High Road; tel: 328 8626) are all worth investigating.

Tickets, however, are not always the easiest thing in the world to come by, particularly for same night performances, and are virtually impossible for the latest Lloyd-Webber extravaganza. The ticket booth in Leicester Square sells half-price (plus 50p) tickets at 2p.m. for same night performances and ticket agencies – which normally charge between 10 and 15 per cent commission – often get returns, so are worth trying if all else fails. Before trying either of these routes, though, would-be theatre goers should check with box offices – not every West End production is an instant sell-out.

As far as music goes, aficionados can more or less take their pick. London has four resident orchestras – the Royal Philharmonic, the Philharmonia, the London Symphony and the London Philharmonic. The **Barbican,** the **Festival Hall** (Belvedere Road, SE1; tel: 928 3191), the **Albert Hall** (Kensington Gore, SW7; tel: 589 8212) and **Fairfields Hall** (Croydon, Surrey; tel: 688 9291) all provide concerts of consistently high standards.

The **Royal Opera House** (Bow Street; tel: 240 1911) is the home of the Royal Opera Company and the Royal Ballet. Same night tickets are not easily come by but 55 amphitheatre seats are on sale every morning, together with seats available in other parts of the house. For opera non-purists, the English National Opera at the **Coliseum** (St. Martin's Lane; tel: 836 3161) has fine productions in English.

And so to alcohol (which really is inordinately expensive in the capital). It would take a very brave man indeed to attempt any sort of comprehensive pub crawl in the city centre – there are hundreds of them; good, bad and distinctly seedy, so it is largely a case of hit and miss. There are, however, a cluster of thoroughly decent pubs, just off the Strand, which are well worth mentioning. Courage's **Lamb & Flag** (33 Rose Street; tel: 836 4108) in Rose Street and Charrington's **White Swan** (14 New Row; tel: 836 3291) are both excellent spots for a little imbibing while not far away, in Catherine Street, the **Opera Tavern** is one of the most interesting Victorian pubs in London.

Further out, the **Cross Keys** and the **Surprise,** both off Cheyne Walk in Chelsea, **The Scarsdale** (23 Edwardes Square; tel: 937 4513) and **The Dove** (19 Upper Mall, Hammersmith; tel: 748 4515) are all particularly well suited to summer quaffing.

Otherwise, it is the wine bar which is receiving most attention these days. Some are quite passable but most, it must be said, are downright indifferent, serving extremely poor wine at extortionate prices. Some of the best in London are run by one Don Hewitson, a New Zealander and ardent wine lover who prides himself on providing a wide choice of good wines at fair price levels. **The Cork and Bottle** (44 Cranbourn Street; tel: 405 6598) just off Charing Cross Road, **Methusela's** (29 Victoria Street; tel: 222 0424) and **Shampers** (4 Kingly Street; tel: 437 1692) are all extremely pleasant, and what's more, the staff actually know something about the wines they are serving – rather a novelty in this age of house red.

**Bill Bentley's Wine Bar** (31 Beauchamp Place; tel: 589 5080) and **Draycott's** (114 Draycott Avenue; tel: 584 5389) in Kensington both serve good wine at reasonable prices although Draycott's is something of a pick up joint for Sloanes. Sloane-y, too, is the **Ebury Wine Bar** (139 Ebury Street; tel: 730 5447) but it does provide some very interesting wines including several uncommon French and a couple of English.

But the real place for wine bars is Covent Garden, a former fruit and vegetable market between St Martins Lane and the Strand. The central Victorian market building is now a popular, verging on the twee, conglomerate of expensive shops and slick cafés, while the piazza, London's first square, hosts a talented array of street musicians (buskers are obliged to audition for permission to play in Covent Garden).

Here it is that London's not-quite-beautiful people sip sweet and sticky cocktails in places like **Rumours** (33 Wellington Street; tel: 580 5796), continually voted 'Cocktail Bar of London' by readers of the *London Standard's* Ad Lib column, and **Palookaville** (13a James Street; tel: 240 3661) just opposite the tube station. **The Crusting Pipe** (Unit 27, Covent Garden Market; tel: 836 1415), **Blakes** (32 Wellington Street; tel: 836 5298) and **Brahms and Liszt** (19 Russell Street; tel: 240 3661) are all equally popular with slightly lesser mortals and, what's more, are all just as crowded.

Stamina (and wallet) permitting, those out for a little late night entertainment could do a lot worse than take in one of London's nightclubs although **Annabels** (44 Berkeley Square; tel: 629 2350) and **Tramps** (40 Jermyn Street; tel: 734 3174) are virtually impossible to get into as far as non-members are concerned, unless, of course, you happen to be one of this season's 'in people'.

Cheaper, though not, I suspect, by much is **Stringfellows** (16 Upper St Martins Lane; tel: 240 5534), a favourite with media celebrities, young executives and last season's 'in people'. A Perrier water here costs around £1.75 but guests

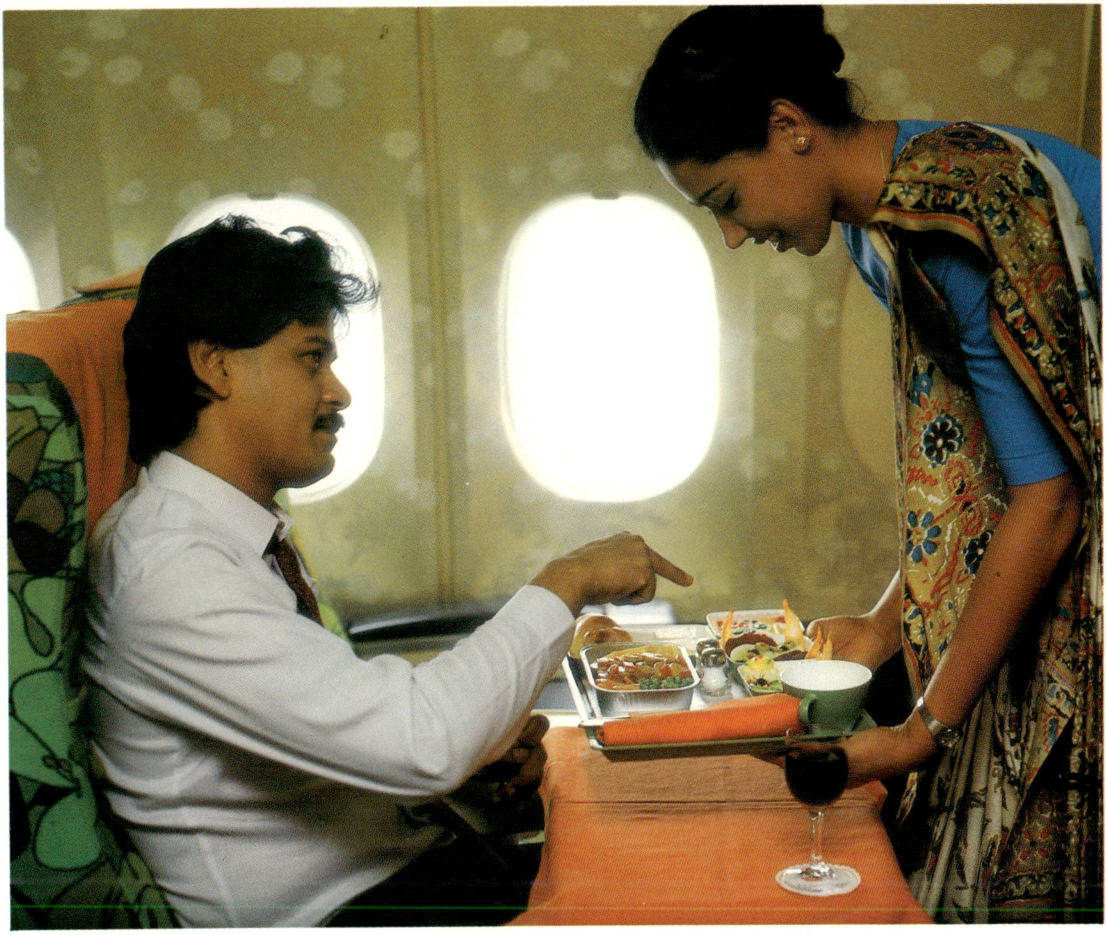

# Biman Executive Class
## only a millimeter behind First Class

Biman Executive Class – a new dimension in service – on our widebody DC 10-30s. Wide seats & leg-space, the comfort of which you find only in First Class, sparkling glass & shining silver, real linen, free drinks, choice of cuisine & electronic headsets for music and movies. On top of that the convenience of separate check-in & luggage entitlement–the same as First Class.

are in with a chance of meeting Peter Stringfellow himself. Music is loud although nowhere near the decibels pumped out at the **Hippodrome** in nearby Charing Cross Road.

For those with a taste for jazz rather than the latest thing in synthesiser technology, **Ronnie Scotts** (47 Frith Street; tel: 439 0747) is a highly respected jazz club featuring some of the best acts in town.

Finally, as dawn breaks, the **Sun Rise,** in Covent Garden's Long Acre, serves bacon and eggs, omelettes, scrambled eggs with smoked salmon and coffee between 2 and 6a.m. and there are some revellers, I'm told, who can actually face such fare at this time of the morning.

# GETTING AROUND

Black cabs, double-decker red buses and the tube – after Big Ben and red-jacketed, busbied Queen's Guardsmen, these are the most popular tourist images of London. They are also crucial to the transport of Londoner and visitor alike.

For a system which is constantly being bewailed by its users, London Transport is nonetheless comprehensive and good. With the aid of a trusty London Underground map, the tube is easily mastered by even the most inexperienced of travellers. Each line is represented by a different colour, and at each entrance there is usually a map of the trains' destinations. The basis for fares changes often, but they are usually based on one's destination. Anyone planning to use the tube and bus with any frequency should invest in a weekly travel card which, for a flat fee, allows travel on both bus and tube. The quality of tube travel has improved recently thanks to an extensive and continuing renovation programme of London's central stations – the bright new tiles make a welcome change from years of soot covered walls. Unfortunately, nothing has been done to relieve the agonies of rush hour traffic when hapless commuters are pressed together in all too intimate contact. Nevertheless, because the tube regularly proves much quicker than land transport during the rush to and from work, it is worth the agony.

*See London from a double-decker bus*

Buses are a good way of combining sightseeing and transportation for the traveller with a bit more time, and the views can be spectacular. All bus stops should provide simplified maps of bus routes together with charts of various destinations and the numbers of the buses that go there. Bus conductors are happy to let you know where to get off the bus if they're asked. For a taste of real London, sit downstairs during the day and listen to the old dears gossip and complain about the weather and their grandchildren.

London transport has an annoying habit of petering out at midnight (1a.m. on Saturday night), at which time taxis become a rare breed. If you do see a black cab, chances are it will be empty but with its lights out (the yellow light at the front of the cab indicates availability), and often drivers will only take late night passengers if the route coincides with their way home. Fares are not outrageously expensive if you do manage to get a cab. Otherwise call a mini cab. Try **Computer Cab** (tel: 286 0286) or **Meadway** (tel: 458 5555). During the day, cab drivers usually know the quickest way around the city's jammed traffic and taxis are thus a good bet for anyone in a hurry. London also has a plethora of hire car firms, including all the big names. Check at your hotel (or in the telephone directory) for details.

# Madrid

**After decades of slumber under General Franco, Madrid is slowly acquiring the characteristics of a modern Western capital – high unemployment, drug problems and bingo. But the easy-going, laid-back mañana mentality makes Madrid a destination to savour.**

**By Maggi O'Sullivan**

There's an Spanish saying that runs: *"To be Spanish is to be proud; to be Madrilenian is a title"*, which even if it was dreamt up by a group of patriotic Madrilenians of a soporific afternoon, sums things up rather nicely. Most of Madrid's four million inhabitants consider themselves to be Madrilenian first, Spanish second – and European a very poor third. It is endearing to hear the locals talk about 'going to Europe' in much the same way that Britons do.

Like most capitals, Madrid has garnered a large portion of its population from the rest of Spain. Every year thousands of Andalusians, Catalonians and Basques troop to what de Musset called *"The Princess of Spain"* to find work. And having been exposed to the lifestyle peculiar to Madrid, few of them choose to leave.

The origins of this lifestyle are difficult to define: more South American than European; more European than South American, the city has fallen strangely out of step with the rest of the Western World. This in turn is hardly surprising considering that democracy and Western mores didn't reach Madrid until 1977 and it has all taken a bit of sinking in. Where foreigners were once dismissed by Franco as undesirable (a British student at Madrid University remembers being chased by an ugly mob after Franco had made a passionate speech urging the good people of Madrid to turn foreigners out of their city) they are now a principal source of revenue. And while Madrid has a long way to go before it realises the full potential of its tourist market – many shops close for four hours in the middle of the day thus throwing away millions of dollars – it has come a long way since the mid-70s.

Slowly but surely Madrid is beginning to catch up. It already has all the things essential to a free and democratic society: high unemployment (official figures put Madrid's at 18 per cent but 23 per cent is probably closer to the mark); serious drug problems (Madrid lags behind on the fashionable drugs scene: heroin is still the 'in' drug here, and punks – who are supposed to be aggressive – prefer to smoke dope or *purro* rather than sniff glue); an organised sex industry (prostitutes advertise their services in a special column in *El Pais);* and a rising crime rate. Strikes (because there is no strike pay) and football hooliganism (because football is still a family game) have not put in much of an appearance here yet.

Unfortunately, and charming as such old-fashioned ideas may be, Madrid still allows itself a month's holiday in the middle of its busiest season. Tourists and businessmen foolish enough to visit this fair city in August do so at their peril – they are likely to find it largely closed. Stores, offices and restaurants shut up shop; everybody disappears to the coast or to their home village to see the family. The Spanish Civil Service stipulates that employees take their full month's leave entitlement between June and September and, needless to say, it takes another full month to get back into the swing of things once they return.

According to Alfredo Araus Ventura of Exposiciones, Congresos y Convenciones – a body set up to advise and encourage trade fairs and conventions – *"The system is ridiculous and outdated. Madrid is paralysed during the August holiday and it doesn't make any sense at all. But to change it, we would have to change so many other things as well. The Education Department, for example, would have to re-schedule the school holidays. There is just so much red tape . . . plus, of course, we are up against a whole mentality."* And changing a mentality, as we all know, requires a great deal of persuasion and time.

Time, though, is something the native appears to have plenty of – although his *sense* of time, it must be said, does tend to be more blunted than that of his American or European counterpart. *"There are two times in Madrid,"* suggests a British ex-pat, *"real time and Spanish time."* Business appointments, for example, are held at Spanish time: you'll be there at 9a.m. sharp and he'll be there around 9.30a.m. – provided, that is, he's a punctual sort of chap. And a word of warning: business hours vary from office to office, particularly in summer when the beloved siesta is at its most popular. So a general rule of thumb is to make all your business calls in the morning.

If the person you want to see is not having a siesta – and this habit *is* slowly being overcome – then he is probably at lunch. Eating is taken extremely seriously here and grabbing a sandwich just won't do. Lunch begins late, around 2.15-2.45p.m. and meanders on well past tea time (afternoon tea at the Ritz is from 6p.m.). Many people go back to the office around 4.30p.m. and work until 8p.m. but such behaviour is by no means guaranteed, so I'd recommend the rule of thumb.

Although Araus is keen to dismiss the 'mañana mentality' as a worn out cliché, it is still very much alive, and unless you impress some sort of urgency on your client you may find yourself drifting uncomfortably close to the end of your stay without having achieved anything.

This lackadaisical attitude to time is illustrated by the experiences of a colleague who had recently moved into a new apartment. He had a telephone installed, and because he worked from home, the phone was in constant use. Two months later he received a puzzled letter from the telephone company telling him that his bill seemed to come to £500 and could this be right?

The banks display a similar lack of urgency: wandering into his bank, the customer joins a queue and is eventually given a receipt for his personal cheque. He then joins another queue to cash his receipt. This laborious process is further complicated by the tellers who hold animated conversations among themselves and show great reluctance to serve anyone if things happen to be getting interesting.

Another curious aspect of doing business here is that despite promoting itself as an international business city, Madrid seems reluctant to converse in any language other than its own. Although the higher echelons of business and industry are perfectly familiar with English, their receptionists are not, so getting through to the top presents a problem. Taxi drivers and shopkeepers certainly speak nothing but Spanish and explaining that you don't understand a word they are saying merely provokes a fresh outburst of equally fast dialogue.

By and large, though, life in Madrid is extremely easy and because much of the day is bound to be appointment-free, the business visitor should have ample time to take in some of the attractions. There can be nothing more pleasant on a hot summer's afternoon than dozing in the Retiro gardens after a heavy lunch, or spending a couple of peaceful hours at the Prado – provided, of course, you keep well clear of the large groups of culturally-underprivileged tramping through the galleries accompanied by vociferous guides and wailing infants.

The Palacio Real on the Caille de Bailén is also worth a visit. It is reserved for official functions these days, King Juan preferring something smaller – and warmer – in the name of socialism, just outside the city. Crammed with beautiful frescoes and furnishings, the palace also houses a magnifi-

*Plaza Mayor, always a popular gathering place, on the feast of San Isidro*

cent collection of tapestries, some dating from the 15th century. Anyone who does go there should wait until early evening because the view from the Plaza de la Armería, just outside gives one of the best sunsets in the city.

All the main plazas in Madrid deserve a second glance: most are well-furnished with imposing statues and tumbling fountains. During the summer, however, some are marred by hideous hardboard pens designed to enclose pageants and open-air theatre. Easily the most attractive square is the Plaza Mayor, plenty of open-air cafés, although it does tend to be something of a tourist trap. This was once the centre of commerce and municipal life, with the odd execution or burning of heretics. Nowadays it has become something of a mecca for gipsies who, carrying the obligatory baby, tell the usual tales of woe: no milk for the aforementioned baby, no food and a husband who has run off or died. They will also try to sell you anything they think you might be persuaded to want, from their grandmothers' gold wedding rings to their grandmothers.

But begging is not really a part of street life in Madrid – gambling, on the other hand, is. Kiosks sell tickets for the *loteria* on every street corner and hawkers weave in and out of the crowded cafés inviting all and sundry to part with their hard-earned pesetas.

Slot machines are extremely popular too – particularly the one-arm bandit variety – but most popular by far is bingo: there are bingo halls at every turn in Madrid and many of the larger hotels hold their own sessions in the evening. There is no class barrier as far as bingo is concerned either, largely because of worthwhile prizes: up to £8,000 in some cases.

What the average citizen really wants is to win a large fortune and retire. There is another revered Spanish saying – and this one came out of my *Baedeker* – which is useful for sayings if little else: *"From Madrid to heaven, and window there from which to look down on Madrid"*. Most people would go along with that, especially the schoolchildren for whom the government recently abolished homework.

# WHERE TO STAY

If there's one irritating thing about Madrid, it's that the beds are of such miserly proportions they are scarcely worth eating breakfast in. Other than that, Madrid provides some of the best, and certainly some of the cheapest five-star accommodation in Western Europe. Prices usually include service, but not the five per cent tax.

The **Madrid Ritz** (Plaza de la Lealtad; tel: 221 2857; telex: 43986), opposite the Prado Museum, is easily the most grand. Built in 1910 under the auspices of King Alfonso III, the Ritz was taken over by Trusthouse Forte in 1982 and much has been done since then to restore the hotel to its former glory. A $6 million renovation programme refurbished the lounge in peach and cream opulence – thick hand-made carpets slide beneath plumped and polished chairs – the small overgrown garden has been clipped and trimmed into a relaxed terraced restaurant and all 156 rooms have been redecorated in Regency-style elegance.

A hotel of the old school, the Ritz has made one concession to the 80s: a sauna, massage and work-out room – but guests are still strongly discouraged from sauntering through the rest of the hotel in anything but the traditional collar and tie.

Single 20,000 pts; double 25,000 pts; suites from 32,000 pts.

Less formal but almost as splendid are the 525-room **Palace Hotel** (Plaza de la Cortes; tel: 429 7551; telex: 22272), just across the square from the Ritz and the **Villa Magna** (Paseo de la Castellana; tel: 261 4900; telex: 22914). Sited on the edge of Old Madrid, the Palace is convenient for the city centre and thus tends to be popular with business visitors. It has a magnificent glass domed ceiling stretching over most of the lounge area which gives it something of the feel of a dignified greenhouse. The front rooms have a particularly lovely view of the Prado. The Villa Magna, on the other hand, has more in common with a mausoleum, with its wide, marble – and usually deserted – lobby presided over by a large sculpture said to be a *"silent witness to the hospitality and devotion that the hotel unfailingly dedicates to its clients"*. Certainly room service is exceptionally fast, although I'm not sure that the absence of mini bars *"so that the client is served rather than serving himself"* is not taking things a bit too far.

Palace Hotel: single 10,400 pts; double 13,000-17,000 pts; suite 21,500-38,000 pts. Villa Magna: single 15,500 pts; double 21,500 pts; suite 38,000-59,000 pts.

Slightly further down the luxury scale, but five-star hotels nonetheless, are the **Eurobuilding** (Padre Damián 23; tel: 457 7800; telex: 22548), located in Madrid's commercial district with one of the best pools in town; the **Princesa Plaza** (Princesa, 40; tel: 242 2100; telex: 44377), Madrid's newest and most modern five-star hotel; and the **Melia Madrid** (Princesa, 27; tel: 241 8200; telex: 22537), which specialises in large conference facilities and is where most of the Spanish political parties hold their conventions. Prices in most of these hotels range from around 8,200 pts for a single room to 28,000 for a suite.

The best of the rest include **Miguel Angel** (Miguel Angel 31; tel: 442 0022; telex: 44235). Single 9,500 pts; double 13,900 pts; plus 5 per cent service and 5 per cent tax; and the **Mindanao** (San Francisco de Sales; tel: 449 5500; telex: 22631) in the university district, known for its excellent kitchen. Single 8,700 pts; double 11,200 pts. The **Wellington** (Velázquez; tel: 275 4400; telex: 22700) is a favourite haunt of bullfighting aficionados, and also of bullfighters who are sound of body, and purse. Single 7,450 pts; double 12,150 pts. The **Melia Castilla** (Capitan Haya; tel: 270 8000; telex: 23142) has been recently upgraded to five-star status, but lacks the class of its sister Melia Madrid. This may have something to do with the prostitutes who flaunt their wares under the hotel's windows.

In a class of its own is the **Hotel Chamartin** (Estacion de Chamartin; tel: 450 9050; telex: 4920) run by the state-owned Entursa. Hotel Chamartin is part of a government-financed extravaganza – the Charmartin Station – which includes four cinemas, a bowling alley, roller rink, restaurants and several cafés. The hotel itself houses conference halls and banqueting rooms of gigantic proportion. Unfortunately the hotel can't provide the sort of personal service and attention to detail offered by the other Madrid hotels because of its sheer size.

If staying at the airport, the **Alameda** (Avenida Logrono; tel: 747 4800; telex: 22255) and the

**Barajas** (Avenida Logrono; tel: 747 7700; telex: 22255) are both recommended. Since the airport is a good 15km from the city, it is not advisable to stay there if doing much business in town. Alameda: single 6,800 pts; double 9,500. Barajas: single 9,550 pts; double 11,950. Tax and service is included in the price.

One of the great pleasures of staying in Madrid is the quality of hotel service. Whether this is because hotels tend to use local people rather than importing foreign labour, or whether it is simply because hoteliers in Madrid have not yet lost sight of their main function – to give pleasure rather than simply provide a service for their guests – service is unusually quick and efficient. And the sulky waitress and surly waiter, common to the rest of Europe, are thankfully few and far between in Madrid.

# WHERE TO EAT

What Madrid excels at, is feeding itself. Not that the capital differs much from the rest of the country in this respect – the cuisine enjoyed here, as with that enjoyed throughout Spain, is *"full of garlic and religious concern"*. There are certain dishes, though, which Madrid claims as its own: *cocido madrileno* – a stew of chickpeas, potatoes, meat and sausage – is one. Then there's tripe à la madrilena made with white wine, cognac, pepper, onion, sausage, ham and spices; *gallinejas* – deep fried intestines; garlic soup à la madrilena (with poached egg and chorizo) and the legendary *judias del tio lucas* – a thick stew made with haricot beans.

Eating out here is cheap – no more than £15–£20 a head even in the most expensive restaurants and at £3 a bottle for a respectable wine, alcohol need not inflate the bill. Prominent among the many excellent restaurants serving international cuisine is **Jockey** (Amador de los Ríos, 6; tel: 419 1003) which is superb and where the callos are exceptional. Founded by one of the greatest names in Spanish cuisine – Don Clodoaldo Cortés – in 1945, Jockey is now run by his son. A meal for two here with house wine works out at around 4,000 pts.

Very similar, though slightly more casual, is **Club 31** (Alcalá 58; tel: 232 0511). Popular with businessmen at lunchtime and with theatre-goers in the late evening, Club 31 has a cheerful atmosphere. Puddings are particularly good here and service is faultless. Again allow around 4,000 pts for two.

**El Amparo** (Callejón de Puigcerdá; tel: 431 6456) is definitely the place for *nouvelle cuisine* although Patrick Buret at the **Ritz** is extremely well-versed in this type of cuisine too. Around 3,000 pts should cover the cost of a meal for two at El Amparo – the Ritz comes slightly more expensive.

**Las Cuatro Estaciones** (Generál Ibánez Ibero; tel: 253 6305) the elegant **Horcher** (Alfonso XII; tel: 222 0731) and **Sacha** (Juan Hurtado de Mendoza; tel: 457 7200) have all earned excellent reputations as purveyors of international cuisine. However, the absolute last word in restaurants of this genre is **Zalacaín** (Alvarez de Baena; tel: 261 1079 or 261 4708). Its popularity is certainly well-deserved – everything is beautifully done, from the elegant decor to the service to the extensive menu which changes four times a year. You are also likely to find yourself surrounded by minor celebrities and major politicians.

For traditional food, **Botin** (Cuchilleros; tel 226 3026) in Old Madrid is probably the best bet. Claiming to be Madrid's oldest restaurant – it began life in the 16th century – Casa Botin serves typically castillian dishes: roast suckling pig, roast lamb and stewed partridge. It also has excellent fish dishes like baby squid in its own ink, clams Botin and baked cantabrian hake. Around 5,000 pts for two, including wine.

Madrid does have an insatiable craving for seafood which is flown in daily from Galicia and the Basque countries in the North. This can be expensive but is usually well worth having – two good places are **La Dorada** (Orense; tel: 270 2004) and **Cabo Mayor** (Juan Hurtado de Mendoza; tel: 250 8776). La Dorada's speciality is bass cooked in the best Andalucian tradition: buried deep beneath large grains of salt and cooked in a wooden box. The Cabo Mayor provides what it calls a 'long and thin' menu which allows customers to sample portions of all the specialities. Reservations are essential at both restaurants.

For excellent food at non-business prices go to any restaurant on Ventura La Vega. The restaurants there are popular with the local community who say that the food is as good as the best home cooking – high praise indeed! Try **El Lucreques** or **El Bilbaino,** where the paella is sublime.

Madrid also has a string of 'ethnic' restaurants, **Mei Ling** (Paseo de la Castellana, 188; tel: 457 6717), **La Casa de Lee** (San Felipe, 4; tel: 279 8454) and the **House of Ming** (Paseo de la Castellana; tel: 261 9827) are regarded as the top Chinese restaurants.

Anyone wanting traditional cocido madrileno should go to **Lhardy** (Carrera de San Jeronimo; tel: 221 3385). *"No visit to Madrid is complete without a visit here,"* says a breathy little booklet produced by the Patronato Municipal de Turismo – they are probably right.

If you care for history with your *vino tinto,* then Old Madrid, with its narrow, tavern-lined streets, is the place to be after dark. It doesn't much matter which of the hundreds of taverns you happen into – they are all much the same; some providing live *organillo* music, most reeking of stale wine and food and all selling the proverbial *tapas.*

The best street for this sort of thing is the cava de San Miguel with places like **La Mazmorra,** the **Meson de Tortilla** and **El Huevo** all specialising in snacks like omelettes, or *tortillas,* and chopped octopus.

But as characteristic and authentic as this old part of the city seems to be, it is not a favourite with the locals – tourists and opportunists seem to have driven them off. The area around the Plaza de Santa Ana, on the other hand, sees few tourists by night and is heavily frequented by young, intellectual Madrid.

The most popular bar/restaurant in this district is **La Trucha** (Manuel Fernandez y Gonzalez, 3; tel: 429 58) which allows you to choose a little of everything on its menu – eels in garlic, fried squid, traditional Spanish smoked sausage, Spanish ham – and wash it down with jugs of fairly decent house wine while watching the locals in action: bawling their orders across the bar and flinging their cigarette ends on the floor.

On the Plaza de Santa Ana itself, the **Café Central** is a relaxed jazz café with live bands every night, which also serves an excellent cup of coffee. Also on the Plaza de Santa Ana is the **Cerveceria Alemana,** where Hemmingway used to while away the hours of the night. It has been discovered by a few dedicated Americans, but has so far evaded the tourist at large. Food, drink and company are all worthwhile.

Of course there is a lot more to do in Madrid by night than drink: there are 30 theatres – 23 of which are commerical, two municipal, two national and three belonging to cultural associations. There are cinemas, mostly showing American films dubbed into Spanish. Film showings don't start until around 10p.m. and provided you don't mind seeing Superman saving the world in Spanish then the **Gran Via** is the best place to go. If you would prefer to see a film in its original form **Alphaville** (Martín de los Heros, 14; tel: 248 7223), and **Pequeno Cinestudio** (Magallanes, 1) show films with sub-titles. **Felipe II** (Fuenta del Berro; tel: 222 5092) also shows films with subtitles for those who like pornography in translation.

Since Franco's demise in 1975, Spanish erotica has come out of the closet. There are floor shows and topless bars galore, among the most popular being **Don 'Q'** (Paseo de la Castellana; tel: 455 7769) and **Montmartre Boite Club** (Libertad; tel: 231 8580). Those looking for closer companionship can check the classified ad section of the daily papers for special messages, or look up telephone numbers in the **Guía del Ocio.** According to a reliable source, the most beautiful women can be found at **Angelo's** bar. However, foreigners should note that the going rate is £100 for them, while for Spaniards it is 10,000 pts.

Madrid claims to have some of the best discotheques and nightclubs in Europe, many of which stay open until 5a.m.; a list of the same can be obtained from the Patronato Municipal de Turismo. I am reliably informed that **Pacha** (Barceló, 11; tel: 446 0137), **Mississippi** (Princesa, 45; tel: 247 5432) and **Rock Ola** (Padre Xifré, 5; tel: 413 7839) are all reasonably lively. For dancing of a more traditional nature, a flamenco club is worth a visit.

One of the most popular with tourists is the **Corral de la Morería** (Morería, 17; tel: 266 3640) just off the Calle de Bailén. The Corral de la Morería is owned by Lucero Teno who, until recently gave stunning displays with the castanets.

*Flamenco: a dance simulating a bullfight*

She no longer plays in public but the flamenco show is still pretty exciting. If you prefer not to eat at the club – and a whole evening of stamping feet and emotional outbursts *is* a bit much – you could try turning up around midnight and taking pot luck. You'll be charged a small fortune for a drink (around 5,000 pts for two if you aren't eating) but it is worth it. A team of appropriately dressed men and women clap and dance their way through a string of loud, emotional numbers, exhausting just to watch. Sit near the front if you can – to appreciate the sheer anguish and pain reflected in the dancers' faces. However, the top Flamenco troupes spend the best part of each year touring, giving only three or four weeks to Madrid a year. When they are in town they usually appear at the **Monumental,** the **Palacio del Progreso** or the **Plaza Color** (a theatre run by the Town Hall). Check the local papers for details.

Travellers with a weekend to spare in Madrid could do worse than spend Sunday at a football game. Madrid's main team – Real Madrid – is excellent, and it is exhilarating to watch them from a crowd of 80,000 supporters. The Madrid basketball team shares both its name and reputation with the football team (it is often forgotten that Spain won the silver medal in basketball in the 1984 Olympics). Basketball can also be seen most weekends.

Finally, if you are not sickened by the sight of blood and find yourself in Madrid between March and June, or from mid-September to mid-October, then go to a bullfight at **Las Ventas** (Plaza de Toros Monumental). The ring itself is stunning, and if the fighting proves too much, the loud and colourful crowd should provide a pleasant diversion from the sport. May is the main bullfighting month, when there are fights every day for three weeks; during the rest of the season they are confined to weekends. March and April are the months when novice matadors, *novilleros,* try to prove themselves on young bulls. In the high season, the names to look out for are Paco Ojeda, Tomas and José Antonio Capuzano, Palomar, and Espartaco. Of the matadors who work on horseback, *rejoneadores,* the Peralta brothers are said to be the best.

# GETTING AROUND

Barajas airport lies 13 km from the centre of Madrid so taxis into town are relatively inexpensive (800–1,000 pts), but check that the meter is turned on.

Getting around the city itself is extremely easy. Apart from its 15,500 taxis, Madrid also provides an excellent and economical underground system which covers practically the whole city for a flat fare of 40 pts. The bus service is equally cheap and efficient: running from 5.30 a.m. to 1.30 a.m., buses charge 40 pts for one journey or you could buy a *bonobus* multiple ticket which would entitle you to journeys for around 260 pts.

Madrid is also served by three mainline stations: Atocha for trains to and from the South and

South East; Principe Pio station for suburban services and trains to and from the North, and Chamartin station for trains to France and Cataluña.

Useful telephone numbers: National Spanish Railway Network (RENFE) 733 3000; metro information 435 2266; bus services 401 9900; teletaxi 445 9008; radiotaxi 404 9000. For further information contact the Patronato Municipal de Turismo, Calle Mayor, 83; tel: 241 9281.

# SHOPPING

Shopping in Madrid is not the easiest thing in the world – largely because so many places persist in closing during the early afternoon. This is particularly true of the Salamanca district although it's probably just as well because this is Madrid's most expensive shopping area. Luxury boutiques and exclusive stores line the Calles Serrano, Goya, Juan Bravo and Velazquez offering made-to-measure suits, haute couture and leather wear at anything but bargain prices. Still, foreign visitors are entitled to a 10 per cent export discount where the value of goods exceeds 10,000 pts (which it inevitably does in the Salamanca district). In theory, the customer fills in a form which is presented to customs officials on leaving Spain and the mount of the discount, minus bank charges, is sent by post. In practice many shops will make the discount at the time of purchase so it is worth looking into.

Less prestigious purchases can be made in the centre of Madrid, principally in the Calle Toledo, Plaza de Progreso, Puerta de Sol, Calle Preciados and the Gran Via. The Gran Via is an especially good bet for electrical goods, furs and inexpensive jewellery. Department stores are not as prevalent as they are, say, in London but the **Galerías Preciados, El Corte Inglés** and **Celso Garcia** have several branches throughout the centre of Madrid. Celso Garcia is particularly good with a branch in the Salamanca district.

But a visit to Madrid would not be complete, as they say in the guide books, without a visit to the **Rastro,** Madrid's Sunday flea-market. The Rastro is the *barrios bajos,* to the south of the city not far from the Plaza Mayor. Here you can pick up 19th and early 20th century handicrafts and an infinite variety of other exotica.

Madrid is particularly keen to make its mark in the fashion world. Once again the Salamanca district is the place for designer wear but the Argüelles area – notably Calle de Princesa and Calle de Arapiles – is the place for young fashion. The **Multi Centro** in Calle de Princesa is one of the best malls for this sort of thing.

Anything 'arty' and you are better off in Old Madrid, there are numerous workshops around the Plaza Mayor, most of which have been owned and worked by the same families for generations. And if you really fancy lugging a guitar back through customs then this is the place to buy one.

*Multi Centro shopping mall is crammed with boutiques*

# Manila

**South East Asia's most disorderly of capitals may be coming apart at the seams, with economic crisis following political crisis in swift succession: but the Filipinos remain the warmest, wittiest and most welcoming of people, greeting adversity with round-the-clock smiles.**

**By Philip Jacobson**

You have to be ready for Manila these days. It was always a fairly challenging city, a flashy, swaggering sort of place, quite unlike other Asian capitals with its strong American flavour. But the past few years have not been kind to the Philippines, and Manila has borne the brunt of the punishment. Alongside an economic crisis of gathering severity came the turbulence and tension generated by the assassination of opposition leader Benigno Aquino in August 1983. Both factors seem certain to plague Manila for some time to come: their combined impact has already scared off a great deal of foreign investment, and with other parts of the region enjoying comparative stability and prosperity, the Philippines today is not exactly enticing to outsiders. And as if that wasn't bad enough, an alarming series of fires in Manila's hotels, from grand to grim, has devastated what was left of the once booming tourist trade.

Now for the good news. Ordinary Filipinos are still a delight to encounter, the warmest, wittiest and most welcoming of people. God knows how they contrive to keep smiling in the face of such relentless misfortune (in addition to man-made troubles, the country has had a basinful of typhoons, floods, earthquakes, even a volcanic eruption, in recent years). But they do, and it is the saving of Manila. Consider, as just one example, the best impromptu test of Filipino cordiality – the evening rush hour in downtown Manila. The sheer strain of coping with one of South East Asia's most disorderly capitals invariably makes itself felt in what would appear to be spectacularly anti-social behaviour. Frustrated motorists career along the grass verges, occasionally mounting the pavement to snatch a few precious yards. Others plunge blindly into no entry streets, headlights blazing. A trifling altercation about right of way assumes such proportions that mass murder seems quite likely (though the era of a gun in every glove compartment has, thankfully, departed – well, more or less).

It is amazingly restful to observe this turmoil from the comfort of an air-conditioned cocktail lounge where, since this is the Philippines, the incomparable ice-cold San Miguel beers are accompanied by pleasing sounds from the finest natural musicians east of Suez. On particularly wearing evenings, it is not unknown for drivers to abandon vehicles en masse in the middle of the road to join

Happy Hour drinkers. In no time, the place is full of small brown people enjoying themselves immoderately, apparently without a care in the world. This defiantly laid-back approach to everyday life worries the Filipinos's starchier neighbours. Why are these people always laughing, always standing complete strangers a drink? Good grief, don't they *know* their country is coming apart at the seams?

They know all right. Anyone with eyes can see that there is very real suffering in the streets of the capital. The truth is that without the charm, high spirits and dignity in the face of hardship and hopelessness of its inhabitants, Manila would be a fearful destination indeed – over-crowded, polluted, always hot and sticky. The gusto with which the people of Manila set about inflicting grievous bodily harm upon each other simply underlines the very real concern for the welfare of visitors. This is one city where round-the-clock smiles for foreigners do not begin to grate. It so happens that the country's political and economic problems have also made Manila one of the best bargains in the region. With reservations managers on their knees for business, determined pursuit of discounts can bring palaces like the five-star Manila Hotel, on the edge of the stunning bay, within range of most travel budgets. And while nobody would call the Philippines a gourmet paradise – too much sub-American cuisine for that – you can now eat pretty well in top restaurants for a few pounds a head.

Those visiting Manila on business will swiftly discover certain immutable facts of life, mostly aggravating. It is particularly important to come to terms with this early on, because letting the city get on top of you is a recipe for a miserable stay. Take the phone system, to use the description loosely. Picking up the receiver at any time of day or night is pure lottery: will you get an outside line, will anything happen after you dial, who is going to answer? The most exotic crossed lines in the world yield a bewildering clamour of static, machine-gun bursts of Tagalog (the national tongue), disconcerting giggles from parties unknown and heart-rending sighs from fellow sufferers. Be prepared for the worst, especially when it rains, and remember that locals often employ human runners for more important and urgent messages.

Many business travellers will become depressingly familiar with the road between downtown Manila, where most hotels are located, and the financial district in Makati. A long, slow drive at the best of times, purgatory in rush hour, it should on no account ever be undertaken in a vehicle without efficient air-conditioning. Staying in one of the good hotels around Makati would eliminate this dreary grind, but like all such districts it virtually empties after work. There are restaurants, bars and nightclubs nearby, but those glass and concrete canyons can become rather depressing for visitors without local contacts to entertain them. There were plans to develop a new commercial centre for big corporations, banks and so on near Roxas Boulevard and the main concentration of hotels, but the economic crisis may have overtaken the project.

As it happens, since air-conditioning is an essential life support system in Manila, enterprising locals economise by conducting their business affairs in the lobbies of major hotels all over town. With such dismal occupancy rates, most managers are grateful for extra takings from sales of coffee and beer and a bit of a bustle to make their place look alive. Be warned that in the office or elsewhere, punctuality is not a noticeable trait of Filipinos. On the other hand, what a joy to be in a country where formal attire for men, from President Ferdinand Marcos on down, means no more than a long-sleeved *barong* – the cool, open-necked shirt worn outside trousers – and well-pressed slacks. I can say with hand on heart that I've never worn a tie in Manila (women travellers who go there frequently say that only cotton will do in the fierce heat and humidity).

As for relaxation, once you've done Intramuros, the old Spanish walled city, Manila has little to offer by way of sights. With taxis and internal air fares so cheap, it makes better sense to take a break away from the heat and hectic pace of the capital. Less than an hour's flight to the North, several thousand feet up in the brooding Cordillera mountains, Baguio City provides almost everything Manila lacks – air you can't see, temperate climate (sweaters needed at night), clean streets, peaceful parks and gardens. Also good hotels, a lively if limited nightlife and a casino where the big wheels converge for serious gambling, accompanied by B-movie bodyguards armed to the teeth. Excellent uncrowded beaches within fairly easy reach of Manila include those of Batangas to the south (Isla Verde has acres of spotless white sand, dotted with little fish restaurants, and wonderful skin diving) and La Union on the north-western coast. The beach at Baung, not far from Baguio City, could

*Manila attempts to get to work*

well be the best in the country.

It helps to remember in dealings of any kind with Filipinos, of all backgrounds, that many can remember much better times for their beleaguered country. In the late 1950s, Manila under Mayor Arsenio H. Lacsan was considered one of the world's best administered cities. Until President Marcos imposed martial law in 1972, a riotous, frequently violent, but essentially healthy democracy prevailed. Since the murder of Aquino, internal pressure for change has produced a relaxation of press censorship and a profusion of organisations opposed to Marcos (you'll see plenty of Aquino posters in Makati). There is absolutely no need to tread cautiously on politics when among Filipinos. Passing around the *chismis* – gossip – is a national pastime, as is the retailing of quite excellent jokes about Marcos, his wife Imelda and their 'magic circle' of cronies. The best are, alas, far too indelicate for these pages, though they often find their way into one or other of Manila's gadfly street journals.

Business travellers staying in Manila will find themselves faced with that all-too-familiar dilemma of big cities – namely, which part of the city to stay in. Hotels in the business district are as luxurious as all good first class establishments should be, but the area is dead after office hours; downtown Manila bumps and grinds through the night, and in the morning you're stuck in a traffic jam miles from that 9a.m. appointment.

If you're in Manila for any length of time it is worth staying in the centre; but for business travellers on short trips the wisest place to stay in Manila is the Makati business district. The four main Makati hotels – the Mandarin, the Peninsula, the Inter-Continental and the Manila Garden – are all within a few blocks of each other.

**The Mandarin** (Paseo de Roxas Triangle, Makati; tel: 816 360; telex 63756) is an elegant and efficient business hotel, with the attraction of a gym for mixed usage – separate entrances and facilities of course. Single 1355 pesos; double 1531 pesos.

Next door is the **Peninsula** (Corner Ayala and Makati Ave; tel: 857 711; telex: 22476), definitely alive with a certain Filipino buzz not really found in the other Makati hotels. The Peninsula has a wide-open, semi-circular lobby – a modern version of the elegant Hong Kong original. It is a meeting place for local businessmen and a good choice for Makati. Single from 1672 pesos; suites from 1936-6952 pesos.

The **Inter-Continental** (Ayala Ave; tel: 815 9711; telex: 23314) is often pretty crowded but has a friendly atmosphere which probably stems from the fact that it is a tourist-style hotel that boasts almost 90 per cent business clientele. There are also groups of tourists to be seen but the hotel is laid out neatly and copes with the mix very well. The Jeepney Café is fun–even if the staff are, as is so often the case with coffee-shop staff, a little slow. Single 1478 pesos; double 1619 pesos; suite 2816-4928 pesos.

The final choice in Makati is the **Manila Garden** (Fourth Quadrant, Makati Commercial Center; tel: 857 911; telex: 45883) a Japan Air Lines hotel which is far from being quiet and serene. In fact, it is positively noisy in that frantic Japanese-tour-group sort of way. Single 1373-1584 pesos; double 1549-1760 pesos; suite 3168 pesos.

There really is only one other choice after weighing up everything Manila has to offer – excluding location and cost – and that's the **Manila Hotel** (Rizal Park; tel: 470 011; telex: 40537). It is elegance itself. Lovely, lofty well-appointed columns, inviting archways, a large marble-floored lobby producing a truly tropical flavour that the slightly shabby Raffles in Singapore and the forbidding Hong Kong Peninsula somehow miss. This elegance is reflected in the prices – single from 1936 pesos; double from 2112 pesos; suites 2640-6688 pesos.

This hotel is as nostalgic and romantic as it's made out to be and even though there is a tinge of pretension it still has endearing Filipino touches.

At the other end of the Bay lies the **Philippine Plaza** (Roxas Bvd; tel: 832 0701 or 593 711; telex: 40443) for anyone who likes to feel securely locked up and safe in a man-made tropical paradise. This hotel is a dream come true, with spectacular features, fountains – almost waterfalls – cascading all around and acres of space. Whoever constructed it obviously had in mind that the guest would be so satisfied he would never wish to leave the hotel. So when he finally decides to leave and has fought his way through security, hailed a taxi for the city and left this showpiece, is he prepared for the cultural shock in store? The Philippine Plaza is not representative of Manila. Single 1390-1566 pesos; double 1654-1830 pesos; suite 3256-7480 pesos.

**The Hilton** (United Nations Ave; tel: 573 711; telex: 63387) is on its own, right next door to the Mabini nightlife zone. Try though it may to build up a family-hotel image, the Hilton's location – convenient for all the government offices as well as Mabini, makes it an ideal hotel for the regular visitor. It's not really a tourist hotel – hordes of Japanese and Australians are not too evident. Mabini really is the life force of Manila, abundant with restaurants, bars and fascinating people. Single 1232-1848 pesos; double 1408-2112 pesos; suite 4648-6688 pesos.

The **Silahis Hotel** (Roxas Bvd; tel: 573 811; telex: 63163) marks the beginning of the tourist heart of Manila, and in the next mile of Roxas Boulevard the Holiday Inn, Sheraton, Hyatt, and Regent are all to be found. This part of town also offers shopping malls, souvenir shops and Western-style restaurants.

The Silahis, which houses the Playboy Club, is locally owned and run by the same group as the Philippine Village, home of Manila's casino near the airport. Single from 1408 pesos; double from 1496 pesos; suites from 1760-2640 pesos. The **Century Park Sheraton** (Vito Cruz Corner M Adriatico St; tel: 506 041; telex: 40489/27791) is working hard at attracting the Arab market. It is a large sprawling hotel that was quite spectacular when it opened in 1976 but is now somewhat overshadowed by the Philippine Plaza.

For the conscientious Hyatt supporter, the **Manila Hyatt** (Roxas Bvd, Pasay City; tel: 831 2611; telex 63344 or 63462) has introduced its impressive Regency Club as part of its present upgrading. Standard rooms are particularly good value, at US$44 for a single or double. Club rooms are pricier at US$93 single, US$103 double. Suites go from $103 to $500.

Finally, the budget-minded businessman

*Manila Hyatt hotel*

could do worse than stay at the **Admiral Hotel** (Roxas Bvd; tel: 572 081; telex: 7420488), a favourite haunt of visiting correspondents. Rooms are comparatively cheap: single 862 pesos; double 968 pesos; and even lower 'summer' rates of single 581 pesos; double 616 pesos.

Travellers should note that hotel bills may be as much as 24 per cent higher than expected, since the 10 per cent service and 13.7 per cent government tax are rarely included in the price. However, 'summer rates' compensate by bringing the official rates down by up to 50 per cent. Given the recent dramatic decline in hotel bookings, the 'summer rate' has been known to linger through the year. These reductions are not always volunteered, so it is worth asking. Hotel bills can usually be paid in US dollars or pesos, but the quoted price is almost invariably in dollars and tends to fluctuate in tune to dollar movements. Our prices have been converted at a rate of 17.60 pesos to the dollar.

# WHERE TO EAT

It rarely takes the visitor to Manila long to notice the ubiquitous mango. It usually makes its first appearance in the hotel room and then reappears through each course of every meal. A typical meal might start with mango and prawn, followed by pork dumpling soup with mango, marinated broiled sirloin steak with mango garnish, ice cream with sweet mango sauce for dessert.

This is not to say that Filipino cuisine is monotonous – far from it – the sheer abundance of seafood alone precludes such accusations. Prawns, in

*Ice cream vendor*

particular, are of a size and succulence unknown in Western Europe. A Filipino friend explained that the warm waters of the Philippines breeds fish with much flesh and little fat, making them particularly sweet and juicy.

Apart from fish, rice is the staple diet of Filipine cooking, and *adobo* is the closest to a national dish. *Adobo* can be either chicken or pork cooked in vinegar, soy sauce, garlic and pepper – giving it a pleasantly tangy taste. Another regular is *bagoong*, a very strong fish paste which is served in a small side dish, often accompanied by sharp green mangos. Vegetables are called *gulay*, and are usually served mixed, often with prawns.

Unsuspecting visitors will be relieved to learn that Filipino food is rarely uncomfortably hot – thanks to an only moderate use of chilli. Travellers who feel betrayed by such lack of spice in foreign climes can console themselves with a *balut* – a fertilized duck's egg, where the embryonic duckling is sucked out through a hole in the shell – this is sold on most street corners and considered a great delicacy and aphrodisiac.

When Filipinos go out to eat, it is usually to a Chinese or Filipino restaurant. **Kamayan** (Quezon Bvd; tel: 994 288) is recommended for authentic Filipino dishes (brave spirits may be interested in Dinuguan, pig's innards stewed in blood and seasoned with chilli). Those who have never entirely mastered the British use of knife and fork may prefer **Sinugba** (Passay Road; tel: 880 298) where food is eaten in authentic Filipino style – with the hands. For Chinese food, try the **Jade Garden** (Makati Commercial Center; tel: 862 319) which is related to the Hong Kong restaurant and said to be excellent.

Should the British businessman/woman be subject to a sudden attack of homesickness, the **San Mig Pub** on Faura Street (tel: 921 3837) serves perfectly respectable draft beer and the fish and chips are reasonable. Other European nationals can find solace at **La Taverna** (Adriatico; tel: 585 372) or at **Weinstube,** among the girlie bars of M.H. del Pilar.

## NIGHT LIFE

Nightlife means all things to all men, and they are all available on Manila's Ermita. The celebrated Strip is held by many Asia hands to be superior even to that of Bangkok. It centres on M.H. del Pilar Street, right in the tourist belt, and is gaudy, raucous and frequently raunchy. Many Filipinos and some visitors find the profusion of go-go bars, short-time joints and massage parlours infinitely depressing. On the other hand, the Strip is perfectly safe, fairly inexpensive – the ubiquitous San Migs cost about $1.00 in most places – and contrives, thanks to the nature of the Filipinos, to avoid the harsher edges of the skin trade elsewhere. The young women in Del Pilar's many welcoming establishments will certainly not object to being bought colourful drinks and will happily consider the possibility of continuing the encounter in more private surroundings.

Fashions and favourites change rapidly in this business, but the **Firehouse** and **Bubbles** (which is British-owned) should suit those who like their bars big, their music loud and wall-to-wall girls. At both places the *mamasan* will helpfully arrange introductions to any of the go-go dancers performing above the bar. If the introduction proves mutually agreeable, it is usually possible to take the girl off for the night for a 'bar fine' of about $10.00. What happens afterwards is strictly between you and your companion, but offers of less than $25 are not greatly appreciated.

Should your needs on del Pilar run to mental stimulation, **Scott's** is where many of the resident ex-pats do their social drinking; and since time immemorial the foreign press have patronised a dark little joint called **The Spiders Web,** where you will find the world's only Scrabble hustlers. Check at the Admiral Hotel for details.

Travellers scanning the local papers are often intrigued by the quantity of advertised fashion shows. These tend to appeal to men rather than women, since the 'show' usually consists of rather young 'models' parading in clothes which would make a bikini seem modest.

As one would expect, the international hotels provide international stars at international prices. It is undeniably pleasant to bask in the glow from a good meal accompanied by plenty of wine while Dionne Warwick sings the blues; but the same act will probably appear at the Folk Arts Theatre later in the week, at a fraction of the price.

# GETTING AROUND

Public transportation in Manila is cheap and plentiful and best avoided by the business traveller. As in most cities, buses run along set routes, but to the foreign eye there seems no rhyme or reason behind these, and the general dearth of bus maps does not make matters any clearer.

The *jeepney* is certainly more intriguing than any bus, though no less confusing. These brashly-coloured jeeps were proudly flaunting their multi-coloured grafittied frames long before grafitti was proclaimed a 20th century art form. Like the buses, the *jeepney* runs along mysterious but preordained routes. Unfortunately, they are more uncomfortable than the buses, often carrying eight people at a time, and are neither a convenient nor comfortable way to travel.

Recently opened is the Manila metro, based on the Belgian model, and using overground trains. It was beautifully efficient when it opened in December 1984, but it is impossible to say how the system will wear under the strain of constant use.

It is possible to hire a car in Manila, and most of the major firms are represented. But car hire is not recommended unless you thrive on aggravation – streets are congested for mile upon mile and remain congested through all hours of the day and night. Should you decide to hire a car despite this, Avis is at P. Casal Street (tel: 741 0394), Hertz at ABC Building, Pasong Tamo Ext. (tel: 868 031).

This leaves taxis as the most convenient way to move through town. Luckily there are taxis in profusion in Manila, and though they are not immune from traffic jams, they are usually reasonably comfortable to be stuck in. Prices are around 30-40 pesos for a journey in town.

Getting into Manila from the airport is refreshingly untraumatic. The airport's proximity to the city centre is certainly an advantage. There are two airport buses that run to the five-star hotels for US$2. Alternatively, most hotels run their own limousines for roughly the same price. A taxi from the airport will cost around 40 pesos.

*City traffic moving freely for once*

**W**HEN you first handle a Patek Philippe, you become aware that this watch has the presence of an object of rare perfection.

We know the feeling well. We experience it every time a Patek Philippe leaves the hands of our craftsmen.

You can call it pride. For us it lasts a moment; for you, a lifetime.

We made this watch for you – to be part of your life – simply because this is the way we've always made watches.

And if we may draw a conclusion from five generations of experience, it will be this: choose once but choose well.

A Patek Philippe – because it's for a lifetime.

PATEK PHILIPPE
GENEVE

Patek Philippe S.A.
41, rue du Rhône – 1211 Geneva 3

KENYON & ECKHARDT, GENEVE

# Milan

Milan has long enjoyed a reputation as Italy's most ambitious and diligent business city. The reality, however, is not only a city where the work ethic and expediency are highly valued but one where la dolce vita can be explored in its broadest dimensions.

By Michael Scott

Among its many foreign conquerers, it was Napoleon who served Milan best. At the beginning of the 19th century he proclaimed Milano capital of the newly founded Republic of Italy. It is a position that every Milanese believes the city has occupied ever since.

Conquerors come and conquerors go – at a steady rate on average of one every two centuries for the last 30,000 years in Milan, whose curriculum vitae reads like a complete potted history of Europe. The pride of the Milanese remains constant, and if today they have to call Rome capital, and not for the first time, they do so secure in the knowledge that in many ways Milan is the real international centre of Italy.

Apex of the northern industrial triangle, fashion and design centre of Italy, commercial and financial hub of the prosperous north, Milan *is* different from other Italian cities, made so by the inventive and industrious approach of its citizens over the centuries.

At first glance, you might not see this. Milan has all the usual Italian trappings: imposing buildings, historical artefacts and art treasures (including the original of Leonardo de Vinci's *The Last Supper),* chaotic parking, lunatic taxi drivers, a gigantic cathedral, an active social hub in the main city square, and a long lunchtime siesta. But you'll have to look hard to find the poverty that is plainly visible in the southern cities, the black-market pedlar at the traffic lights, the high level of street crime. You will see people lounging the day away at pavement cafés, but they will mostly be tourists – the Milanese work hard.

To some this makes Milan a joyless city, but the term is only relative. In the same way, the people of Milan are dour in their speech and manner, with few of the extravagant gestures of their southern kinfolk. Compared with your average Swede, they are still pretty florid.

And to a visiting businessman it is a positive boon. The dreaded phrase 'an Italian promise' did not originate in the boardrooms of Milan. Here the local businessmen like to make appointments well in advance, to stick to them, and to mean what they say at them.

Any visitor seeking to find the heart of Milan without delay is favoured by the way the city's geography has evolved. It is centred on the cathedral square (Piazza del Duomo), with a more or less logical pattern of streets radiating out from the hub, and a series of three major ring roads (the Cerchia die Navigli, the Viale and the Circanvalazione Esterna). The first of these follows an ancient waterway, and defines the limits of the old city – an inner circle that contains most of the Milan the non-resident will ever require to be well acquainted with. Herein lie the opera, the most select shops, the best restaurants, and most of the nightlife. Elegant streets, many reserved for pedestrians, line the pavements with often breathtaking window displays, while apartment and office blocks turn their backs. The outermost *circonvalazione* is much newer, a major highway designed to keep heavy trucks and other through traffic out of the city.

Despite this apparent logic, time and pedestrian precincts have added enough twists and turns to make driving in the middle of Milan a task best left to the experienced. The plentiful taxis are painted a vivid, aggressive yellow, and most are driven in a manner that lives up to the colour. It is not unusual in the rush hour to have to placate your driver, who will loudly insist that the cars (quite legitimately) in his way are obviously not driven by Milanese. *"Are they tourists?"* I asked an elderly driver. *"No – they're foreign . . . from Pisa, Genoa, Turin."* The scorn in his voice was palpable.

Unless your business is directly concerned with fashion or finance, you are more likely to be travelling beyond the inner circle, into one of the vast industrial complexes that surround the city. Here big, well-signposted roads radiate from Milan; access is rapid and simple, and driving is no problem for anyone prepared to keep up with the flow. Be reminded that almost all Italians are keen sporting drivers, and that Milan is the only city in the world to have a permanent purpose-built grand prix circuit within the city limits. It is in the Parco di Monza, and you can even drive a few laps of the circuit yourself – in the wheeltracks of Ascari – for a small fee.

Social and cultural life revolves firmly around the centre of Milan, overseen by the Duomo, third-largest cathedral in the world. It is an imposing edifice indeed. Built over 500 years and fully completed in 1897, it reflects a variety of styles, and is distinguished less by the size of the rather overly ornate Gothic facade than by the 135 marble pillars and reputed 2,245 statues that thrust up to 350 feet in the air. You can join their lofty view point, either by climbing 258 steps or taking the L.2,000 elevator ride to the cathedral's roof-terraces. On a clear day the views extend to the Matterhorn and the

*Milan's cathedral is the third largest in the world*

Alps, 75 miles away to the northwest, and across the plains of Lombardy to the Po river in the south. But Milan is the centre of an industrial society, and one's view is more usually confined by haze to the sprawl of the city itself.

Despite the ecclesiastical power of this immense building, mammon is never far away. The Piazza del Duomo is the dead centre of Milanese street life. Here, booksellers purvey international magazines, antiquarian books and hard-core pornography, all sharing the same shelves cheek by jowl (if that is the expression), apparently unaware of any incongruity.

Jewellery and clothing shops ring the square, the smartest of them in the magnificently glass-vaulted Galleria Vittorio Emanuele, where are also the city's most expensive pavement cafés, tables glassed off from the throng.

Milan's proudest possession is not, however, the cathedral, but La Scala opera house, in front of its own piazza just off the corner of the cathedral square. The opening of the season in December provides the big night of the year for Milanese socialites, and if you prefer all-in wrestling to opera, do be careful who you tell.

High fashion looms large in the Milanese legend. The majority of the most exclusive and expensive boutiques are hard by the Scala around the Via Monte Napoleone, where the elegance of the fur-coated window-shoppers is scarcely more mundane than the supreme chic of the displays. Prices are astronomical, putting even Paris fashions in the shade. Yet the Milanese couturiers do offer something more. As LA fashion buyer Frank Dover put it: *"These are clothes that a woman can go on wearing as long as she can still fit into them. Paris provides street fashions, that you can wear only for a season or two. Milanese clothes are classical, and they don't date as fast as other high fashion."* The big fashion shows are in March, for clothing and for the shoes and leather goods for which the city is justly famous.

Art lovers will find a feast, with some galleries standing out from the general high standard: the Poldi-Pezzoli Museum for early Renaissance paintings, and a Botticelli Madonna, the Brera Palace and Sforza Castle the Venetian and Lombard schools, and the Modern Art Gallery, with its significant collection of 19th and 20th century works.

Philistines of the technical age need not fear the approbrium of their hosts, though. Milan is proudest of its adopted son, Leonardo da Vinci, and has devoted an entire wing of its fine Museum of Technology to scale models of some of his remarkable futuristic inventions. The display includes Leonardo's helicopter, operated on a sort of aerial Archimedes screw principal (far-sighted or far-fetched?), a perpetual motion machine that nearly works, along with various ingenious military, excavating and water-control machines that cannot fail to impress.

Further evidence of the genius of Leonardo is a short step away, at the convent of the church of Santa Maria delle Grazie, where his best-known work – *The Last Supper* – has survived almost 500 years and a direct hit by a wartime bomb. Today

*Elegant arcades are the place for a pleasant stroll*

the mural is a murky remnant, in spite of several attempts at restoration, and is half hidden by the scaffolding of the latest attempt. Its power is sadly dimmed by the fact that one can barely see it.

What of street crime, the bugbear of Italian cities? The Milanese point to women walking freely round the city squares at night, wearing fur coats. Five years ago, they say, nobody would have dared to go out looking so well-off, for fear of being robbed. Now – well, see for yourself.

Milan's conquerors stretch from the Etruscans to the Hapsburgs: but the city has emerged intact. A clue to how they did it may be drawn from the role they played with Italy's last dictator. Although they helped Mussolini into power in the early years of Fascism, the Milanese were among the first and most effective to turn against him when German troops occupied Italy. While the battlefront was still in the south, escaping Allied prisoners could find sanctuary and assistance from the Milanese underground, and the city liberated itself before the arrival of the Allied troops.

The Milanese are proud of this record. To others it might indicate expediency above loyalty, reflecting a happy knack of getting in good with the winning side well in advance of events.

Be that as it may, it is an approach to life that has served Milan well over the centuries, summed up well if unwittingly by a hotel executive's statement, sweeping but true. *"Milan. . .Milan is not the south of Italy."*

Indeed, it is not. And if it is not the centre of Italy either, well, that's only the official view.

# WHERE TO STAY

Milan is undoubtedly a business city *par excellence;* straightforward, plain and hardheaded, it is in many ways a un-Italian city. Its old centre is small and compact, much altered and rebuilt since its days as a dukedom when da Vinci himself walked the streets. Not much that he would recognise now though, for Milan is filled with modern buildings, grandiose 19th century developments, and not a few ugly reminders of the 1940s. Some of these are hotels and if you fancy old-style living then there are a few to choose from. But there are also a large number of uncompromisingly modern hotels, and a few inexpensive places too.

Although in most cases Milan offers as good a mixture of everything as you are likely to need (shops, restaurants, bars), there are basically only three areas for hotels: motels and some modern chain hotels are located outside the city; several more are to be found in the roughly circular old town; and the majority are within a short walk of the main rail station.

Flying into Linate airport on Alitalia's blue riband service is easy and swift. You can then take a taxi or a bus to the central city – about 20 minutes on a good day. The SEAV airport bus costs L.1,700 and takes you either to the central station or on to the one-time Alitalia centre at Garibaldi Station where you will find the large, new **Hotel Executive** (Viale Sturzo 45; tel: 026 294; telex: 310191 Hotexe). This modern boxy structure is an efficient operation with a shopping arcade, spacious lobby and a stairway leading to its own convention centre, and restaurant. There's a garage for 500 cars, and next door is the Francesco Conti Club with two pools and a gym. Prices L.165,000 single and L210,000 double.

Definitely grand old-style is the **Excelsior Hotel Gallia** (Piazza Duca d'Aosta 9; tel: 62 77; telex: 311160), beside the station. It has 248 rooms and 15 suites and is part of the Meridien empire. The area around the central station is not as seedy as most similar Italian city areas and the Excelsior definitely raises the tone, although its piped music doesn't exactly add class. Very spacious, very much the grand deluxe five star place and its restaurant echoes the overall sumptuousness.

But if you want to impress, you should consider one of the two CIGA properties – The **Principe e Savoia** (Piazza della Republica 17; tel: 62 30; telex 310052). or the **Palace** (Piazza della Rebpubblica 20; tel: 63 36; telex: 311026). I recall staying at the former some years ago and friends actually came in to gape at the large rooms. And there are now two satellite hotels well worth considering. The **Hotel Diana Majestic** (Vale Piave 42; tel: 34 04; telex: 203404) with 102 rooms and five apartments is charming and overlooks a garden – important if you hate traffic noise for much of Milan *is* noisy. There are five conference rooms, and you can entertain at a garden bar during the warm months.

The slightly unfortunately named Annex has been re-designed and is now the **Duca di Milano** (tel: 62 84) which houses 50 small apartments and guests may use the facilities of the main hotel next door plus those at the Principe e Savoia. Rates at the Principe L.210,000 single and L.320,000 double, plus taxes.

A small yet very well designed hotel in the centre of Milan is one I consider a real 'find'. It's the modern **Hotel Florida** (Via Lepetit 33; tel: 271 6910; telex 314102) and is a good place for someone on a budget. Rooms are plain, certainly not large, so are public areas. But it's a friendly place for someone who just wants to perch for a while.

Another good small property is the **Hotel Ambasciatori** (Galleria del Corso 3; tel: 790 241; telex: 315489) close to the handsome covered arcades around the spun sugar spires of the cathedral. Again basic accommodation at a reasonable rate – expect to pay L.78,000 for a single, L.117,000 for a double with breakfast.

A little out of the centre, but with the regular shuttle bus connections to the station, is the **Hotel Leonardo da Vinci** (Via Senigallia 6; tel: 026 407; telex: 201211). The main attraction for business visitors is the large conference complex – over 40 rooms holding from 15 to 1,000 people; there are also eight tennis courts and a covered heated pool. Rates from L.132,000 single and L.184,000 double including breakfast.

Although it preserves a somewhat kitsch foyer and public rooms, the **Hotel President** (Largo Augusto; tel: 027 746; telex: 20111) is totally modernised above the ground floor. Rather a formal style prevails in this central hostelry with its restaurant views of the cathedral's spires. Garage, walking distance from many major attractions, rooms are soundproofed. Rates are from L.170,000 single, L.210,000 double.

Finally, another bargain – the compact 45 room **Hotel Flora** (Via Napo Torriani 23; tel: 659 9561; telex:312547 Flora 1). It's typical of Milan's small modern hotels, straightforward and without frills yet it offers a central place to lay a busy head. Rooms are small but well equipped and air-conditioned. Rates are from L.62,000 single with shower, L.91,000 double, breakfast extra.

# WHERE TO EAT

The thing the Milanese are justly proud of in their rather grey and constantly moving city, are the restaurants. There are so many, and often of such high quality, that any listing is inevitably going to be incomplete.

A general rule of thumb seems to be: stick to the many Italian special dishes on offer and you are unlikely to go far wrong. Even the snack bar at the rail station serves excellent pasta. Hotel restaurants are kept very much on their mettle too – Hilton's **Da Guiseppe** (Via Galvani 12; tel: 680 598) boasts a restaurant that has gained awards.

If it's atmosphere you are after then the **Ali Matarel** (Via Laura Solera Mantegazza 2; tel: 654 204), in a corner of the old city, is perfect: a crowded, charming place, with neat, pink-clothed tables. Here you can tuck into such mouthwatering examples of *cucina Milanese antica* as *tortelli*, or that corn pudding so popular in the north – *polenta 'alla fine del mondo'* – or snails. Closed Tuesdays, no cards, menu at fixed price of L.30,000.

In the elegant 19th century gallery linking the Duomo to the Scala theatre is **Savini** (Galleria Vittorio Emanuele; tel: 805 8343), a holdover of high-class cooking, well recommended by the *Michelin Guide* and classed as one of the top 20 restaurants. Here you will dine on wonderful Milanese specialities – and French and the so-called 'international' dishes if you like. But stick to the home base and order the *ossobucco, or the costoletta,* or for that matter, the staple of the city, *risotto Milanese.* All very grand, in a setting that is genuinely Milanese. From L.50,000 – service extra – closed Sundays, takes all cards.

**Down Town** (tel: 800 148) is a neighbour of the Savini, but not so grand, nor so expensive, with a menu starting around L.32,000. There's a plentiful cold buffet table as well as dishes of local origin. This sensible restaurant takes most credit cards and is open on Sunday when many establishments are closed. One of the nicest things about eating in the Galleria area (a style that American cities have tried – unsuccessfully – to ape in similar modern developments) is that the parade of Milan swirls about you and after dinner there's nothing nicer than taking an expresso and watching the daily *passeggiata.*

A small and decidedly atmospheric place – straw covered bottles, artefacts and country flummery filling every corner – is **La Porta Rossa** (Via Vittorio Pisani near the via Locatelli; tel: 670 5932). But don't be put off by the décor – sit down and fill up on solid Puglian specialities . This is the place to try southern food, helped down with wines from the same part of Italy.

Nearby, in a small spot in the wall, the **Trento** is a restaurant specialising in mountain cooking – *Cucina Trentina* says the sign that means rabbit

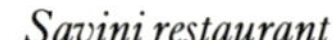

*Savini restaurant*

with *polenta* and thick goulashes. For a taste of Naples though, try **Anna and Leo** (Via Tadino; tel: 279 870), where the fish is fresh as it can be and the shellfish all alive. No cards, closed Sundays.

The renowned rooftop restaurant at the **Palace Hotel** is supplemented by a no-less smart **Casanova Grill** on the ground floor. International selections with daily choices from the chef in a sophisticated setting. All credit cards, and reservations are suggested – open every day. The service is very good – but then you expect to find smooth attendance in such a city.

A last note – if you only want a snack then try local cafés. Head along the Via Brera – where there are all sorts of eating places and pedestrian streets – and you will come across **Geni's** where there's a clearly priced lunchtime *tavola calda* as well as coffee, wine and beer. I also popped into **Crota Piemunteisa** (Piazza Beccaria 10) for a ham sandwich and more of the wonderful coffee that Milan makes so well.

# NIGHT LIFE

The Milanese make the most of their time off and popular pursuits range from cheering the local team at the stadium (football is a fever in Italy), to driving to the nearby Alps for a spot of skiing, to relaxing by the glorious lakes just north of the city. A useful publication is *Milano Weekend* which covers weekly events and is on sale at most bookstands. The fact that it is printed in Italian is no real drawback as the listings are easy to follow. It also lists cinemas showing films in English – notably **Cinema Anteo** (Via Milatto; tel: 659 7732); **Cinema Paris** (tel: 655 5534) and **Cinema Centrala** (tel: 874 826). *Il Giornale* also lists a score of small houses under the heading: Sexy Cine. Beside the regular cinema listings of first and second releases there are art houses showing unusual films. Seat prices range from L.2,500 to L.6,000.

There is of course a vast range of television programmes but the numerous stations do broadcast almost exclusively in Italian. Plays, too, are a problem if you aren't fluent in the language although a recent trip to Milan revealed a number of imports from the UK and the US. *Richard III* was at the **Manzoni** (Via Manzoni; tel: 799 171), *Saint Joan* at the **Teatro Nazionale** (Via Rovellg; tel: 872 352), *The Real Thing* at the **Piccolo** (Piatta Filodrammatici, tel: 803 659), and, if you haven't already seen the latest Broadway hit you could catch it at the **Teatro Nuovo** (Piazza San Babila, tel: 700 086).

Of the theatres the best known is 'of course' **La Scala** (Piazza della Scala; tel: 807 041), home of opera and ballet and a must for anyone who wants to see not only a great theatre but the beauties of Milan on parade. You can obtain tickets from the theatre when available (big name events tend to sell out ahead of time, but there are still many things that don't). Prices are not always sky-high – a recent visit gained a seat for less than L.16,000 in a top section. La Scala's opera season runs from December to July. There are also many concerts at such centres as the **Angelicum** (tel: 632 748) and the **Conservatorio** (tel: 701 705).

But just strolling in Milan, particularly the old city, can be a very pleasant experience – remember, though, that Milan is hardly a warm spot in winter. The Milanese love to loaf along the galleries in smart clothes, and there is a definite sense of a café society. There are numerous small art galleries showing a wealth of works – listed in the guide magazines – and they are usually free.

There are a number of pleasant bars, some offering piano entertainment, and hotels too will often have their own entertainment so you don't even have to stir if you don't want to. There are also a number of night clubs, some offering shows such as the **Astoria** (Piazza Santa Maria Beltrade; tel: 872 166), **Maxim** (Galleria Mantoni; tel: 700 528), and the **Venus** nightclub with striptease. Almost all will take the range of credit cards. A literal flood of discotheques is on offer and you may be hard put to know which to choose. Very popular and much more friendly are the jazz bars known as locales. Some offer food, others just drinks.

The great attraction for those with a bit of time to spare is still the surroundings of Milan – in a short hour's drive you can be in ancient cities or in the mountains and there are many good places to stay and eat, often at surprisingly low prices. There are good rail connections too – try Stresa on Maggiore, or the town of Como, for a break. Rail prices are reasonable (as are the public transport trains and buses – a flat L.500).

# GETTING AROUND

Milan may be a small city, but it is a monolithic nightmare when trying to get from one end to the other. Streets are circuitous one-way labyrinths, littered with manic drivers and maniac pedestrians. Taxis may be plentiful, but their drivers are experts in the art of taking the foreign passenger for a long, expensive ride. While the cost of such ventures may not worry the expense-account happy businessman, the danger of being late for appointments is reason to be wary.

That said, Milan does have a fine and comprehensive public transportation system, the ATM (bus and tram) and the Metropolitana Milanese (MM) subway. Tickets for the ATM must be bought in advance from bar *tabacchi* and newsstands which display an ATM sign. It is often more convenient to buy a day ticket from a main underground station or the Tourist Office, as this allows unlimited travel on ATM and MM. The metro is easy to use, as it has two lines only: M1 and M2, both running from 6.20 a.m. to midnight. Since parts of the centre of Milan have been closed to traffic, public transportation is often the quickest way to get around. However, should you decide to take a taxi, they are yellow, have meters and can be hailed on the street. Otherwise, you can ring for a cab at the following numbers: 6767, 8585 or 8388.

Should you choose to hire a car, all the usual firms are represented: Avis (tel: 6981), Budget (tel: 670 3151), Europcar (tel: 607 1053) and Hertz (tel: 20 483); but prices tend to be high. A Milanese tour book is emphatic about the dangers of leaving anything in the car, unless it is in a guarded car park. Also, watch out for *divieto di sosta* – no parking – and *rimozione forzata* – tow away – signs.

Getting into Milan from the airports is relatively easy. The Linate Airport serves domestic and European flights, and is only seven km from the centre. There is an airport bus which leaves every half hour, and taxis are numerous. Malpensa Airport is used for most international flights, and is 50km from the city. Again, there are plenty of taxis as well as an airport bus, which runs to the Stazione Centrale, stopping at the Porta Garibaldi Station on the way.

*Buy your ticket before you board the bus*

# New York

Some say it is the greatest city on earth, others that it is the most vivid and lurid display of modern man's moral decline. But nobody can accuse New York of being boring. Visiting businessmen are advised to leave their preconceptions behind.
By Michael Leapman

New York does not yield its secrets easily. First-time visitors can get badly disoriented, partly because so much seems superficially familiar from television and the movies. You ought to feel at home but you don't. As a rule of thumb, I submit that the average business visitor, staying perhaps a week, will not begin to experience any kind of rapport with the city until his or her third visit at the earliest.

Yet once that intimacy is achieved, no place is easier to tune back into. New York wears its heart on its sleeve (or more literally on its souvenir *"I Love New York"* T-shirts). To fall into its mood at an instant, the visitor has only to buy on arrival a handful of key publications – the *New York Times, New York* magazine and maybe the evening *New York Post.* It will seem as though you have never been away.

Doing just that on my most recent visit I discovered that a sleeping passenger on a subway train had been set on fire by a neighbour; that a jilted lover was holding his ex-fiancée hostage in an office skyscraper on Fifth Avenue; that the New York Yankees baseball team were performing dismally and drastic remedies propounded; that there were still disputes about plans for Westway, a major highway along Manhattan's western edge; and that joggers in Central Park were now carrying weights, called Heavy Hands, to strengthen their arm muscles as they ran.

All familiar and welcoming yet of course the city does not in truth stay static. Changes – some transparent and others more subtle – are in train all the time.

The trouble is that there is seldom consensus among New Yorkers about what the changes are, what they signify or what stage they have reached. Take, for example, the case of Columbus Avenue, the northern stretch of Ninth Avenue, a block west of Central Park. When I first went to live in New York in 1970, my apartment was just off the Avenue, then a decidedly downbeat thoroughfare lined with dim Irish bars, junk shops, cheap snack booths, small shops selling shoes, vegetables and hardware.

Today there are singles bars, boutiques and *nouvelle cuisine* restaurants with neon-lit windows, Star Wars decor and plenty of elegant bustle. Its place in the city's social geography was crisply explained to me by a native: *"Nowadays it's only tourists that go to Greenwich Village. New Yorkers go to Columbus Avenue."*

But do they? An alternative view, put to me by an equally qualified observer, is that Columbus Avenue has come and gone, now patronised chiefly by the *"bridge and tunnel crowd"* who drive in from the New Jersey suburbs and in whose company no trend-respecting Manhattan-dweller would care to be seen. Things move so fast on the New York cultural circuit you have to keep your eyes peeled to distinguish the *nouveau chic* from the old hat.

My second friend's theory is that the fashionable action has moved to the Lower East Side and East Village, around St. Mark's Place and the Public Theater, where Manhattan bulges and the avenues are known by letters (A, B, C, D) as well as numbers. But for all I know by the time you read this the scene may have passed from there also.

One thing people still do go to Columbus Avenue for is ice cream. America has a long-running love affair with the stuff, investing it with sensuous qualities that quite escape us from lesser nations. When one entrepreneur comes up with what is widely accepted as the ultimate in cool, creamy delight, it merely presents a challenge to the next one to concoct something still more wonderful.

The hottest ice cream emporium just now is Steve's on Columbus Avenue. His gimmick is to mix the substance with M&Ms (Smarties) or chopped candy bars of the customer's choice, for around $2.50 a time. Not being a New Yorker I found the price and the sickly concoction a bit over the top, but as an intrepid reporter it's my duty to tell you about it.

I think my first friend was being a bit unfair to Greenwich Village when he wrote it off as a place for the cognoscenti to be seen. I was taken down there one evening and given a choice between dining at Forlini's, a large and gaudy Italian restaurant in Baxter Street, serving large and gaudy portions, and the Pink Tea Cup on Bleeker Street, specialising in soul food from the southern states. I picked the latter and tasted some splendid smothered chicken – fried chicken with a spicy gravy – with candied yams and black-eyed peas. It is a small, unglamorous restaurant with no drinks licence, but you can take in your own wine and beer.

Such café-style proletarian places with minimal decor are coming into vogue. One of the busiest – hard to get into without a reservation – is Guido's Supreme Macaroni Co. on Ninth Avenue near the bus terminal. The restaurant is at the back of the pasta store, which you have to walk through to get to it. Further west is the Empire Diner on

*Wall Street Stock Exchange*

10th Avenue and 23rd Street, with simple meat-and-potatoes food to match the art deco.

Sloppy Louie's on South Street, in the new seaport museum area, was closed for refurbishment on my previous visit but is now open again, as studiedly unglamorous as ever, still serving splendid fresh sea food, as is its marginally up-market neighbour Sweet's. Both restaurants close early in the evening and for part of the weekend, so ring before you go down there.

For those having business in the Wall Street area I recommend a visit to the seaport museum. After years of waiting, it has become a well-planned conservation area with its 19th century warehouses restored to reproduce a small part of what was New York's main maritime area until the big liners began to berth on the West Side, in the Hudson River. A first class film and slide show, lasting an hour, gives an interesting account of the seaport's history with some unusual audio-visual gimmicks – a kind of indoor *son-et-lumière.* If you need to justify time spent on a visit to South Street, an extra consideration is that it embraces a lively shopping area specialising in food and gifts of the kind a business visitor might want to take home for the family.

What other changes? I was sad to see that Rogers Peet, my favourite source of low-price clothing, has finally closed after numerous liquidation sales, leaving empty its premises opposite the Public Library on Fifth Avenue. This means that the best remaining source of cut-price suits are the upper-floor workrooms on Fifth Avenue between 14th and 23rd Streets, although Alexander's, next to Bloomingdale's on Lexington Avenue and 59th Street, still offers good value.

From cheap clobber to pricey culture, the Museum of Modern Art has expanded its galleries allowing an extensive display of the fabulous collection of works by Picasso, Matisse, Modigliani, Jackson Pollock and so on. I especially enjoyed the extended photographic gallery, with space to do justice to some marvellous images of 20th century America.

Potentially the most radical change in mid-Manhattan is a new Marriott hotel on Broadway just north of Times Square, a district dominated for most of this century by the Broadway theatres and, most conspicuously, the sleaze of the sex industry. The city's planners hope that the hotel will drive away the porn shops, peep shows, strip theatres and explicit cinemas.

So it might, although there is no sign of it so far and I'm not at all sure it would be a good thing in any case. Like Soho in London, New York's Times Square area is a self-contained, defined vice area, easy to avoid if such excesses give offence. If the sex businesses are forced out they will for sure go somewhere else to satisfy the clear demand, spreading the pollution further. More than any other city in the world, New York will always respond to market forces.

That, of course, is what makes it such a splendid city to do business in. It is a place where to return phone calls is the rule rather than the exception, where there is no two-hour void in the middle of the day as executives linger over liquid lunches, where businessmen arrive at the office early and leave it late. New Yorkers are as intense about doing business as they are about their social life and their conspicuous consumption: it is a less often remarked upon aspect of the city's energy but, when all is said and done, represents the most powerful reason for the business traveller to love New York.

# WHERE TO STAY

The most controversial of New York's ever-rising hotels is the **Marriott Marquis** (tel: 398 1900; telex: 82907), a towering structure designed to play a key role in the revitalisation of Times Square.

The controversy exists because while economists have delighted in the idea of such a glittering money-spinner in a soiled area, the purists have objected because the Marquis' construction meant the destruction of part of the theatre district. Money won and the iron ball swung. The site houses 1,878 rooms, four restaurants, (including a 900-seat revolving rooftop) and a new theatre. Single $200; double from $225; suites $400-$3,500.

Another new hotel is the **Novotel** (tel: 315 0100) on the West Side of Broadway between 51st and 52nd. Preliminary rates for its 470 rooms are $90-$125 single, $110-$145 double and $195-$500 for a suite. Like all midtown hotels, the Novotel is well off for access to the theatre, business and Fifth Avenue. Even better off though is the **St. Regis Sheraton** (Fifth Ave. & 55th St; tel: 753 4500; telex: 148368) which remains a relative unknown on the NYC hotel map even though it has been sitting elegantly just off Fifth Avenue since 1904.

It has recently undergone a $25 million facelift which covered everything, including its 525 rooms, 84 of which are suites. These run around $125-$185 single, $145-$205 double and $225-$700 for suites. Its King Cole restaurant is guaranteed to make merry old souls of anyone – entrees from $18 to $28.

There's little to pick and choose between the hotels along Central Park South. It's a good neighbourhood – providing you don't stumble through the park after dark – and names such as **The Plaza** (Fifth Ave. and 59th St; tel: 759 3000; telex: 236 958), the **St. Moritz** (50 Central Park South; tel: 755 5800 ; telex: 668840) and the **Essex House** (150 Central Park South; tel: 247 0300) make for fine company. But the **Ritz-Carlton** (112 Central Park South; tel: 757 1900; telex: 971534) had the right idea when it switched from being the Navarro. A good view over the park can make a hotel room in this strip and the Ritz-Carlton installed picture windows to get the message across. It's also owned by the same John Coleman who gave Washington D.C. the Ritz-Carlton (formerly the Fairfax), and Chicago, the Tremont and Whitehall, and who is also giving Manhattan the Jockey Club bar and restaurant. Room rates run $165-$210 single, $185-$235 double and $400-$850 for suites.

There's a small band of New York hotels that might be termed 'the unknown élite,' mainly because they've never had a song named after them (Pennsylvania 65000 was the Statler's phone number) or had a movie filmed there (the Plaza has been a virtual soundstage over the years). These plush establishments include the **Mayfair Regent** (tel: 288 0800; telex: 236257) on Park Avenue at 65th St. (rates $145-$730); the **Regency** (tel: 759 4100; telex: 147180) on Park Avenue at 61st St. ($145-$750), the **American Stanhope** (tel: 288 5800; telex: 224244) on Fifth Avenue at 81st St. ($145-$600) and the **Westbury** (tel: 535 2000; telex: 125388) on Madison Avenue at 69th St. ($135-$700). In all these hotels, the room rates are higher than average – although you'll be lucky to find a decent room in New York for less than three figures – but the premium is generally reckoned to

*The Plaza hotel*

be well worth the degree of comfort served.

There are also smaller hotels with around 200 rooms which are located a walkable distance from the busy midtown areas.

If I had to recommend a bargain, that would be tough. For starters, I'd stay well clear of the fantastic rates offered by the **Milford Plaza** (tel: 869 3600; telex: 177610) (single $66-$81, double $80-$99). It is not a bad hotel inside, and with so many Broadway cast parties held there you might catch a glimpse of Anthony Quinn or some other pseudo-European. The reason the Milford Plaza bathes its exterior in white spotlights is that, on Eighth Avenue at 45th St., it's in the heart of kill city. That's the bottom line.

The **Omni Park Central** (tel: 247 8000; telex: 424434) has had its teething troubles since taking over the old New York Sheraton. But its management, Dunfey, has invested very heavily in restoring what was a profitable but dowdy hotel. Dunfey also did a fine job restoring the Berkshire Place on East 52nd St. so the Omni ($95-$450), on Seventh Ave. at 56th St. might be worth watching.

I'll try and narrow this race to four: the **Parker Meridien** (tel: 245 5000; telex: 640205), the **Sheraton Russell** (tel: 685 7676; telex: 421308), the **Kitano** (tel: 685 0022; telex: 424429) and the **Empire** (tel: 265 7409; telex: 428190). The last has also undergone a renovation. It sits slap next to Lincoln Center in the fashionable Upper West Side and is a stone's throw from some of New York's liveliest nightlife. It's only 20 minutes walk from midtown, or a short cab ride, and has a multilingual staff. I can't vouch for comfort and service but the location is outstanding, as are the prices: single $65-$85; double $70-$90; suites $75-$140.

The Kitano is a gracious Japanese hotel with only 112 rooms. It is situated in the quiet Murray Hill area (on Park Avenue at 38th St.), has a highly-rated Japanese restaurant (Hakubai). Single $85-$90; double $105-$115; suites $270.

The Sheraton Russell might as well drop the Sheraton tag. Hardly anyone knows it exists, never mind the fact that it's a little sister to the Sheraton giants uptown. With Chippendale furnishings, a concierge, an English-style bar and fresh flowers all over, it can rightly claim to be European-style – and it is also in quiet Murray Hill, on Park Ave. at 37th St. The rates are up there, but so is the hotel: single $169-$190; double $179-$210; suites $230-$340.

The Meridien has a vast, high-mirrored hallway running from West 57th St. to the main entrance on West 56th. It also has a classic nouvelle cuisine restaurant and access to the Club La Raquette health club in its basement. The rooftop pool affords the views, rich Europeans afford the rates: single $135-$195; double $155-$215; suites $235-$450.

A mention should go to the **Vista International,** 3 World Trade Center (tel: 938 9100; telex: 223120) because it's the only real hotel in the Wall Street area, but I'm not so keen on an area that dies after dark and at weekends.

The cantilevered bulk of the 34-storey **Grand Hyatt** (tel: 883 1234; telex: 645601) is hard to miss, hanging out as it does over 42nd St. above Grand Central Station like a celestial conservatory. Until 1980 this was the Commodore, then Gruzen and Partners remodelled it using lavish amounts of light brown marble and making sweeping statements in its spatial atrium with cascading waterfalls etc.

Special people get special treatment in the Regency club on the 31st floor. To gain this particular ground it is necessary to use a personalised key in the lift – 1,407 rooms including 87 suites. Single $135-$165; double $155-$185; suites $300-$2,100.

Top politicians stay at the other Hyatt-linked property, the **United Nations Plaza** (tel: 355 3400; telex: 126803) at 44th and First Avenue across the road from the UN. Hyatt International Corp. manage this award-winning skyscraper (which is in fact two towers) but it is owned by the State of New York.

This is an imposing place and not a little confusing both inside and out, but in the nicest possible way – concealed lighting and green baize along the corridor walls lead one to wend, rather than walk, and to develop a certain affinity with snooker balls.

Guest rooms start on the 28th floor; the nether region is offices. The Plaza Tower, with its own lobby and security, is largely given over to long-term lets. Complimentary use of the health club, the 44-foot heated swimming pool and of a limousine service to Wall Street and the garment district. A special package at $99 per night, single or double, fills the place up at weekends. Single studio $100, double $145, Regency club singles $145, kings $205. Suites from $250 to $645. The latter price is for the Ralph J. Bunche Suite much favoured by Mrs Thatcher.

# WHERE TO EAT

Add together all the consulates, missions and other corners of 'foreign territory' within the boundaries of New York City and the total number of countries represented would top the 100 mark. Run up a list of 'non-American' restaurants, though, and the figure would be doubled.

There are Vietnamese restaurants tucked away in the backyard of Chinatown; Brazilian in the middle of midtown; Thai on the Upper West Side, Indian and Ukrainian on the Lower East. And the fashionable stretches of Madison Avenue and the East side in the 40s and 50s is the home of haute cuisine: **Lutece** (249 E. 50th St; tel: 752 2225), **Le Cirque** (58 E. 65th St; tel: 794 9292), the **Four Seasons** (99 E. 52nd St; tel: 754 9494) *et al.*

Two additions to New York's already packed restaurant scene are the **Sea Grill** (tel: 246 9201) and the **American Festival Café** (tel: 246 6699), although they're not really new at all. Huddled in the sunken area facing Rockefeller Center's Prometheus Fountain, these two eateries have replaced the **Promenade,** which, it is said, shut down to bust a labour contract. But that's for unions and management to fret about – in the meantime as far as the customer is concerned the two replacement restaurants are exquisite. The Sea Grill is slightly more expensive, asking $24 for its striped bass, $17 for wall eyed pike, and $18 for 'Local Duckling'. But the lobster consommé is reasonable at $4.50 and the mousse of salmon and scallops, served with a light sweet mustard is well worth the $7.75. Next door, the Festival served up traditional American fare: steamed mussels for $6, barbecued ribs for $7 and a creamy chilled corn and crab soup for $4.50. The burgers come in at $8.75, which is a little stiff compared to normal city prices ($3-$6) but these whoppers do weigh half a pound. The Festival also boasts a fine selection of beers, including New Amsterdam, the only beer brewed in New York – a glowing amber ale with a fine yeasty taste. Both these restaurants are open in-doors and out, May to September, indoors year-round.

If you prefer a musical interlude with your meals, then New York has plenty to offer. Catch Bobby Short on the piano at the **Café Carlyle** (tel: 744 1600) in the Carlyle Hotel on Madison Avenue at 76th St., Tuesday-Saturday. Entrees in the café – mainly steaks, chops and seafood – start at $16 but there's a $20 cover charge.

Across the park, next to Lincoln Center home of the Metropolitan Opera and the New York Philharmonic on West 65th St. is **Maestro** (tel: 787 5990). Maestro features a band of strolling opera singers but they'll perform anything from Tosca to Cole Porter on request. The menu's musical theme offers such 'Overtures' as smoked trout and horseradish for $5.50 and cold poached salmon for $5.25; such 'Centre Stages' as roasted herb chicken for $13.50 and veal scallopini with morel mushrooms for $13.95 and such 'Grand Finales' as peach melba – but of course – for $3.95 and white chocolate mousse for $4.95.

On a more frugal note, the **Clam Broth House** in Hoboken, N.J., (tel: 201 659 2448) a few minutes across the Hudson from Manhattan, offers cheap seafood and cold beer in a pub-like setting. The food is filling but average and the decor is spartan – but Frank Sinatra began his singing career here as a strolling waiter/minstrel, and the Clam Broth House is a good, let-your-hair-down place in which to relax. The broth, by the way, is free.

One only wishes Greenwich Village could still live up to its reputation. Sadly, its main thoroughfares are now festooned with pizza parlours and *souvlaki* huts, but just to the north a taste of Andalucia is to be found at **Spain** (tel: 929 9580) just off Sixth Avenue, on West 13th St. The cocktail lounge in the entrance looks very ordinary but a narrow corridor opens out into a splendid white stucco dining room. The paellas could feed a bull, and at least two humans, and cost $12-$15. The lobster in green sauce is similarly priced while such entrees as shrimp in a garlic sauce run at only $3-$4. Good prices and prompt service.

Some other recommended hunting grounds:

Chinatown: Forego the queues in the main drags and cross to East Broadway and **Little Shanghai** (tel: 925 4238). Like all the best Chinese restaurants, it's a case of lots of food, little money. Three people can gorge for $30.

Italian: **Le Cirque** (58 East 65th St; tel: 794 9292) is expensive but still serves some of the best food in town.

French: **Café des Artistes** (tel: 877 3500), on West 67th, next to Central Park. Low-key with entrees $14-$20. Excellent fish casserole.

Indian: I've yet to work out the difference between *pekora* and *du piazi* in a midtown Indian. On the Lower East Side, East Sixth St. between First and Second Avenues, is the Indian Strip, or Little India, a splurge of simple curry-houses. **Panna** and **Ganges** (tel: 228 3767) both merit further investigation but bring your own wine – and dress down.

Irish: **Moran's Chelsea Seafood** (tel: 989 9225) on 10th Ave. at 19th St. has been around for donkey's years. Expect to pay up to $20 for lunch and not much more for dinner.

Japanese: Best for a business lunch is **Nada** (tel: 838 2537) on 50th St. and Lexington Ave., or the restaurant in the **Hotel Kitano** on Park Ave. at 38th. In both cases, lunch comes at around $13-$15 a head.

Steaks: **Gallagher's** (tel: 245 5336) on 52nd St. and Broadway is *the* place. A traditional sports hang-out, the restaurant is happy to sell you some of its special sauce – but don't ask for the recipe, you won't get it.

Restaurants occupy 34 of the *Manhattan Yellow Pages,* so there's plenty to choose from. Time consumed choosing where to eat, though, is time which could be spent on consuming, so the best way to choose a restaurant in Manhattan is – fast.

*Chinatown*

# NIGHT LIFE

The combination of AIDS paranoia and Mayor Ed Koch's determination to clean up central Manhattan has thrown the sleazy side of the city's nightlife into some confusion. The notorious Plato's Retreat, which once featured such cultural highlights as Ladies Amateur Oil Wrestling and S & M Fantasy shows, was closed at the end of 1985.

The Koch campaign may well curtail some of the city's more exotic forms of nocturnal entertainment, but it will make little difference to the more conventional visitors' nights out on the town. For them the lavish Broadway shows (now terrifyingly expensive at between $45 and $60 a ticket), the innumerable late night jazz clubs and the 24-hour-a-day throb of Manhattan's entertainment industry are enough to provide even the most demanding out-of-towners with nights they will never forget. Whatever the world's other business capitals claim, New York has no peer when it comes to wild nights on the town – and the business traveller's main problem is to remain coherent at working breakfasts.

Not surprisingly, perhaps, there are more escort services in New York than there are yellow cabs. A recent issue of *Screw* – the bible of New York sleazies – listed over 300 ads for all sorts of services rendered – straight and gay – from professional ladies of the night to those boosting the housekeeping money.

Those in search of close encounters of the non-professional kind should try their luck at one of the city's many singles' bars. Though a bar's popularity may change with the season, the cluster of bars on the Upper East side, between Third and First Avenues, remain an established hunting ground. The famous **Thank God It's Friday** bar (or T.G.I. Friday's to those in the know) can be found on First Ave. and 63rd St. while the equally (in)famous **Maxwell's Plum** is on block further north; both bars have been favourites for over ten years.

A reliable source says the bars on 57th to 59th streets, between Second and Fifth Aves, are full of attractive and 'quite willing' women, and men. **The Trattoria del Pino** on East 59th and Third Avenue (tel: 688 3817) comes particularly recommended. Further west, the **Hard Rock Café** (221 West 57th) has perfected the art of the pick-up by allocating a space for name and telephone number on the inside of their matchbooks, which makes for easy passing in the crowded bar. As a quick rule of thumb, the amount of plastic visible is directly proportional to the amount of success in a singles' bar.

Lest it be said that New York does not cater to all tastes, the **Erotic Baker** (246 East 51st) has multi-flavoured goodies in shapes which leave nothing to the imagination. Rum-filled testicles cost ¢75 each, while a heart shaped cream cake topped by a breast (or anything else you may desire) costs $12.00. They also bake non-erotic cakes to order.

New York also offers a multitude of sensual pleasures of a more aural nature; music lovers have

*Bright lights on Broadway*

been known to call it the centre of the universe, with good reason. The quality and quantity of classical music in the city is simply staggering. Pavarotti graces the Met with regularity, as do the other Big Names. Juillard students give free performances in the Alice Tully Hall, and there is always the acoustic delight of Carnegie Hall. Half price tickets for music and dance bought at a TKTS booth in Bryant Park at 42nd St. and Ave. of the Americas (tel: 382 2323).

For the jazz fiend, New York is tantamount to Nirvana. On my last visit Tommy Flanagan, Miles Davis and Art Blakey and the Jazz Messengers were in town on the same night. Of the old clubs, the **Blue Note** (131 West 3rd Street; tel: 475 8592) is not what it used to be, with new decor of mirrors and slatted wood, but the **Village Vanguard** (160 Bleeker Street; tel: 255 4037) is as smoky and cramped as ever, and the greats can still be heard there. Check the *New Yorker, New York Times* or *New York* magazine for details of who's playing where.

## GETTING AROUND

New Yorkers take taxis more habitually than any other race on earth. This is probably due to the fact that traffic and parking are so obscenely difficult that many New Yorkers never bother learning how to drive. Public transportation, like most things in New York, is a monolithic parody of itself. The city is swallowed by a gargantuan network of subway and buses, which run, graffitied and efficiently, through both day and night. Yet congestion in the city is such that even this multitude of modes of transport seems hopelessly inadequate, when stranded on a corner on a freezing night.

Getting into New York from JFK or La Guardia airports poses few problems. There are taxis galore, and should you arrive expense-account in hand, they are the way to go. Ask the driver to take the most scenic route, for the first-time view of that much-vaunted skyline. Expect to pay around $15 from La Guardia; $27 from JFK.

Otherwise there is the JFK Express (dubbed The Train to the Plane) which leaves at 20-minute intervals from 6 a.m. to 11 p.m. and costs about $5. It takes about an hour to get to West Fourth Street in Greenwich Village, from where you can change to the A Train, or get out and catch a taxi. The train to the plane is a good way of aclimatising to New York quickly – since it is perfectly safe, and manned by ticket collectors carrying batons and guns.

Of course, the major hotels all have airport buses.

Once in New York, the most convenient way to travel is by taxi. Taxis are another good form of initiation into New York life. If you're lucky, the driver will speak English – so you may understand him as he curses at all and sundry. If not, you can try to guess the obscenities in Spanish, Polish and a multitude of other tongues. Taxi prices are not cheap, and they seem to rise more quickly than inflation.

Despite its reputation as a war-zone manned by gangs, rapists, murderers and other ogres, the New York subway is said to boast an average of only four deaths a year. Underground it is a grim, concrete jungle, smelling faintly of urine and rats, but this does not prevent commuters using it in their hundreds of thousands to circumvent the trafic above ground. The famed A train is the most civilised of lines on the run from West 72nd to West Fourth Street, though it gets a bit seedy further up town. My worst personal New York subway story is of a friend who accidentally took the D train to the South Bronx. On alighting onto the street, she was immediately relieved of her watch, jewellery and wallet. Her assailants then escorted her to the police station, explaining that she was in the wrong part of town (and that they had her name and address, should she see fit to file a report of theft).

Most of the underground route maps were vandalised years ago, so it is best to check which train to take, and where to change before venturing underground. The subway token costs ¢90, and is valid on buses and underground.

The city buses are a more clement means of transport, and since the city tends to run in straight lines, the routes are not difficult to decipher.

All the major car hire firms are represented in New York, but the frustration of manoeuvering in New York's perennial traffic jams is a high price to pay for the freedom of one's own car. All hotels have details of car rental.

# Paris

**The Paris of cinema and contemporary song may be a city of soft-focus romance but for the visiting business traveller it is a formal and often aloof capital.
Yet Paris is as sordid as it is chic, as vulgar as it is sophisticated and as nationalistic as they come.
By David Owen**

“*Cars, homosexuals and part-timers,*” says Alain Paucard, author of the obnoxious *Guide Paucard des Filles de Paris,* are the three things which have changed the face of Parisian prostitution. Cars because they permit the brief, tolerably discreet encounter favoured by the home-bound commuter; homosexuals simply because there are now more male prostitutes, transvestites and trans-sexuals than ever (of some 8,000 bodies for sale in the Paris area, around 4-500 are reckoned to be male and 7-800 transvestites/ indeterminate); and part-timers because, in the author's doubtless authoritative view, *"you can catch everything from them."*

The serried ranks (and I have seldom seen ranks so serried) of 300-francs-a-throw *chandelles* in the doorways of the rue St Denis and Pigalle are a far cry from the city of sauce and romance depicted by the tourist brochures. Both, nevertheless, have their basis in fact. Paris is as sordid as it is chic, as vulgar as it is sophisticated. Patrons of the much-vaunted TGV (high-speed train) service from Lyons emerge from the station's striking art nouveau facade into the scheduled-for-redevelopment Ilôt Chalon, still reputedly the city's worst heroin *(drépeau)* blackspot. The most stylish café in the classiest area may even today front a wc *à la Turque* you wouldn't wish on the neighbour's cat. And an evening stroll in the Tuileries is sure to be punctuated by glimpses of men relieving themselves against the nearest tree. Nor is the scabrous, disreputable side of the city a purely 20th century phenomenon, as evidenced by the poems of Villon and Baudelaire and the novels of Hugo. But whether positively or negatively, the atmosphere is constantly charged, making Paris, in my view as a card-carrying francophile, amongst the most exciting cities of all to live in and to visit.

Of course, to the hard-pressed businessman on a tight schedule, Paris may seem like just another city. To do it justice, one must be prepared to 'waste' time dawdling, browsing, *traînant dans les rues.* Anywhere will do. Among better-known haunts, the Beaubourg area around Centre Pompidou is a seemingly inexhaustible repository of exuberance and vitality, as epitomised by the brilliantly-conceived Stravinsky – Rites of Spring fountain. For sheer sustained elegance, I know of nowhere that can match the rue de Rivoli, while a stroll around Pigalle makes Soho look positively pedestrian. Perhaps the most restful corner of the city (in stark contrast to the unspeakably ugly Invalides nearby) is the garden of the increasingly popular Musée Rodin, where the work of the master sculptor vies for your attention with the chatter of clusters of English *au pairs.* And cemetery-lovers should on no account forego the chance to lose themselves (literally) in the vast and wonderful Cimetière du Père Lachaise, final resting place of innumerable national and international heroes from Chopin to Piaf, Oscar Wilde to Racine, Molière to Jim Morrison, as well as a sizeable colony of (predominantly grey) cats.

While it is not usually necessary to light the blue touchpaper and retire, the average French businessman should be handled with care. Business is conducted *"with a strict formality,"* according to Mike Garner of the Franco-British Chamber of Commerce and Industry, with the stilted, traditional style of correspondence (still very much *de rigueur* in Paris) anathema to today's breed of no-holds-barred go-getter. The best advice is be prepared to take things slowly. In a country where it takes six months to set up a company (although delays are reportedly diminishing) and where distribution networks can involve as many as ten middlemen, patience is essential. Without it exasperation will quickly set in.

It will also considerably smooth the path to a successful outcome if *monsieur* can proceed in his own language. Paris is arguably the only city in western Europe to attach more importance to its traditions than does London and amongst the most important of these in the face of rampant Americanisation and pervasive *Franglais* is the French language itself. While an *homme d'affaires* may outwardly deride one's stuttering rendition of *La plume de ma tante* (and if not the average shop assistant certainly will), the effort will be deemed a courtesy likely to stand one in good stead in future dealings.

If there is anything Parisians take more seriously than their language it is food. Not just purveyors of *haute cuisine* with which the city is incomparably well-endowed but everything down to the humblest staple of the Frenchman's diet: the *baguette,* Paris consumes about 60,000 *baguettes* a day – a huge total, but considerably fewer than the one million plus regularly devoured in the loaf's heyday during the 1950s. Sociological factors – Parisians have grown wealthier for one – are clearly partly to blame for the decline. But *baguette* connoisseurs are quick to point the finger at the spread of certain insidious practices such as the use of bean flour or acid to speed rising, employed by unscrupulous boulangeries to cut costs. Cheesemakers have succumbed to similar pressures. Of some 2,000 brands of Camembert commercially available, only 25 have been accorded an *appellation d'origine controlée,* an unmistakable mark of quality. Look for the words *fromage fermier* or the initials VCN on the label. Even so, the cheese business is holding its own: per capita consumption is around 17 kg a year of the 700 or so cheeses available.

Meanwhile, Paris is increasingly the focus of the intensifying political confrontation between François Mitterand's internationally acclaimed but domestically unpopular brand of socialism and the re-emerging forces of the right, spearheaded in the capital by mayor and presidential aspirant Jacques Chirac.

*Art Nouveau on the street*

In Paris, their rivalry is most apparent in the additions proposed by both to the city's architectural heritage. Mitterand has won most of the headlines if not the plaudits for his plan to employ Sino-US architect I M Pei to build a 60-foot glass pyramid in the Louvre courtyard. Meanwhile Chirac's brainchild, the Paris-Bercy Omnisport Palace has both provided much-needed sports facilities and proved a drain on the city's finances. Chirac is now turning his attentions to the run-down largely immigrant communities to the east and north of Paris – no doubt a shrewd move with elections in mind. One such is the Goutte d'Or ghetto in the 18th *arrondissement* where they say conditions are so bad that many prostitutes patrolling the area use old paraffin cans for lack of running water.

The existence of such *quartiers* coupled with worsening unemployment has incited a resurgence of racism in France, particularly evident in the big cities with their comparatively high concentration of immigrants. National Front leader Jean-Marie Le Pen is undoubtedly a charismatic figure and his party polled higher in Paris in the 1984 elections for the European parliament than the 10 per cent it recorded nationwide (a recent survey suggested as many as 27 per cent of the electorate agrees with his fundamental policy of repatriating France's four million immigrants). Even relatively prosperous immigrant areas such as the recently-established oriental community south of the Place d'Italie are the object of widespread resentment and suspicion. The story goes that this Parisian 'Chinatown' has a phenomenally low death rate because the *cartes d'identité* of deceased legal immigrants are swiftly purloined by those without entitlement to stay.

*Even the bread shop is a work of art*

Racism is not the only ugly aspect of present-day Paris. It is also an increasingly violent city. While a New Yorker would consider the Paris métro a haven of peace and tranquillity, the 1984 tally of 2,943 muggings will do little to reassure a bourgeoisie which traditionally lives in terror of venturing underground.

The city is in addition fast acquiring a reputation as a soft touch for international terrorist organisations. Within two days of arrival I had read reports on terrorism in Europe in *Le Monde*, Euro-terrorism in *Libération* (together with an interview with Eugenio Etxeveste of the Basque terrorist organisation ETA) and a profile of the police's 'Mr Anti-Terrorism', Robert Broussard, in *Le Figaro.*

But for all this and despite the gradual erosion of many former 'pillars' of the Gallic lifestyle (garlic and red wine are both losing ground and the makers of 'Gauloises', the archetypal, some would say unsmokeable, French cigarette, have felt constrained to launch the decidedly more genteel 'Gauloises Blondes' in a bid to resuscitate flagging sales), I can report that that indefinable but unmistakeable Parisian atmosphere remains intact. Though the all-American influence from hamburgers (McDonald's is back after the home office enforced name change to O'Kitch in 1981) to Hemingway (a bar in the Ritz, no less, still commemorates him) strengthens daily with the dollar, it is not every city which would countenance a 60-foot glass pyramid at the heart of its national gallery.

Clearly the decision to surrender Paris to the Nazis rather than risk wholesale devastation, controversial as it remains, was fundamental to the preservation of the city's unique charm. The grandiose continuity of Haussmann's mid-19th century design to modernise the then riot-torn capital, exemplified in the boulevard which bears his name (now the city's main shopping thoroughfare), remains for all to see. And, while the present artistic and cultural life of the city may not quite match the glory, glory days either side of 1910 when the likes of Apollinaire, Jarry and Picasso would frequent cafés like Le Lapin Agile in Montmartre, Paris is still Mecca for a sizeable cross-section of the artistic and thespian community. *"Everyone can come here and find himself,"* said Lawrence Durrell in an interview with *Passion* (the brashly informative English-language monthly which is a must for anyone contemplating a lengthy stay). *"It's a kind of gluepot which works for everybody."*

# WHERE TO STAY

I arrived in the Hotel Inter-Continental hot on the heels of two US businessmen, one evidently in Paris for the first time, the other an old hand. I presume that the newcomer had been passing inane remarks of the type *"Gosh, they have cars here!"* all the way from the airport, since when he came out with *"I never expected this,"* the old hand stopped dead in his tracks (prompting your correspondent to take rather hasty evasive action) and let out, *"Hell, it's not Ice Station Zebra here."*

The higher the dollar climbs the more US businessmen come to appreciate that Paris' luxury hotels have little in common with Ice Station Zebra, nor indeed Paris itself with the North Pole. In December 1983, US business accounted for 4.5 per cent of total commercial activity in France, according to US Chamber of Commerce estimates. The current proportion must be considerably higher, if the number of New York/Texan accents in hotel foyers is anything to go by.

In franc terms, the dollar is worth twice what it was four years ago. This perhaps explains the hefty price hikes which many luxury hotels have been able to post over the past few years. Americans are paying the same in dollars for their room in the Ritz as they were in 1980.

Chances are discount hunters, whatever the currency, will be out of luck in May/June and September/October when Paris is by all accounts completely full. At other times, much depends on the conference situation – Paris still hosts more 'salons' than any other city – with cut-price rooms once again difficult to come by when a big event is in town. Best bets out of season are the clutch of 900-room plus hotels like the Montparnasse Park and the Méridien Paris, which are likely to be under the most pressure to fill beds when businessmen are thin on the ground. Elsewhere, chains like the Holiday Inn are trying to standardise discount practice by offering cuts to clients guaranteeing a certain number of room-nights and agents. Meanwhile, the gaudy Nova-Park Elysées is more likely to offer upgraded accommodation and the archetypal Parisian hotel, the George-V, disregards them on principle.

In a city of over 30 luxury hotels, space does not permit a comprehensive guide. Still less in view of the plethora of two-four star establishments, the bulk of which provide perfectly adequate accommodation very cheaply. Expect to pay up to F300 for two stars, up to F400 for three stars and F650-800 for four stars. Local knowledge recommends the Hotel **Washington** (43 rue Washington; tel: 561 1076; telex: 260717), very cheap for a room in the chic eighth *arrondissement* and the **Hotel Taranne** (153 Bvd St. Germain; tel: 222 2165; telex: 250302) in lively St Germain des Prés where they serve breakfast all day long for the benefit of lie-abed night clubbers.

Nor are the luxury hotel rates extortionate, in view of the immaculate standard of service which most provide. Beware of mark-ups however – you can find yourself going through francs like water with injudicious use of bar or room service facilities.

Undoubtedly, the best-known of the old school of Paris hotels are the **George-V** (31 Arc George V; tel: 723 5400; telex: 650082) and the **Crillon** (tel: 265 2424; telex: 290204). Both are now the property of chains (THF and Taittinger respectively) and both are excellently situated for business and nightlife alike, with the George-V a stone's throw from the Champs Elysées, and the Crillon on Place de la Concorde. Whereas the George-V, despite possessing a number of charming suites, could frankly do with a facelift, the Crillon has benefited from extensive modernisation and refurbishment and can now offer quite the most sumptuous non-suite accommodation in the city. Prices for George-V: single F1,100; double: F1,470; suites F3,050-8,050 (service extra). Prices for the Crillon: double F2,000 (approx); suites F4,000-6,000.

**The Ritz** (tel: 260 3830; telex: 220262) and the **Meurice** (tel: 260 3860; telex: 230673) both enjoy similar reputations for tradition and luxury.

*The Ritz hotel*

The Ritz, on Place Vendôme, is noted for its inimitable style and immense bathtubs, while the Meurice, nearby on the rue de Rivoli, combines opulence with a unique air of history, the legacy of such regular patrons as Rudyard Kipling, Alphonse XIII of Spain and Liza Minelli. Prices for the Ritz: single F1,500; double F1,900; suites F6,000-30,000 (service 15% extra). Prices for the Meurice: single F1,472; double F1,883; suites F3,680-6,600 (service included).

Two hotels much-favoured at present amongst the jet-set are the **Bristol** (112 rue du Faubourg, St Honoré; tel: 266 9145; telex: 280961) and the **Nova-Park Elysées** (51 rue François-I; tel: 562 6364; telex: 643189). The Bristol combines old and new with class and originality (many bathrooms have their original Lalique windows), though, if you are not careful, you may glimpse Sacré-Coeur from the sixth-floor swimming pool. Prices: single F1,060-1,460; double F1,460-1,960; suites F4,500 (service included, tax 18.6% extra). Subtlety is not the Nova-Park's strong point. From the outrageous entrance to the foyer, fetchingly fitted in purple and mauve and crammed with display cases, the hard sell is much in evidence. However, it does boast an unrivalled range of facilities, with the Wall Street Corner business services section of particular interest. Prices: single F1,558-1,689; double F1,840; suites F2,309-23,880 (service included, tax 18.6% extra).

The **Concorde La Fayette** (tel: 758 1284; telex: 650892) is one of a clutch of similar hotels offering the efficiency and value-for-money typical of the best large-scale (900 rooms plus) establishments. Prices: single F1,100; double F1,250; suites F2,000-6,000 (all inclusive). Similar prices and accommodation can be obtained at the **Meridien Paris** (tel: 758 1230), the **P.L.M. Saint-Jacques** (tel: 589 8980) and the **Montparnasse Park** (tel: 320 1551).

Of hotels bearing the names of well-known chains in the city, the **Inter-Continental** (tel: 260 3780; telex: 220114) is in a class of its own for decor and comfort. Sited in rue de Castiglione, just opposite the Meurice, it is particularly noted for its seven courtyards and magnificent Napoleon III salons, a favourite venue for conferences and fashion shows by the likes of Yves St Laurent. Prices: single F1,269-1,432; double F1,432-1,830; suites F2,338-8,283 (all inclusive).

The **Holiday Inn,** (Place de la République; tel: 355 4434; telex: 210651) represents outstanding value to the travelling businessman (in part, no doubt, because it has yet to attain a four *étoiles de luxe* status). Elegantly housed in a building designed for the 1867 Universal Exposition, it nonetheless has a tendency, like other Holiday Inns in my experience, to swamp the visitor with sales literature and forms to fill in. Prices (including breakfast): single F740; double F970-1,070; suites F1,200-2,000. The **Hilton Paris** (18 av de Suffren; tel: 273 9200; telex: 200955) has undergone an extensive and much-needed renovation, with the new rooms a large improvement on the former impersonal, rather tatty accommodation. Service is however excellent – viz (in answer to a request for a typewriter), *"Certainly sir. English or French keyboard?"* Prices: single F935-1,122; double F1,116-1,323; suites from F2,484.

**The Sofitel Bourbon** (rue Sainte-Dominique; tel: 555 9180 or 01 725 1000 for UK reservations; telex: 250019) is one of a clutch of prestigious Sofitel hotels, aiming at low-key luxury in elegant surroundings. Set unobtrusively in a quiet street in the diplomatic heart of Paris, the hotel has become a favourite with people looking for first-class service away from the hustle of the bigger chain hotels and the lunacy of the Paris traffic, yet is within walking distance of both the Latin Quarter and the Eiffel Tower. As well as 112 discreetly comfortable bedrooms and four suites, the hotel also boasts a top-class restaurant, Le Dauphin, which has earned one Michelin star. Prices: single F940-990; double F1,080-1,150; suites F2,200 (breakfast F65 extra.)

Finally two personal favourites **Hotel Raphael** (17 av Kléber; tel: 502 1600; telex: 610356) is a charming and richly decorated establishment near Étoile, boasting a concierge who will proudly show you the Turner at the rear of the foyer if you say you are English. Prices (all inclusive): single F640-1,030; double F700-1,090; suites F1,210-1,880. **L'Hotel** (13 rue des Beaux-Arts; tel: 325 2722; telex: 270870) is a tiny hotel of unmatched charm and intimacy where Oscar Wilde died. As it boasts only 26 rooms, chances are you will need to book at least a month in advance. Prices: single from F500; double F1,200; suite F2,500.

# WHERE TO EAT

From the depths of Paris' well-heeled 16th *arrondissement* comes the secret of the new French cooking. *"In recent years many more chefs have dared to personalise their work,"* says Henri Faugeron, owner of the acclaimed **Faugeron Restaurant** (tel: 704 2453). Joel Robuchon, *cuisinier par excellence* at the equally celebrated **Jamin** (tel: 727 1227) just up the rue de Longchcamp, concurs: *"We always try to come up with something a bit different,"* though he adds that the base of his creations will always be found in traditional *haute cuisine.*

The pair of them represent the cream of the new wave of French chefs who have seen fit to take traditional cuisine by the scruff of its neck and inject it with a measure of flair and originality. The welcome result is that the business traveller cum *bon vivant* has a selection of absolutely top class restaurants to choose from on his visit to Paris.

Take Henri Faugeron's *le salmis de pintadeau aux raviolis de lentilles.* The basic guinea fowl with lentils is a standard French family dish. But, says Faugeron, *"everyone knows pasta is good with guinea fowl"* – a thought which led him to try combining the three elements in an appropriate and original way. He is equally ready to use new or unusual ingredients. The fish in his *le capitaine au citron et poivre vert* hails from the coast of West Africa and has only recently become available in local fishmongers. His menus are also noted for the occasional touch of humour: *les parfaits "époux" chocolat et menthe* is so-called because of mint's folkloric reputation in France as an aphrodisiac.

Expect to pay around F400 for a full (five-course) meal at Faugeron plus wine. However, the good news for lunchers is that he offers by common consent the best business menu in town at a very reasonable F165 plus wine and service. When it comes to reservations (as with all the much-in-demand restaurants here enumerated), one of two

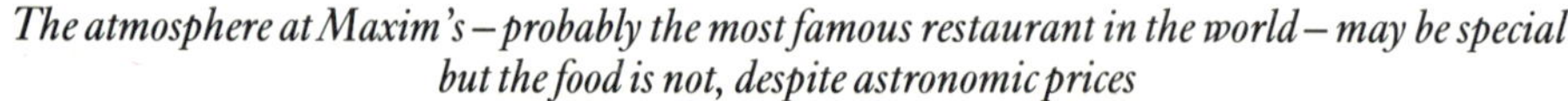

*The atmosphere at Maxim's – probably the most famous restaurant in the world – may be special but the food is not, despite astronomic prices*

tactics should be adopted. Either reserve three-four weeks in advance (waiting lists are generally particularly long for dinner) or ring up the day before you wish to go and hope for a cancellation.

Robuchon, a native of Poitiers, eschews regional dishes on the grounds that "a *bouillabaisse in Marseilles tastes entirely different from one in Paris*". Instead, his menu consists of largely self-styled dishes derived from a traditional base – such as *medley d'huîtres et de noix de St Jacques au Caviar* – coupled with a sprinkling from his *haute cuisine* repertoire. Whatever your preference, Robuchon aims to ensure that all elements of a dish are mutually indispensible; sauces are there to reinforce not to smother, he maintains – a philosophy which his *bohémienne de filets de rougets à la fleur de thym* amply justifies.

The decor of this unpretentious little restaurant is predominantly pink with chintz upholstery and mahogany trimmings – a fitting setting for what will probably be one of the best meals of your life. My *rôti d'agneau aux herbes, en croûte de sel* was succulence itself. Chances are you will pay over F500 plus wine for a full meal at Jamin but it will be worth every centime, meanwhile for lighter diners there are menus at F340 and F390 and a lunchtime business menu at F145. Service is quite impeccable.

A further half dozen or so Parisian restaurants can live in such company, amongst them, the **Taillevent** (tel: 561 1290), **Le Grand Véfour** (tel: 296 5627), the celebrated **La Tour d'Argent** (tel: 354 2331) and the **Archestrate** (tel: 551 4733).

Such is the renown of Claude Terrail's La Tour d'Argent that an exact replica was recently opened in the Otani Hotel, Tokyo. As a result, it is arguably overpriced (expect to pay up to F700, sometimes more) but a cut-price menu is available and a visit remains, by all accounts, an unforgettable experience. Particularly recommended – *canard au sang.* Still more superlatives are expended in gourmet circles on Jean-Claude Vrinat's immensely civilised Taillevent. You can still escape for under F600 a head including wine from a quite outstanding list (though not if you select Château Lafitte Rothschild 1937 at F4,900 a bottle) and the service is noted for giving the impression that your table is its exclusive concern.

Some might find the ornate decor of Le Grand Véfour, recently renovated with reinforced glass after a bomb blast, a trifle overpowering with their *tournedos Palais Royal.* However, for those who revel in authentic 19th century surroundings it is well worth a visit – even at F500-550 plus wine for a full meal. Meanwhile, the pricey Archestrate is still considered the pick of the capital's *cuisine nouvelle* restaurants. Those endowed with particularly adventurous palates might, for example, be tempted by *langoustines en papillote de poireaux.* I am told the *patron* worked in the same restaurant as Henri Faugeron and Joel Robuchon for a spell in the late 60s. Some restaurant that must have been!

Few would wish or could afford to patronise such establishments at every meal. Bearing in mind there are literally thousands of restaurants and cafés in Paris where one can eat both cheaply and well, here are a few names to conjure with when something rather less elaborate is called for. **La Coupole** (tel: 320 1420) in Montparnasse is a huge café, much-frequented by the artistic community around the turn of the century, where you can eat simple French food in the company of ordinary Parisians (particularly recommended lunchtime Sunday). By contrast **Pacific Palisades** (tel: 274 0117) is fast acquiring a reputation as a place to be seen. Its relaxed California-style atmosphere has been known to attract the likes of Duran Duran and Roman Polanski of an evening. Finally, for those on the most spartan of expense accounts, **Chartiers** on rue du Faubourg Montmartre is an experience not to be missed. The cavernous hall is crammed with tables and once inside (you will have to queue) you cannot but admire the speed and prodigious memories of the waiters. Food is basic but tasty and it is still possible to eat (and drink) one's fill for under F50.

Doyenne of the Paris jazz circuit and owner of the **New Morning** (tel: 523 5141) the capital's premier venue, Iglal Farhi, sees her club as functioning more like a theatre than a cabaret.

*"The music is the main attraction. When it finishes, people leave,"* she elaborated over the din of Jaco Pastorius's bass guitar.

*The Moulin Rouge in Pigalle*

Jazz has enjoyed a marked revival in Paris in recent years, re-establishing a following as devoted as that of the 50s and 60s which prompted a number of US musicians, amongst them clarinetist Sidney Bechet, to make it their home. New clubs such as New Morning itself, **La Chapelle-des-Lombards** (tel: 357 2424) and **Le Petit Opportun** (tel: 236 0136) (run by Bernard and former trapeze artist and stunt-woman, Mariane) have sprung up to replace the old standards like the **Blue Note** and **Le Chat Qui Pêche**. All regularly present musicians of the highest calibre, although New Morning (founded in 1981 after the success of a similar venture in Geneva and holding around 500) is the only one with capacity for the really big names. Recent attractions have included Pastorius, Art Blakey and Roy Buchanan.

For those who prefer a more energetic evening, Paris is tolerably well-imbued with nightclubs. Arguably the pick of these are the relative newcomer **La Piscine** – a disco complete with swimming pool in a huge loft adorned with mosaics (tel: 380 5099), **Le Garage** (tel: 225 5320) a haunt of Jean-Paul Belmondo and supposedly members-only, and **Les Bains Douches** (tel: 887 3440) a trendy dive in a former Turkish bath where the Rolling Stones have been known to perform impromptu concerts. Premier gay club at present is **Le Look** near Les Halles.

Those seeking more traditional entertainment might consider a night at the incomparable Paris opera or indeed the theatre, which *Passion* describes as *"the healthiest and proudest French art form today"*. Sam Shepard is just about taking over from Ariane Mnouchkine (purveyor of Shakespeare Oriental style) as the name on everyone's lips, although the range available from the highly traditional **Théatre de la Ville** to the stage where American playwright Richard Ledes presents plays in his apartment on the rue St Martin, should cater for all tastes. **Théatre de Temps** (tel: 355 1088) and **Théatre de la Bastille** (tel: 357 4214) are usually well worth checking out. (A full listing of programmes for theatre, cinema etc. can be found in the weekly *Pariscope,* on sale in kiosks throughout the city.)

The range of cinema available in Paris at any one time is simply outstanding. New American films often reach Paris before London and scores of old classics from *Les Enfants du Paradis* to *Lolita* are seemingly permanently on view – though you may have to travel to some fairly obscure areas to find them. A favourite cinema is **La Pagode** (tel: 705 1215), the brainchild of director Louis Malle. While it won't actually transform an indifferent film into a masterpiece, this cinema, brought to Paris piecemeal by an Orientophile in 1896, will do nothing to detract from your enjoyment.

Others might prefer the type of variety entertainment provided by the likes of the **Folies Bergères** or the **Moulin Rouge,** while TV addicts may be interested to learn that there's a home-produced soap opera, *Rue Carnot,* on the air – albeit on France's subscriber channel Canal Plus.

For those in search of more tangible pleasures, I am reliably informed that a bar called **Le Sherwood** (3 rue Daunous) is usually full of habitués in search of a shoulder to cry on. In similar vein, it seems you will never leave **Le Bleu Nuit** (12 rue des Vertus) unaccompanied, unless you are Quasimodo or wearing a three-piece suit.

# GETTING AROUND

There are currently more French drivers in Formula 1 than any other nationality – a fact readily comprehensible to anyone who has hired a car in Paris and lived to tell the tale.

While I exaggerate, the high accident rate is a powerful argument against renting a car in Paris itself. Add to that affordable taxis, efficient public transport and a VAT rate of 33.33 per cent on car rental (parking is less of a problem) and the case against begins to look overwhelming.

There is little to choose between the majors on price. While Avis tends towards the cheapest daily rate, Europcar adds less per km. All things considered, savings made by shopping around are minimal. Expect to pay F165-175 (plus F2 per km) including tax for a Group A Fiesta, rising to F745-770 (plus F7.50-8 per km) for a Mercedes 280SE. A typical Escort or similar works out around F210-220 (plus F2.60-2.90 per km). Hertz: (tel: 574 97 39); Avis: (tel: 550 32 31); Europcar: (tel: 563 04 27).

Taxis are plentiful and reasonably priced. A typical city centre trip should come to between F20-25 and most go by the meter (although there is a tendency to go from A to B by other than the shortest possible route and/or to 'misunderstand' the stated destination. If in doubt, write it down. A cab from 'centre ville' to Orly should be between F90-120 and to Roissy (Charles de Gaulle) F120-150 (the latter compares with F28 for a bus to Porte Maillot on the outskirts of the city and F21 for the metro to Gare du Nord).

The Paris métro is extremely efficient and tolerably pleasant – although you should keep a tight grip on any valuables (avoid if you can the infamous no. 4 line between Pte d'Orléans and Pte de Clignancourt). To navigate successfully you will need to know the appropriate terminus on the line you require. Flat rate is F4.20 (F4.60 – First class) but if you are planning several rides, a weekly *carte hebdomadaire* is good value at F37. You will need a passport photo.

There are those who swear by the Paris bus service. Métro tickets are valid but I must confess to never having mastered the intricacies of the routing system.

*Though transport is not a problem, Paris is a city which should be explored on foot*

# Rio

**Rio is the Jekyll and Hyde of Latin America, its urbane loveliness often obscuring the ugliness within. Visiting businessmen would do well to remember that its alma mater remains the university of the jungle, and are advised to watch their step and their wallet.**

**by David Owen.**

I was feeling smug as I strolled out of the Hotel Meridien onto Avenida Atlântica, seduced by first impressions. So this really is the teeming, exuberant metropolis in its setting of unparalleled natural beauty promoted by travel agents, I mused, as I meandered along Copacabana. Ten minutes and two colloquies later, I was having second thoughts.

*"What's that? Shit!"* I was first startled from my reverie by the boisterous attentions of a shoeshine boy. Sure enough, my right shoe was spattered with an indeterminate, gelatinous substance, deftly deposited by my tormentor on his approach. Removal of the 'shit' was swift and inexpensive. But such is the preponderance of these infant opportunists that it makes sense to wear Hush-Puppies.

No sooner had I shaken off one hard-sell exponent, than I was assailed by two more. It is customary for Carioca ladies of the night to hunt in pairs, I was belatedly informed. Not taking no for an answer, one rummaged through my pockets while the other rummaged through my trousers. I emerged, my virtue intact, but about 50,000 cruzeiros the poorer.

Rio is the Jekyll and Hyde of Latin American cities, its urbane loveliness often obscuring the ugliness within. Visiting businessmen would do well to remember that Rio's alma mater remains the law of the jungle.

Thieving will probably prove the major problem. The precautions are obvious: be alert everywhere from hotel to beach; use safe deposit boxes; never carry more cash than is immediately needed; guard against external manifestations of wealth. But they should be rigorously applied – particularly as one can expect little help from the police. An acquaintance recently returned nursing a gash in the back of his neck, the legacy of an attempt on his gold chain while he was sunbathing. Buses may prove a false economy as pickpockets are common and 'hold-ups' frequent. Beaches make easy pickings, and no one in their right mind will take anything of sentimental or monetary value. So great is this problem that the Caesar Park hotel in Ipanema employs private security guards to patrol its beach.

Rio sprawls along Brazil's east coast – a long, thin strip of a city (24 km long and only three to 16 km wide) separated by mountains and hills from the rest of the country. Writers have waxed lyrical about Rio for centuries, eulogising its sparkling blue seas, majestic grey mountains and lush, tropical foliage. It comes as a surprise, then, that many of Rio's beaches are man-made – the land reclaimed from the sea by a Dutch engineer, the golden sands imported. And even these gleaming beaches are not as they seem from the distance – covered, as they are, in orange peel, wrapping paper and crushed tins.

The capital city for 125 years (until 1959), Rio was first settled by the French, and though the Portuguese took possession of it in 1567, the French continued to invade until the 1710s. The city still shows signs of its colonial roots – mainly in the centro – in the old buildings, the requisite abundance of churches and monasteries and in some of the elegant wide streets. The Avenida Rio Branco, in particular, is reminiscent of old Europe, and is often referred to as Rio's Champs Elysées.

Politically Brazil is in a state of flux. While the death and subsequent apotheosis of Trancredo Neves were potentially disastrous for Brazil's fledgeling democracy, the avuncular Sarney, whom nobody (least of all himself) expected to accede to the presidency, nipped an explosive situation in the bud by adopting a low-key approach and pledging to execute the policies of his ill-fated predecessor.

Modern Rio runs at a frenetic pace. You really do take your life in your hands whenever you cross the street. Red lights appear purely decorative and speed is of the essence. Even if you stick to the pavements, your path is often obstructed by chaotically parked cars, or bollards designed to prevent such transgressions but equally obstructive. Pollution is appalling for a coastal city although, as often as not, the fumes are of alcohol rather than carbon monoxide: Brazil prides itself on having saved $3.5bn in oil imports in two years by producing vehicles to run on sugar-derived alcohol.

To keep up, Cariocas resort copiously to their best-known national product – coffee. Many think nothing of a daily fix of 15-20 *cafezinhos* – immensely strong, immensely sweet and generally downed in one gulp. I found the city's inhabitants chauvinistic, fervently patriotic, at times maddeningly puerile (*"If I didn't litter the streets, what would the roadsweepers do?"*), at times enigmatically worldly-wise. *"Ten um jeitinho"* (there's always a little way) is a catchphrase which owes more to the power of the bribe in Brazil than the Carioca's instinctive optimism. There is also more than a hint of racism, witness the common view of the Amazonian Indian as a hopelessly backward dunce, and a string of cheap jokes about blacks – a white runner is a jogger; a black runner is a thief – are popular. And some amateur sociologists propound (seriously, as far as I could tell) that the reason there are fewer blacks than usual in the national soccer team is that hard times have driven blacks to robbery at times when they used to play football in Copacabana. Though whites comprise 54 per cent of the population at present, by the end of the century coloureds will predominate.

But the good-humoured, relaxed side of the national character generally comes to the fore in business dealings. Businessmen invariably adopt the laid-back approach, often taunting the more serious, rolled-up-sleeves attitude of their archetypal São Paulo counterparts. Despite – or perhaps because of this attitude, however, at least half of Rio – the zona sul – has remained as affluent as in the boom years of the 18th century, when the city was the main port serving the rich mines of Minas Gerais.

While the *favelas* (slums) grow poorer by the day and the heavily-industrialised zona norte (which most businessmen will traverse only twice – to and from the airport) seems ever more drab and depressed, Brazil's shaky economic position has done little to curb prosperous Rio's inimitable style. Appearance is everything – which helps keep the upmarket shopping malls of Ipanema (specialising in fashion and jewellery) in clover. It also contributes to the spectacular nature of much of the nightlife on offer.

Brazilian entertainment is synonymous with samba. Of course, should your visit coincide with the renowned Carnival – Shrove Tuesday and the three days before – your exposure to samba will be complete. Gyrating samba schools (often with hundreds or thousands of members – men, women and children) take over the streets to compete in their scant, garish, glittering costumes. So intrinsic is Carnival to the Carioca soul, that the Sambadromo (Rua Marques de Sapucai, Cidade Nova) is a permanent building – a concrete tribute to pleasure. But Carnival is the worst time, bar none, to do business in the city.

Less glamorous than Carnival, but more beautiful in its own, quieter way is the festival of Iemanjá, the Macumba Goddess of the Sea. On the night of December 31 the beaches of Ipanema, Copacabana and Leblon fill with people carrying candles, often dressed in white, waiting to make their offerings to Iemanjá. Local fishing boats crowd close to the shore, bedecked with streamers and other regalia. Just before midnight the offerings are made – flowers and such – and thrown into the sea where they drift together until dispersed by the tide. Macumba is the spiritual religion of Brazil – an odd marriage of South American catholicism, African voodoo and Indian magic. The Catholic

*Cinelandia in downtown Rio*

church would dearly love to ban it (especially since many of the spirits share the names of Catholic saints) but its following is too strong. There are Macumba ceremonies held throughout the year, and many hotels offer night tours. Unfortunately these are not usually genuine, and it is not safe to attend the real thing held in the *favelas.*

The closest the foreigner can safely come to Macumba is at the São Cristóvão market, where each Sunday morning an old man sits on a chair handling live snakes and performing other tricks, circled round by children and adults. The market is full of such treasures, if you don't mind hunting for them through dust and dirt. There is stall after stall of brightly striped hammocks, second hand bicycles, lace, clothes, records, skillets of cooking food, sacks of beans and spices, and endless aisles of meat (though the sight of so much unrefrigerated meat hanging in the open may be a bit rich for some – not to mention the pig's head swinging in the breeze). It is a true people's market – for the people of the north east of Brazil, with none of the tourist trappings of Ipanema's Hippie Fair. The market is open every Sunday until 3 p.m. It is best to go by taxi as the buses can be complicated, and it is not so far from the zona norte.

For a different taste of authentic Brazil, go to a football game at the Maracana Stadium. Even if the football is not brilliant (though with Zico and company it usually is), the crowd will provide ample entertainment. Elaborate drumming from the stands is an integral part of any football game, as is loud booing at every opposition move. At half-time the fans parade from one side of the stadium to the other swinging giant team flags, accompanied by the drums. The 200,000 seat stadium is the largest in the world. On the day I went, Flamengo (the local team) was convincingly outplayed by a fourth-rate team. The fans remained loyal through the first half, but by the beginning of the second had begun to boo their own team. By the fourth quarter the two men on my right were engrossed in a violent argument – *"It would have been better if they'd given the game away and not played"* said one. *"No,"* said the other, *"they should have died in a bus crash on the way to the game and been spared this disgrace."*

Though Rio may conjure up scenes of idyllic repose – luxuriating on sandy beaches or by hotel pools – chances are you will return exhausted, like me, by the city's vitality. While the beach is indeed an integral part of the Carioca lifestyle, don't expect to find peace and quiet there. If the parading bikinis are not enough to set your pulse racing (and it is not for nothing that one of the prime fashion lines is called Bum Bum – though European women should note that these are worn by old and

*Corcovado*

young, fat and thin, and that they will feel more uncomfortable and conspicuous in a modest one-piece), the raucous attentions of the vendors, selling everything from coconut milk to shrimp kebabs, certainly will.

The famous Christ figure, inaugurated in 1931, must be caught in two minds as He peers down at the city from the summit of the 2,400 ft Corcovado mountain. The splendid panorama laid out before Him may resemble the Garden of Eden. Closer inspection reveals it is the world's most beautiful concrete jungle.

# WHERE TO STAY

The pace is so fast in Rio that comfortable lodgings are essential. The city's hotels are generally good by European standards, and superlative by Latin American ones. It is not a good idea to stay in the city centre unless on the shortest of business trips (i.e. one night), since the area is moribund after dark, and you will waste valuable time and money trying to escape to the zona sul for the evenings. Many of Rio's hotels line the crescent of the Copacabana coast, separated from the beach front by the Avenida Atlântica. Although the hotels are often the height of elegance, the Avenida itself becomes progressively seedier as it winds south. The bars along the far-southern end are full of transvestite hookers – who may be beautiful but should not be touched.

The prominent **Meridien** (Av. Atlântica, 1020; tel: 275 9922; telex: 02123183) is the most practical for the business traveller in need of a trouble-free stay (though the lifts can be infuriatingly slow). Ideally situated for both Copacabana and Leme beaches and a ten-minute taxi ride from the city, it also boasts Rio's best-equipped business centre. From the glassed-in walls of the hotel's pool terrace, guests can watch the less fortunate as they are subjected to the attentions of vendors and pick-pockets on the beach below. Ask for a room on the beach-side – the views are spectacular and bear a suspicious resemblance to Rio's most popular postcard. Unfortunately, the sea air cannot be enjoyed since the rooms are air-conditioned and the windows do not open. Single Cr$ 757,000-964,000; double Cr$ 826,000-1,033,000; suite Cr$ 723,000-3,443,000.

Also in Copacabana is the luxurious but expensive **Rio Palace** (Av. Atlântica, 4240; tel: 521 3232; telex: 21803). All of the 400 rooms have private balconies with sea views – of Copacabana or Ipanema beaches; and visitors are spoilt for choice of chlorinated water between the hotel's two swimming pools. Facilities are excellent for both business people and tourists, and the banqueting rooms are superb. The Palace is a favourite with visiting celebrities and, perhaps not surprisingly, it is also the base of Rio's Foreign Press Club. Single Cr$ 757,000-1,102,000; double Cr$ 895,000-1,239,000; suite from Cr$ 2,203,000.

Overlooked by the Rio Palace but in no way overshadowed by it is the **Caesar Park** (Av. Vieira Souto, 460; tel: 287 3122; telex: 021 21204). The Caesar Park has the advantage of being in Ipanema – where the shops are more stylish and the streets are less harried than in neighbouring Copacabana. Although the hotel only opened in 1978, it has the sophistication of a more mature establishment. Single Cr$ 895,000-1,033,000; double Cr$ 1,033,000-1,170,000; suite from Cr$ 2,410,000.

The closest hotel to the centro is the going-to-seed **Gloria** (Pria do Russel 632; tel: 205 7272;

*Rio Palace hotel*

telex; 2123623). Once one of Rio's most luxurious properties, the Gloria's decline is best documented by the fate of its private beach – which was recently annexed by city landscapers. Now hotel guests must walk across the Flamengo Park to get to sand and surf. With 700 rooms, the Gloria is Brazil's biggest hotel. However, you still run the risk of rooming in all too close proximity to a plane-load of US package tourists – which is how the hotel keeps up its occupancy rate. Single Cr$ 434,000; double Cr$ 551,000; suite Cr$ 613,000.

Two establishments which have seen better days are the **Nacional** (Av. Niemeyer; tel: 322 1000; telex: 021 23615) and the **Copacabana Palace** (Av. Atlântica, 1072; tel: 257 1818; telex: 021 21482), though each has its attractions. The Copacabana Palace, now fallen from grace, was once a hotel of world ranking, though it still has a charm somewhat lacking in the great new moderns. Rooms are comfortable and the swimming pool is the largest in Rio. A recent preservation order may yet allow the Copacabana Palace to restore its former glory. Single Cr$ 689,000; double Cr$ 929,000; suite Cr$ 4,820,000. The Nacional hosts Rio's annual film festival and is reckoned by many to have the best conference facilities in town. There are also the usual slew of nightclubs, restaurants, saunas and swimming pools. Single around Cr$ 482,000; double around Cr$ 516,000; suite around Cr$ 689,000.

The Nacional shares this distinction, in my view, with the **Sheraton** (Av. Nieymeyer, 121; tel: 274 1122; telex: 021 23485) and the **Inter-Continental** (Av. Prefeito Mendes de Morais, 222; tel: 322 2200; telex: 021 21790). Both have recently been refurbished, and while the Sheraton is better value, the Inter-Continental is undeniably plusher. With a beach to the front, a golf course to the back and ample private grounds surrounding, the Inter-Continental is a resort in the true sense of the word. There are also swimming pools (three), tennis courts, a gymnasium and sauna. Not surprising that this should then be the base for the Brazilian Grand Prix. All three are situated beyond Leblon and are hence inconvenient for the centro – a 30-minute cab ride away. Sheraton: single from Cr$ 620,000; double from Cr$ 723,000; suite from Cr$ 1,033,000. Inter-Continental: single from Cr$ 757,000; double Cr$ 826,000; suite from Cr$ 1,790,000.

Also worthy of note is the **Everest Rio** (Rua Prudente de Morais, 1117; tel: 287 8282; telex: 02122254), superb value and popular with long-stay visitors. Meanwhile, the best value in town at around Cr$ 275,400 a night is the three-star **Astoria** (Rua Republica do Peru; tel: 257 8080). No frills here but most amenities, including pool and sauna. Ask for a room in the new wing, dating from 1984. Those planning a long stay should also note the presence of Apart-hotels; self-contained apartments complemented with hotel-standard services in which 30 per cent discounts are normally available for long-stay guests.

A note on exchange rates. While hotels can offer only the official rate, anybody in his right mind uses the 'parallel' market, at a saving of around 10 to 20 per cent. Porters and receptionists are happy to give directions for the nearest outlet – in Copacabana, though, there is a good cambio at Irmãos Campos on Av. Rio Branco. It is advisable to change money a little at a time because the cruzeiro tends to depreciate quite rapidly and it then matters less if you are robbed. On changing money, most Cariocas cache their money around their person (usually in their underwear) before venturing onto the street.

# WHERE TO EAT

Cariocas eat late. Enter a restaurant before 9p.m. and you will eat alone – but chances are you will eat well, and cheaply. In Rio you will never pay over Cr$ 344,000 a head and often under Cr$ 68,800. If you do need to keep costs down, one legitimate method is to sample the local wines – which can be excellent. For white, try Lejon or Chilean Santa Emiliana, while a reliable red is Grand cru Fasana. Brazilian champagne is quite palatable too, though unimaginatively dubbed M. Chandon.

Staples of the Brazilian diet are rice, *'feijoadas'* (black beans), and meat – lots of it. Fellow carnivores should not leave without visiting a *churrascaria* where, for a flat rate, waiters repeatedly appear with plates of barbecued meats until you tell them to stop. **Leblon** (tel: 247 4022) is the most popular and arguably the best. Seafood is also outstanding, as one might expect. **Marimbas** (tel: 231 2338), a new restaurant near the Rio Palace hotel, has received good reports but my favourite is the **Cabaça Grande** (tel: 231 2338), tucked away in a backstreet behind the docks. Its *Moqueita de peixe* – a quintessentially Carioca fish stew – is especially delicious.

Best for business lunches in the centro, Rio's business centre, is the **English Bar** (tel: 224 2539). The restaurant and small pub bar downstairs have a surprisingly authentic, relaxed English atmosphere – making a welcome break from a frantic city. For those who find the thought of eating English food abroad barbaric, there is a vast menu of European specialities at the restaurant upstairs, including the national dishes of Spain, Portugal and, yes, England. Another favourite, for the businessman in a rush, is the **La Mole** chain, famous for bringing cheap food to Copacabana and serving plain but palatable dishes at under Cr$ 34,400 a head.

At the other end of the spectrum, there are three luxury restaurants in Rio which stand out from the pack. All are French, two are in hotels. **Le Pré Catelan** (tel: 521 3232) in the Rio Palace hotel manages, against all odds, to seem like a real restaurant instead of an institutional appendage to a hotel. Subtlety and surprise are the main elements of the fine *nouvelle cuisine* menu. And the claim that the food rivals the best in Paris is no idle boast – the restaurant is orchestrated by Gaston Lenotre (Parisien chef *par excellence*).

The Meridien's **St Honore** (tel: 275 9922) is presided over by another world-renowned chef – Paul Bocuse. The menu is smaller than Le Pré Catelan's, but no less excellent for it. The restaurant sits on the top of the Meridien and has what are arguably the most sweeping views of Rio. It makes for an impressive and enticing business lunch, especially since the pre-set lunch menu is not outrageously expensive.

**Troisgros** (Rua Custodia Serrao, 62; tel: 226 4542 or 246 7609) is named after its chef and owner, Claude Troisgros. The restaurant sits, undramatically, in a small side-street. Since it opened in 1984, Troisgros has enjoyed an unsullied reputation for *haute cuisine.* One would, of course, expect nothing but the best from Claude Troisgros, who comes from a family of distinguished French chefs, and who headed the kitchen at Le Pré Catelan before opening his own restaurant. Troisgros combines traditional French cooking with Brazilian ingredients – a combination that is both refined and exotic.

My own preferred haunts lie in the Botafogo area. **Ô Xente** specialises in black cuisine from the Brazilian north. It serves the best *Vatapá* (a spicy fish casserole) in town and is fetchingly decorated in graffiti and cardboard macaws. Just along the street is the **Aurora** (Capitão Salomão, 35) an undeniably pretentious haven of the city's intelligentsia which also happens to serve superb and inexpensive food. Perhaps the least subtle item on the restaurant's jokey menu is Catfish à la Sarnay – a reference to the Brazilian premier's walrus moustache.

Further points on food: I recommend the copious use of the *zumo* (juice) bars, to be found on every street corner. To Europeans, used to a staple of re-constituted orange juice, this fresh, ice-cold drink is quite another order of reality. Nor is there any need to be wary of ice cubes; water in Rio is, generally, safe. Also beware Brazilian condiment pots: the 'salt cellar' usually contains toothpicks.

# NIGHT LIFE

Visitors to Rio soon learn that Brazilians love to play – and while the city centre sleeps through the night and weekends, the rest of the city throbs with insomnia. Samba is the most popular form of entertainment for foreigner and Carioca alike. The best regular show available is the weekly performance of the highly-rated Beija-Flor school at **Morro da Urca** (halfway up the Sugar Loaf; tel: 791 1571) on Mondays at 9.30 p.m. Failing that, visit **Oba-Oba** (Visconde de Priajá, 499) at Largo Humaita for a dazzling mélange of local dance music.

For those in search of mellower fare, a string of excellent jazz clubs has opened since 1984, the pick being **People** (Av. Bartolomeu Mitre; tel: 294 0547) and the **Tinker** (Rio Design Centre, Leblon; tel: 294 6494). Discos are plentiful and popular. **Help** (Av. Atlântica, 3432; tel: 521 1296), touted as the largest in South America, has quickly established itself, while **Crepusculo de Cubatão** (Rua Barata Ribeiro 543; tel: 237 1924), part-owned by Great Train Robber Ronnie Biggs, has successfully targeted the early 30s market. Those in search of greater exclusivity can arrange for nightly membership of some of Rio's private clubs – **Hippopotamus** (Rua Barão da Torre; tel: 227 8658), **Règine** (Hotel Meridien; tel: 275 9922) or **Le Streghe** (Praca General Osorio; tel: 287 1369) through their hotel.

Rio must be the most licentious of all nominally catholic cities. Chances are that, as a foreigner staying at a large hotel, you will be sought out by prostitutes and such, whether it be in front of the hotel or at a club or bar. The best places for a pick-up are the bars from Rua Duvivier to Av.

*Rio nightlife is colourful and noisy*

Princesa Isabel. **Barbarella** (Av. Princesa Isabel) comes highly recommended. The girls are said to be the most beautiful in Rio – quite often upper-middle-class girls looking for pin money and, perhaps, an affluent foreign husband. For the disinterested foreigner it is an amusing place to watch humanity in action, but drinks do cost more than at the ordinary bars.

That said, my favourite Rio evenings have been those spent wandering from bar to bar, chatting, staring and downing *caipirihanas*, the exquisite cocktail of cachaça, limes, sugar and ice which rivals *cafezinho* as the national dish. The Grotto de Urca and the magnificent yellow café opposite the Opera House are particularly pleasant.

*Buses are not recommended*

# GETTING AROUND

Arriving at Rio's international airport for the first time can seem like a very, very bad dream. After surmounting the difficulties presented by customs and passport officials, the weary passenger is met by uniformed men grabbing at luggage, large women crammed behind small booths shouting and waving money, and a general sense of unease. It is a relief, then, to find that travel into the city is relatively easy. Take an official taxi (Cootramo or Transcoopass), and pay by voucher, in advance (thus avoiding being taken for a ride). There are also two buses: the inter-airport bus, a comfortable, air-conditioned, tinted glass affair that takes you to the Santos Dumont Airport downtown, from where you can catch numerous city buses or taxis; or there is a bus which goes to all the major hotels in Copacabana and Ipanema. The only problem with the buses is that they are subject to the occasional ambush.

Once in Rio, taxis are the usual and best means of transport for visitors. They are also inexpensive (around Cr$21,000 from Copacabana to the centro; under Cr$69,000 for the airport run). Meters have fallen hopelessly behind inflation, so charts are used to escalate the actual reading. If in doubt, ask to check the chart yourself – it pays to ensure that flag '1' is showing. Flag '2' is 20 per cent more expensive and only applies after 11 p.m. on Sundays and holidays and beyond Leblon.

Hire cars (some would say for the foolhardy) are freely available, with outlets principally clustered along Avenida Princesa Isabel. A small Volkswagen from Hertz (tel: 275 4996) costs US$17 a day, plus US¢9 per km, or US$104 per week with the same mileage rate. The same car from Avis (tel: 542 4249) costs US$16.90 a day, and US¢8 per km. The weekly rate is US$101.50, plus the same rate for mileage. Most of the major hire firms do not accept cash payment, though the choice of credit cards accepted is vast. Since most locals harbour dreams of being racing drivers, however, driving in Rio is not for the timid.

As for the buses – they provide an insider's guide to Rio that most business travellers are not likely to want. Certain routes are better than others: the buses from Copacabana to Rio Sul and Urca are generally safe. But even more than in New York, it is imperative to dress for the street if taking public transport: leave valuables behind, and beware of pickpockets at the turnstiles. Avoid at all costs route 553, which traverses one of the worst *favelas;* and the St Theresa tram should be approached with caution. Oddly enough, the metro is clean, reliable and safe, perhaps because at present it is confined to the journey between Botafogo and the centro.

# Rome

**Neither Mediterranean nor North European, Rome suffers from something of an identity crisis – even Italians are at a loss to swear to its true character. Yet such is the mystique of the Eternal City that it remains the unquestioned business capital of a nation, and spiritual capital of a religion.**
**By Simon Inglis**

There was a poll in Italy recently to determine in which cities it was best to live, in terms of hospitals, transport, education and so on. Rome, the capital, came in 35th place. But the poll also revealed that there wasn't a town or city south of Rome which fared any better: Italy remains a nation divided not only into two, the North and South, but also into several different parts based on regionalism.

So the Milanese ridicule the Romans and the Romans deride the Neapolitans. *"Let's just say they have a healthy disregard for each other,"* said one member of the British Embassy's commercial staff.

Primarily, until the rise of Mussolini, Rome was a large town of some 400,000 souls. But since the war the population has exploded to over three million, the largest in Italy, and the city cannot cope.

Its administrators strain under the burden of not only supporting the city but also the surrounding Lazio region, the central Government and Parliament with their accompanying hordes of civil servants, and some 1.3 million visitors every year, most of whom flock to Rome as the spiritual capital of Roman Catholicism.

In addition to this there remains the centuries-old problem of maintaining two delicate balances. The first lies between the worldwide demands and responsibilities of the Vatican and the needs of a secular capital with European commitments. The second is between the need to preserve and conserve ancient and Renaissance Rome while at the same time modernising the city's overall infrastructure.

This divergence of interests is exemplified by the existence of a Communist-led city council in the midst of what is basically a stronghold of conservative civil servants.

It is a blend of characteristics quite unique in the world; as if the city was a *mélange* of Jerusalem, London, Washington and Athens. To confuse the issue further, I found very little agreement about the city from either residents or foreign businessmen. If it is true that wherever there are two Jews there are three arguments, the same goes for Romans and their opinions.

Some despise the city as a place to live in – accommodation costs are very high, for example, while basic salaries are low – and they condemn its people for their shallowness. *"They are trashy in their taste and their thinking,"* said a businessman from Florence. *"Despite all this ancient grandeur they are just materialistic."* Rome, he said, is neither Northern European, like Milan, nor Mediterranean like Naples.

But then, only 46 per cent of Rome's residents were actually born in Rome. The majority are immigrants, sucked in from the North to the city's bloated (and, I am told, frequently corrupt) bureaucracy, or drawn up from the impoverished South.

This might be the perfect recipe for expansion, were there jobs to be had in Rome. But there aren't, and the city has spread out into a series of hastily built suburbs, lacking in proper roads or sewers, where disaffection grows in the face of civic helplessness.

But there are encouraging signs.

A plan called the Rome Capital Project which, typically, awaits proper funding, proposes a series of developments for urban renewal, international exhibition halls and theatres, and perhaps most exciting of all, the development of the almost forgotten River Tiber into a recreational and navigable asset.

All that is for the future. For the time being Rome's biggest fillip has come from the Government-backed *Cassa per il Mezzogiorno.* This agency has poured money and resources into the South of Italy, which geographically takes in all the country up to a line roughly 30 kilometres south of Rome.

Several industries, notably centred upon electronics and pharmaceuticals, have been set up with state aid in those Southern outskirts. There are also increasing numbers of joint British and Italian ventures, Westland helicopters with Augusta, for example. The manufacturing will actually take place in Milan, but as is common, the finance is engineered from the capital.

Similarly, Austin-Rover and General Motors moved to Rome in the last decade, not because the market is centred there but because that is where the regulatory problems have to be overcome.

Rome continues to be the communications centre of the country, with a particular interest in telecommunications, and, out at Mussolini's Cinecitta, the Hollywood of the Tiber, Rome keeps hold of that glamorous film-star connection which so revitalised the city in the late 1950s and early 1960s, the heyday of *La Dolce Vita* along the Via Veneto.

In fact, during the 1970s Cinecitta was turning out more full-length films, especially for television, than Hollywood.

But most of the wheeling and dealing in Rome involves administration. If a product is made in Milan or Turin it is almost certain that its fate will lie in negotiations held in Rome. Compared with the Milan trade fair, said one businessman, Rome's fair is *"like a village fête"*. But in Rome lies the political clout. Even quite small Northern businesses, I was told, maintain an office or an agent in the city.

Apart from the obvious need for the bureaucrats to justify their existence (as well as pay for their sea-side villas and mistresses) there is perhaps an historical reason for this relationship between Rome and the North. One theory has it that after the unification of Italy in 1870 the government decided that for the sake of stability it would keep all big industry away from the seat of power, thus avoiding potential disruption from any dangerous working class activism.

True or not, the division of responsibilities is decreasing, with Rome catching up quickly on the production side. It is now the third largest industrial centre in Italy, after Milan and Turin.

A symbol of this regeneration is the South Western development called EUR, an acronym for the *Esposizione Universale di Roma.* This was originally developed as the futuristic site for Mussolini's 1942 World Fair, cancelled when war broke out.

For many years after the war the area was a deserted and almost forgotten adjunct of the city, but since Nervi built his impressive sports palace there in 1959, and more especially with the recent siting of several major Italian and Roman companies in EUR, this concrete and marble landscape of Fascist pomposity has come to life as a vital breathing space for Rome's cramped facilities.

At lunchtime, in fact, it almost seems quite human, and even if business does not take you there it is well worth a visit.

Wherever you are in the city however, modern

*Throw a coin in the Trevi Fountain to ensure a return to Rome*

business methods are not the main key to success. Rome retains its old-boy network and thrives on personal influence.

For example, everyone will tell you that a foreign business must operate through an agent in Rome, someone who has a foot in the door of the politicians and bureaucrats. But although most foreign companies use Northern agents, it often transpires that they don't have any real influence South of Florence.

*La Bella Figura* is still important, according to some Rome experts. This means, said one, *"Making a big splash"*. It entails looking good, not stinting with the drinks, not cutting corners, and flattering the ego of your opposite number. One journalist cynically commented that it also requires having a beautiful secretary, though he added that in Rome, the plusher the office and the more expansive the talk, the more suspicious you should be.

Rome is also, according to another regular business traveller, a much harder place to do business in than the North. Less English is spoken and more personal contact is expected (hence the need for an agent). One foreign correspondent in Italy also told me he found the Romans slower, less business-like and less punctual than their fellow Italians.

I saw his point a few days later when a city official invited me to his office for a certain day. I arrived only to find the building closed.

Office hours, in addition, dictate that you should do most of your work before 1p.m. From then on your contact may either be at a long lunch, or, as is apparently common, in the late afternoon he may be working at another job altogether.

*"How else does a minor civil servant afford a BMW and a town flat for his mistress?"* suggested one official.

Once you fulfil your appointment, however, the Romans couldn't be more charming or gracious hosts. It is not so much that they suffer from any laid-back *mañana* syndrome as the fact that Rome as a city gives anyone a valid excuse for lack of organisation.

Physically it can be an exhausting place. For the visitor, walking is compulsive, yet the cobbled streets play hell with the soles of your feet, and simply crossing the road can be a major adventure. Until you get the hang of it I would suggest crossing alongside one of the natives.

The timing of your visit could have a marked effect on your stay, especially since most hotels are more geared towards either the very affluent guest or the tourist, and during Easter and the summer months rooms can be difficult to book. During August much of Rome closes down anyway.

But what of the pleasures of Rome? What are the factors which compensate for your aching feet, your frustration with bureaucracy and the Mediterranean office hours?

As a place of historical interest Rome needs no testimonial from me, and you probably won't get one from a Roman either. For the majority, places like St. Peter's and the Colosseum are, apparently, 'just there'. Always have been and always will be.

Thus it is commonplace to see baroque churches covered in graffiti, or, as I saw one day with great horror, young Romans playing frisbee and football in the atrium of the Pantheon, one of the best preserved ancient buildings in the world. No one stopped them, not even the passing *carabinieri,* and I, on behalf of Western Civilisation, did not have the guts.

This carefree attitude seems to extend to the snappily-dressed politicians, who you can see with their lackeys loitering around the Parliament building puffing on cigarettes and eating ice-creams as they wait for their limousines.

In contrast, the city has a violent edge. Terrorists gunned down a professor at the university while I was in Rome, and street crime, mainly perpetrated by drug addicts, is a daily topic of conversation. For example, no-one ever leaves his car-radio in a parked car, and many use heavy-duty chains to supplement their steering locks.

So many precautions, yet thousands of motor cyclists zoom about the city without wearing crash helmets.

I cannot explain it, nor do I know whether to believe the pessimists or the optimists who talk about Rome. From a human angle, life in the city appears to be deteriorating quickly, with little hope

*Rome is a city of churches as befits the cradle of Christianity*

of change unless the government invests in Rome the kind of money which a capital city merits.

From a business point of view, however, there is no doubt that the prospect looks better now than for many years.

My most memorable prospect of the city was at sundown, a view of the skyline from Rome's highest hill, the Quirinal. St. Peter's in the distance rose high above a sea of aerials, church towers and roof gardens, bathed in a glorious pink-blue light such as I have never witnessed before.

Backed by a symphony of church bells and hooting horns, this was a vista hypnotic enough to make anyone forgive Rome all its faults, and explain to me at least why all those disgruntled individuals I had spoken to have stayed in the city, and probably always will.

When the Sheraton Roma charged L.5,000 for some lemon tea to accompany breakfast (ordinary tea would have been inclusive) I realised what the man had meant about looking out for hidden charges.

At some hotels you may even have to pay extra for air-conditioning (L.15,000 at the Hassler Villa Medici for example), at most of them breakfast is extra (L.17,200 at the Hilton, whether you eat anything or not), and there might also be a token L.1,800 room tax added on. Check all this, and find out if service and VAT are included.

Above all, because of the year-long tourist demand, book well in advance if it is humanly possible. There are surprisingly few luxury or chain hotels and cross-town traffic being what it is you will not want to find yourself on the wrong side of town for business.

Or on the wrong side of the hotel. Good views can transform your stay, while front-facing rooms in cheaper hotels can be very noisy at night.

If you have appointments near the airport, perhaps in the EUR district, there is the **Parco dei Medici** (Viale Castello della Magliana; tel: 5475; telex: 613302), with rooms from L.89,000, but it is particularly isolated. Also tucked away, but popular for its conference and health club facilities is the new **Sheraton Roma** (Viale del Pattinaggio; tel: 5453; telex: 614223). Regular free buses run into town and to the airport, but for room prices of L.140,000 upwards you might wish to get closer to the noise, smell and excitement of the centre. The Sheraton could be anywhere, and Rome is not just anywhere.

On the North Western side of the city, perched on Monte Mario overlooking the city, is the resort hotel **Cavalieri Hilton** (Via Cadlolo; tel: 3151; telex: 610296). Keep at least one night free for the Pergola restaurant or the Oyster Bar. Prices from L.175,000 to L.250,000.

That the more modern hotels are outside the centre is purely a matter of space and planning permission. For the real grandeur of Rome there are several older, smaller and in many cases more luxurious hotels within walking distances of the sights.

**The Grand** (Via Vittorio E. Orlando; tel: 4709; telex: 610210) is the most impressive, founded by César Ritz in 1894, with a foyer of palatial dimensions and decor. One of the CIGA chain, its immaculate service and facilities – Le Rallye grill room for example – merit the highest prices, from L.200,000 for a single up to L.441,600. If you can't stay there at least visit this contender for Europe's most lavish hotel. It's like being in a period drama.

On a smaller scale, but equally favoured by royalty and diverse celebrities (from Chaplin to Nixon), is the **Hassler Villa Medici** (Trinita dei Monti; tel: 679 2651; telex: 610208). Overlooking the Spanish Steps, this outwardly ordinary hotel has popular restaurants on its patio and roof top. Some of the fittings are rather too classically fussy for my liking, and my latest information has it that credit cards are still not accepted here. Check first though, because it's a gem. Prices from L.122,000.

A few doors away, on the Via Sistina, is the highly regarded **Hotel de la Ville** (tel: 6733; telex: 611676), an 18th century building with a surprising amount of space behind its small facade. Rooms from L.185,000 to L.250,000.

Among the Via Veneto hotels are the **Ambasciatori Palace** (tel: 473 831; telex: 610241), the **Excelsior** (tel: 4708; telex: 610232) and the **Flora** (tel: 497 821; telex: 680494). The Excelsior, also a CIGA hotel, is, in its dated way, the most lavish of the three, resembling the Grand and almost matching its prices.

*The Excelsior hotel on the glamorous Via Veneto*

Nearby, at the entrance of the stunning Villa Borghese Gardens, is the **Eden Hotel** (Via Ludovisi; tel: 474 3551; telex: 610567). Popular with Americans, it has been completely renovated, with a marble entrance way but less heavy-handed rooms. The penthouse restaurant offers a panoramic view of the city. Single rooms start at L.160,000, doubles at L.250,000.

The only really modern hotel in the centre is the **Jolly** (Corso d'Italia; tel: 8495; telex: 612293), one of an Italian chain; reliable, good value (L.66,000-181,000) but somehow . . . not Rome.

I feel the same about the **Hotel Bernini Bristol** (Piazza Barberini; tel: 463 051; telex: 610554). But plain and uninspired though the facade and interior may be, this is a popular deluxe establishment in a prime location, with rooms from L.170,000 to L.275,000. You might get more modernity at the Sheraton, but you'll soon spend the difference on taxis.

Of the countless smaller first class hotels in Rome, several are favourites among visiting businessmen. I like the **Hotel d'Inghilterra** (Via Bocca di Leone; tel: 672 161; telex: 614552), close to the Spanish Steps. Once the guest house of a noble family, it has developed a reputation for housing actors and writers, including Alec Guinness, Henry James, Mark Twain and Ernest Hemingway. Maybe that's why I felt at home here. The English bar used to be a favourite among British embassy staff. Small and friendly, rooms cost from L.141,000-L.187,000.

Other smaller hotels worth trying are **Boston** (Via Lombardia; tel: 473 951; telex: 680460), the **Sitea** (Via V.E. Orlando opposite the Grand; tel: 475 1560; telex: 614163), which is second class but reliable at only L.58,000 to L.97,000, and, with its enviable view of Imperial Rome, the **Forum Hotel** (Via Tor de'Conti; tel: 679 2446; telex: 6880252). Rooms here cost between L.90,000 and L.173,000.

Visiting British businessmen seem to like the **Marini Strand Hotel** (Via del Tritone; tel: 672 061; telex: 612295) – half the clientele at any one

*Eden Hotel*

time are said to be British – though having seen the garish interior I cannot quite understand why. Other smaller hotels to note are the 19-room **Gregoriana** (Via Gregoriana; tel: 679 4269; no telex), and for cheaper accommodation on the Via Veneto the **Hotel Alexandra** (tel: 461 943).

Finally one rather special hotel, the **Lord Byron** (Via G. de Notaris; tel: 360 9541; telex: 611217). Part of the Relais et Châteaux chain, this converted mansion in the quiet Parioli district – a five-minute taxi ride from the centre – is probably the most attentive, relaxing hotel I have ever stayed in. No detail is too much for the staff. The restaurant is superb and the bedrooms have fresh flowers, crisp linen hand-towels, marble baths, digital safes and electronically operated shutters. I cannot fault this hotel in any respect, which is probably why it costs between L.260,000 and L.320,000.

For a complete list of hotels and prices write to Ente Provinciale Per Il Turismo di Roma, *Via Parigi 11, Rome.* Otherwise, beware of guide prices (mine included), as costs fluctuate according to the season and the included extras.

# WHERE TO EAT

«*Notoriously uninteresting,*" said one correspondent commenting on Rome's restaurants. The average Roman, he said, hardly bothers eating out – except perhaps on Sundays when the family might drive out to a rural or seaside *osteria.*

*"Life in this city is really about eating,"* insisted another foreign resident, *"and more precisely, eating out."*

*"It all depends on what you're used to,"* commented another foreigner . . . . well, me actually. It is my contention that if you're accustomed to the quality and diversity of restaurants in London, for example, then Rome is indeed parochial and limited in comparison, even with other Italian cities like Milan and Turin. But if you genuinely crave Italian food then you should have no complaints, as long as you take the right advice.

Unfortunately, therein lies a problem, since every visitor and every local has his own, very different list of favourites.

Example: *"If you do nothing else you simply must go to Sabatini's* (S. Maria in Trastavere; tel: 588 307)," I was told by a gourmet before leaving London. *"Sabatini's?"* said two other regular visitors. *"That's for tourists. There are much better places nearby."*

Nevertheless I went to Sabatini's, and I would have tried it had they accepted my particular credit card. Therein lies another problem. Some restaurants only accept Diners or American Express, and several enjoy such a brisk trade that they simply don't feel the need for any credit provision.

There is a third irritation. Because of union agreements every public establishment in Rome has to close for at least one day a week. Fair enough, but which day? Many choose Sundays or Mondays, but plenty more close on other days. So always check beforehand on methods of payment and opening days, and if possible book in advance. Despite what the aforementioned correspondent told me, I rarely saw an empty restaurant.

Now for the good news. There are so many *trattorias, ristorantes, pizzerias* and *osterias* in the Rome area – over 5,000 by one estimate – that you need never eat badly, or necessarily at great cost.

The recommended **Romolo's** (8, Via di Porta Settimana; tel: 588 284) in the Trastevere district, for example, charged me L.37,000 for a full meal with wine. With its own delightful vine-covered courtyard, Romolo's is reputed to have been the meeting place of Raphael and his mistress, Fornarina. Other visitors mentioned are Michelangelo and Kirk Douglas (local restaurants seem to delight in name dropping). Although traditional Roman dishes form only a small part of most restaurants' cuisine I would suggest at Romolo's the *fettucine,* the region's main contribution to that long list of pasta varieties.

For pure Roman fare, **Checchino dal 1887** (30, Via Monte Testaccio; tel: 576 318) is the most popular locally, but you have to like offal. In a similar price range, also with a pleasant outdoor arbor, is **Otello alla Concordia** (81, Via della Croce; tel: 679 1178) near the Spanish Steps. Friendly and unpretentious, if you can get a table for lunch sit outside and be prepared to take your time. Like most Roman restaurants the service declines noticeably during the tourist season, and may cease altogether in August, when half the city escapes to the countryside.

Most guides agree that **La Carbonara** (23, Campo de'Fiori; tel: 656 4783) and **Osteria dell'Antiquario** (27, Piazza San Simeone) are also worthwhile for unfussy, but quality traditional cooking.

I would add **L'Orso 80** (Via del Orso; tel: 656 4904 or 757 1710), where the fish, seafood, fruit and vegetables are laid out as for a market stall. The staff show an attitude common to these smaller *osterias;* boisterous almost irreverent, and quite capable, as I witnessed, of smoking over the food one minute before serving up a delicacy with charm the next.

A few yards away is the **Hosteria dell'Orso** (25, Via dei Soldati; tel: 656 4221, evenings only) which is the complete opposite. Set in a 15th century Renaissance *palazzo,* the atmosphere is more rarified, the bill will be twice the size of its neighbours, and well-heeled American tourists will sometimes form most of the clientele (Aristotle Onassis was the celebrity guest here). Upstairs is the Cabala nightclub.

Also with dancing and music at hand, but with a spectacular over-view of the city as a bonus, is the **Pergola,** at the Cavalieri Hilton Hotel (Monte Mario; tel: 3151). Regarded by some as one of the top five restaurants in Europe, despite the rather sleazy modern decor, the menu here is relatively simple and the presentation perfect. So restrained is the lighting that at night it's difficult to determine where the dining room finishes and the twinkling city begins.

The Pergola is indicative of how Rome's higher ranking restaurants are to be found increasingly in hotels. **Le Rallye** at the Grand Hotel (tel: 4709) has the longest tradition, going back to 1894, and boasts particularly fine hand-made pasta (as well as royal and rock star clients). **La Cupola** at the Excelsior Hotel (Via Veneto; tel: 4708) is, I believe, more inventive, allowing you to pick between classics and *la nuova cucina* variations, but my favourite is undoubtedly **Le Jardin,** the small basement restaurant at the Lord Byron Hotel (Via Giuseppe De Notaris; tel: 360 9541).

One critic deems it to be the best in Rome, and who am I to argue? Classified as a Relais et Châteaux, Le Jardin's cuisine is as light, delicate and refreshing as the restaurant itself; frivolous some might call it, pretentious maybe, but if this brand of *nouvelle cuisine* is a rip-off then I am a willing victim. I sampled Rabbit Pie basilicum-flavoured, pancakes with mushrooms and shrimps, baby lamb with honey and some iced nougat in hot caramel sauce which was so good I almost forgot myself and wiped the plate clean.

All these hotel restaurants will charge from L.60,000 to L.80,000 per head, including wine.

There are other, more famous establishments. **George's** (7, Via Marche; tel: 484 575) is excellent – the *gazpacho* particularly – as is **El Toula** (29, Via Della Lupa; tel: 678 1196), where I recommend the *Insalata Toula* and any of the desserts. **Ristorante G. Ranieri** (26, Via Mario dei Fiori; tel: 679 1592), founded by Queen Victoria's chef, is favoured by discerning Romans, not only for its *lasagne verdi* (the house speciality) but also for its restful atmosphere.

For a city built around a river, Rome seems curiously unimpressed by the potential of the Tiber's banks. I found only one decent riverside restaurant, the **Isola del Sole** by the Scalo de Pinedo. Run by a friendly Argentinian, this floating restaurant is perfect for warm afternoons. Meals cost around L.20,000 per head. The fresh air is free and, for Rome, decidedly welcome.

*Find time to relax in a pavement cafe*

After a few days you may get tired of predictable Italian menus, in which case be wary of alternatives. I once sought out a highly recommended Chinese restaurant, just for a change, and was bitterly disappointed. Instead, try those Italian places which offer alternative dishes. For example steaks are best at Tuscan restaurants, such as **La Fontanella** (86, Largo Fontanella Borghese; tel: 678 3849) . . . visited by the Kennedys and **Nino's** (11, Via Borgognona; tel: 679 5676). The latter is also good for a Roman speciality, *Giovedi Gnocchi,* small dumplings in a rich sauce, served only on Thursday.

It is to the eternal credit of the Romans that Messrs McDonald and Wimpy have so far proved unable to establish a foothold in the city, the reason for this being, in addition to the respect with which Italians hold proper cooking, the existence of hundreds of stand-up snack bars, which apart from slices of pizza, often serve a very passable hamburger.

You can also get quick and cheap meals at cafés. The **Café de Paris** and **Babington's** are among the most famous but I prefer the more down-to-earth **Pantheon.** Homesick Americans might prefer **The Cowboy** (68, Via Francesco Crispi), while even Italians in a hurry flock to places like the **Piccadilly** (Via Barberini) or the **Alemagna Tea Room** (Via del Corso) for a wide selection of pastas and delicatessen snacks.

Somewhere on these pages I had to use the words 'When in Rome . . .' Well, if the Romans do enjoy a weekend trip to a countryside restaurant, you might wish to do the same. The canal-port of Fiumicino (by the airport) has several commendable seafood restaurants, as do the seaside towns of Ostia and Fregene. A short train ride to the unspoilt wine-producing town of Frascati is also a great escape from the tourists and traffic.

Finally, ignore at your peril the ice cream at either the **Gelateria Tre Scalini** (Piazza Navona) or at the **Piazza San Calisto** (Trastevere). After the joy of a *Gelato Tartufo* I know of only one other experience so sensual on a sunny afternoon.

# NIGHT LIFE

Twice I walked up the Via Veneto at night and not once was I molested by a *paparazzo* or lured into a seething den of iniquity. No sign of Clint Eastwood or Sophia Loren either. So what happened to *La Dolce Vita,* celebrated by Fellini and envied by the more austere Northern Europeans in the post-war era?

All gone, or just resting?

Rome, it has to be said, does not pulsate with night life. The posturing of the promenaders is still there, but nowadays more around the Piazza del Popolo than on the Via Veneto. And around the Via Condotti and the Spanish Steps there is a cast of thousands, all dimly lit by Rome's quite appalling street lighting.

But the real stars of the night remain the buildings and the open spaces; the Trevi Fountain in its spotlit glory, St Peter's, the Piazza Navona, and the Capitoline Hill. With such magnificence all around, it is tempting to ask, who needs anything more to heighten the senses?

Of course man cannot live on past glories alone, and in Rome it is also true that man can barely get intoxicated without a huge expense account.

*"I know of no other city in the world where liquor is so cheap in the shops and so expensive in the bars,"* said one visiting businessman, and he should know, he sells gin. A general comparison is that for one measure of spirits in a medium to high class bar you could buy a whole bottle in the corner shop.

Tax was one explanation for prices like L.10,000 for a gin and tonic in **Harry's Bar** and L.5,000 for a beer at the **Sheraton** (though the same small bottle at a snack bar costs only L.1,500). Someone else told me it was just greed.

*The Coliseum is among the ancient monuments floodlit by night*

One resident of Rome explained it thus. The average Roman is not a heavy spirits drinker. A night out for him is more likely to be spent in a drawn out dinner, starting at around 9 p.m. and finishing in the small hours. Thus wine comes before whisky, and is often followed by a *digestif,* either Sambuca or Fernet Branca, the latter of which tastes appalling but settles the stomach.

Those Romans who do mingle and pose in café society are, however, likely to be seen at either the **Canova** (Piazza del Popolo), which offers a choice between chrome and velvet bars, a pavement terrace or a traditional courtyard, or, in the same piazza, the **Rosati.**

The former working class district Trastevere has also lured the chic Roman away from the Via Veneto. In the Piazza Santa Maria, opposite Sabatini's, are more basic but lively cafés: the **Bar di Marzio** and the **Galeassi.**

I found the liveliest atmosphere around the Via Condotti, where you can window shop, eye the passing Italian youths as they eye the passing young tourists around the Spanish Steps, and pop in and out of a mixture of bars.

The **Antico Café Greco** (86, Via Condotti) is one of Rome's oldest bars – favoured apparently by D'Annunzio and Goethe among others – where the decor is pleasantly dated and the prices are very reasonable. At 55, Via Condotti is the **Baretto,** a tiny bar favoured by glamorous Romans but best during the day. Above all there is in this area and Trastevere a chance to get away from those rich tourists, and journalists like myself, who congregate around the Via Veneto in the hope of bumping into one of the stars of the Italian Screen.

Not that you should avoid the Via Veneto completely. You can even get a guide who will lead you past the Café de Paris, Harry's or the Doney, showing you where Richard Burton and Elizabeth Taylor used to meet, where King Farouk of Egypt used to idle away his exile and where Sinatra had a bust up with Ava Gardner. Appropriately, the street is overlooked by the American Embassy.

Of Rome's surprisingly few night clubs, the current place to be seen is apparently **Bella Blu** (21, Via Luigi Luciana) in the residential Parioli district. This was set up by Marina Lante della Rovere, a count's wife whose autobiography was a sensational and racy account of the real *Dolce Vita.* Film stars and Roman aristocrats gather at the club, and if your dress and face fits you too can enter to watch them at play.

A few doors away (at 52 Via Luigi Luciani) is **Much More,** somewhat noisier and younger-at-heart. Also out of the centre is the **Pergola** which in midweek can be extremely dull but is convenient after a meal or if you are staying at the Hilton.

Back to the Via Veneto district is **Jackie O'** (11, Via Boncompagni), one of the clubs set up by Beatrice Jannozzi, the woman who has supposedly brought *La Dolce Vita* into the 80s, filling her bars with Hollywood stars and international playboys. Jackie O' is apparently less selective than it used to be and I would not recommend eating there.

For less glitter but more refined music, try **Club 84** (84 Via Emilia) or the excellent **Mississippi Jazz Club** (16, Borgo Angelico).

Don't expect to find a red light district. With the Vatican breathing down the city's neck, and a clause in the Concordat (the agreement between the Pope and the Italian parliament) which seeks to preserve the sacred nature of the city, Rome is conservative. The only floorshow worth noting is at **Paradise** (97, Via Mario de'Fiori), where some top names perform and there is also a disco and restaurant. Your first drink, if you are not dining, will cost you about L.25,000, going down to a mere L.18,000 for the second.

But the best view I had at night was from the piano bar at the **Fontana Hotel** (96, Piazza di Trevi), set in a converted 13th century monastery and overlooking the spectacular Trevi Fountain. Now there is really beauty in the buff.

# GETTING AROUND

The Rome traffic really is a revelation, even in the small hours. Traffic lights and road markings are barely acknowledged, while the narrowest streets are often congested with tiny battered Fiats and motorbikes. On my last visit the arrival of the Queen of the Netherlands almost brought the centre to a complete standstill.

And at night when the city is plunged into almost Dickensian gloom – apart from the beautifully illuminated fountains and ruins – it becomes impossible to read the quaint marble-inscribed street names, with their SPQR headings.

*Despite Rome's reputation for traffic chaos and crazy drivers, getting around is no worse than anywhere else*

I would not therefore advise anyone to hire a car. One businessman I met who was offered a vehicle took an hour to find a parking space and missed his appointment. There is a plan to pedestrianise the centre, though even this may be difficult to implement since existing pedestrian only signs are widely ignored anyway.

But however chaotic Rome traffic may seem, the drivers are in fact superb, exploiting every gap and space with enviable accuracy. I still cannot believe that I have never seen an accident in Rome, however small.

Taxis are good and on par with London prices. Drivers sometimes add extras for any conceivable excuse (especially on trips to the airport), though I never paid more than L.17,000 for a cross-town trip. Beware however of bogus yellow taxis, without a sign on the roof. *"Oh, it must have fallen off,"* one cowboy reportedly said.

A small underground system helps. It took 22 years to build and the escalators must be the slowest in the world. I also find the bus system cheap and easy to use. Each ride costs L.400 with a ticket bought in advance.

# Seoul

**As unlikely host of the 1988 Olympic Games, Seoul is busy shedding its role as the emotional home of the Cold War and donning the guise of a modern business capital. Whether this change of identity succeeds in the long run remains to be seen.**

**By Karen Zagor**

The tit-for-tat boycotts of the Olympics in 1980, when the Americans boycotted the Russian event, and in 1984, when the Russians did the same to Los Angeles, are now firmly lodged in the pages of history, filed under *"the messy inconsistency of contemporary sporting politics"*. The 1988 Olympics provide an opportunity for both nations to participate, but the enormous irony of the location is impossible to ignore; for whatever South Korea has become in the intervening years, it will always be seen as the emotional heart of the Cold War.

The political import of the 1988 Olympics should not be underestimated. Since the killing of 11 Israeli athletes at the Munich Olympics in 1972, the games have shown a disturbing tendency to mirror the stage of world politics. And the Montreal Olympics were such a financial fiasco that only two countries were willing to bid for the '88 Games: South Korea and pre-Khomeini Iran. At the end of the Los Angeles Olympics, the president of the International Olympic Committee, Spain's Juan Antonio Samaranch admitted that another boycott or similar disaster in 1988 could be critical, throwing the entire Olympic movement into question.

Beyond the obvious Cold War associations, Seoul is an odd choice of venue for many reasons. South Korea has no diplomatic relations with the Soviet Union, nor with China. Its relationship with its bordering Northern namesake is quirky and tense (visitors find little comfort in the local custom of describing Seoul as *"five minutes by bomber from the North")* and its government is generally regarded as repressive, right wing and under the thumb of the United States. South Korea would hardly seem the ideal spot for a reconciliation between East and West, nor for that stability so crucial to the 1988 Games.

But the South Korean attitude towards the Games, officially at least, is happily oblivious to the greater political issues. Sensitive questions are answered by referring to the philosophic nature of the Games. According to an official South Korean document, *"To build a peaceful world, a primary goal of the Olympic Movement, is the unwavering and historic desire of the Korean people. With this lofty goal in mind, we adopted 'Harmony and Progress' as the motto for the 1988 Olympic Games."* It would seem cruel to remind them that the original Olympics, spanning 1,169 years, came to an end in AD 393 because of corruption, commercialism and political poisoning; which reached a peak when Nero himself, not hitherto renowned for his athletic prowess, participated in the Games, winning each event he entered.

Yet there is also cause for hope of success for the 1988 Olympics. In 1983 it seemed that relations between North and South Korea could never improve, after Pyongyang took responsibility for a bomb in Burma which killed five members of the South Korean cabinet. Only one year later, however, the South accepted aid from the North when a flood devastated the country. Since then there has been a cautious but positive dialogue between North and South. Already discussions to form a joint North/South Korean team for the Olympics with the North hosting some winter events have progressed beyond anyone's wildest dreams. Even if nothing comes of these talks, their very existence is encouraging. So, too, is the series of arranged meetings between families separated by the North/South divide.

The Olympics, then, may be a God given opportunity for reconciliation, both on the national and international circus. But whatever the Games do or don't achieve, the business traveller to Seoul in these pre-Olympic years should have nothing but thankfulness for the powers that chose Seoul as the site for the 1988 Olympics. English-speakers are proliferating at a remarkable rate, concrete sky-scraping eyesores are being transformed by excellent landscaping. Seoul has caught Olympics fever, using the Games as an excuse for phenomenal civic improvement. And each improvement makes the city a better place to do business in; Seoul is swiftly changing from an unappealing destination to a rather pleasant one.

It used to be that foreigners returned from Seoul with the impression of dust, more dust and air pollution. South Korea is a highly industrialised country, and its industries mainly burn fossil fuels. Hardly surprising, then, that Seoul's air had the highest sulphur dioxide content of any major city in the world, according to a World Health Organisation report in 1978. Furthermore, the Han river was described as being incomparably worse than the Hudson River in New York by Professor Kwon Sook Pyo, the director of the Institute for Environmental Research at Yonsei University. Efforts are now being made to clean the air and river before the all-important Games, and the added irritation of dust should settle when the frenzy of building, above and under ground, subsides as the Olympics' facilities are completed.

But the greatest promise of improvement lies in the new underground railway. The existence of this railway was crucial to the success of Seoul's bid for the Olympics in 1981. Accordingly, Seoul has spent more than half its annual income since 1979 on the railway to ensure its completion in time. The economic planning ahead is typical of Seoul's attitude to the Games. It is the reason that most of the newly built facilities, such as the 100,000 seat stadium and Olympic Village, will be completed in time for a trial run at the 1986 Asian Games, unlike the 1976 Montreal Olympics, where the stadium was not completed until the very last minute. This forward planning is also the reason Seoul can hope to make a profit from the Games, where Montreal made a loss of US$ 1 billion. Revenue will come from television rights, sponsorships, ticket sales and a lottery. The lottery went into effect in 1983, incorporated into South Korea's already well-established housing lottery, with the profits being split 6:4 in favour of the Olympic committee. In the first year the lottery raised US$10 million for the games, and it is expected to raise US$40 million by 1988.

This pragmatism is a national characteristic, cultivated by centuries of Confucianism – whose values dominated the country for 600 years, until the Japanese invasion at the start of this century. The traditions of Confucianism are most apparent in business, where respect for age, seniority and authority is automatic, and rank and the family unit are all important. South Korean businesses, even the family-owned conglomerates, the *chaebols,* practise an enlightened nepotism. It is possible to rise through merit alone, but family connection is highly respected. Thus Chung Ju Yung of Hyundai and Lee Byung Chullof Samsung have prepared their sons to take top positions in their companies. There are, of course, problems inherent in this system: for example, it is claimed that the financial collapse of the Kukje Group was partly the result of complex family rivalries, which over-rode the good of the company.

Confucianism is also behind the formality in Korean business dealings. Foreigners are forgiven lapses in customs; but try to remember to use both hands when handing anything to a South Korean

*Parliament building*

businessman. In business dealings, remember that a person's rank is more important than getting the correct full name. The Korea Guide, distributed by the Seoul Tourist Board, sums this up aptly: *"When one calls on the home and wishes to speak to the wife of Vice President Chung, you would not refer to her by name but would ask for the mother of the son of Vice President Chung. Hence the importance of having a son in the family because now the wife has a position."* Hence, too, the relative unimportance of the woman's position in South Korean society, another hold-over from the Confucian years.

Industry has benefitted from the Confucian emphasis on education – which has produced an educated and rigorously disciplined workforce. Conversely, widespread education has sown the seeds of social discontent, creating higher expectations than can be presently fulfilled. Student demonstrations such as the occupation of the US Information Service library building in Seoul, have become the annual norm, with demands for a more equitable distribution of wealth and rapid institution of reforms. These demonstrations are treated with surprising indulgence. *"After all, they are all our children"* is an oft-heard refrain. And children are all important in the Confucian family.

Recently there has been widespread talk of political reform; and the government has fostered this with the promise of 'democratic' elections at the end of 1987, when President Chun Doo Hwan has said he will step down. Again, the impetus is said to be the forthcoming Olympics.

All in all, South Korea has made a remarkable recovery from the devastation of the Korean War of 1950-1953. In the years since the War, the South has become a model of the possibilities for Third World countries, with its burgeoning electronics, chemical and steel industries. One can only hope, then, that in its political and economic sectors, and in the hosting of the Olympics, it will find that balance between Yin and Yang, chaos and order, the symbol on the national flag.

## WHERE TO STAY

Seoul's hotel rooms are multiplying so quickly it's hard to keep pace: 661 rooms were added in 1984, and another 10,000 are expected by 1987, making a total of over 33,000. This will still be insufficient to cope with the Olympic hordes (it is hoped that the surplus of some 16,000 people will be absorbed into private homes and Korean inns – *yokwan*) but it should more than cover the business traveller's needs.

At one time the **Lotte** hotel (1 Sogong Dong, Chung-Ku; tel: 77 110; telex: 23533) was the only hotel in Seoul to rank as world-class. The abundance of shops and leisure facilities (including indoor running track and golf driving range) are enough to seduce an endless stream of visitors. The décor is delightful or gaudy, depending on your taste in white columns, gilt ceilings and mirrors; and the rooms are plush and comfortable. Single and double 88,000 – 141,000 won; suites 176,000 – 1,056,000 won.

Standards at the Lotte have in no way declined, but it has been joined in quality by several other hotels, thanks to the aforementioned bullish travel trade. The **Chosun** (87 Sokong Dong, Chung-Ku; tel: 77 105; telex: 24256) is linked to the Lotte by an enclosed square, complete with cafés. Known to locals as 'the foreigners' hotel' because of its popularity with visiting businessmen, the Chosun is the smallest of Seoul's three most central hotels. The rooms are large and comfortable and beautifully decked out for the business traveller, with telephones sitting at proper no-nonsense desks in each room. For some reason there are no less than 31 airline offices in the hotel – I'm not sure what this signifies. There is also an outdoor swimming pool, but alas no health club at present. Single 79,000-101,000 won; double 88,000-110,000 won; suites 242,000-704,000 won.

The third centre-city hotel is the **Plaza** (23, 2-KA Taypyung-Ro, Chung-Ku; tel: 77 122; telex: 2615), which sits on the main square, opposite the town hall. Although the Plaza has no health club, there is a health centre close at hand, and the hotel's excellent business services (including telex, extensive secretarial and translation facilities) more than compensate for this oversight. Single 78,000-92,000 won; double 92,000-132,000 won.

Seoul's other major hotels are all a good 15-minute taxi ride from the city centre, but the quiet of the Namsan Park area more than compensates for the drive. The recently opened **Hilton** (395, 5-KA Nadaemun-Ro, Chung-Ku; tel: 753 7788 or 753 3788; telex: 26695) was the site of the 1985 IMF-World Bank meeting. Its extensive conference and banquet facilities can cope with vast numbers, and there are all the usual features of Hilton hotels, including a health club and indoor pool. The Hilton sits on the city-side corner of Namsan Park, near the railway station. In preparation for the IMF meeting, the area surrounding the hotel (which was less than beautiful) was bulldozed and landscaped, and is now one of the more agreeable parts of Seoul. Single 66,000-92,000 won; double 79,000-111,000 won; suites 176,000-888,000 won.

The **Hyatt** (747-7 Hannam-Dong, Yongsan-Ku; tel: 798 0061/9; telex 24136 or 24537) is most enjoyable during Seoul's summer, when the hotel's two outdoor swimming pools, tennis courts and extensive gardens can be enjoyed. The rooms are being completely overhauled in time for the coming Olympics, which should add to the Hyatt's charms. Single and double 95,000-114,000 won; suites 167,000-678,000 won.

Equally lovely is the **Shilla** hotel (2 GA Jangchung-Dong, 100-202 Chung-Ku; tel: 233 3131; telex: 24160) set in 23 acres of landscaped gardens. The Shilla seems to have taken on the refined air of its neighbour, a former state guest house, which now houses the hotel's restaurant and banquet rooms. The Shilla's lobby is large and airy, though the rooms seem small in contrast. It is a favourite with visiting diplomats. Both the Shilla and the Hyatt run free shuttle buses into the town centre. Single 88,000-106,000 won; double 97,000-123,000 won; twin 106,000-141,000 won; suites 220,000-1,056,000 won.

Further into the park there is the **Sheraton Walker Hill** (San 21, Kwangjang-Dong; tel: 445 0121 or 445 0131; telex: 22228), named after an American general captured during the Korean War. The Walker Hill started life as an R&R base for GIs, and it is still a good place for recreation, being more resort than city hotel. The Walker Hill has all of the trappings of a resort hotel, as well as an extensive conference centre. But its location, a good half-hour from the city, makes it better for conventions than for a short business stay. Service is slick, but some of the star-spangled entertainment can be trying on a weak stomach. Single and double 88,000-97,000 won; suites 176,000 won.

However, for a taste of true decadence, I recommend the **Ambassador** (186-56 Changchung-Dong, 2-KA, Chung-Ku; tel: 261 1101; telex: 23269). The Ambassador has the full complement of international restaurants and business facilities. But the hotel's Finnish-style sauna, complete with jacuzzi, cold and mineral water pools, massage and barber's parlour, make the Ambassador a delight to return to at the end of the day. Rooms from 84,000 won.

In most hotels there is usually a 10 per cent

*Sheraton Walker Hill hotel*

service charge on room prices, though the custom of tipping on top of this has been dropped for the Olympics. Hotel prices are often quoted in US$. We have converted at a rate of 880 won to the dollar.

# WHERE TO EAT

Not long ago, Seoul had a reputation for some of the worst food in the world. The reputation was deserved; a general dearth of refrigeration coupled with poor sanitation did much to wreak havoc with the Western stomach, and Imodium or Arret were the only worthwhile condiments at a Korean meal.

Times have changed for the better. South Korea is learning to cater to the outside world; and while the results are rarely gourmet by international standards, they are perfectly adequate and enjoyable, and more important, they are largely safe for the foreign visitor.

Korean home cooking is fairly plain, but elaborate meals are usually served to visitors. The basic everyday meal consists of white rice, a meat or fish soup and *kimchi,* Korea's national dish. Kimchi consists of cabbage, radishes and other vegetables, pickled in brine with bright red hot peppers. This red pepper makes its appearance in many Korean dishes, especially the soups. Of the more elaborate dishes, *bulgogi* (beef ribs marinated in soy sauce, sesame and various spices, cooked over a charcoal fire) and *shinsollo* (a casserole of vegetables, meat, fish and eggs cooked with pine and gingko nuts – a favourite with royalty in bygone years) are particularly popular.

A feast day foreigners may well want to miss is Bok Day. On this day, it is said, Korean families go on a picnic, accompanied by the family dog. Prior to the barbecue the dog is strangled, according to ancient custom. It is then cooked on an open fire and served as the main course. But the government is trying to eliminate dog and snake from the capital's diet in preparation for Olympic visitors.

More savoury meals can be had in the city. The highest quality cuisine is served at the more cosmopolitan hotels. The Chosun's **Ninth Gate Restaurant** (tel: 77 105) has basked in its fine reputation for many years. The menu changes daily, and the food is universally good. The wine list comes particularly highly rated. In the same class are **Hugo's** at the Hyatt (tel: 795 0061), the **Prince Eugene** at the Lotte (tel: 77 110) and the **Celadon** at the Sheraton Walker Hill (tel: 444 8211).

The Hilton's **Seasons** (tel: 753 7788) has quickly risen to the top of the hotel restaurant list. The restaurant serves primarily French cuisine. My *boeuf bourguignon* was mouth-wateringly good, but the menu changes frequently so it is difficult to make recommendations. The buffets at the Hilton's other restaurant are varied and good.

The **Golden Dragon** restaurant at the Sheraton Walker Hill (tel: 444 8211) is a Chinese restaurant worth travelling for. Other good bets are the Italian restaurants at the Hotel Lotte, though by Milanese standards the food is a bit on the bland side.

For a break in a steady diet of hotel fare, the **Moghul** (Chung-Dong, near the Korea Exhibition Centre; tel: 541 1257) serves good, authentically spicy Indian cuisine. It's a fair way from the city centre, but the mutton buffet at the weekend is worth an excursion.

Another favourite is the **Chalet Swiss** (tel: 792 1723). For some reason Swiss food comes into its own in Third World countries. There are the expected array of fondue dishes, but the restaurant seems to have access to high quality cuts of meat (usually the preserves of the international hotels). The Chalet's proximity to the cluster of embassies makes it particularly crowded at lunchtime.

The **Nam Mun** in Sam Chung-Dong (tel: 722 3423) is a favourite with Korean food aficionados, though it is somewhat off the beaten tourist track. The menu is usually set, but it is possible to arrange a special menu in advance. Reservations are crucial for both lunch and dinner.

The **Dae Yun Gak** in Sam Chung-Dong (tel: 778 2377) is a favourite with the resident expat community. The setting alone is a meal in itself. Set in many acres of lush parkland are numerous small bungalows, where the meal is brought and cooked. Not surprisingly, the Dae Yun Gak is a haunt of courting couples; but it is also appropriate for a confidential business meal.

For a joint Japanese-Korean meal try the **Ban Po Hae Gwan** (tel: 593 6895) not far from the Palace Hotel. Japanese food is served in the basement, Korean on the first floor, and a mixture of both can be arranged in the private dining room in the basement. The food is excellent and reasonably priced, but the staff is not known for its linguistic ability.

While most hotels stock a good cellar of foreign wines, domestic wine is the staple outside hotel walls. Visitors should note that Korean reds are virtually unpalatable; white wines are better, but not by much.

# NIGHT LIFE

Old Korea hands with a penchant for the less savoury things in life bewail the passing of Seoul's curfew. In the good old days, or so they say, the price of a woman was inversely proportional to the hour of night: the later and closer to curfew the lower the price.

But curfew ended in 1982, and it is generally agreed that things aren't what they used to be. Many would say that's no great tragedy. Still, a country which housed Japanese invading forces for well on 30 years, and has catered to the US military since then, is bound to have ample entertainment for the world weary; and the demise of curfew has done nothing to lessen the ranks of women in need of 'taxi money'.

No story of Korean nights would be complete without the *kisaeng* – the Korean equivalent of the Japanese *geisha* girl. The *kisaeng* tradition covers many centuries, and is steeped in local folklore: stories of battles won and emperors tamed because of the intelligence, charm and beauty of the *kisaeng*. The *kisaeng's* role is to soothe and entertain – and in general one shouldn't expect more than that from a *kisaeng* house. Seoul's best known *kisaeng* house is **Samcheong-gak** (tel: 762 0151), where décor and dress are traditional, but the number of visitors (up to 100 at a time) makes it somewhat impersonal. Unfortunately, local connections are necessary for the most authentic of *kisaeng-jip*.

A more modern version of the *kisaeng* can be found at the **Tiger House,** otherwise known as **Tiger Kang and Her Cubs** (tel: 752 7706) opposite the Chosun hotel. Traditional entertainment in the form of food, drink and female company is provided here, but for a pre-arranged price the women there are willing to do more than talk.

Seoul's equivalent of Bangkok's Patpong is in Itaewon. The most usual Itaewon final destination is the **US Sportsmen's Club,** which tends to cater to the international crowd during the week, but is largely the preserve of US servicemen at the weekend. Its popularity is due, in part, to the exceptionally low price of its beer.

Further upmarket are **All That Jazz** and the **Jazz Messenger.** The music at both these clubs is less raucous than at the Sportsmen's Club; but neither establishment could be said to play a single bar of jazz.

**Sam's Place** and the **Grand 'Ole Opry** on the other hand, are country and western bars which actually provide music of the same. Of the other establishments that cluster along the Itaewon strip and surrounding side-streets, suffice it to say that the area is known locally as the MSR (Military Supply Route), with good reason.

Locals, however, tend to take their entertainment in Myongdong or Yongdong. Yongdong is

*Have a flutter at the Walker Hill*

being touted as 'a new city' within Seoul, and is particularly popular. The steady stream of tourists in the next few years for the International Monetary Fund-World Bank conference, the Asian Games and the Olympics should do much to bolster Seoul's nightlife.

But, as in most Asian cities, the international hotels are unlikely to be ousted from their position of prominence in the night-time entertainment. The Sheraton Walker Hill resort is said to have the best nightclub in the city.

# GETTING AROUND

The monolithic size of Seoul often takes the unsuspecting newcomer by surprise. The fact that Seoul is one of the most densely populated cities in the world – rivalling Hong Kong in that respect – is little known to Westerners. And though the business district is a compact area in the city centre, negotiating the city at large can be bewildering at first. A fact not helped by the manic speed with which all South Koreans seem to drive.

Normal taxis are metered, and relatively inexpensive (around 600 won for the first kilometre, and 40 won for each 500 metres thereafter), but they tend to be unkempt and uncomfortable and extraordinarily difficult to hail downtown. Covered taxi stands are liberally scattered around the city, and make welcome havens from Seoul's more rugged weather; but pandemonium breaks loose if more than one person needs a cab. The 'call taxis' are larger and better cared for – pessimists say they offer a better chance of survival in the event of a crash. They cost around twice as much as regular taxis, and can be found circling the larger hotels. Business travellers are advised to trust the *kae-in* taxi drivers, whose yellow shirts and jackets are adorned with safe-driving badges.

Most of Seoul's population rides the buses – a fact which is all too apparent to anyone seeking a seat. The buses hurtle along at breakneck speed, and are worth avoiding both as a passenger and a pedestrian.

But the underground is Seoul's pride and joy. At time of going to press the first stage of the underground has been completed, and the entire network should be running by 1987. With all the money, time and care that has been poured into the system, Seoul's underground should be a pleasure to ride.

Car hire has also benefitted from the bullish tourist market. Hertz has recently opened an office in Seoul, and there is also an Avis licensee: Korea Rent-a-Car. Check at the Hotel Lotte (tel: 752 1851) for details.

Transportation from the airport is also progressing apace. Taxis take around 25 minutes to reach the city centre, and cost around 5,500 won. A sign outside the arrivals hall gives the correct fare to the major hotels. But the queue for taxis can be appalling, and at night it is even worse. There is, however, an airport bus (#601) which runs to downtown hotels. It costs 500 won, an appealing price, but unfortunately there is no luggage compartment on the bus, so the ride is less than comfortable.

When planning a trip to Seoul, try to avoid flights with morning arrivals. Seoul is prone to heavy fog which sits on the airport year-round, and it is all too usual for flights arriving before 10 a.m. to be diverted to Pusan.

# Singapore

**Much of the Oriental mystique and charm has been rationalised out of free-market Singapore. But Singaporeans are proud of their thrusting business capital where the skyscrapers rise amid restful, crime-free and tree-lined boulevards.**
**By Nick Hanna**

Singapore rates as one of the success stories among Asia's new industrial nations. It seems to work: a thoroughly-planned, efficient, clean and apparently prosperous society where the only blemish appears to be a largely demolished culture.

Prosperity has come at a price, though, as Singaporeans are quick to concede. A decade of meteroic growth has seen offices, shopping centres and hotels going up at a frantic rate and the older buildings disappearing like dust. In fact, according to residents, it is not at all unusual to see the ball and chain at work one day, then, two months later, the same plot grassed over and ready for sale.

It appears to have taken the dwindling of the tourist dollar to make the city stage wake up to the fact that its invaluable cultural heritage was being decimated by the bulldozer. Tourists expecting to find Asia were instead confronted by a typically Western city, only cleaner. Their numbers declined (although they're now creeping back up again) but the concensus remains that without its super-abundance of tropical greenery, Singapore would exist merely as one dense concrete and glass shopping mall.

This is where a Special Task Force in Tourism comes in. As their report notes: *"As a result of our modernisation programme, we have removed aspects of our Oriental mystique and charm which are best symbolised in old buildings, traditional activities and roadside activities such as the pasar malam (night markets)."* On the question of culture it's worth noting that Singapore is still a comparatively young nation (founded by Stamford Raffles around 165 years ago), and philistine though I may be I would rather be walking down one of Singapore's restful, crime-free, tree-lined boulevards than through the noisy, traffic-clogged, polluted and often squalid streets of some other Asian capitals, culture or no.

Nonetheless, Singaporeans are proud of their professional symphony orchestra, and point out that you can still come across authentic Chinese street opera in the old districts.

In 1985 the government embarked on an ambitious restoration programme for 'vernacular' architecture. The lynchpin of this is the Emerald Hill project, right in the centre of the tourist enclave of Orchard Road, where a whole street is restored with its original 30s façades. The showpiece of the project is the Peranakan Museum devoted to the culture of the Straits Chinese.

The critics, predictably, say too little, too late. To this Mrs Pamela Lee, Divisional Director of Development for the Singapore Tourist Promotion Board, replies: "*Name one Chinatown in the world that is of equal size and significance to Singapore's. Look at Vancouver, San Francisco, London's Soho – do you think these are real Chinatowns? Ours is never going to be as good as it could have been if we'd started earlier, but what is there is sufficient in scale and dimension to make good.*"

The Emerald Hill project is a pilot for the complete restoration of Chinatown itself but the problems are enormous; houses in old Chinatown weren't built to last and many are falling down. And then there is the question of who is going to live there: young Singaporeans now established in the new housing estates are unlikely to want to return to the cramped conditions endured by the older generation.

But Joseph Kong, Deputy Director of the Singapore Tourist Promotion Board, suggests that the government has clearly signalled its intentions: "*The preservation of Chinatown is now very high on our list of priorities.*" He says that it could well become the prototype for other preservation schemes which might take place in Little India and the Malay Kampong settlements.

The STPB is also pinning its hopes on a major feature film about Singapore which is intended to glamorise it as a tourist destination in the same way that *The World of Suzie Wong* and *Love Is A Many Splendoured Thing* projected a romantic image of Hong Kong in the late 50s.

Will this idea of making a feature film have the desired effect? Mr Kong believes that "*the launch of Hong Kong's tourist industry was helped enormously by these two films. A good film will contribute substantially to the public awareness of Singapore and it's a very cost effective means of publicity for us.*"

Steps are also being taken to jettison the myths that the city state's hotel rooms are expensive and that the physical dimensions of the place limit its attractions to those of a stopover destination. But it remains quite true that Singapore's attractions are not on the grand scale: rather they tend to be dispersed all over the city. High on the list are the sights, sounds and smells of Chinatown, Serangoon Road ('Little India') and Arab Street, or visits to the Bukit Timah Nature Reserve and the Jurong Bird Park.

And if you're only going to see one thing it should be the Haw Par Jade Collection in the National Museum. The remarkable scope and diversity of this collection has earned it the distinction of being one of the best-known in Asia, if not the world. There are 385 pieces (although not all on display at once) ranging from three-coloured Burmese jade to Chinese jade and beautifully-sculptured pieces in jasper and aventurine.

Singapore's urban landscapes may not have the architectural merits of LA or Houston, but they certainly put them up quickly – and it sometimes shows. As one local architect explained, there is so much building going on that young architects are being given the opportunity to work on major projects soon after qualifying, whereas anywhere else they would need to wait years to take on that much responsibility. It was, he said, an exciting place to be. However, because of problems associated with the new buildings, the government has imposed a quota on construction companies to make them employ more labourers from Hong Kong in an effort to improve the quality of workmanship.

Apart from the new skyscrapers in the business district, the main focus of development is around Marina Bay; it's here that the massive Raffles City development, comprising the 73-storey Westin Stamford hotel, the 28-storey Westin Plaza hotel, and a 42-storey office block, is being constructed.

When it is completed the Westin Stamford will be the tallest hotel in the world and – together with the Plaza – will completely dominate the sky above Raffles' once-secluded French Renaissance Palm Court, which seems a shame.

*Skyscrapers are springing up all over Singapore's business district*

Another multi-million dollar hotel and shopping development, the Marina Centre, is taking shape on reclaimed land in the same vicinity. Its cornerstones, three de-luxe hotels, the Marina Mandarin (640 rooms), the Pan Pacific (850 rooms) and the Oriental (527 rooms) all feature roof-high atria.

It's interesting to note that although Singapore is held up as a shining example of free market capitalism, in fact the government sector accounts for upwards of 40 per cent of the economy. Government policy is to roll one massive project on after another; for instance, the labour force which was employed on the construction of public housing is now being absorbed by the Mass Rapid Transit (MRT) project. On two of the city's main axes there are huge building sites every quarter of a mile or so as construction of stations for this enormous MRT project – the government's biggest ever investment – progresses.

The State reaches into every aspect of people's lives and the government's heavy-handed attitudes and Confucian paternalism tend to stifle spontaneity, creativity and individuality, as Singaporeans themselves are the first to admit.

No doubt there's a rational explanation for it, since Prime Minister Lee Kuan Yew's policies are nothing if not rational – like, for instance, making every citizen undergo an annual medical check-up known as the IPPT, or Individual Physical Proficiency Test, in the interests of a healthy nation. No problem, you might think – except that if you fail the IPPT you have to go to an army camp for a week to get fit again.

In response to charges of being out of touch with the electorate, the government has established a Feedback Unit to involve people more in the policy-making process; whether this will meet the expectations of a younger generation looking for a more liberal atmosphere remains to be seen.

Following the talks on Hong Kong's future, the Singapore government set about building an enormous number of expensive condominiums to house an expected influx of Hong Kong Chinese. That influx hasn't occurred. Indeed, quite the reverse, since Singapore may now find itself with a diminished role in the region as Hong Kong undergoes a boom in tourism, financial services, transportation and trade, thanks to its position at the back door of the largest market in the world.

But Singapore still hopes that the financial community will move in its direction in the mid 1990s as confidence in Hong Kong diminishes prior to the 1997 handover. At present, Singapore businesses are among the leading investors in China itself, having pumped over S$900 million in the last five years into joint ventures or partnerships in hotels, warehouses, light industries and oil-based servicing projects.

One of the main stumbling blocks in terms of Singapore taking over from Hong Kong as a leading financial centre, however, is the high rate of corporate tax (40 per cent compared to Hong Kong's 15 per cent). But resident businessmen still claim that it's a great place to do business; you can move money in and out with no restrictions, there's very little government red tape, the public service really is a public service, and they work hard on your behalf.

Another advantage is that if you're thinking of setting up and staying for any length of time then bargain rates can be negotiated on accommodation and office space (as with hotel rates). The cost of living, however, has otherwise become very high for visitors and locals alike.

Growth areas in the Singaporean economy include shipping (it ranks as the world's second busiest port), financial services, construction, and insurance. An asset which it will never lose is its strategic location. In addition, Singapore's offshore sector caters to the financial needs of neighbouring countries such as Thailand, Malaysia, and Indonesia. Although the latter would rather not have to rely on the city state's services, they find they can't do without them because Singapore is always several steps ahead. Now, for instance, they lead the region in providing computer expertise.

By the standards of Silicon Valley, much of Singapore's manufacturing industry is still low to medium tech, but the government's intention is to move towards the higher value end of the semiconductor industry, and they take great pains to stress Singapore's positive moves in this direction. A US$40m investment by telecomms giant AT&T, for example, got bigger headlines on the front pages of the national dailies than it did in the *Business Times* – which is not unusual, since it's government policy to make the public more 'business-aware', as indeed they are.

The availability of cheaper components and a good infrastructure have recently prompted companies such as SGS Semiconductors, Nixdorf, General Motors, and Silicon Systems, amongst others, to step up their investment in integrated circuit manufacturing in Singapore. The island's semi-conductor industries produce around five per cent of the worldwide total output worldwide $57 billion.

Another breakthrough was the recent production of Singapore's first chips designed by local engineers. However, moves into more volatile sectors such as electronics and financial services mean that the government is less confident about predicting future trends.

# WHERE TO STAY

So many new luxury hotels or extensions to existing hotels have recently opened in Singapore that it's likely to remain a buyer's market for years to come.

What's more, another 11 new hotels, representing a further 4,463 rooms, are due to come on stream by mid-86 and that's not even including the giant Raffles City and Marina Square developments, between them accounting for a further 4,070 rooms.

Although the major hotels claim occupancy rates in the high 70s, a more reliable figure would be around 60-65 per cent, so discounting is widespread. Indeed, hotel brochures put out by the Singapore Tourist Promotion Board's overseas offices in some cases already have '40 per cent discount' stickers on them, so the message should be clear to everyone by now. (Prices quoted here are the official rates only.)

Older hotels are having to upgrade their facilities to compete with so many new hotels. The Mandarin recently completed a S$4m renovation programme, the Ming Court has been refurbished, all the rooms at the Goodwood have been completely renovated, and even Raffles has had to start improving previously somewhat tatty facilities.

One of Singapore's best is still the peerless **Shangri-La** (22 Orange Grove Road; tel: 737 3644; telex: 21505). Situated just beyond the top end of Orchard Road, the Shangri-La is set in several acres of tropical park, offering something of a retreat from city life. It is equipped with a health centre, a biggish pool, tennis and squash courts, a 24-hour business centre and comprehensive conference facilities. Standard single-double (main block) S$180/S$215; S$300 respectively for pool-view rooms in the Garden Wing.

On the opposite side of Orchard Road, near the various food and handicraft-orientated attractions surrounding the Tourist Board's offices in Tanglin Road, are the **Marco Polo** (247 Tanglin Road; tel: 474 7141; telex 21476), the **Pavilion Inter-Continental** (1 Cuscaden Road; tel: 733 888; telex 37248) and the **Boulevard** (40 Cuscaden Road; tel: 737 2911; telex 21771), previously the Hotel Malaysia.

Surrounded by four acres of tropical greenery – amongst which a Japanese garden is to be found – the Marco Polo is considered to be one of the best, and has a reputation for particularly welcoming and personalised service. Spacious rooms, big working desks, moveable phones and a well-run business centre are other aspects of the Marco Polo designed to attract the business traveller. Standard single/double from S$180/S$210; executive suites S$380-420.

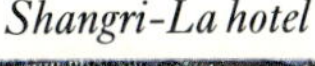

*Shangri-La hotel*

In the stakes for the most prestigious lobby the Pavilion Inter-Continental is currently streets ahead, although no doubt it won't remain so for long. Their enormous John Portman-designed atrium, with four glass elevators in the middle and chrysanthemums and other tropical plants draped over several storeys, is designed to impress even the most hardened critic of the 'You've-seen-one-atrium-you've-seen-them-all' school of thought.

There is a branch of Maxim's in the hotel, as well as all the usual business and health facilities for winding yourself up on one hand and winding down on the other. Standard single/double S$180/S$220; executive suites from S$500.

The nearby Boulevard, which is the revamped Hotel Malaysia with a new wing and second pool added, has caught atrium-itis too, although not on quite such a grand scale. Business class rooms, which cost from S$230-260, overlook the new pool. Standard rooms cost from S$155 for singles, S$185 for doubles.

The **Ming Court,** again in Tanglin Road, (tel: 737 4411; telex 21528), has undergone a facelift but still retains traditional black lacquered Chinese furniture in the rooms and a Ming Warrior to scare off over-rapacious taxi drivers at the front entrance. At lobby-level, the Jade Lounge, which features a crooner at the piano every night, has been recently redecorated in handsome green and gold tones, and re-landscaping around the pool has prettied up the garden area. Standard single/double from S$175/S$175 rising to S$230-S$255 in the Business class Taipan Club floor.

Further down Orchard Road is the 435-room **Hilton** (581 Orchard Road; tel: 737 2233; telex 21491), which charges S$160 for singles, S$185 for doubles. The Hilton has an Executive Business Centre with full secretarial services and a reference library, as well as 12 Givenchy-designed executive suites (prices from S$450) which feature personal butler service and whirlpool baths.

Clustered around the junction of Scotts Road and Orchard Road are the Royal Holiday Inn, the Hyatt Regency, and the Dynasty.

The **Royal Holiday Inn** (25 Scotts Road; tel: 737 7966; telex 21818), with its somewhat incongruous Austrian-style decor, charges from S$157 for singles, S$177 for doubles, or S$225 and S$255 for executive suites.

Over the road at the **Hyatt Regency** (10 Scotts Road; tel: 733 1188; telex 24415), singles cost S$190, doubles S$220, or S$290 and S$320 respectively in the 320 rooms which comprise the recently-completed Regency Terrace, which has the added bonus of an attractively-landscaped pool area, tennis and squash facilities and what is said to be the most extensive fitness club in Singapore.

No one could possibly mistake **The Dynasty** (320 Orchard Road; tel: 734 9900; telex 36633) for any other hotel, not only because of its grandiose, Imperial Chinese-inspired lobby, but also thanks to the fact that it must be the world's only pagoda-shaped skyscraper. Facilities include a 600-seat ballroom, Chinese gardens, and one of the very few pavement cafés in Singapore (the Café Boulevard at the Ming Court is another). Standard single/double: from S$190/S$220; executive suites from S$500.

A totally different atmosphere prevails at the **Goodwood Park** (22 Scotts Road; tel: 737 7411; telex 24377). The Goodwood has a rich, colourful history, having been built for use as a German social club, occupied by the Japanese during the First World War, used as a war crimes court after the war, and even being converted to an electricity sub-station at one point during its lifetime.

The Goodwood's 235-rooms have recently been refurbished to unusually high standards using restful, pastel fabrics and beechwood furniture, and there are two swimming pools to choose from. Singles from S$245, doubles from S$275. For curiosity's sake you might like to know that to experience the ultimate in opulence and stay in the Goodwood's Brunei Suite will cost you S$3,000, or just over £1,000 per night.

Another of Singapore's more famous hotels, the **Mandarin** (333 Orchard Road; tel: 737 4411; telex 21528), located right in the middle of Orchard Road, has also recently completed a renovation programme, with the lifts, telephones and swimming pool all having been revamped.

Until the Westin Stamford arrived the Mandarin, with 1,200 rooms, was Singapore's largest hotel, and offers the full range of services that you would expect from a hotel of this size, including banqueting and conference facilities, numerous restaurants (including the 'Top of the M' revolving restaurant on the 38th floor), fully-equipped health club, and a more than efficient Executive Services centre. Standard single/double from S$180; executive suites S$250; senior executive suites S$320-350. Reservations also through HRI in London on 01-583 3050.

Perhaps Singapore's most celebrated hotel is **Raffles** (3 Beach Road; tel: 337 8041; telex 21586), which has been coasting along contentedly on its worldwide literary reputation since a resurgence of interest in the history of the hotel during the 1960s.

In 1981 it was declared a historical landmark, and it was decided to build an extension behind the original hotel, although this idea has now had to be shelved because of the current surplus of hotel rooms in the city. Instead, Raffles has concentrated on upgrading existing facilities for their 1986 100th anniversary celebrations. Standard single/double S$150/S$170; superior Palm Court rooms S$180-S$200.

One of the smartest of Singapore's latest batch of luxury hotels is the **New Otani** (177A River Valley Road; tel: 338 3333; telex 20299), located on the banks of the Singapore River overlooking Chinatown. Although only a couple of minutes away from the central business district; it's not particularly convenient for the tourist area around Orchard Road, and in a city where prestigious lobbies are *de rigueur,* the New Otani suffers from the drawback of a lobby on the seventh floor which has to be reached via lifts. Taxi drivers tend to be somewhat bewildered by its location and the lack of any visible lobby.

However, all this is made up for by the exceptionally high standard of the rooms, which have immaculate marble bathrooms, tea and coffee making facilites, and, thank goodness, balconies – which is a real luxury after some of Singapore's enclosed rooms. Superior rooms single/double S$190/S$210; deluxe S$210/S$230; executive suites S$450.

Another new hotel is the 354-room **Furama Singapore** (1 Fu Tong Sen Street; tel: 533 3888; telex: RS 28592), also conveniently close to the business district, although for some odd reason the entrance seems to have been put at the back of the building. Superior single/double from S$150/S$170.

But the focus of attention in Singapore's hotel business is now increasingly being directed away from Orchard Road to Marina Bay, located midway between the business and shopping districts.

Singapore's hoteliers have survived (just) the first wave of staff movements caused by the opening of new hotels in the last year or so, but over the next few years visitors may well find themselves experiencing deteriorating standards of service and the closure of facilities due to lack of staff.

*Raffles hotel*

24-hour coffee shops may become a thing of the past – already the Marco Polo has closed its La Pinata café between 1a.m. and 6a.m. Room service will most likely end at midnight. Valet car-parking, in-house laundry and elevator staff will disappear in many hotels.

Singapore's hoteliers face tough times until the end of the decade; the good times are definitely over.

# WHERE TO EAT

In Singapore you may find yourself not so much eating out as eating in, since some of the best restaurants are to be found in hotels. However, despite the fact that Singapore has managed to destroy its cultural heritage, this hasn't, luckily, had any effect on its culinary skills, which are of a high standard.

An enormous variety of specialised cuisines are available, including Malay, Javanese, Sumatran, several regional Chinese styles, Indian, Japanese, Thai, Korean, and Vietnamese amongst the Oriental cuisines, plus a smattering of European restaurants and an ever-increasing number of American fast food outlets.

The bewildering array of Chinese food avail ble in Singapore includes provincial cooking from Szechwan, Hokkein, Canton, Shanghai, Swatow, Teochew, and Beijing; of these Cantonese and Szechwan are the two most popular with Singaporeans.

One of the more authentic Szechwan restaurants in Singapore is the **Min Jian** at the Goodwood Park Hotel (tel: 737 5337). Szechwan cuisine combines contrasting hot, sweet and sour flavours in such dishes as sautéed prawns with dried red chilli, or long-standing favourites like the delectable camphor and tea-smoked duck with five-spice sauce.

Unlike many Chinese restaurants, which seem to seat about a thousand people, the Min Jiang is at least on a human scale; the silk paintings, lanterns and classic but restrained red, gold and jade decor contribute to the atmosphere of understated sophistication. The cost per head is around S$40-50 excluding drinks.

Trends towards healthier eating aren't solely confined to Occidental chefs: the Shangri-La Hotel's **Shang Palace Restaurant** (tel: 373 7644) recently acquired one of Singapore's best chefs, Mr Peter Tsang, who specialises in what might be called *nouvelle* Guangdong food, which uses more steaming and less frying than normal.

Hallmarks of Peter Tsang's style are less use of oil and carbohydrates, low salt and no monosodium glutamate. Some of his creations include Phoenix Jade Roll (braised sliced chicken and broccoli roll), braised bamboo pith stuffed with mixed vegetables and hot sweetened water chestnuts with cream. Meals at the re-vamped Shang Palace are likely to be expensive, but you're paying for what Singapore's top food writer, Violet Oon, describes as *"very fine quality cooking with the touch of an artist"*.

Still on the health theme, the **Royal Holiday Inn** (tel: 737 7966) recently introduced a Gourmet Health Menu which features foods low in calories, sodium, fat and cholesterol.

At the opposite end of the scale traditional French provincial cooking can be found at **Chez Bidou** in the Ming Court Hotel (tel: 737 1133) where, apart from the food, the main attraction of the restaurant is Monsieur Bidou himself, who emerges from the kitchen wearing his chef's hat to sing ("*C'est si bon, Chez Bidou, Chez Bidou*") to a piano and accordion accompaniment. Good entertainment value.

No round-up of restaurants would be complete without mentioning the **Harbour Grill** at the Hilton (tel: 737 2233), where what they like to call *cuisine en évolution* is served efficiently and imaginatively.

For a change of style, though, north Indian food is the speciality of the **Maharini** (tel: 235 8840) in the Far East Plaza, and in a new branch at the Boulevard Hotel, renamed the **Mayarani** (tel: 732 6179). The quality of the food is more or less the same in both branches, although the atmosphere and service at the new Mayarani seem to be distinctly lacking. Around S$70 for two. Other recommended north Indian restaurants include the **Omar Khayyam** (tel: 336 1505) and the **Moti Mahal** (tel: 221 4338).

For sheer ambience and novelty value it would be hard to beat **Trader Vic's** (tel: 338 3333) at the New Otani, where, in an atmosphere which can only be described as expense-account South Pacific, you can try starters such as Trader Vic's titbits (fried shrimps, spare ribs, crab rangoon and sliced pork), and main courses which include curries, Chinese seafoods and house specialities such as bamboo tahitian chicken of chippewa steak with wild rice.

Trader Vic's isn't cheap (around S$100 for two excluding drink) but then their Gin Slings are a considerable improvement over those served at Raffles, where demand is such that they now mix them in a giant urn without, apparently, remembering to put equivalent quantities of gin in. Afternoon tea in the **Tiffin Room** at Raffles is likewise a big disappointment (although the room itself is worth going to have a look at).

To find out where Singaporeans eat when they want a cheap night out and to make a change from all those air-conditioned restaurants, visit one of the open air food markets known as hawker centres.

Instructions clearly spelt out in English to explain to the first-timer that you may sit at any table without obligation and order dishes from any of the dozens of surrounding stalls as you wish; one of the most popular hawker centres for visitors is the **Rasa Singapura,** located behind the Tourist Board's offices on Tanglin Road.

Hawker centres are particularly good for *satay,* the Malay national dish which consists of marinated chicken, mutton or beef, roasted or skewered and served with a spicy peanut sauce. They also provide a wide choice of both Indian and Chinese food.

# NIGHT LIFE

"Nightlife? What nightlife?" is the most common reaction on asking ex-pats what goes on in Singapore in the evenings. But it isn't that nothing happens so much as what's happening isn't particularly visible. Some of the better nightclubs, for instance, are hidden away on the third or fourth floors of shopping centres, so you wouldn't necessarily find them unless you knew where to look.

Most of the big hotels have either private clubs or discos, or both. Two of the best are **My Place** at the Boulevard and **The Library** at the Mandarin. But if you're looking for a pick-up then the low-life **Rasa Sayang** bar at the Tropicana (Scotts Road) or the slightly more salubrious **Copacabana Disco** in Orchard Towers will cater for the needs of those on a moderate budget (S$100-150 per night).

Contrary to popular opinon, Singapore is not altogether sinless, and as well as a plethora of escort agencies found in and around the shopping centres (S$100 an evening, triple wages for overtime), there are any number of seedy institutions lurking down back alleys, amongst them well-organised Chinese brothels, hostess bars, and the like.

Singapore's infamous transvestite population is no longer to be found in Bugis Street which once featured some of the most devastatingly attractive boys in Asia – and they now tend to be in a different place every month, until the police get too interested.

More celibate and cerebral entertainment can be found here too, of course – relaxing over a few beers at the cosy **Bistro Toulouse-Lautrec,** for instance, listening to some of the best jazz musicians in town as well as visiting virtuosi. The Toulouse-Lautrec is on the fourth floor of the Tanglin Road shopping centre, there's no cover charge, and beers cost S$7.

*Dynasty hotel*

Live contemporary music and visiting rock bands can be found in the currently trendy **Rainbow Room,** behind the Ming Court.

If you can bear the thought of 'Instant Asia' shows then the Mandarin, the Hyatt and Raffles all stage them; the Mandarin every night except Monday, the Hyatt on Tuesdays and Fridays, and Raffles nightly. The Mandarin also operates the **Neptune Theatre-Restaurant** on Collyer Quay which serves Chinese food to the accompaniment of Koreans slaughtering Malay songs, Taiwanese murdering Chinese opera, and the young Singaporeans doing their version of *Flashdance.* Ask for a table near the back unless you are stone deaf – the Chinese like their music LOUD.

Perhaps the most chic nightclub in town is the **Top Ten,** which opened recently in Orchard Towers, having been converted at a cost of some S$2m from what used to be a cinema. A classy joint if ever I saw one, and admission costs (S$15 on weekdays, S$25 at weekends) aren't that high.

But even the Top Ten has to be reached by walking up escalators which have long since been shut down for the evening and past rows of shuttered-up shops. Perhaps it's all a ploy to make people think there's no nightlife in Singapore.

# GETTING AROUND

The Singapore government rarely makes mistakes – or admits to them – but one it did make recently was to increase the price of diesel fuel by 600 per cent and the price of cab fares by 50-150 per cent. Results: commuters deserted taxis in droves and business was so bad that the government, in an unprecedented move, reversed its policy within just four days and approved a 20 per cent cut in fares.

From the taxi drivers' point of view the damage had already been done: the newspapers devoted numerous column inches to the plight of drivers falling behind on repayments and having their cabs repossessed.

For the visitor, and Singaporeans who can afford the new fares, it means there's no longer any problem whatsoever finding a cab. Since the price hike, one businessman told me, he had found himself arriving 20 minutes early for all his appointments, as there are no longer queues at cab ranks.

All the government controlled NTUC Comfort cabs, which account for 7,000 of Singapore's 11,600 cabs, display a 20 per cent discount sticker on the front windscreen. Taxis at hotel ranks don't give the discount, although any cab hailed in the street or from a normal cab rank should do so. Short to medium journeys around town are still good value by international standards at around S$3-6 per journey.

Singapore taxi drivers, like their counterparts all over the world, will try it on if they think you don't know the ropes. Once I complained that the fare was too high and the driver pulled out his chart again to find the right price in the discount column, this time using a torch to help him read it better. All very plausible, except for the fact that it was broad daylight.

There is one place where you will emphatically not get 20 per cent off, and that's on journeys into town from the airport (the discount is still applicable for the journey out).

It's easy to see why: one evening I counted 450 taxis waiting along the 3km of airport approach road, and a further 150 waiting outside the terminal itself. Although it seems incredible that over 600 taxis should wait in line for up to four hours to get a fare, it dramatically illustrates the predicament facing the cabbies.

There is, anyway, little choice in the matter since the only alternative is a bus service which is by no means ideal. The buses are non-air-conditioned, not as frequent as they could be, and stop often, taking up to 45 minutes to get to the town centre.

The air-conditioned bus service which used to run into town in half an hour has been 'indefinitely suspended', presumably to make people use taxis and the MRT is not due to reach the airport for years.

Around town there is a comprehensive bus network, but there's little point in trying to master the routes when taxis are still comparatively cheap.

In an effort to cut down on pollution and private car use the government introduced surcharges for people wishing to drive into the Central Business District during peak hours (a system which has been so successful it is now being copied by Bangkok and Jakarta), and so taxi rides into the CBD between 7.30 and 10.15 a.m. and out again between 4 and 7p.m. will cost extra.

Should you need to drive yourself around Singapore, there are few problems. Car hire rates are reasonable, traffic is well behaved, and roads are clearly signposted in English.

## SHOPPING

«Why aren't you out shopping?*" one Singaporean asked every time she rang me at the hotel, adding: "*Go out and buy something, we need visitors to do more shopping.*" Unfortunately the only items I found worth buying were bootleg cassettes on TDK tape, and although I bought several dozen of those I don't think it's quite what my friend had in mind.

It's not that there isn't plenty to buy in Singapore, it's just that what's available doesn't necessarily represent a bargain anymore. You can get everything you want – but at a price. Singapore is now more expensive than either Bangkok or HongKong, largely because of the high cost of shop rentals, which are passed on to the consumer.

However, with the opening of new shopping centres (particularly Raffles City and Marina Square, which will double existing capacity by 1990) rental costs will come down, as they have already started to do, and prices should tumble rapidly. Then Singapore will be not only a pleasant but also a competitive place to go shopping.

One of the ideas suggested by the tourism task force is to motivate shop staff more by giving them commission on sales, as happens in Hong Kong, where shoppers are continuously harassed to buy.

Most of the big shopping centres are in Orchard Road. A Tourist Board leaflet, *Ivory and Incense,* explains where else in town you can find ethnic Oriental artefacts such as Chinese quartz eggs, hand-tooled Indian leatherwork, Muslim basketware, Nonya jewellery, and so on.

Department stores have fixed prices but elsewhere bargaining is the order of the day. Although most Westerners find bargaining a pain in the neck (which it often is), a good way to go about it is to make up as many outrageous reasons for paying as low a price as you can; the entertainment you thereby provide will often work to your profit.

# Sydney

**With the Pacific Basin now earmarked by economists internationally as the focal point of 21st century development, Australia's premier city is poised for great things. For the moment though it is a relatively unspoiled city that is just the right size and possesses just the right balance of development and preservation.**

**By Carol Weingott**

Sydneysiders appear happy with their lot: prosperous looking homes, cars, catamarans, wives. Their city confirms the conceit, or perhaps spawns it – the gifts of sun and harbour being perfected by the strategical implant of Bridge and Opera House.

But as Londoners are not English, Sydneysiders are not Australian. They are Italian, Eastern European and Asian. And the volume of the take-away trade in rice cakes and dim sums attests to the Asian influence. But, according to one resident of Sydney's considerable Asian community, it is not quite like this. *"Australians don't have many original ideas. Overseas people think we're slobs – we follow English fashions and American technology."*

Still, the Lucky Country appears to be on a winning streak, 25,000 millionaires (at the last count) can't be wrong and a not uncommon weekly paypacket of $380 goes a long way to suggesting a country rich in resources and brimming with the good things in life for those fortunate enough to live there. It is indeed a country where first generation fortunes are being accumulated by taxi drivers and milkmen. Or in the words of one senior airline executive: *"It is the last optimistic country left on earth where mobility between streams is easier than anywhere else."*

It is also an adventurous New World country with strong native opinions: *"Australia sort of eats itself, we're quite isolated."* Shades of the dingo, the baby and Ayers Rock. It is a country on a surfboard wearing a sweatshirt proclaiming "GO for it Australia." It is a country where everybody got very cross indeed with Rupert Murdoch when he renounced his citizenship in order to become an American and acquire six television stations.

Melbourne, of course, is nowhere: *"It is a town prone to avoiding a challenge."* Sydney, on the other hand, is *"The Society Capital of the Southern Hemisphere."* It is the home of landmark suburbs like Kings Cross, *"the most exciting square mile in Australia,"* and with 80,000 residents, the most densely populated. And Bondi? *"A sort of Kings Cross on the wave-strewn golden sands with joggers in the a.m., tits at midday and drugs at night."* And Manly: *"Oh that boring extremity."*

It is a city of parochial suburbanites; aspect is very important in Sydney, you see. And nowhere are people more parochial than in the wealthy Eastern suburbs especially Double Bay (double pay) which gets the best of the sunshine, the less ferocious morning sun, and prime harbour views. And there's Rose Bay and big yachts and small yachts, and Watson's Bay with Doyle's, Australia's most celebrated seafood restaurant, where business visitors will invariably be taken for lunch. The great grandparents built a hut on the beach in the early 1800s and sold fish from it. Sitting virtually on the beach (with its own wharf and taxi ferry from Circular Quay) 180 years on, eating superior fish and chips and drinking champagne, makes for pleasant memories indeed.

Eastern Bay Yuppies, like an increasing number of Australians, prefer to drink wine. From being the 10th biggest drinking nation in 1975, Australia is this year predicted to fall to 18th: the bellyfulls of middies are losing rapid ground. So are the beer guts that used to protrude over the male Sydneysider's 'uniform' of walk shorts and long socks or that other uniform of stubbies, thongs and zinc on the nose.

The Double Bay Yuppies are in any case more likely to want to sip vitamin cocktails before teeing off at the Royal Sydney Golf Club (a five-year waiting list, $800 annual membership and written rules stipulating no Jewish members). Visitors will be pleased to hear they can play golf all over Sydney at many public courses for as little as $3.50 for 18 holes.

The other thing about Yuppies – a notion which has just hit Sydney – is that they are big car spenders, brash and extroverted ones. *"They buy an exciting two-door coupé listed at $93,489 for their own use and a four-door saloon at $76,829 for the missus,"* said an Eastern Bay dealer. *"And if they're after a Rolls, they've got to add the price of a uniformed driver. This is a must."*

The real reason behind Sydney's more civilised drinking habits, however, uniformed drivers and general wealth aside, was the introduction of random breath testing in 1982. The restaurants say they're feeling it.

The good life of the Eastern Bay is mirrored on the other side of the harbour – in the south where the *nouveau riche* started building their own paradises in the 1950s and 60s. The North Shore is the home of decent family life while the west suffers from *"that strong and nasty afternoon sun and unattractive housing."* Wherever you are though, the waterfront is the thing – $5 or $6 million for a piece

*Sydney landmarks: the Harbour, Bridge and Opera House*

of it at Hunter's Hill. Nearly waterfront, a four bedroom, three bathroom job at Vaucluse or Point Piper goes for a 'song' at $750,000. Or there are the new Quay apartments where the two-storey penthouses have mezzanine sitting rooms with 8.5 metre tall windows framing the Harbour, the Bridge, and the Opera House – the three wise men and the best public relations structures known to man.

The quality of the 'inner life' of this New Country which hasn't had time to indulge in introspection (thus being forgivably brash, speaking too loudly) is reflected in its meagre graffiti: *"Real punks can't spell cappochino"*. Does this bespeak of cultural misery and facile middle class insularity? Is this an unspeakably retarded continent or an island? Is this the place that so decimated 250,000 black Australians by the 1920s that today you simply won't see them? But you may hear them. Listen for the Aboriginal desert band Coloured Stones or the Warumpis (mixed West Coast sounds, reggae and pop) or No Fixed Address. Or go to the Opera House, you must anyway, and try to catch the Sydney Dance Company at work.

Which takes us back to the Harbour, to the 'coathanger' as Sydneysiders curiously refer to the Bridge, to the eerie Lady Lunar of the park, her face always white, ghostly, a moonstone grimacing above the shark-laden waters. The Harbour is the sort of place that's high on imagination, just like the cannabis and heroin importers/exporters of whose stock 8.6 tonnes of cannabis and 209 kilograms of heroin was seized on the waterfront between April 1981 and April 1984. Police believe such quantities are too great for the local market: the speculation is that NSW is a transhipment point.

Crossites (as they like to be known) say the drug problem is relatively recent. *"In the past there were always a few drunks about but now there are zombies. You get bashings and puddles of blood."* The garbage is the other problem.

The Kings Cross Chamber of Commerce wants the City Council to designate the Cross an Official Tourist Zone – to arrange for garbage removal at weekends when the area is at its busiest.

Even more telling of the infancy of Sydney's infrastructure for coping with visitors is the fact that its first currency exchange facility (a Thomas Cook outlet near the Hyatt in Kings Cross), aside from banks was apologetic on its first day of business in May 1985, explaining an hour and a half after opening that: *"We're still waiting for the van to come from the West."*

*"When do you expect it?"*

*"Oh, it's on its way, it depends on the traffic."*

# WHERE TO STAY

With financially optimistic Sydney intent on doubling its number of hotel rooms by the end of the 80s, not to mention the rapid growth and popularity of serviced apartments, business travellers can expect to be spoilt for choice. That the hotels are bound to wage an unholy battle to maintain what in 1985 were only marginally healthy occupancy levels, at *"just over 70 per cent"*, goes without saying. And whatever becomes of mid-winter discounts, known to run as low as 50 per cent, is anyone's guess.

What can safely be said though, is that the market is facing an unprecedented shakedown. During the past few years the city's older, more established hotels have been preparing for it with a bout of lavish facelifting: $9.5 million at the downtown Hilton International; $9.3 million at the Sheraton-Wentworth; $8.6 million at the Holiday Inn Menzies; $7 million at the Hyatt Kingsgate and $6 million at the Boulevard.

A large percentage of the funds has gone on pampering business travellers. Teleconferencing facilities, for example, are now provided by the Hilton, the Sheraton-Wentworth, the Inter-Continental and the Hyatt Kingsgate, while the Hilton and Sheraton-Wentworth also have Newscan, a 24-hour news service flashing up on your television screen direct from the AAP newsroom. All in all, a far cry from the situation a decade ago when visiting executives had to scan the likes of the *Sydney Morning Herald's* classified ads for a part-time secretary.

The wooing of the business traveller began in earnest as a counter-measure to the expected impact of the 620-room Regent's arrival early in 1983 and that of the Inter-Continental two years later. And with a 600-room Nikko Hotel (owned by Japan Air Lines) due on line in 1988, the wooing can only be expected to continue.

Sydney has proved big enough for its luxury hotels to market themselves effectively as being in specific locations; the business district, the night-life zone, the shopping heartland and, of course, the beach. Anyone with business on the North Shore would be understandably attracted to the **Manly Pacific** (North Steyne, Manly; tel: 977 7666; telex: AA73097), as would anyone from the frozen wastes of the Northern Hemisphere during summer: it is, as it proudly bills itself, *"Sydney's only international hotel on the beach"*. It is a modern property with a number of restaurants and bars and plenty of healthful diversions including: a heated, roof-top swimming pool, a spa and health club and facilities for golf, tennis and the ubiquitous bowls. The six-mile crossing from Manly to the business district on Circular Quay shouldn't put anyone off – ferries cross frequently taking a scenic half hour to do so while the hydrofoil takes just 15 minutes. Single $85-$98; double $98; suites $130-$200.

The 'traditional' business hotels are the Sheraton-Wentworth, the Menzies and the Hilton. The **Sheraton-Wentworth** (Phillip Street; tel: 230 0700; telex: AA21227) enjoys a reputation as a classic hotel with some of the city's finest conference facilities. Since the Sheraton group took it over from Qantas in 1982 they have gone to considerable lengths to upgrade all facilities while maintaining a formal, but never intimidating, air. The hotel is well-geared to the needs of the business traveller, efficient, discreet and above all, quiet: this is a particularly solidly-built hotel where there is no risk of intruding noise – but there's no pool. Single $100-$125; double $110-$135; suite $180-$230.

The **Holiday Inn Menzies** (Carrington Street; tel: 20 232; telex: AA20443), rates as Sydney's most senior luxury hotel. It is said that each time a new hotel comes on the market the Menzies appears to fall out of favour but, according to management, the regulars always return. Before Holiday Inn took up management, what the regulars returned to was undoubtedly Sydney's most traditional atmosphere: a hotel all dressed up in dark wood, red leather chesterfields and crystal. What happens under new management, for whom the Menzies represents a second step into Australia (the group has a management agreement on a Surfers Paradise hotel), depends on how the $14 million earmarked for further upgrading is spent. The 441-room hotel has six restaurants and an astonishing 17 bars. Single $77-$89; double $87-$99; suite $180-$400.

Hilton International have two properties, with the **Airport Hilton** (Levy Street, Arncliffe; tel: 579 0122; telex: AA70795) having room to spread itself about. Keen sportsmen may well prefer it for its swimming pool, squash and tennis courts, jogging parkland and the 18-hole golf course across the road. A complimentary shuttle bus runs into town every 20 minutes. Single $79-$81; double $92-$106. The downtown **Hilton** (Pitt Street; tel: 266 0610; telex: AA25208), on the other hand, is convenient for shopping; department stores, shopping arcades etc. are literally just steps away as the hotel is sited atop offices and shops. The 36th floor has been given over to an Executive Club: 14 guest rooms, a 12-seat board room and a private lounge and library. The Hilton has an arrangement with a fitness centre on the 18th floor, its own outdoor pool and a Juliana's nightclub. Single $110; double $125; suite on request.

The **Inter-Continental** (Macquarie Street; tel: 230 0200; telex: AA176890) artfully incorporates one of Sydney's most historic landmarks, the three-storey, colonial-style Treasury Building, into its public areas and conference and banqueting facilities. With its usual, faultless style, Inter-Continental offers two restaurants, two bars, a cocktail lounge, a swimming pool and health club. Many rooms have superb views of the Opera House and the nearby Botanical Gardens. Single $100-$125; double $160-$190; suite $250-$300.

Equidistant between the business district and Kings Cross lies the **Boulevard** (William Street; tel: 357 2277; telex: AA24350), a subsidiary of the Southern Pacific Hotel Corporation which owns the large Travelodge chain. Rooms have gained a much needed new lease of life from extensive renovations and rate as very pleasant indeed, some with fine views of the domain, others of the harbour. Special features include an in-house sauna and an Eastern-style bath house. The hotel does a lot of business with nearby companies based in Alexandria and Waterloo. Single $98; double $104; suite prices on request.

Visitors determined to soak up all they can of the Kings Cross flavour will no doubt head for one of the trio of hotels in the immediate vicinity. The most visually imposing of these is the **Hyatt Kingsgate** (Kings Cross; tel: 357 2233; telex AA23114) which rises 33 floors to give sweeping views across the city. In its renovation programme Hyatt added an extra floor to its Regency Club, the

*Circular Quay is Sydney's business district*

'hotel within a hotel for business travellers' and installed a new business centre. Extensive use of marble, glass and chrome in the general refurbishment has lifted the hotel beyond its former 'racy' categorisation, though the passing parade of the Cross goes by just as saucily as ever. Beneath the hotel there's a 40-unit shopping complex incorporating a health and fitness centre. Single $97; double $103; suite $170-$190.

At the opposite end of the Cross lies the **Gazebo** (Elizabeth Bay Road; tel: 358 1999; telex: AA21569), favoured by the likes of airline crews. It has a swimming pool and all the usual amenities and comes a price cut below other hotels offering similar services. Single $75-$84; double $80-$90; suite $94-$280.

The most salubrious of the Cross Hotels is without doubt the small and select **Sebel Town House** (Elizabeth Bay Road; tel: 358 3244; telex: AA20677), a member of the Leading Hotels of the World. The guest list reads like a *Who's Who* of the entertainment industry with every leading light ever to have visited Sydney likely to have their name in the guest book. Service is extremely discreet and the message service exemplary, but business facilities are somewhat limited, though most requirements can be met 'by arrangement'. The sense of being in a private home has much to do with the fact that the 164 rooms and suites are distinctively detailed (traditional timber panelled walls and the like) and staff have been taught the value of leaving guests, celebrities or otherwise, in 'tranquil seclusion'. There is none of the usual fuss about *"just checking your mini bar"* at 7.30 a.m. Rooms at the back overlook the marina at Rushcutter's Bay where there are facilities for squash, tennis and jogging. Single $104-$120; de-luxe with dressing rooms $108-$124; suite $190-$550.

The **Regent** (George Street; tel: 238 000; telex: AA3023), in the Rocks area where the convicts first pitched tents, has won several awards for excellence in the accommodation stakes since it opened in 1983 and is a regular host to business and community leaders. Much is made of this hotel's spacious rooms and their generally very appealing views over the harbour and city. It is an enormous shame though, that balconies weren't included in the plans – also that the generous windows can't be opened. Such minor irritations aside, service is impeccable and commendably personalised with extras like the placing of an Australian wild flower on the pillow each evening, while a bottle of mineral water and a sachet of dried fruits find their way onto the bedside table. The business centre has an extensive reference library, well-stocked with journals such as the *Harvard*

*Business Review*, the *Financial Times* and the *Wall Street Journal.* Six restaurants and bars include the celebrated Don Burrows Supper Club. Single $125-$160; suite $225-$290.

Among the city's burgeoning crop of serviced apartments (available by the day, week or month) are the **Cliveden** (Bridge Street; tel: 235 1333; telex: AA27750), where studios are available from $40-$60 a night, and the **Hyde Park Plaza** (College Street; tel: 331 6933; telex: AA22450), with a selection of one and two-bedroom suites from $75-$110 a night. The Hyde Park Plaza has all the amenities of a hotel plus convenient extras like guests' laundromat, sundecks, spas and saunas and a variety of meeting and convention rooms.

In a not dissimilar vein, Sydney has scores of motels, the two largest concerns being Flag Inns consortium and Homestead. The latter is represented worldwide by Best Western. Such properties are not in the least seedy in the American sense and are available from upwards of $30 a night.

# WHERE TO EAT

The *Sydney Morning Herald's* food critic Leo Schofield has all rights to presenting *the* authoritative guide to Sydney's cuisine sewn up in his *Good Food Guide* ($8.95 and worth it). This deals with around 400 of the more than 2,000 places listed to eat in the Yellow Pages in an intelligent and discerning way. It also carries 12 maps locating all the main restaurants, from 'the best Thai tucker in town' and 'Moussaka at midnight' to 'Yumma yum cha'.

Australians like to eat out and they also like to eat Chinese, Vietnamese and Japanese, often married with Western seafood. Chinatown exemplifies this sort of cuisine, naturally enough, and positively leaps with *dim sum* eateries and roomy Cantonese cafés. A gentleman named Dominic Choy is responsible for the two reliably excellent **Choy** restaurants (Belmore Road, Randwick; tel: 399 6387) and **Choy's Inn** (Hay Street, Haymarket; tel: 211 3661). The Randwick establishment gives formal service (staff in black and white) in elegant pink and grey surroundings. The menu is largely of the predictable deep-fried and sweet and sour variety, but executed with care. A meal for two, with drinks extra, costs around $24, reservations are recommended. The Chinatown branch lists 25 dishes on a blackboard menu and is much less formal. It is also open later, 2a.m. Fridays and Saturdays as against 11p.m. at the Randwick branch. For authentic Malay satays, the **Satay Stick** (Goulburn Street; tel: 211 5556), does nicely, but for grander fare try the **Malaya** (George Street, City; tel: 211 4659; and Mount Street, North Sydney; tel: 924 306). This restaurant has been serving sambals and laksas for 21 years at its city branch and certainly knows what to do with the *ah sam* fish. As with the majority of Sydney's restaurants, the Malaya's hours aren't conducive to late-night dining, 11.45 a.m.–3 p.m. and 4.45–10 p.m.

According to the experts though, quite simply the finest Chinese restaurant in Sydney is the **Imperial Peking Harbourside** (Circular Quay West, the Rocks; tel: 277 073) whose success can be rated by the fact that despite having seating for 400, booking is essential. Here you can delight in shallot cakes and mermaid's tresses in architect-turned-restaurateur Kenneth Lai's *"elegant, evocative and contemporary series of interiors"*. There are million dollar views of the Opera House, though two can dine for around $40 plus drinks. There are other branches – at the Hilton hotel (tel: 267 2555) and Double Bay (corner Knox and Bay Street; tel: 316 1057) with basically similar menus and reputedly outstanding Peking duck.

Traditional Australian food of the meat pie and sausage roll variety is still widely consumed despite the Asian palate invasion. Cakes and pastries, particularly doughnuts (pineapple), are also firmly established favourites. Cake shops, ice cream parlours and pastry saloons (if you please) exist on every corner though they may be disguised as milkbars and dairies. A 'café society' appears to be well-established to take in such establishments plus trendier, student places. The Bring Your Own (BYO) wine factor and absence of VAT (under review at the time of writing) undoubtedly figure in the popularity of such places. Among the most conspicuously popular are: **Hot Gossip** (Oxford Street; tel: 336 702) for home-cooked meals and fruit shakes, and **Café Deco** (Flinders Street, Taylor Square; tel: 357 5056) for cappuccinos.

Fast food has been refined to something of an art form by the likes of **Harry's Café de Wheels** (no phone, in a battered caravan) near the entrance to HM Naval Dockyards, Garden Island. Here such celebrities as Cilla Black and Des O'Connor have been known to spoon a mess of green peas beneath the lid of a good hot pie in the early a.m. Pies being to Sydney what submarine sandwiches are to New York, there are nonetheless hamburger chains, **Hungry Jacks** and **McDonalds,** plus pizza chains, **Ely's** and **Pizza Hut.** The hot dogs and waffles touch is provided by **Jilly's Roadside Diners** – red, white and blue caravans – and there's a Danish waffle bakery in Kings Cross. Sandwiches are sold everywhere, often with rather indifferent (marbled) brown bread, though **Big Al's Sandwich Joints** (at a bar in the MLC Centre and the American Express Tower) serve imaginatively-filled specimens which don't have this defect.

As one would expect, the seafood is generally excellent and easily available in Sydney with hundreds of little restaurants, fish and chip shops and stalls serving oysters, prawns and all manner of fish. At the top end of the scale are the establishments run by the Doyle family plus some 20 others deemed 'excellent' by Leo Schofield and his researchers. If you can't get into **Doyle's** (tel: 337 2007), the best bet is **Dory's** (Rose Bay; tel: 327 6561) which in fact used to be a Doyle's. Around $38 for two, plus drinks. Expect to pay $50 for two without wine at Doyle's.

Sydney's restaurateurs have woken up rather late to the fact that it is both desirable and possible to dine outdoors for much of the year. Star practitioners of the art are the gentlemen responsible for the Yellow Book in Marbella, one of Europe's most glamorous resort restaurants. They sold up and returned to Sydney to set up an equally starry establishment, also called **Yellow Book,** at Potts Point (tel: 358 6162). Upstairs is a Beardsleyesque black and yellow room where the specials include lambs' brains milanese with a sauce ciboulette and rolled lamb loin filled with prunes and walnuts. Around $50 for two, plus drinks. The outdoors and generally lighter eating goes on downstairs in the **Garden Café** at lunchtimes (and evenings) at around $28 for two plus drinks. **Eliza's** (Double Bay; tel: 323 656) has a very green courtyard and ritzy regulars including politicians at leisure.

The art of formal dining has long been held to be the province of the Berowa Waters Inn (Berowa Waters; tel: 456 1027), 40 kms from Sydney in a spectacular bushland setting. Schofield calls it *"the most inventive cooking to be done in Australia"* and a *"trailblazer"* in Sydney's restaurant development. Offal and shellfish are perennial favourites with the cuisine described as French-derived, delicate and often surprising in terms of combinations. Around

*Eliza's Restaurant*

$100 for two, wine extra, reservations essential.

Business lunches are big business with top of the line being **Simpson's** (Ash Street, City; tel: 232 4533) with a regular clientele of lawyers/brokers/bankers and, appropriately, politicians: the site used to be the Liberal Party headquarters. The food is imaginative French/Italian (broad spinach noodles with *"an intense meat gravy with pieces of duck and bone marrow"*). Around $50 for two, booking recommended.

Besides the few hallowed names already mentioned, there are a vast number of restaurants aspiring to present *haute cuisine* under the broad banner of brasseries. Exemplars of this art are the three Kiwis running the **Bayswater Brasserie** (Kings Cross; tel: 357 2749) in a row of converted terraces. In the noisy, tiled central area or the back garden you can sample imaginative cuisine like kingfish in orange sauce and quail with pickled baby aubergines. Service is said to be the friendliest in town. No bookings, around $28 for two, plus drinks. In the same category come restaurants offering Italian/pasta dishes among the best of which are: **Pulcinella** (Bayswater Road, Kings Cross; tel: 358 6530), **Mario's** (Stanley Street, East Sydney; tel: 331 4945) and **D'Arcy's** (Hargrave Street, Paddington; tel: 323 706).

The John Cadman Cruising Restaurant (Embarkation, New Beach Road, Darling Point; tel: 329 287) is a Sydney institution providing spectacular sights though not, according to Schofield, spectacular food. He advises diners to *"keep it simple – a plate of oysters and grilled fish"*. Booking two weeks ahead, fixed price $65 for two, plus drinks.

Anyone with the time and the money for a gastronomic weekend could do no better than travel the 120 kms from Sydney to the Blue Mountain Edwardian-style restaurant and guesthouse **Glenella** (Blackheath; tel: 047 878352). Anyone planning to stay the Saturday night will need to have made a reservation at least six months in advance – though mere diners won't, of course, be kept waiting that long. Glenella's food is described as *nouvelle* French along the lines of braised sweetbread with fennel entrées and stuffed fillets of flounder with shellfish mousseline and cream sauce. Around $60 for two, plus drinks. Accommodation, $45 double.

Finally, what to drink? Australia's classic reds – Penfold's Grange Hermitage and Lindeman's Rouge Homme – are available at the best of the licensed restaurants as are the famous whites – Houghton's White Burgundy and Tyrrell's Chardonnay Semillion, and a wide range of unknowns. Anyone seriously interested in getting to know the unknowns would be well-advised to take a course at Australia's recently-opened first full-time wine school (The Rocks; tel: 241 3230) where there are evening and weekend courses from $30.

# NIGHT LIFE

Cities that inveigle you to live into the night have simple, stardust-in-the-eyes techniques, like long-lit neons and a surfeit of restaurants and cabs. All the more so if they are being a nation's Big Smoke. Such a one is Sydney. The big bait of Kings Cross lures very well, drawing hundreds of gawping groups from the outback and inordinantly curious non-Antipodeans. It is all quite understandable – (the most densely populated square mile . . . etc) and of course it has all the neon and most of the cabs.

If the evidence of the growing drug problem (the pincushion business) and the weekend garbage doesn't bother you, and you've an eye for massage parlours, sex shops and beckoning, blemished women, then this is the place for you. If, on the other hand, you're simply after people, this is still the place for you. There aren't any other 'crowds'. But walk purposefully, especially if you're a woman, and avoid eye contact and all those other New Yorkesque routines. Anyone earnestly and safely seeking a 'good time' should refer to the list in the back of the official *Sydney Tourist Guide: "Reserve your companion, Asians and other nationalities too"*.

For Sydneysiders and lucky guests, nights are likely as not to revolve around barbecues and beach parties, the corks of native champagne bottles whizzing precariously close to the bared and half-bared, all-bronzed bodies that have spent the late evening bobbing about the harbour on all manner of boards and yachts. Sydneysiders are 'into recreation' with leisure being of such importance that terms like the City to Surf Run have evolved quite naturally to describe what happens when executives quit their offices at 4.30p.m. – having started the working day at 8.30a.m.

Open-air-minded visitors who don't get invited to barbecues and beach parties should find plenty of consolation in the range of other spectator sports: night trotts and greyhounds at Harold Park, racing at Rosehill or Randwick, bowls, basketball and indoor tennis at the **Sydney Entertainment Centre** (tel: 325 757), Aussie Rules, and motor racing at **Amaroo Park** (tel: 679 1121).

There is, too, Dame Edna's *"sport of the brain"*, as epitomised by the first-rate entertainment provided by Australian films. With the 'cultural cringe' of the 60s banished by a decade of government support for the arts in general, some sectors are positively thriving, namely music – jazz and rock. For jazz, the **Don Burrows Supper Club** at the Regent (tel: 238 0000), has the city's premier reputation to protect. Here, presided over by the King himself, you may catch the number one group, Galapagos Duck. Other jazz spots include: the **Basement** (Circular Quay; tel: 279 727), the more formal **Old Push Restaurant** (St George St; tel: 272 588), and the **Orient Hotel** (George and Argyle Streets; tel: 272 464). Plushest of the real jazz 'pubs' is the **Marble Bar,** a painstakingly-restored Victorian tavern carved out beneath the Hilton (tel: 266 0610 ext. 6085). The jazz starts around 7 p.m. weekdays and Saturday afternoons.

The most boisterous of the rock music is found at the **Manzil Room** (Springfield Ave, Kings Cross; tel: 358 3318) and the **Coogee Bay Hotel,** south of Bondi (tel: 665 000). Less proletarian is the red-plush-couched **Stranded** (Pitt Street; tel: 232 5170) which only *sometimes* has bands, and the **New York Tavern** (corner of York and Market; tel: 291 618) which definitely has bands (and a disco) Tuesday to Saturday.

The pub scene is generally pretty appalling – a large central bar with stools at it, tiled walls all around and a large piece of lino for standing. A distinctive legacy from the days of the 'six-o-clock swill' when rapid, urgent guzzling was all there was to it. Among the very few pleasant bars are the **Customs House Hotel** (Macquarie Place) frequented by City workers, and the **Lord Nelson Hotel** (Kent Street, the Rocks).

Places which could pass for cruisy 'singles' bars include: **Kinselas** (Bourke Street, Darlinghurst; tel: 331 2699), which used to be a funeral parlour and now also runs to a theatre restaurant with late night cabaret/comedy and fringe shows;

*Sydney bars are only for the extremely thirsty*

**Rogues** (Oxford Square, Darlinghurst; tel: 331 1523), a big international-style club for big spenders; and **Arthur's** (Victoria Street, Potts Point; tel: 358 5097) where new-wavey people and visiting pop celebrities go to sit decoratively in 50s-style laminex booths. The views over the city and Wolloomoolloo are good, so is the music.

Other fringe venues open and shut in converted warehouses all the time – for these check with the *Sydney Morning Herald* or *Stiletto,* the 'artsy' magazine. Big names sell out quickly and re-sell dearly: tickets for the 1985 Springsteen tour were changing hands at $75 – up from $25 – in no time at all. Much the same can be said of big shows at the **Opera House** (tel: 205 88). Where you are more likely to be able to get in without pre-booking is at the **Conservatory of Music** at the edge of the Botanical Gardens. This romantic edifice, formerly government stables, lists what's on outside: free lunchtime performances are not uncommon and you can hear quite clearly from the gardens. Mainstream theatre exists at **Her Majesty's** (tel: 231 3411), **Theatre Royal** (tel: 231 6111) and half a dozen others. The two respectable places to gamble are the **Empress Club** (Darlinghurst Road, Kings Cross; tel: 358 2197) – minimum stake $5, maximum $300 – mostly card games in luxurious surroundings and an à la carte restaurant till 6 a.m.; and the **Barclay Club** (Bayswater Road, Kings Cross; tel: 358 1992), from 3p.m. seven days.

# GETTING AROUND

The prospect of crossing such a sprawling city as Sydney (a distance of around 70 miles) would indeed be defeating were it not for the excellent public transport system which has evolved through necessity. Over a million Sydneysiders get to work on its trains, buses and ferries.

The downtown, miniature Underground covers the City stops of Wynyard, Town Hall, Museum, St. James, Circular Quay and Martin Place in a loop known as the City Circle. One-trip or Day Rover tickets can be purchased on the spot. The system is brisk and efficient, though somewhat scary, as it consists of noisy double-decker, stainless steel carriages. The broader Sydney Metropolitan Rail System links the City Circle to 180 urban and interurban stations, the intricacies of which are thoroughly explained in the weighty tome *Gregory's Sydney by Public Transport* – 180 pages with a decent map for $5.

There are both government and private buses, including the free bus (route 777) which runs a circular route around the inner city every 10 minutes, 9.30a.m. – 4p.m. weekdays. Buses are cheap (20 – 40 cents in the business district) and keep long hours. A trip to the far northern beaches takes half an hour.

The 6,000 non-polluting liquid gas taxis are generally easily available, changeover shift excepted, and cost 80 cents at flag-fall with 50 cents for each subsequent kilometre – add 60 cents for phone bookings. Inveterate taxi users should investigate various credit card schemes run by most of the city's 10 companies: two of the largest are Taxi Credit (tel: 922 3075) and Cab Charge (tel: 331 2124). The airport trip costs around $10 by taxi but by the public airport bus the fare is $2, by either means of transport the trip takes 30 to 40 minutes depending on traffic.

Car rental is a thriving business with a good selection of independent firms competing with the majors (Hertz, tel: 669 0066; Avis, tel: 430 488 and Budget, tel: 339 8888) who claim a 50 per cent share of the market. Among the independents likely sounding bets include: Pam's Rent A Car (tel: 358 7011) with Valiants/Holdens/Fords from $14 a day and Thrifty Rent-A-Car (tel: 357 4055) which provides non-smoking cars plus a booklet of sightseeing/restaurant and hotel discount vouchers at competitive rates. Details on all aspects of travel from the Travel Centre of NSW (Spring Street; tel: 231 444; telex: 22611).

The pleasantest way to get around Sydney though, is on its harbour. Ferries and hydrofoils depart regularly from Circular Quay to the harbour-side suburbs: to Manly 80 cents or $1.50 on the hydrofoil; Cremorne 60 cents; Taronga Park Zoo 60 cents. Those who want to sail themselves should investigate Waltons Hire Boats (tel: 969 6006) for yachts, cruisers, windsurfers and catamarans. A 17-foot yacht costs $15 an hour or $60 a day for five people with a 25-footer going for $110 a day for eight people. Booking is a minimum three hours ahead.

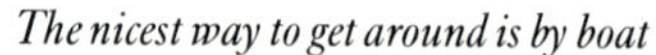

*The nicest way to get around is by boat*

# Tokyo

**The most reassuring aspect of doing business in the teeming, alien technopolis that calls itself Tokyo is that the Japanese are the world's most generous hosts. But the first-time visitor is likely to feel desperately foreign in this most overachieving and stress-ridden of cities.**

**By Michael Scott**

When a Japanese saws wood, he cuts on the pulling stroke. A Westerner, however, cuts on the push.

To an observer, the two styles look the same. But they are fundamentally different.

This is a telling observation on the difficulties facing a *gaijin* (foreigner) in Tokyo. Superficially, everything is very similar to home-town. There are no difficulties in, for example, finding a hotel, catching a taxi or even using the subways. It is only when things go wrong that the size of the culture gap becomes obvious, and you feel really, desperately, foreign.

However, increasing exposure to the foibles of the West, combined with a natural courtesy that is almost overwhelming, has made life much easier for foreigners in Tokyo in the last decade.

This fact is reflected in many ways. The first time I visited Tokyo, in 1973, my six-foot plus frame and manly full beard just about stopped the traffic, and I became accustomed to being followed around by giggling groups. Now the traffic has stopped purely due to congestion, but I can pass apparently unnoticed through the central city.

More tangible benefits are that Engrish (sorry, English) is much more widely spoken, after a fashion; and even the infamous subway system holds few fears, with station names reproduced in English, and the crowds reduced by the addition of a number of new lines.

It all makes Tokyo easier to manage, but no less alien than before. The impenetrable language, the desire to do things in groups rather than alone, a dislike of direct questions and answers, and a pathological fear of embarrassment for themselves or their guests weighs against a growing air of cosmopolitanism, and a wish as well as a need to integrate with the Western commercial world.

A desire to do things in groups? An item in today's *Japan Times* (one of four English-language dailies published in Japan) describes how a new national gymnasium in the suburbs was opened by 5,000 people, adding Japanese inflexions to a no doubt rousing version of Beethoven's Ninth.

Of course, there is a proverb to cover it, sometimes directed against individual overachievers: that a person who rises above average will be knocked down again (the original concerns wooden stakes and mallets).

A British interpretation of the same concept would (indeed does) drag everybody down to the level of the least competent. Thus a fast runner should be forced to wear lead shoes, and a particularly clever person hit on the head frequently. In Japan, however, suppression of the individual works differently. It elevates the average to a high state of achievement, and makes teamwork the keynote of the Japanese economic miracle.

Perhaps this talent for living close together has something to do with the precarious nature of life. Like fish seeking safety in numbers from predators by schooling together.

Tokyo is a city waiting for a major earthquake, which is now overdue. It is not without trepidation that I write this on the 37th floor of one of the scores of gigantic American-style hotels. The last big 'quake was in 1923, and they are said to happen on average every 60 years. Perhaps this is why a chart of rail distances from Tokyo via bullet train carries the disclaimer: 'Information in this brochure is subject to change without prior notice.' In view of this very real danger, the recent addition of large numbers of skyscrapers to the skyline, especially in the Shinjuku district, as the city centre gradually moves west, is rather hard to understand. (Forthcoming Japanese proverb: A building that rises above average will be knocked down?)

Tokyo is the capital of Japan in every sense of the word, an enormous city teeming with people (27 million in a 30-mile radius of the central Imperial Palace, 12 million within the city limits). A crowded technopolis, where conformity is not only enshrined but quintessential: where tradition and the ultramodern co-exist with surprisingly little friction, and where a visitor can all too easily find himself figuratively as well as literally lost.

It became the capital (after Kyoto) during the Shogun era, when the most powerful of them, Tokagawa, moved in with tens of thousands of camp followers. Until then, it had been a fishing village called Edo, commanding a natural harbour and dominated by a feudal castle.

By 1700, the population had climbed to one million, and when imperial rule was restored to Japan in 1868, and the country opened its doors to foreigners, it was renamed Tokyo (Eastern Capital).

The centre then was the Imperial Palace, still residence of the long-lived Emperor Hirohito – but even his palace is a recent reconstruction, for Tokyo has over the years been victim to a number of disasters both natural and otherwise – most recently the earthquake of 1923, and the US firebombing of 1945.

Like London, Tokyo is made up of a series of villages that have grown together. Indeed, this conurbation extends far beyond Tokyo, so that in a 50-km trip south to Osaka, one never leaves the urban sprawl. Unlike London, these 23 separate centres are not particularly distinct from one another, and the city is amorphous in character. Modern buildings are side-by-side with small wooden houses, even quite close to the centre.

In fact, the concept 'centre of town' is difficult to define. The city is based around the Imperial Palace, true, but there are several other areas which today could equally well claim to be the modern centre . . . such as the Ginza, the main shopping area; Shinjuku, with its cluster of tall buildings; Kyobashi, where the government buildings are situated; or Marunouchi, where many multi-national corporations have their headquarters.

The bright lights are wherever you happen to be: streets lit up at night with the trade names of products that have become internationally famous . . . Sony, Brother, Mitsubishi, Nikon, etc – along with the lights of the restaurants and nightclubs which cater to the crowds of stress-ridden, overachieving Japanese businessmen, who temper their diet of extremely hard work with a variety of after-hours activities ranging from simple group singing in special bars to the pursuit of fleshy pleasures at 'love-hotels', all accompanied by the consumption of lots of very, very expensive whisky.

The price of an evening's drinking is just one of the things that make it daunting for a Western businessman to join in – some bars, indistinguish-

*The Ginza shopping district*

able from others, are intended purely for expense account drinkers, with prices adjusted accordingly to anything up to £20 a glass. Fortunately, Japanese business etiquette dictates that their guests should be cared for carefully, so you are not likely to be alone most evenings, and will either be an expense-account guest, or be shown more economical places of recreation. Indeed, some bars will decline to serve Westerners, because of their fear of embarrassment should there be any difficulty with an unexpectedly large bill at the end of it.

The same thing applies to the massage parlours and love-hotels. Rather than risk any difficulty with the police, the Westerner is likely to be told 'Japanese only', unless he is escorted by a regular patron.

The Japanese will go to great lengths to avoid giving offence, or alternatively losing face. This principle expresses itself in extreme forms of politeness that you would do well to emulate. It is wise to give profuse thanks for even quite small favours, and to repeat those thanks on the next meeting. It is a good idea to master a few Japanese phrases, which will impress your hosts no end, simply by your having made the effort. Words such as the general purpose *domo* (not unlike the Italian *prego,* serving as please, thank you, hello and good-bye), or the more formal *arigato* (thank you), *sumimasen* (to get attention or service), *oishii desu* or *gochisosama* (that was delicious), and the vital *ryoshusho o kudasai* (please give me a receipt) will all elicit a giggle of admiration.

Anyone tempted to titter at the funny Japanese way of speaking English, meantime, would do well to reflect that every schoolchild has to master not only three different ways of writing Japanese, incorporating upwards of 2,000 Japanese and Chinese symbols or cryptograms, but also the Roman alphabet.

Other aspects of good manners that surprise Westerners are the number of times people bow to one another. In hotels, department stores and business meetings heads will be bowed to you frequently, and you should respond with an equivalent bow before imposing your own Western standards and shaking hands. This can lead to difficulties. On my most recent visit, I bent to pick up my case from the ground before leaving a dinner engagement, whereupon everyone else in the room also bent down low in response.

In fact, it is often good policy to sit back and let things happen. There is much in this very alien way of life that will otherwise take you by surprise. For example, the blessing of a business association in a Shinto temple. To the heathen Occidental, this may seem very odd indeed. Try not to show it, for this would cause embarrassment. Instead, relax, and accept the offer of a stool if you have difficulty in spending a lot of time on your haunches. I did not and suffered the consequences by being barely able to walk for several minutes after a recent hand-clapping Shinto session slotted into the middle of the day. This was a paradox, since part of the blessing had been designed to make my travels go smoothly.

In a people whose technology leads the world, simplicity and humility are an unexpected element. Yet they are inescapable, and should be related to on the same level. Showing photographs of your home town or your family would not be appropriate at a high-powered meeting in New York, but is quite normal here. This simplicity is charming, and if you are not able to find it so, then try and suppress your feelings.

All this simplicity and charm, however, can get on your nerves, and (more to the point) waste a lot of your time. It is not uncommon to find that speculative meetings that initially appear encouraging are instead simply a sort of blind. For example, if you are trying to sell something to a firm which does not want to buy it, or, as in my case, to obtain information from a firm unwilling to divulge it, rather than tell you so from the outset, the Japanese prefer to go through the motions of an inevitably abortive meeting.

Thus you may find yourself punctiliously fetched from your hotel, and then kept waiting for a time before meeting the wrong person, and obtaining yet another equivocal reply. Then you will be politely driven home again. A few days spent doing that, and you start to wish that they had rather adopted the British method of simply not returning your call.

No doubt this time-wasting is one reason why the Japanese work so hard. Office hours are officially nine to five, with an hour for lunch (with flexi-time variations meaning some offices start at 8 a.m. and others at 10), but working late at the office is more often the rule than the exception, as they compensate for time lost.

Hard work is a Japanese tradition whether it's in the rice paddies or in a multi-storey office block, so there is no shock to their culture in that. And there is enough flexibility in the Japanese way of life to accommodate a lot of modern Western life without sacrificing strong traditions. Even so, Tokyo is in a state of flux, with a rising youth cult eagerly embracing the American ways.

It is now rare to see women dressed in kimonos in Tokyo, though the Geisha girls are still in evidence, shuffling prettily along in the late afternoon to keep their trysts with rich businessmen patrons or (alternatively) tour-groups. The latter are surprised at the innocence of the entertainment at Geisha houses . . . games of marbles with chopsticks, or recitations of folk poetry. One suspects the former have a more salacious time, but you will not see it for yourself.

On the other hand, McDonald's are in Tokyo in an increasingly big way, as are pizza parlours, coffee shops, English-style pubs and the like, especially in Harajuka, a very youthful area where the black limousines of the top businessmen are replaced by snappy turbocharged two-seaters. European cars are real status symbols, with BMW and Mercedes Benz now having replaced the Americans, ever since the quality of Japan's own cars surpassed the monsters from the US.

Tokyo's own Disneyland opened in 1983, and soon after it broke records set in the States with 110,000 visitors in one day.

At the moment, this change has been achieved with remarkably little agony. It is difficult not to predict social upheaval in the future, a favourite hobby of the worried older generation. One of the biggest changes is the liberation of women, which is still several light years behind Europe, but is proceeding apace. It is not unknown for women to occupy executive positions, and the office working *sarariman* (salary-man) now has an equivalent in the *OL* (Office Lady). It means that visiting businesswomen are accepted with a semblance of equanimity, and one sees women dining without men, and enjoying the nightlife in a way that would have been unthinkable 15 or 20 years ago.

To them, no doubt, it is a great relief that Tokyo has the lowest crime rate of any big city in the world. There is a strong but in no way oppressive police presence, and your Tokyo lawman is closer in spirit to a mild-mannered London bobby than a heavily armed New York patrolman. There are police-boxes at many street corners, happy to serve as givers of directions. Gun laws are extremely strict, petty crime is as rare as violent crime, but drug-taking is now on the increase because of the proximity of sources of prime opium and marijuana in South-East Asia.

Another dissimilarity with big Western cities is the efficiency with which everything works. Telephone boxes are everywhere (Y10 for three minutes for a local call), and I have yet to find one that is out of order, let alone vandalised.

This is not so surprising in a city where high technology is celebrated with great gusto. Tokyo takes childish delight in such things as the musical staircase at the Sony building in the Ginza (each step sound a different note on an electronic scale), and the electrical and electronic bazaar at Akihabara must be seen to be believed. There, with all the atmosphere of a French fresh-food market, you can bargain over the price of a personal computer or a washing machine, or choose from among numbers of stalls selling micro-chips, transistors and other esoteric micro-electronic components.

So what are we to make of a people who drive cars called Gloria and Cedric, which chime maddeningly every time they exceed the 100km/h speed limit; who are prudish enough to paint over the pubic hair of English-language *Playboy* and *Penthouse,* yet read comics of astounding ultra-violence; who are shy and over-polite to the point of being irritating, yet who watch TV game shows like the infamous *Endurance* – a contest of suffering endured; whose spirituality embraces several religions in their daily life, but whose materialism knows no bounds; whose national identity is strong and traditional, yet who have taken to burgers, Disneyland and golf with an almost frightening fervour?

Money is one thing, and friendship is another – not least because of the Japanese preference for doing business with people with whom they can socialise (the British penchant for talking about the weather is a great asset in Japan). They are futhermore the world's most generous hosts, so it is easy to like those who like you.

But the ultimate message of Tokyo lies in its adaptability.

Tokyo was once the archetypal polluted city, and was famed for the provision of coin-operated oxygen dispensers at street corners, for those overcome by the fumes of the dense traffic. Now the traffic is denser still, but there is no exhaust smell from the serried ranks of idling Toyotas fitted with emission-control equipment to the strictest standard in the world.

And perhaps this is the ultimate message. Japanese society has been dragged from the feudal to the frantic in the space of just over 100 years. The Japanese have learnt fast, and made deliberate adjustments to avoid the modern ills that have crept up on the cities of the Western industrial revolution. It is this that makes them such formidable business competitors, while it is their lingering traditions, still relatively fresh, that keep them remote from the West.

They are happy to be junior partners to the US, and indeed eager to remain in the position, for to threaten the West too much would be to change their role and jeopardise their prosperity. And when the going gets sticky, they retreat behind the wall of courtesy and restraint that is just as impregnable as if it were made of rudeness and arrogance.

The country that rises above the average will get beaten down again. Modern Japan is intent on making sure it does not happen to them for a second time.

# WHERE TO STAY

A city without a clearly defined centre, Tokyo has hotels dotted all around, with the emphasis on monstrous towers in the American style – with a speciality of service above and beyond the call of duty.

It seems that all of the hotels are over-staffed – by European standards, at any rate . . . the best of them have girls whose main, indeed only, function is to bow to you at the lift doors on the lobby floor. There are also excellent executive facilities, and health facilities and a selection of restaurants that would take more than a week to exhaust.

However, you must pay dearly for the privilege, with rates for the top properties averaging out at around Y20,000 for a single room without breakfast.

The best hotel in Tokyo is commonly held to be the **Okura** (2-10-4 Toranomon, Minato-ku; tel: 582 0111; telex: J22790 HTLOKURA). With superbly appointed rooms, and an atmosphere of unhurried efficiency, it is easy to see why it has been rated as one of the best in the world. Single from Y17,500, double from Y26,000.

But others are not far behind. Traditionally completing the trio are the **Imperial Hotel** and the **Capitol Tokyu.** The Imperial (1-1-1 Uchisaiwaicho, Chiyoda-ku; tel: 504 1111; telex: 222-2346 IMPHOJ) was established in 1890, in a famous building by Frank Lloyd Wright. Today it has added a tower wing to its new modern building, and its location on the edge of the Ginza is an asset. Single from Y19,500, double from Y23,500.

Not so the Capitol (2-10-3 Nagatacho, Chiyoda-ku; tel: 581 4511; telex J24290 CAPTEL), formerly the Tokyo Hilton. Close to the heart of Akasaka, an area rich in hotels, it is tucked away in a quiet enclave next to a shrine. Rooms are Western in size, but have a touch of Japanese character, with sliding paper screens over the windows. Single from Y20,500, double from Y26,000.

Bidding fair to join the top trio is the new **Hilton** (6-6-2 Nishi-Shinjuku, Shinjuku-ku; (tel: 344 5111; telex: 232 4515). It is a 38-storey tower block among many, in the Escher-like multi-level landscape of Shinjuku, but is trying hard to make an instant reputation for itself. Single from Y18,000, double from Y19,500.

But none of these can rival the **Akasaka Prince** for sheer beauty. It rises over Akasaka like a stark modern sculpture, and was designed by Kinzo Tande, famed for his Olympic stadium swimming pool, among other things. The high design is carried through within, with an austere white marble lobby, and stark, efficient modern interiors. (1-2 Kioicho, Chiyoda-ku; tel: 234 1111; telex: 232 4028). Single from Y18,000, double from Y25,000.

And who can ignore the **New Otani** just next door (4-1 Kioicho, Chiyoda-ku; tel: 265 1119; telex:J24719 HTLOTANI), its new tower having made it the largest hotel in Asia. Indeed, this is one of its problems. With its lower prices and enormous capacity, it suffers from the dreaded tour groups, and the lobby is invariably packed with people. On the other hand, it does have its own 400-year-old garden, which is generally amazingly deserted. However, the slightly smaller rooms tend to be a bit claustrophobic, and on a recent visit I was unable to make my sealed cabin cool enough for comfort. Single from Y14,000, double from Y21,500.

All of these, by the way, also offer Japanese-style accommodation, at a hefty premium . . . no less than Y60,000 for the lovely Akasaka Prince, for instance.

But if you're going Japanese-style, then why go to an American-style hotel in the first place? At a traditional *Ryokan,* your room is your castle. You are allocated a maid, who serves you meals in your room, and only the bath is communal. Prices range from around Y13,000 per person if meals are included, and from around Y3,500 if not. Try the **Meguro Gajoen** (1-8-1 Shimo-Meguro, Meguro-ku; tel: 491 0074) for fine if rather faded traditional interiors, or (in Shinjuku) **Yashima** (1-15-5 Hyakunincho, Shinjuku-ku; tel: 364 2534).

However, *Ryokans* are not recommended for first-time visitors to Japan, who will already have enough culture shock to cope with.

There are large numbers of cheaper hotels, tending towards the functional, and culminating in the 'capsule hotels', where, for around Y3,000, you get a slot in the wall a little bigger than our penultimate refrigerated resting places.

You're bound to prefer one of the quieter, smaller hotels, not least because you can stand up and walk around in the rooms, though in some places (not recommended here) this is only just the case.

The **Palace Hotel** (1-1-1 Marunouchi, Chiyoda-ku; tel: 211 5211) is a star in this category, with a calm atmosphere and fine views over the Imperial Palace gardens. Single from Y14,500, double from Y19,000. The **Hotel Kayu Kaidan** (801 Sambancho, Chiyoda-ku; tel: 230 1111; telex: 232 3318) is an Okura-chain hotel, also quiet and relatively small by Tokyo standards. Single from Y8,500, double from Y13,500. The **Gajoen Kanko Hotel,** next door to the Meguro Gajoen Ryokan is described as 'eccentric' (1-8-1 Shimo-Meguro, Meguro-ku; tel: 491 0111; telex: 246-6006: single from Y5,000, double from Y8,000).

# DOING BUSINESS

A recent survey in Australia revealed that the majority of executives in the 67 top corporations think that the Japanese are untrustworthy and unethical in business dealings; that they do not honour contracts; that Japanese negotiators deliberately arrange meetings at night, when visitors are jet-lagged; and that they say 'yes' when they really mean 'no'.

This has not been my experience. Rather the reverse. My contacts in Japanese publishing have exceeded their promises, have always been decisive, and paid up on the nail. They have even sent me gifts to show satisfaction on completion of various jobs.

The truth probably lies somewhere in between – but one thing does seem likely – that the problems experienced by the Aussie tycoons are a reflection on themselves, and their lack of sympathy for the Japanese etiquette of business.

Doing business in Tokyo is hedged with vital patterns of behaviour, and these are trampled at your peril. The exchange of gifts is just one sign that the Japanese prefer these dealings to be on a friendly basis, under which heading would also come the ability to renegotiate unexpired contracts to match changing circumstances, and a degree of loyalty that can sometimes be almost sentimental.

*Bond trading room at the Stock Exchange*

The first rule is that you should stock up on duty free whisky (three bottles per foreign passenger), to dole out to suitable recipients. A bottle of Chivas Regal is highly valued in Tokyo.

The next is that you have business cards printed with a Japanese translation on the reverse side (JAL offer this service, as do the business centres in the main hotels). This is an essential courtesy, since the exchange of cards is almost a ceremonial rite – the recipient of yours will hiss with respect as he reads your title (his own will be absolutely as grandiose as his job allows), then leave your card on the table in front of him for a short time.

Meetings are conducted in the presence of many witnesses, who often take no part at all in the proceedings. They are rather different from the give-and-take dialogue of the West. Rather, they are a series of considered counter-presentations. Thus you may receive no reply at all to a series of suggestions, but should not then make the mistake of repeating them, only louder. Silences are less embarrassing to the Japanese than to Westerners and you should let them run their course.

Meetings generally take place not in the protagonist's office, but in special rooms set aside for the purpose (this is because even quite senior executives tend to share crowded office space with their subordinates). Surprisingly, these rooms are not always private. It's not unknown for two rival supplicants to conduct meetings in the same room.

As to saying yes when meaning no – there is a semantic reason. The Japanese *"yes"* – an explosive *hai* that punctuates each and every conversation – does not mean *"I agree,"* but *"I am listening."*

There is another good reason – good manners. It is impolite to refuse, so do not set much store on the words: *"We will consider your proposal."* Only if a rider is added, such as: *"in a positive manner"*, can you expect a subsequent response.

Another curious factor is the extreme shyness even of people in quite senior positions. This is also 'good manners', but can unfortunately manifest itself in something approaching brusqueness and even off-handedness.

Business relationships are cemented after hours in men-only drinking sessions. Be warned – few Japanese people have the same head for liquor as do Westerners, becoming rapidly red in the face and a bit tipsy. If you feel like doing the same, try not to get too loud, except in a sing-along *karaoke* bar.

If things go well, you will get a gift in return for your bottle of whisky. To be safe, this requires reciprocation with a gift of equivalent value, as well as making sure to express great gratitude, and to repeat your thanks at your next meeting. This in turn evokes another gift to you . . . and so on.

Still . . . that's business in Japan.

# WHERE TO EAT

A big prawn, uncooked, is soaked in liquor. Then you take it in your hands, bend the tail back to meet the head, and bite into the plump flesh. It is delicious.

Just one thing is difficult to stomach. The prawn is still alive . . .

This meal, the most alien I encountered during my most recent visit, was the one that set the tone. To make the most of what is available in Tokyo, you must suspend all culinary preconceptions, and be bold. And remember that it's all very good for you. All Japanese look young, few are overweight. The food is the reason why.

With 45,000 restaurants, eating out in Tokyo offers such variety one barely knows where to begin. The same is true when looking for a restaurant by oneself . . . or would be, but for the excellent habit of having window displays of models of the various dishes executed in an amazingly appetising looking plastic.

*Looks good but tastes a bit chewy: plastic replicas in restaurant window display*

You need a basic knowledge of Japanese food – delicately flavoured and decoratively arranged small portions of curious substances, ranging from raw fish to bean curd to balls of rice. Cooking is avoided – a quick singe sometimes, more usually none at all. But raw fish is much nicer to eat than it is to contemplate, though even the most sanguine of Westerners is permitted to blanch at some things – like leathery herring roes, chewy abalone and the like.

Japanese restaurants tend to be of a particular type. *Sashimi* restaurants serve raw fish with abstruse salads; *sushi* bars serve rice balls topped with similar delicacies; *sukiyaki* and *shabu-shabu* are thinly sliced beef barely cooked with fungus and greens in a soyish broth – all done at your table; *tempura* is sea-food fast-fried in a light and frothy batter; *soba* and *udon* are noodles, sometimes eaten in a thin hot broth, sometimes cold.

Japanese food being expensive, there are probably more Chinese restaurants in Tokyo, popular for entertaining or just a quick bite. The food has a distinctive Japanese taste to it, compared with the Chinese restaurants familiar to a Westerner, for instance, and price and quality vary widely. Some are really exotic: the live prawn dish, for instance, was Chinese rather than Japanese.

There are many Korean barbecues, where thinly sliced beef is served raw. Some of it is intended to be eaten that way, but gas burners at each table are for the purpose of quick-cooking the cheaper or fattier cuts.

Curry and rice is popular, again distinctively Japanese, though there are a number of authentic Indian restaurants. Grilled eel is a favourite speciality elsewhere.

There are also Italian, French and other foreign restaurants, some classic, others adding a Japanese touch. More recent is the advent of US-style fast foods – McDonald's, Colonel Saunders, pizza and the like.

Another thing to remember before going into detail is that beef is an expensive luxury. It is either imported from the US, or comes from Kobe, where the beasts are massaged and given fodder soaked with *sake* for that ready-marinated taste. Shrimps, prawn, crayfish, lobster and the like, on the other hand, are the common food of the common man.

It is hard to supply listings, because they would fill the rest of the book. Tokyo eats out a lot, and each area has a copious supply of usually small restaurants. It depends where you are staying, given the distances involved between the major centres. Indeed, the typical large hotel has a large number of restaurants anyway, mostly of very high quality – and prices, (no less than 37, at the New Otani hotel, for instance), so pot luck, relying on price as a guide to quality, or using of one of the recommended guide books, are your best substitute for a Japanese host.

Snacking alone is picturesque, and less fraught than you might fear, at Chinese or Japanese noodle restaurants, or Japanese *yakitori* (fried chicken) places, dozens of which cluster under railway arches, especially in Shinjuku and Roppongi.

For the adventuresome, some quick pointers: Japanese haute cuisine (*kaiseki ryori*) can be sampled at great cost (Y8,000 to Y10,000) in a very traditional Japanese atmosphere at **Takamura** (3-4-27 Roppongi, Minato-ku; tel: 585 6600), or with only a slight drop in quality at **Tatsumiya** (1-33-5 Asakusa, Taito-ku; tel: 842 7373) amid furnishing of splendid Japanese antiques.

*Tempura* treats at the famous **Ten-Ichi** (6-6-5 Ginza, Chuo-ku; tel: 571 1949, or others in the 10-restaurant chain): and at **Tsunahachi,** (3-31-8 Shinjuku, Shinjuku-ku; tel: 352 1011); *sukiyaki* and *shabu-shabu* at **Shabusen** (Ginza Core Building, 5-8-20 Ginza, Chuo-ku; tel: 572 3806) or **Hassan** (Denki Building basement, 6-1-20 Roppongi, Minato-ku; tel: 403 833), costing Y4,000 to 6,000.

The dreaded poisonous *fugu* fish is for the very brave – you should be served enough of the poisonous part to numb your lips, but preferably not enough to kill you. Try it raw (*fugu-sashi*), at **Santomo** (6-14-1 Ueno, Taito-ku; tel: 831 3898) or more cheaply at **Nibiki** (3-3-7 Shitaya, Taito-ku; tel: 872 6250).

Live prawns? They're at the gourmet Chinese restaurant **Hai-Whan** (Akasaka Floral Building 4-5 floors, 3-8-8 Akasaka, Minato-ku; tel: 586 5666), representative of a rare Cantonese 'yet quivering' school of cuisine.

Recommended guide books, both with the essential maps: *Good Tokyo Restaurants,* by Rick Kennedy (Kodansha International), and *Tokyo,* by Judith Connor and Mayumi Yoshida (Ryuko Tsushin Co Ltd).

# NIGHT LIFE

The most surprising thing about Tokyo night-life is just how soon you have missed it. The more traditional or authentically Japanese an entertainment, the earlier it closes, with theatres and concerts finishing at about 9 p.m., and many restaurants and bars closing at the same time.

Although this is changing to a small extent – especially in youth-oriented areas like Roppongi and Harajuku – there is a counter-move that has recently forced the areas of ill repute to shut up shop by midnight. So while some of the discos go on later than before, the 'pink' (Japanese for blue) cabarets close earlier than ever.

Most business entertaining takes place in bars – and is an important element of wheeling and dealing. Beware of those around the Ginza area especially, which have prices tailored for free-spending expense account executives. But all of them are expensive by British and other standards – even the pub-like café bars.

Hostess bars supply you with a girl to make conversation and massage the egos of tired businessmen. Usually, this is all that will be massaged, apart from your credit card, and in any case few speak English. If you're still keen on the experience, why not try the **Mikado** (2-14-6 Akasaka, Minato-ku; tel: 583 1101), where you see a cabaret as well. The world's largest cabaret, no less, with you just one among 1,700 guests.

Traditional bars, called *Nomiya,* offer snacks and often private rooms, with the Mama-san in frequent attendance. My favourite is **Tagawa** (3-17-7 Akasaka, Minato-ku; tel: 583 6692), where traditional authenticity extends to menus written on paper made from shaved wood, and camphor-wood toothpicks with the bark still on.

Japanese beer is rather good, to those with a taste for lager, and the beer halls are interesting. One such, rich in tradition, is the **Azumabashi Beer House** (1-23 Azumabashi, Sumida-ku; tel: 622 0530). One big advantage... beer is cheap.

For a truly alien experience, you could try a *karaoke* bar, where special 'dub' records have

*Red lights a-go-go in Shinjuku-Kabuki-cho*

soundtracks but no vocals. Patrons take turns at the microphone to sing favourite popular songs (song-sheets provided), to the unrestrained applause of all present. Truly, the Japanese abandon their shyness and restraint when they have a drink or two inside them.

For other quite incomprehensible experiences, you could try *Kabuki* or *Noh* theatre, where the tradition and pageantry are so slow moving that they are losing popularity even with the Japanese. Maybe you'd be better off watching *Sumo* wrestling, at **Kokugikan** (2-1-9 Kurumae, Taito-ku; tel: 866 8700). The best seats are already block-booked well in advance, but tickets are available at the stadium. Then again, it is televised daily on NHK during tournaments, and again in the evening on TV Asahi, with slow-motion replay a big help in following bouts that can be as short as 10 seconds.

Roppongi and Shinjuku are the places for discos, costing Y3,000 to 4,000 for entry, often including some free food and drink. Most close at midnight, but **Tokio** (Aizawa Bldg Bl, 5-9-12 Minami-Aoyama, Minato-ku; tel: 407 1805) and **Cleo Palazzi** (Shadai Bldg Bl, 3-8-12 Roppongi, Minato-ku; tel: 586 8494) both stay open until the small hours, and are amenable to foreigners. Another popular with *gaijins* is **Lexington Queen** (Daisan Goto Bldg Bl, 3-13-4 Roppongi, Minato-ku; tel: 401 1661).

Cabarets and live music shows are often slightly inferior imitations of what you would see in the West. There are some real peculiarities – not least the **Cavern Club** (Roppongi Hosho Bldg 3rd floor, 7-14-1 Roppongi, Minato-ku; tel: 405 5207), where a (nearly) lookalike Beatles group sings (nearly) passable versions of Beatle songs. The **Live Inn** (Ekimae Kaikan 8th floor, 1-3-1 Dogenzaka, Shibuya-ku; tel: 499 5205) features a variety of music, often with foreign bands.

Finally, sleaze.

Anyone who has admired the Japanese appetite for the fleshpots of the rest of the world will not be surprised to learn that similar proclivities are displayed at home, in spite of more or less strict laws to the contrary. Also, anyone familiar with just how impenetrable the Japanese can be when they want will not be surprised at how these activities are kept to themselves.

Escort services are call girls, and those advertised in the *Tour Guide* (a free publication distributed by the major hotels) are tailored for foreigners. Then there are 'fashion massages', which is another name for a salacious massage parlour. *Toruko buro* (Turkish baths) add some splashing around and soapy slithering to the experience, though (following, apparently, protest from the Turkish Embassy) these nowadays often go under the name of 'Soapland'. Then there are the 'Love Hotels' – Disney-like fantasies like fairy castles, or beached ocean liners, where couples are admitted for short-stay visits (minimum two hours for about Y8,000).

Since 1985 police have cracked down on the Kabuki-cho area of Shinjuku, which used to be the centre of sleaze. It still goes on, but must nowadays close down at midnight.

The informed Japanese *roué* now goes beyond the city boundaries, to the Kanegawa area of Kawasaki, about 25 minutes to the west by train. There, the Turkish Baths of **Hori-No-Uchi** have received favourable reports. But, like everything else here, prices are high – anywhere between Y20,000 and 40,000.

# GETTING AROUND

Tokyo is an endless and featureless city, beset by equally endless traffic jams. Street name signs are in short supply . . . indeed many streets lack names, and the man who sallies forth without a map is asking for trouble.

How your taxi-driver finds his way to your destination is something of a mystery – and since few of them speak English, you are advised to carry both a Japanese-language card of your hotel and of your intended destination, lest he become as lost as you are.

Taxis are numerous and rather expensive, especially when the meter ticks away in one of the perpetual traffic jams (it soon becomes clear why the locals call the many elevated Expressways 'Slowly-Roads'). Cost is Y410 to 470 for the first two kilometres, Y80 for every extra 425 metres and three minutes, rapidly mounting up to Y1500 to Y2500 for average cross-town trips.

Car hire is reasonable, from firms like Mazda or Nissan, but driving here is more than somewhat daunting, unless you know the city well, because very few direction signs are bi-lingual. The Japanese drive on the left side of the road, but are very polite and tolerant towards drivers who become confused.

Most of the 12 million inhabitants travel by train or subway, which are quick and efficient, although unbelievably crowded in morning and evening rush-hours.

The subway runs along 10 colour-coded lines (the trains are painted to match the maps), and stations have bi-lingual signs, so there is no special difficulty for Occidentals, and this should be your preferred means of transport. Fares are between Y120 and Y330, with tickets issued by slot-machines or available at station booking offices.

In addition there are the railways . . . the Japanese National Railway (JNR), and a total of 19 private companies. In town, they supplement the subway system and you should know about the JNR *Yamanote* loop line, and the *Chuo* line heading out west. Even Tokyo residents do not know all of the private lines, and you should either live without them, or seek advice on the ground.

Finally (actually, first), there is the matter of travelling the 56km from Narita Airport to Tokyo.

A taxi will cost between Y15,000 and Y17,500 – OK for small groups, but no quicker than the 60 to 80 minutes taken by the frequent orange limousine buses. These cost Y2,500 to TCAT (Tokyo City Air Terminal), located near the Ginza, and Y2,700 for the less frequent services to the principal hotels.

There is also a private railway line run by the Kaisei Electric Railway. The 'Skyliner' train costs Y1,600 and takes an hour, but runs only to the Ueno district, north of central Tokyo, so is only convenient and economical if you're heading there anyway. Meantime, JNR's direct line to Tokyo main station is still in the planning stages.

*Tokyo on the move*

# Washington

The US capital is known as something of an anthill, the ants being the politicians, wordsmiths, lobbyists, lawyers, aides and specialist cranks on Capitol Hill. But Washingon DC, with a 70 per cent black population, also sets something of an example in cautiously harmonious living.
By Karen Zagor

On a recent visit to Washington a white friend of mine, fed on tales of theft and violence, found himself lost in the wrong part of town in the witching hours. On a narrow side street he passed a group of tough-looking young men. They followed him. The faster he walked the faster they followed, until he could feel their breath on his neck. Suddenly, as my friend prepared to meet his maker, there was a loud "*boo*" behind him. By the time he'd recovered from the shock they had disappeared, leaving only the echo of their laughter.

This is the lighter side of a serious problem. Washington is a city with two distinct personalities. By day it is the urbane home of government, national and international, with the life in the Capitol having a cast of thousands: at the last count the bureaucracy of Capitol Hill was close to 12,000. Around the politicans and their aides swarm an equal number of lawyers, and their aides. Add several contingents of lobbyists, bus-loads of tourists and a perpetual flood of protesting students and you are left with terrifying numbers of people, especially when the offices empty for lunch. Although all of Washington's city officials are black, from Mayor Barry to the Chief of Police, day-time Washington is a white city, governed by a white man in a white house.

At six o'clock each evening Washington's transformation begins, as the daytime and city workers, mainly white, wend their way towards leafy suburban homes. The city is then left to its residents for the night. The official population of Washington is 70 per cent black, and the official population of Washington is poor. There are a few white enclaves: Georgetown is a favourite for university students, Preppies and Yuppies, while the area around the Capitol is starting to attract legal and political interns and young couples, but the residents tend not to venture too far afield after dark. There is an understandable tension between city blacks and their privileged and more affluent white neighbours. Although I have walked through most of the city unmolested, there are many sections where whites are not made welcome. As with all US cities, tales of mugging and racial violence abound.

The average business traveller will have little cause to see this more sour side of Washington. There are enough clubs and bars in Georgetown, Capitol Hill and 'the 19th Street Corridor' (the business area) to keep the reveller in good spirits all night long. And for those of a more cultural bent, the Kennedy Center houses the National Symphony, as well as opera, ballet, chamber music and a cinema. There are several theatres, including the National which has been at the same location since 1835 and presents pre and post Broadway plays.

When John F. Kennedy dubbed Washington "*a city of Southern efficiency and Northern charm,*" he was probably being somewhat facetious. The North is no more known for its charm than the South for its efficiency. But Kennedy was also making a valid point about Washington. 'DC' (as the capital is often called to avoid confusion with Washington state) is unique in its blend of Northern and Southern characteristics.

Efficiency is generally expected in the United States of the 1980s, but the essentially Southern soul of DC often takes the visitor by surprise. The grandeur of the lofty marble buildings with high windows, Corinthian columns and sweeping drives, would put the set of *Gone With The Wind* to shame. Indeed, it is often said that after politics, the second biggest thing in Washington is white marble.

Much of DC was built to the designs of Thomas Jefferson, the nation's third president, and a fine architect. Jefferson was responsible for some of the South's best architecture, including the beautiful University of Virginia. The city was originally planned in 1791 by Pierre L'Enfant and George Washington himself, before any people moved in. Their plans were never fully implemented and Washington ended up growing from generation to generation. However, the city's overall structure of circles and parks linked by diagonal avenues has much to do with the original plans. While other US cities have expanded upwards, Washington has kept its character thanks to a strictly imposed height limit on buildings. It is fitting that the Washington Monument still dominates the skyline, as it has for nearly 100 years.

Along with DC's Southern splendour goes Southern hospitality. This often gives the city a disarmingly provincial air – hardly surprising when you consider that Virginia sits hard by across the Potomac. For an international centre, Washington is remarkably unsophisticated. There are, of course, nightclubs, bars and fine restaurants. But for real adventure you must go to New York. Washington may be an international city, but it imports most of its cosmopolitan characters.

Cynics might find it appropriate that Washington's location was the result of a com-

*The White House is Washington's number one tourist attraction*

promise. At the first US Congress meeting in 1789 (held in New York, the temporary capital) the Northerners and Southerners could not agree on a capital city, and Philadelphia was finally accepted until a solution could be reached. For ten years Philadelphia remained the capital of the US. Eventually Thomas Jefferson (a Virginia agrarian liberal) and Alexander Hamilton (a New York Federalist and fiscal conservative) came to a compromise. If Hamilton's Northerners would agree to a capital on the banks of the Potomac, Jeffersons's Southerners would accept Hamilton's proposal that Federal government assume the war debts of the 13 original states. Although George Washington chose the exact site for the capital, he never held office in it: Washington was named after him in 1799. Kennedy's description of the hybrid city nearly 200 years later would doubtless have pleased the city fathers.

Because of its location, DC does not suffer the bitter extremes of weather of other Eastern cities. Winters tend to be more wet than white, summers more humid than hot. But autumn is glorious, with fierce orange, gold and red leaves battling against the marble buildings. Spring is equally magnificent, but more fragrant. The Japanese cherry trees along Pennsylvania Avenue and the Jefferson Memorial are truly spectacular in full bloom, and the Southern magnolias can make the bleakest street a thing of beauty.

Washington's planners intended the city to be a great commercial centre, as well as the seat of government, and the site on the Potomac was chosen accordingly. But the city's planners made one crucial mistake – they did not take into account the fact that the Potomac River is virtually unnavigable. While river transportation is no longer crucial to commerce, Washington has never become a major business town. It is politic for most large businesses to have representatives in DC, but the true muscle of any company is usually located elsewhere.

Whether you visit Washington for a month, a week or only a day, there are certain sights which it would be almost criminal to neglect. A good place to start is Lafayette Square, just opposite the White House. Whoever placed the statue of Lafayette in the corner of the square to be completely overshadowed by a giant bronze statue of Andrew Jackson on a horse must have had an odd sense of humour. The square is full of trees and grass and has benches to rest weary legs. There's an old Washington saying that "*the squirrels are in Lafayette Park, but the nuts are across the street*". Whatever one may think of the present US administration, it is worthwhile crossing Pennsylvania Avenue for a tour of the White House. You won't see the president, he is kept at a safe distance from the public and usually travels to and from the White House by helicopter, but you will be able to visit all the rooms on the State floor.

For a closer examination of the US government at work, a trip to Congress on Capitol Hill is essential. If there's an important debate you're likely to see such political celebrities as Edward Kennedy, Gary Hart and Jessies Helms and Jackson. I think the most beautiful building on the Hill is the Library of Congress with its mosaic murals, marble floors and carved balustrades; but a famous guide book describes it as "*a florid Italian Renaissance building*".

Great powers have always collected art, and the powerful of DC are no exception. The art museums in the city are among the finest in the world. The best known is the Hirshhorn Museum with over 6,000 paintings and sculptures, including Rodin's *Burghers of Calais,* Matisse's *Backs,* and a superb collection of modern American masters. Another favourite is the East Wing of the National Gallery. Designed by I.M. Pei, in the shape of two interlocking triangles, the building itself is a tribute to modern American architecture. Inside it is all light and air, and makes a perfect setting for the excellent collection of modern art.

Because Washington is America's city of history, a list of things to see would be endless. But if I had time for just one sight, it would be the Vietnam Veterans Memorial in Constitution Gardens. Designed by Maya Lin, the V-shaped black granite monument is stark and simple. The first wall starts low with few names for the early years of the war, reaching a peak (and an angle) in 1968 when the names reach over your head, then gradually dying down the second wall to the end of the war. There are 57,939 names with room to add more should other deaths be discovered. The nation is only slowly and painfully coming to terms with Vietnam – it took nearly ten years to erect this monument to its dead. This may seem a needlessly sombre way to end a trip to Washington, but no one can hope to understand the current political and social mood of the United States without some understanding of this most painful chapter in modern American history.

# WHERE TO STAY

I used to joke that the hot hotel in Washington was the Best Western Iron Horse. For the uninformed, this specimen of Americana stood equidistant between a mass of grimy Amtrak marshalling yards and Route 50, a six-lane highway from Washington to Annapolis, Maryland. The distance was about 20 feet.

Today, I might still have to resort to humour, for Washington has gone hotel-crazy, adding about 40 in the past decade. It shows no signs of stopping. Hyatt has moved in; Hilton International has unfurled its Vista flag; Ramada chose Washington for one of its top-line business hotels. And Marriott, which calls Washington home, has exploded to 10 hotels in its own backyard.

All this should make recommending a Washington hotel a formidable task, but perhaps not. We all have our favourites. Although Washington is no midtown Manhattan at rush hour, it can grow pretty hectic, making the small, uncrowded luxury hotel a haven for the business traveller. Washington abounds in these.

You don't just stroll into the **Hampshire Hotel** (1310 New Hampshire Ave, NW; tel: 202 296 7600) in the city's West End. You appear at the door, knock, and the desk clerk buzzes you in. Like many other small Washington hotels, the Hampshire was once a somewhat bland apartment building, with large square windows; concrete and clay. But inside is different. The lobby is a mite tight, but the rooms are large and well-fitted. Decor is what Americans call European, which means more cloths than vinyls, more earth tones than electrics. All 82 rooms are suites, some with balconies. Its three meeting rooms fit five to 40, and there's the popular French creole-style Lafitte's restaurant. Single $85; double $116-136.

Another all-suite hotel, the **Canterbury,** lies a stone's throw away (1733 N St, NW; tel: 202 393 3000; telex: 469373), at the West End, towards 'Embassy Row' and the White House. Surprise, surprise: it's an old apartment building. The Canterbury already has a fine restaurant in Chaucer's and, as the name might suggest, beef and venison are the orders of the day. The Canterbury also has big rooms, big beds, big rates: $140-$340.

Farther over towards the White House (1200 16th St, NW; tel: 202 347 2200; telex: 248879) stands the **Jefferson.** This is not – repeat not – an old apartment building. Instead, it's a plush little 112-room hotel that has been peddling comfort since 1925. No two rooms are identical. One boasts a four-poster bed and a grandfather clock, another rich mahogany furniture and crystal chandeliers, a third is decked out in a soft eggshell blue and white with lace all around. Until recently, the Jefferson had only 100 rooms, before it took over a neighbouring apartment house and recreated the main building. A single room goes for $135-225 in this gem, but once you've strolled into the tranquillity of its rooms, with homely low ceilings and carpets that, as a British colleague once put it, threatens to suck your shoes off, then you'll be hooked for life – or at least the duration of a business trip. Suites cost $200-350 for a parlour with one bedroom, $375 and up for a parlour and two.

You could walk past the **Dolley Madison** (1507 M St, NW; tel: 202 862 1600; telex: 710822 0145) and miss it. That's your first mistake. Your second would be to assume that – just because the Rolling Stones took it over entirely on a Washington pit stop and were later copied by The Who – this hotel is home for a bunch of cacophonic rock musicians. Sorry. The loudest thing in the Dolley is the placid tick-tock of an antique clock in the equally antique library, a sombre pit stop for day's end where the business world sips tea and rests among voluminous armchairs, Chinese screens and mahogany writing desks.

Single rooms go for $135 doubles from $150, junior suites for $300, one-bedroom suites for $350 and luxury suites for $550. The hotel's restaurant serves breakfast and lunch but not dinner. For that, you must cross the road to the **Madison** (15th and M Sts, NW; tel: 202 862 1600; telex: 64245 or 7108220145), which is not so much the Dolley's sister hotel as its great aunt.

The Madison has not got the quiet of its niece, but it does have the sumptuous furnishings, and

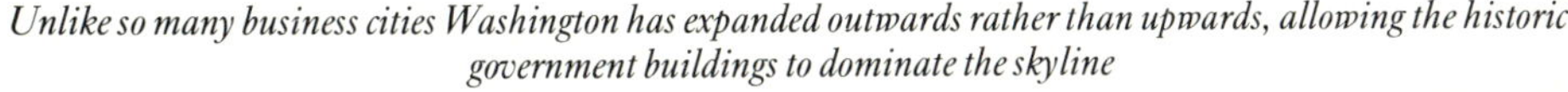

*Unlike so many business cities Washington has expanded outwards rather than upwards, allowing the historic government buildings to dominate the skyline*

the Montpelier Restaurant is regarded as one of the most comfortable in Washington. Both hotels are close to a foreign newspaper stand (we're still around Embassy Row) for out-of-country publications. Each of the 370-room Madison's televisions shows round-the-clock cable news and coverage of proceedings at the House of Representatives, and at the front desk stock market quotations are rattled off when trading finishes.

The sad aspect of the Madison is that it pumps aggravating muzak through its main corridors. If this music be the food of love, thanks, but I'll starve and go celibate. Rates run from $135 for one person to $525 for a two-bedroom suite. The Madison Suite, a living room with one or two bedrooms, comes in at $995-1200.

No prize for guessing that the **Henley Park Hotel** was also once an apartment block. Built in 1918 at Massachusetts Ave and 10th St, NW (tel: 202 638 5200; telex: 904059), round the corner from Washington's new convention centre. Its Coeur de Lion restaurant serves up everything from swordfish to a fillet steak, and the chef awaits instruction if the preparation is not your cup of tea. Speaking of cups of tea, Marley's lounge is the afternoon retreat for many a local businessman (or woman). Room rates start at $95-140 single, $115-160 double. Suites run from $175-360.

**One Washington Circle** (the address doubles as the name, tel: 202 872 1680; telex: 440546) doesn't advertise itself as a former apartment building, but don't hedge your bets; it certainly looks like one. It has just been renovated, but has kept the West End Café (this one is also in Washington's West End), a popular supper club. A nice touch is the weather report with morning wake-up call. Single $120-190, double $117-242.

The Grand Dame of Washington's hotels is the **Mayflower** (1227 Connecticut Ave NW; tel: 347 3000; telex 892342), where they have spent $59 million on restoring it to its former glory. It looks effortlessly elegant, flags flapping outside and palms and ferns lying placid inside. The first big to-do for this socialite hang-out was the inaugural ball for President Calvin Coolidge in 1925, but it was at the repeal of prohibition that the Mayflower played its trump card. It applied for, and acquired, liquor license number one, and promptly started a tradition of tea-dancing in the Café Promenade. If there's one drawback, it's that the main lobby is lined with moderately-sized convention rooms, so it can become noisy. The cost of the 46,000 square feet of Italian marble paving the bathrooms should be taken care of by room rates: single $106-200; double $126-220.

Other fine hotels are not mentioned in any detail here. The **Vista International** (1400 M St, NW; tel: 429 1700; telex: 440237), for example, looks spanking new but inexorably plain from outside, but its atrium lobby has rooms overlooking a multi-level courtyard, giving the air of a studio set or an operatic stage. The **Dupont Plaza** (1500 New Hampshire Ave; tel: 483 6000; telex: 904 053) has proved popular because it is central and on two Metro lines, and then there is the **Watergate,** (2650 Virginia Ave; tel: 965 2300; telex: 197 691), famed for ever after Tricky Dicky Nixon's men were nabbed there while snooping on the Democrats. The stately **Hay-Adams,** (16th and H Streets NW; tel: 638 2260; telex: 7108229543) receives gilt-lined guests, as does the **Ritz-Carlton,** (2100 Massachusetts Ave, NW; tel: 293 2100; telex: 7108229228), with its oh so lah-di-dah Jockey Club restaurant, and the **Hotel Washington,** (Pennsylvania Ave, NW; tel: 638 5900; telex: 7108220105), has an immensely popular rooftop restaurant. The **Georgetown Hotel,** (P. St. NW; tel: 293 3100; telex: 887800) is good for those wanting to mix business with night-life, the **Sheraton Carlton** (16th St. NW; tel: 638 2626; telex: 440650), is as good a Sheraton as exists, and the **Shoreham Hotel,** (Calvert St. NW; tel: 234 0700) which is spending almost $30 million on renovation, swings and dances along every night in its Marquis lounge. Finally, the **Four Seasons** (Pennsylvania Ave; NW; tel: 342 0444; telex: 9040084) has, in Aux Beaux Champs, the people's choice as the best restaurant in Washington.

# WHERE TO EAT

There was a time when it was almost impossible to find a decent, moderately priced restaurant in Washington.

Top of the line, yes. With Aux Beaux Champs peddling lamb, veal and roast pigeon from its post in the Four Seasons Hotel, and the Jockey Club in the Ritz-Carlton Hotel serving up crab cakes that

*Georgetown is where the Yuppies hang out*

would melt even the most stoic and conservative – translation: Republican – of palates, Washington has always been on a par with, say, New York. But mid-range? Certainly not.

The tide, however, is turning.

Cuisines of other countries, not just the traditional steak, chops and seafood of the US, are sprouting up all over Washington. Now, the District of Columbia has Afghan and Korean alongside French and Italian, Vietnamese and Middle Eastern alongside Indian and Chinese. To paraphrase *Washington Post* food critic Phyllis Richman, it seems that every time a war breaks out somewhere, Washington celebrates by opening a restaurant.

Why the city has suffered this famine for so long is open to question. Politicians, Washington's principal populace, have never been known as the most discriminating eaters and will usually look for a simple meal to settle stomachs ravaged by the Capitol Hill cocktail circuit. And unlike New York to the north, Washington has never really received a mass influx of immigrants.

But to search for answers would be folly. Better not to look a gift horse in the mouth; better to give it its nose bag, and go eat.

There are several ways to find a satisfactory Washington restaurant. The best is to pick up a copy of *Richman's Best Restaurants (& Others) in Washington D.C. & Environs. "The only thing we're lacking,"* says Richman, *"are some more Italian restaurants and some Scandinavian. And we could do with a delicatessen or two. But we have everything else."*

So they do. The area known as Adams Morgan, to the north-west of the city centre, is fast taking over the role of ethnic Bohemia from Georgetown, and has not yet been burdened by the polyester of tourism. Around here can be found **Mama Ayesha's Calvert Café** (1967 Calvert St, NW; tel: 232 5431), a Middle Eastern restaurant specializing in lamb broth and pastries. Dinner here will rarely cost more than $18 a head.

Two of the city's finest Italian restaurants are close by. **Petitto's** (2653 Connecticut Ave, NW; tel: 677 5350) specialises in concocting forms of pasta dishes, while the antipasto – a watercress salad with bacon and fresh mozzarella – starts off the meal perfectly. With a fine selection of house wines, dinner prices start at around $15 a head. Regarded by some as the best seafood restaurant is

**Vincenzo's** (1606 20th St, NW; tel: 667 0047) just off Dupont Circle. Try the linguini tossed with clams or mussels, or perhaps the whole red snapper. Price for two runs upwards of $60.

Hotel restaurants can be a funny bunch, principally because they are only part of a larger whole, and lack individual personality. Still, the **New Leaf** in the Shoreham Hotel serves a tasty tournedos and caps dinner with a shimmering soufflé of either strawberry, banana or rum and raisin – or a combination of all three. The rack of lamb is also recommended. Around $60 for two.

Other frontrunners in the hotel category include **Chaucer's** in the Canterbury Hotel, the **West End Café** in One Washington Circle, and the **Tabard Inn** (1739 N St, NW; tel: 785 1277), a reclusive little place downtown that has been known to follow an American tradition of strange concoctions – goat cheese and walnut with noodles, for instance.

Another of Richman's projects is the restaurant guide she oversees twice a year for the *Post.* The autumn guide is a general reference but the spring version takes on a theme. "*Last year,*" says Richman, "*it was dieting. The year before, seafood. But this time round, we're going outdoors, to sidewalks, gardens and rooftops.*"

The good part is that most of them are turning at last to what is termed 'New American' cuisine. This basically means jazzing up local ingredients. In the past, restaurants had tendencies to throw down a steak with a side of fries. Now, chefs are showing more imagination, such as chicken stuffed with zucchini, or fish salad with fresh corn. Best bets for such are **Nora's** (2132 Florida Ave, NW; tel: 462 5143), **Sholl's Cafeteria** (1990 K St, NW; tel: 296 3065) and the **Foggy Bottom Café** (924 25th St, NW; tel: 338 8707). You should get change out of $25.

Outside the city, two restaurants can be recommended. **L'Auberge Chez Francois** in Great Falls, Virginia, requires reservations two weeks in advance (tel: 703 759 3800) and for good reason. Speciality of the house is the *saumon soufflé de l'auberge,* a salmon steak topped with a mousse made from pike. Dinner costs around $20.

The other is the **Inn at Little Washington,** in Washington, Virginia, (tel: 703 675 3800). American fare again, with the chef preparing such dishes as duck with raspberries or a delicate corn mousse. Entrées cost $15-18. Reservations should be made two weeks in advance.

For those desperate to sample the headiest American entertainment delights in Washington there is really only one address. It is National Airport, where they will catch the half hourly shuttle to La Guardia airport, New York, run by Eastern and New York Air.

This is not to say you cannot have the night of your life in Washington. It is just to say that it requires more planning: in New York, the lazy reveller need only hit the Second Avenue piano bars. Three weeks later, when their entertainment value begins to pall, there's always Broadway, not to mention the city's score or so of decent nightclubs.

Washington has bars, too, and they must be regarded as the principal source of ready entertainment, certainly the launch pad of an evening on the nation's capital.

If you want to inhale the heady atmosphere of the White House and its media court, visit the **Class Reunion** at 1726 H Street (tel: 298 8477). This is a Washington version of London's sodden El Vino wine bar, habitat of Fleet Street's legendary Lunchtime O'Booze.

Try to shout down *Washington Post* luminaries boasting about their latest blow for democracy and free speech. Ogle the comely young women sipping daquiries who, without your intervention, might become their victims.

When things go sour there, if they do, hobble on down Pennsylvania Avenue for a couple of blocks to 15th Street, and enter the Las Vegas, Diamond Lil style interior of the new **Old Ebbitt Bar** (tel: 347 4800). For those who remember Washington's old Old Ebbitt Bar – a dusty, noisy cave, with the cadaver of some long dead, tusked animal projecting from the wall above the bar – the new Old Ebbitt is a surprise: there seem to be around 16 bars and restaurants, with room for around one million customers.

But you can eat and drink well there – the 'Raw bar', as the Americans call oyster bars, is particularly good. In the evenings it is filled with Preppie young women from the White House,the

Treasury and points beyond. An engaging fixture is barman Grant, a refugee from the old Old Ebbitt who bears a passing resemblance to the tusked Leviathan which used to hover above him like the creature in the Thurber drawing.

If a light evening meal with drink is your fancy while you consider how best to tackle the evening, **The American Café** on the corner of M Street and Wisconsin Avenue, Georgetown (tel: 337 3600), is interesting. This is also the local HQ of the corn-fed Preppies from Georgetown University.

If you wish to concentrate your evening's bar and restaurant entertainment in one area, Georgetown is it. Specifically, that stretch from 29th Street to 36th Street and M. This covers everything from the elegance of the **Four Seasons Hotel** to rowdy bars like **Annie's,** on the M-Wisconsin intersection (tel: 333 6767).

Within a short walking distance there is **Blues Alley** (tel: 337 4141), a jazz club in a lane between M Street and the river, and **Charlie's** (3223 K. St NW; tel: 298 5985), a nightclub owned by guitarist Charlie Byrd. Both are to be recommended. Nearby, for those who like to drink, dance and eat, there is **F Scott's** at 1232 36th Street (tel: 965 1789). This has the reputation of attracting fun-loving young women, but I think that's largely alarmist talk.

For mysterious reasons Washington is a great centre of country music.Two of the radio stations here play nothing else, and there are several clubs where banjo and fiddle music are the *specialité de la maison.* Chief among those is **The Birchmere,** over the 14th Street Bridge in Alexandria, Virginia (tel: 549 5919), a $12 or so cab fare. If your tastes are more sedate there is always something worth seeing or hearing at the **Kennedy Center** theatres (tel: 254 3600) and **American Film Institute** cinema.

It's nice to dine afterwards on the roof, and watch planes skim in over the 14th Street Bridge to land at National. That's if the wind's in the right direction. If it's not, they will be taking off towards you. (Of course, if you really want a heady night's entertainment, you will be peering out of one at the Kennedy Center.)

# GETTING AROUND

Washington is afforded the luxury of three airports: National, Dulles and Baltimore Washington International (BWI).

National is one of the world's busiest airports, although handling domestic flights only. The reason is clear: sitting just across the Potomac River, it is but a 15-minute drive from downtown Washington, a $10-15 taxi ride, or an 80 cent Metro subway ride. It is not uncommon for a flight to abort a landing when it finds another plane on the runway. Studies show that schedules should be directed to Dulles or BWI, but the airlines are naturally reluctant to sacrifice the convenience of National.

BWI is a shiny airport that never seems to be busy. This is where elephants go to die. Outside rush hour, it is a 45-minute ride from downtown Washington. A bus service between airport and the Capital Hilton costs $9. Taxi fare costs from $40-50 and should be agreed upon before departure; a limo costs $45. There is an Amtrak station nearby with trains running every hour, but a bus connection is necessary from the airport.

Dulles is also a $40 taxi ride and a $9 bus ride. Like BWI, it is not the most hectic airport this side of the Mississippi.

Within the city limits, taxis cost a $1.70 basic rate, with 75 cents charged for additional passengers and a 65 cent surcharge during rush hours. The Metrobus service covers most of the city, with a basic fare of 80 cents, 85 during rush hour. Its schedules connect with Washington's Metrorail service, a bright new subway plan that covers most of the downtown area and is still reaching out to suburban districts.

The best way to ride the Metro is to buy a Farecard from a machine that will take up to $20. Any purchase over $10 gets a five per cent bonus. Computers automatically mark your card when it is inserted at the entrance and exit gate.

At Union Station, Amtrak has services to all the major points in the US.

**Research**
**by Karen Zagor**

**Picture credits:**
Aspect Picture Library (pp. 299, 301).
Graham Boynton (pp. 63, 64, 67, 69, 70, 71, 72, 74).
Richard Dewing (p. 242).
Mike Roles Studio (pp. 198, 205).

**The following photographs were supplied by The Imagebank:–**

Sebastiao Barbosa (p. 255).
Morton Beebe (pp. 99, 102, 163, 267, 295).
Bernard van Berg (pp. 45, 92).
W Beust (p. 121).
Ira Block (pp. 117, 119).
Peter & Georgina Bowater (pp. 87, 89, 94, 95, 105, 109, 114, 155, 177, 178, 179, 181, 182, 285).
John Branigan (p. 298).
Joseph P Brignolo (pp. 25, 158).
Gerald Brimacombe (pp. 275, 277).
John Bryson (pp. 18, 68, 241, 283).
Wayne Caravella (p. 83).
Bill Carter (p. 313).
Stephen Carter (p. 187).
Luis Castaneda (pp. 207, 209, 214).
Andy Caulfield (pp. 129, 130, 281).
Flip Chalfont (p. 55).
Kay Chernush (p. 81).
Alain Choisnet (pp. 243, 249).
Gianalberto Cigolini (p. 223).
L Dennis (p. 238).
R Eisele (p. 165).
Paul Elson (p. 49).
Fbueno (p. 230).
Cliff Feulner (pp. 53, 54, 146, 245, 265).
Brett Froomer (pp. 15, 41, 44, 86, 270, 305, 308).
Ted Funk (p. 111).
Aram Gesar (p. 97).
Michael Going (p. 38).
Larry Dale Gordon (p. 257).
Paolo Gori (p. 159).
Adelheid Heine-Stillmark (p. 190).
Peter Hendrie (pp. 290, 293).
Francisco Hidalgo (pp. 140, 203).
L Hughes (pp. 200, 299).
Jawitz (p. 317).
R Kledrowski (p. 17).
Kasho Kumagai (p. 185).
Don Klumpp (p. 66).
Harvey Lloyd (p. 268).
Terry Madison (p. 215).
David J Maenza (pp. 56, 189, 225, 228).
Richard & Mary Magruder (pp. 149, 253).
Brad Martin (p. 231).
Leo Mason (p. 289).
Patti McConville (pp. 79, 90, 135, 139, 264).
Mike McQueen (p. 23).
Randy Millar (p. 47).
James Montgomery (p. 43).
Cara Moore (pp. 251, 254).
Marvyn E Newman (pp. 73, 196, 306, 309).
Nick Nicolson (p. 226).
Richard Nowitz (p. 259).
Obremski (p. 137).
Dave Paterson (pp. 107, 108).
Nick Pavloff (p. 144).
Robert Phillips (pp. 151, 315).
Jake Rajs (pp. 101, 311).
Paul van Riel (pp. 246, 287).
Fulvio Roiter (p. 213).
Marc Romanelli (p. 235, 237, 261, 262).
Guido A Rossi (pp. 127, 132, 273).
Al Satterwhite (p. 279).
Juergen Schmitt (pp. 219, 220, 221).
Marcel Isy Schwart (pp. 26, 28, 31, 291).
Allen Seiden (p. 157).
Erik Leigh Simmons (p. 231).
Michael Skott (p. 123).
Paul Slaughter (p. 61).
G M Smith (p. 145).
Marc St Gill (pp. 147, 153).
John Lewis Stage (pp. 39, 75).
Ted Streshinsky (p. 271).
H Sund (p. 217).
Chris Turner (p. 195).
Alvis Upitis (pp. 59, 233).
H R Uthoff (pp. 115, 124).
Anne van der Vaeren (p. 52).
Amedeo Vergani (pp. 116, 169, 170, 175, 248).
Charles Weckler (pp. 77, 167, 172, 297).
Jules Zalon (p. 37).